Weimar and Now: German Cultural Criticism
Martin Jay and Anton Kaes, General Editors

Hollywood in Berlin

Cover of feature issue on America, *Internationale Filmschau*, 1 June 1921.

Hollywood in Berlin
American Cinema and Weimar Germany

THOMAS J. SAUNDERS

UNIVERSITY OF CALIFORNIA PRESS
Berkeley   Los Angeles   London

University of California Press
Berkeley and Los Angeles, California

University of California Press
London, England

Copyright © 1994 by The Regents of the University of California

Library of Congress Cataloging-in-Publication Data

Library of Congress Cataloging-in-Publication Data

Saunders, Thomas J.
    Hollywood in Berlin : American cinema and Weimar Germany / Thomas
J. Saunders.
        p.   cm.—(Weimar and now ; 6)
    Includes bibliographical references and index.
    ISBN 0-520-08354-7
    1. Motion pictures—Germany—History. 2. Motion pictures,
American—Germany—Influence. 3. Motion pictures, German—United
States—Influence. 4. National characteristics, American, in motion
pictures. 5. National characteristics, German, in motion pictures.
I. Title. II. Series.
PN1993.5.G3S34 1994
791.43′0943—dc20
                                                                93-38196
                                                                CIP

Printed in the United States of America

1 2 3 4 5 6 7 8 9

Contents

Illustrations

Acknowledgments

Numerous persons have contributed to the making of this book. It is a pleasure to acknowledge my indebtedness to them for counsel, support, and criticism.

For assistance with sources and helpfulness in other ways I would like to thank the staff of the Bundesarchiv in Koblenz, Potsdam (formerly the Zentrales Staatsarchiv) and Berlin (formerly the Staatliches Filmarchiv der DDR), and of the Deutsches Literaturarchiv, Marbach; Wolfgang Jacobsen and Werner Sudendorf of the Stiftung Deutsche Kinemathek, Berlin; Robert Fischer of the Landesbildstelle Berlin; Eberhard Spiess of the Deutsches Institut für Filmkunde, Frankfurt a.M.; Hans Bohrmann of the Institut für Zeitungsforschung, Dortmund; Katherine Loughney of the Motion Picture Division of the Library of Congress, Washington; Leith Adams of the Warner Bros. Archive, Los Angeles.

For the inspiration of their own scholarship as well as the benefit of their suggestions and encouragement I am grateful to Sabine Hake, Victoria de Grazia, Thomas Elsaesser, Eric Rentschler, Gary Stark, Denise Youngblood, and especially Anton Kaes. I have also appreciated the support of my colleagues in the department of history at the University of Victoria. The friendship and hospitality of Annette and Heinrich Bader, Christina and Klaus Dordel, and Kathy and Christian Methner have made visits to Germany pleasurable as well as profitable.

Special thanks are due Modris Eksteins, who supervised the dissertation upon which this study is based. To his patience, encouragement and wisdom no less than his model as a scholar I owe a great deal more than an acknowledgment can repay.

The Social Sciences and Humanities Research Council of Canada and the President's Committee on Faculty Research and Travel at the University of Victoria generously provided funds which made this project possible. The *Journal of European Studies* has graciously permitted the use in chapter six of material originally published in volume 17 of the journal. Edward Dimendberg and Rebecca Frazier at the University of California Press have been friendly and helpful in seeing the manuscript through the publication process.

My wife, who for too many years has endured the manuscript in everything from my state of distraction to my absences, and has not only maintained her sense of humor but has also helped to maintain mine, cannot be adequately thanked. I acknowledge her support with deep gratitude.

This book is dedicated to David Mundell, who to my great sadness did not live to see it completed. His sometimes skeptical questioning in its early phases was as much a source of inspiration as his friendship and his faith in me.

T. J. S.
University of Victoria

INTRODUCTION

Before the First World War European observers prophesied that the twentieth century would be dominated by the United States. By virtue of population, resources and entrepreneurship the New World was predestined to eclipse the Old World. Although full realization of this prophecy came only after 1945, America's participation in the Great War set the stage for what was to follow. The interwar period witnessed Europe's first serious reckoning with American economic, diplomatic and cultural influence. Capital and merchandise were the visible accoutrements of American power. Behind them loomed management principles, advertising methods, labour relations, social values and moral standards. However isolationist its foreign policy, the United States exported its entrepreneurial, social and cultural norms. Europe experienced an unprecedented onslaught of what Germans dubbed *Amerikanismus* (Americanism) and *Amerikanisierung* (Americanization).[1]

This onslaught was effected by a variety of means and media, from travellers' reports and visits of American celebrities to American loans and symbols of prosperity like the Model T. But for the broad mass of Europeans the main agent of Americanization was the moving picture. Still a curiosity at the turn of the century, by 1918 the cinema was an ubiquitous and influential public medium. Parallel with America's rise to global importance, it emerged as the dominant form of popular entertainment and enlightenment. As a vehicle for exporting the American way of life and stimulating demand for American products it proved unrivaled. Hollywood became the promotional guardian of the American dream and the primary instrument for domesticating American culture in Europe.

Hollywood's monopolization of the international film market

has never been a secret. Yet until very recently the profound ramifications of that monopoly have not been seriously investigated. Only with the waning of American power since the 1970s has the phenomenon of cinematic monopoly been treated as an historical "accident" which requires explaining. While film scholars are examining the consolidation of the studio system and narrative tradition which via Hollywood standardized much of global film production, cultural historians have begun to consider the meaning of Hollywood's hegemony for both American and non-American viewers. In the study of European film cultures there is growing recognition that to treat Hollywood as extrinsic to national cinemas is simply inadmissable. Be it French, German, British, Italian or even Soviet, the culture of interwar cinema was first and foremost American.[2]

Since the Great War the moving picture and Hollywood have become so rooted in Western culture and cultural mythology as to appear eternally synonymous. Three-quarters of a century later it requires considerable effort to imagine a world not yet frozen on celluloid and celluloid not dominated by the American model. Yet despite the historical simultaneity of cinema's rise to public importance and American domination of the medium, this symbiosis was not always operable. The generation which survived the war, still intensely engaged in assimilating the cinema's multifaceted import and just recently exposed to the full weight of American culture, only gradually conceded an inescapable tie between the moving picture and its American variant. What in retrospect appears to be the initial phase in a preordained process constituted then a cultural revolution.

The emergence of cinema to prominence in the public realm represented in itself a dramatic breakthrough. Technologically, film was born of the second industrial revolution in the last third of the nineteenth century. Socioeconomically, its appearance coincided with a massive wave of urbanization. For populations experiencing unprecedented geographic and in turn sociopsychological uprootedness, the motion picture provided community, moral guidance and education as well as entertainment, all at a moderate cost. It thereby took its place alongside the press, military service and universal education as an indispensable means of public indoctrination, vaulting within a generation of its development to the front rank of the mass media. Who was to control this public force, at whom and to what end it should be directed, and to what extent it could influence viewers, became unavoidable issues. Contemporaries debated the relationship between art, politics, technology, commerce and human progress in light of cinema's pervasive impact. Caught between the drive to exploit and the urge to understand or control, they became embroiled in a contest to determine cinematic agendas.[3]

After 1918 mapping these agendas became inconceivable without reference to Hollywood. In the postwar decade Europe experienced a massive invasion of American culture, spearheaded by the motion picture. Jazz bands, sports heroes, troupes of dancing girls, movie stars and tycoons were its personal representatives. American literature, fashions, mores and aspirations were its commercial and ethical counterparts. In the face of this onslaught Europe began to question its cultural resilience. Americanization became a buzzword. To some it promised excitement and revivication for cultures mired in the past and bankrupted by war. To others it portended the leveling of centuries of cultural development. For both, America became caught up in domestic debate about cultural values and direction in which the cinema was already enmeshed.[4]

Two decades earlier neither the American nor cinematic challenge to European culture had provoked such intense debate. Nor had they been recognized as siamese twins. At the turn of the century the United States began to occupy the European mind primarily because of its burgeoning economic power. Thereafter, travel reports and early photojournalism began to present a mosaic of industrial advance, bustling cities, endless landscapes, the cult of technology and efficiency, and the triumph of mass culture. Youthful, wealthy, optimistic, and supremely self-confident, America became a prototype for future societies.[5] Cinema increasingly breathed life into these visions and disseminated them to a mass public, but it did not create them. Indeed, if there was correspondence between European attitudes toward cinema and the United States it lay in the assumption that neither had a serious contribution to make to culture.[6] To the extent that the motion picture did stir general debate, American film was not a primary concern. Before World War I French producers dominated international film markets, their closest rivals being Italian, American and Scandinavian companies. Controversy about the cinema assumed more generic than national characteristics, focusing on the threat of film to literature, theater and the social order. In sum, images of the United States began to haunt or enchant Europe independently of the growing preoccupation with film.[7]

Only after the outbreak of European war did the fusion of American and motion picture challenges occur. Independently, both the cinema and its American variant entered new historical phases. A combination of unprecedented official respect for the power of the moving image and mass enthusiasm for motion picture entertainment made it an indispensable component of national self-awareness and self-projection. At precisely this moment there occurred a fundamental shift in the international film balance. French production suffered a calamitous decline, occasioned in part by failure to protect key personnel from enlisting. The Italian industry also experienced a setback and, like the French, did not regain its place on the international market. Economic and social pressures of European mobilization and the disruption of previous trade patterns permitted Hollywood to become the principal supplier for European movie theaters and win primacy on the world film market.[8]

Before the war, Germany, though the foremost power in Europe, relied overwhelmingly on imported motion pictures to supply its cinemas. It now proved the primary European beneficiary of the market revolution. Cut off from previous sources of supply in enemy countries, it belatedly developed a production sector to match its national power. While the constellation of forces which has ever since encouraged equation of the motion picture and Hollywood took shape, Germany laid the foundation for an international cinema profile. The coincidence of Hollywood's rise to global dominance and Germany's emergence as the leading European producer determined the pattern of international competition in the subsequent decade. It meant as well that Germany's postwar version of a common European experience—inundation by American motion picture entertainment—acquired unique accents.

The first of these was temporal. Whereas in western Europe the war brought an avalanche of American movies, Germany became increasingly isolated from international trends and witnessed dramatic expansion of domestic film output. While American exports established a firm position in Europe in the latter stages of the war and fortified it immediately thereafter, the German market belonged overwhelmingly to domestic producers.[9] Motion picture import remained illegal until 1921 and of limited profitability until 1924 because of the postwar inflationary spiral. Thus Weimar's initiation into American movie entertainment came late and after a considerable hiatus. American movies had been shown in German theaters until the middle of the war, but the intervening break gave the Weimar encounter with Hollywood considerable novelty.

The second distinction concerns the volume and breadth of American impact. Not only did Hollywood's inroads come late, but they never assumed the dimensions familiar elsewhere. American companies dumped large quantities of movies in Germany, established their own distribution companies and gained influence in German production. Nevertheless, Hollywood never won the control in Germany which it wielded almost everywhere else. At no time did American feature film imports constitute a clear majority of German market offerings. A significant indigenous alternative to Hollywood survived throughout the Republican era. Though overseas competition eliminated domestic production of short entertainment films, in the newsreel and documentary department native producers more than held their own. Despite extreme economic vicissitudes, German producers retained a position from which they recovered control of the domestic market with the advent of talking motion pictures.[10]

The third peculiarity of the German situation is qualitative. Weimar's reputation is not purely posthumous. Germany not only boasted the largest and healthiest film industry in Europe at the end of the war, but it won international recognition almost immediately with a series of outstanding motion pictures, beginning with *Madame Dubarry* and *Das Cabinet des Dr. Caligari*. Notwithstanding American inroads and theft of talent, a tradition of excellence persisted through the remainder of the decade. In the latter half of the Weimar era the films of G. W. Pabst and Fritz Lang, not to mention the experiments of Leopold Jessner, Bertolt Brecht, Piel Jutzi and Robert Siodmak, testified to ongoing artistic ferment. German filmmakers continued to contribute substantially to the development of cinema as an art form and exercised considerable influence abroad.[11]

Together these features anchor Weimar cinema's historical reputation. After the war Germany was the one nation which could pretend to present a European answer to Hollywood. For a fleeting moment in the first half of the postwar decade it even appeared to mount a frontal assault on American hegemony. For a comparably brief period in the second half of the decade it became the rallying point of a pan-European movement aimed at checking American inroads. However beleaguered, it thus presented a commercial as well as artistic alternative to American domination.[12] That achievement has made it a cynosure of historical interest. Legendary in its own time for historical authenticity, artistic stylization, interiority and exploration of the uncanny or bizarre, it continues to fascinate. In the annals of cultural modernism it stands for many of the progressive, experimental features attributed to Weimar culture. In the history of film it retains paradigmatic importance for thematic and stylistic peculiarities which anchor a national cinema and for advancing the cause of film art through participation in Expressionism and *Neue Sachlichkeit*. In the history of interwar Germany it tells a tale of inwardness, horror and retreat from the present into a glorified past parallel to the path from Republic to Third Reich. In each respect it points beyond itself to larger concerns.[13]

Historiographically, Weimar cinema has both profitted and suffered from its notoriety. Siegfried Kracauer's classic *From Caligari to Hitler*, written in the aftermath of World War II, established a much-criticized but still influential precedent by using the film record to shed light on German history. Kracauer posited a relationship between Weimar cinema and the rise of Hitler by treating the former as a reflection of the national psyche. He aimed, in short, to link cinema to the German (psychic) *Sonderweg*.[14] Shortly thereafter Lotte Eisner's study of Expressionist film established historical interest in this narrow slice of

Weimar cinema. Though, unlike Kracauer, more interested in artistic than psychological predispositions, she too made reference to characteristics of the German soul.[15] Together, Kracauer and Eisner have largely set the agenda of subsequent research, particularly through their periodization and film selection. Quite apart from the seemingly inexhaustible attraction of motion picture Expressionism, Weimar cinema remains a study in German peculiarities. At its most provocative this approach has yielded reconstructions of the commercial imperatives, intellectual assumptions and sociological base which formed the creative context of contemporary filmmaking.[16] In more derivative forms it has created a pantheon of classic films and directors, a type of Whig history of cinema which leads from the postwar historical spectacles of Ernst Lubitsch and Richard Oswald, through the Expressionist and stylized works of Paul Wegener, Paul Leni and Robert Wiene, the *Kammerspielfilm* of F. W. Murnau and Lupu Pick and the mythical epics of Fritz Lang, to the realist works of *Neue Sachlichkeit* by G. W. Pabst and Joe May. Prominent directors and pioneering films present a succession of thematic and technical advances in the evolution of cinema.[17]

Although more than four decades after Kracauer a new synthesis of Weimar cinema remains to be written, scholars have recently begun to chip away at accepted wisdom. In Germany, cinema's relegation to inferior status among academic disciplines means that much of the best work is being done by archivists and private researchers, struggling against time and financial constraints to find and preserve primary material from the silent period. Despite extensive material losses and the high cost of preserving what is extant, considerable empirical research has been undertaken. At Anglo-American universities the explosion of interest in film has been spurred largely by literary and theoretical concerns in the history of popular culture. In the last decade and a half new vistas have been opened on Weimar cinema from a number of perspectives—literary, proletarian, feminist and political.[18] Lacunae have been filled in our understanding of the production process by studies of leading personalities.[19] Moreover, investigation of the early confrontation between film and literature has assisted the task of integrating cinema history into the wider sweep of German culture in the first third of the century.[20] Nonetheless, obstacles to a successful synthesis remain. We have neither a social nor an economic history of Weimar cinema, nor a systematic investigation of film criticism, advertising or censorship. Nor do we yet have an overview of production patterns which pays serious attention to the fact that Germany was Europe's leading motion picture manufacturer and exporter, not just a specialist in Expressionist stylization, historical drama and experiments in social realism.[21]

Nonetheless, it is clear, as Wolfgang Jacobsen and Erich Rentschler have recently argued, that the main features of Weimar cinema were neither Expressionism nor *Neue Sachlichkeit* but thematic and stylistic eclecticism, a blend of kitsch, realism and expressionism with German accents but anchored in international narrative and identificatory modalities.[22] Categories borrowed from literature and art do scant justice to the outpouring of sensationalist serials, detective movies, military farces, operettas and documentaries. They also fail to integrate the motion picture into the broader stream of popular culture. Moreover, the overwhelming national bias of research has marginalized Germany's function as the meeting place of cinematic currents from east and west, primarily from the Soviet Union and the United States. For most of the 1920s Germany drew about half of its feature film releases from foreign producers and devoted intense effort to expansion of its foreign market, primarily in the United States. Weimar cinema, like Weimar culture in general, was as much international as German.[23]

The specific issue of Hollywood's global ascendancy, surely one of the most remarkable and unavoidable facets of twentieth century culture, has only recently been broached as an international concern.[24] In the last decade studies of Australian, Italian and British film have acknowledged that domestic developments took shape in dialogue with, reaction against and imitation of Hollywood.[25] The balance has begun to shift away from national exclusivity to consideration of the international context within which it was defined. This is not to deny that cinema came to maturity during decades which witnessed the zenith of European nationalism. Even before 1914 relatively free exchange took place amidst sharpening commercial rivalries as industrialists recognized that trade followed moving images as much as the flag. Apart from its economic importance as a consumer of capital, source of employment and contributor of foreign credits, film served to indoctrinate, pacify and educate, and thereby to nationalize the masses.[26] In the course of the First World War control of the mind became another weapon in national arsenals. Governments realized the cinema's potential to influence attitudes and enlisted it in propaganda efforts to justify belligerence, defame the enemy and entertain the home front or soldiers behind the lines. Cinema became a national resource.[27]

All this being said, film's global ramifications—ideological, commercial and cultural—were evident from its infancy. Cinema was, as it remains, the first and most consequential medium to transcend geographic, linguistic and cultural barriers. No other mode of communication has enjoyed such catholic impact, speaking directly to persons of diverse national, social and ideological backgrounds. Particularly in the first three decades of this century, the era of screen silence, the cinema offered the closest approximation to a universal language—Esperanto based on images.[28] Moreover, international film exchange became the norm almost from the moment of the medium's birth. Before World War I European audiences saw, apart from the preponderant French films, English, Italian, American and Scandinavian pictures. Different countries gained genre-specific identities—Italy in costume spectacle, the United States in slapstick and westerns, Denmark in chamber drama—but the market was not characterized by chauvinism.[29]

Scholarly inclination to treat film movements in national context, despite long awareness of American hegemony in the golden age of silents, is rooted in circumstances created by the Great War. The decade after 1918 has been dubbed the era of national cinemas: producers in each country allegedly cultivated, and their audiences preferred, domestic film styles.[30] While neither arbitrary nor accidental, that designation pays tribute to the contemporary drive—through product differentiation, experimentation and borrowing from other art forms—to stake out unique national property, artistic and commercial, in a highly supranational medium under American control. As much ideal construct as reality (the paper answer to Hollywood's celluloid imperialism), it confirmed the disregard of film for national boundaries.[31] Subsequent preoccupation with uniquely accented motion pictures—in the German case, historical epics, Expressionist experiments, chamber drama and the socially realistic films of the second half of the era—therefore follows a logic rooted in American hegemony after 1918. Without adopting its chauvinism, scholarship has accepted its organizational principles. None of the categories traditionally employed in study of Weimar cinema is sufficiently rigorous to permit unambiguous application to more than a fraction of total domestic production, but each, significantly, sets Weimar cinema apart from Hollywood.[32] For contemporaries, the national cinema had limited historical significance without reference to American film. National identity and cosmopolitanism posed not conflicting options but dialectical poles marking off the real and rhetorical space within which they located Weimar cinema. Historical concern for national identity testifies to the tenacity of perceptions rooted in the 1920s—recognition of America's thematic and stylistic primacy but rebellion against its hegemonic pretensions.[33]

The German confrontation with Hollywood took place in an international context whose main contours have long been familiar. Already in the course of the war American motion pictures made enormous, irreversible inroads on French, British, Italian and Scandinavian markets. The United States emerged from the war without film rivals, dwarfing all other nations in every department from the size and number of its theaters to production figures and the salaries paid its screen stars. It produced several times the number of feature films annually as Germany, its closest rival. With a population less than double that of Germany it had roughly four times as many movie theaters.[34] Although Germany escaped the initial onslaught thanks to the blockade and an import ban, when Hollywood gained access to the German market at the beginning of the new decade it rapidly made up for lost time. Within three years it had eliminated German production of entertainment shorts, won direct control of roughly forty percent of the feature film market and gained a hand in domestic production through branch operations in Germany. Berlin, the center of European film production and culture, attracted a stream of American stars and moguls with production or distribution plans and contracts with which to enlist talent for Hollywood. Germany was thus belatedly but thoroughly integrated into the network of international cinema culture of which Hollywood was capital.

Hollywood was essential to German cinema experience in the 1920s because its product, advertising and personalities enjoyed international primacy. Sheer magnitude, its outstanding feature, was not, however, its only component. The German (and European) experience of Hollywood was stamped, as contemporaries gradually realized, by complementarity between the motion picture and American culture. Motion pictures quickly became the most pervasive and persuasive of America's contributions to European culture because cinema epitomized American culture in its mass orientation, tempo, monumentalism, sensationalism and profit urge.[35] In short, Hollywood's dominance signified correspondence between the medium and the American message. Not only did Hollywood bring to more Europeans than ever before "live" impressions of the New World, giving visual contours to the American dream—the moral, social and economic foundations of beauty, success and happiness, it also introduced and recycled interminably a formula for motion picture entertainment rooted in American assumptions which established itself as *the* mode of filmic discourse. This symbiosis of broad cultural and more specific dramatic-filmic conventions lent potency to Hollywood's presence. It made cinema a major pillar of the American imperium in the postwar world.

Historical treatment of responses to Hollywood in interwar Europe has essentially followed the lines of the cultural debate about America and Americanization. This highlights conflicting attitudes toward consumer culture, social leveling, traditional literary or artistic forms and the encroachments of technology. The debate about American cinema becomes a microcosm of this larger discourse. Hollywood represented the erosion of traditional distinctions between culture and commodity, art and artifice, personal creativity and assembly-line production, the fusion of high and low culture, and a catalyst for formation of a homogenized mass culture, what D. L. LeMahieu has termed a "common culture." Reactions to it appear, on the one hand, as a final, futile effort to reverse the tide of history and, on the other, as enthusiasm for cultural modernity.[36]

To the extent that Hollywood's presence in Germany has received historical attention, emphasis has fallen on its distance from classical Weimar cinema and fascination for literary intellectuals. Thomas Elsaesser situates Germany's assimilation of Hollywood in the domestic tug-of-war between market imperatives and the quest for artistic self-realization. Recognizing classical Weimar cinema as a "self-conscious attempt at bourgeois cinema," Elsaesser argues that Hollywood represented the challenge of the mass market and a particular formula for relating art, technology and commerce. Weimar's search for a synthesis of these components appropriate to the demands of the cultural establishment yielded a transitional cinema, experimental and lacking solid commercial underpinnings. Unlike the American model, in Germany the relationship between artist and medium remained unstable.[37]

Use of American cinema as a point of contrast for domestic agendas is homologous to the appropriation of Hollywood for extra-filmic purposes by literary intellectuals. Anton Kaes has situated fascination with *Amerikanismus* within the broader *Kinodebatte*, specifically the process by which literary intellectuals came to terms with popular culture. Left-leaning cultural critics and writers flirted with Hollywood as part of their rebellion against bourgeois cultural norms. Weary of a cultural establishment whose credibility had been severely shaken by the Great War, these persons found escape in American westerns and comedies. Here Hollywood enjoyed the attraction of the other—distant, exotic, modern and anarchic—and immediacy as an entertainment industry catering to the mass need for distraction.[38]

The agendas pursued in classical Weimar cinema and in the *Kinodebatte* are the essential points of departure for any discussion of Hollywood's place in Germany. If not always explicitly directed at American cinema, they heavily shaped German discourse on American film. Yet neither perspective is wholly satisfactory, for neither does full justice to the historical location of Weimar cinema. Only a small proportion of the feature films made in Germany in the 1920s belong to what we now identify as classical Weimar cinema. Moreover, those literary intellectuals intrigued by the films of Charlie Chaplin or Douglas Fairbanks represent only one window on Weimar's encounter with Hollywood. American motion pictures became such an integral part of domestic movie culture that dialogue between Hollywood and Berlin was sustained across an enormous spectrum of commercial, artistic and national interests. Discourse on American film was riven with the competing ambitions of businesspeople, filmmakers, critics, censors and intellectuals. Its vital context was an ambitious domestic cinema, a culture industry with interests to legitimize and defend, which fought self-consciously to carve out cultural space for itself.

Research on Hollywood's role in other nations has taken American ascendancy for granted while seeking the specific sources of that ascendancy. Peter Stead and Paul Swann have rationalized the popular demand for American film entertainment in interwar and postwar Britain.[39] James Hay has recently examined the process by which interwar Italian audiences identified with and found significance in American movies.[40] Hollywood's attraction for the European avant-garde has been explored by David Shi and Thomas Elsaesser.[41] Barry Salt has undertaken the arduous task of evaluating Hollywood's impact on European filmmaking practice by comparing evolution in shot lengths and rhythms.[42] Whatever their precise focus, thematic, technical or intellectual, these analyses concur that Hollywood's meaning was determined by the context in which it was received as well as by its own signifiers.[43]

As already indicated, the German context differs in essential respects from that of its European neighbors. In the first instance, one cannot assume American primacy. Germany boasted a vigorous, initially quite independent motion picture culture, which like no other of its time presented a counterpart and challenge to Hollywood. Contrary to practice elsewhere, in Germany there is occasion to rationalize the relative unpopularity of American motion pictures. This, plus the fact that in the early 1920s Germany appeared a potential threat to Hollywood's international hegemony, shaped domestic discussion of American cinema in distinctive ways.[44] Moreover, within the macrocosm of nation, context was anything but fixed or homogeneous. Quite apart from the multiplicity of interests noted above, context shifted over time with the advance and recession of Hollywood's presence as well as the fluctuating fortunes of the German film economy. What follows analyzes the changing contours of discourse on American cinema in Weimar Germany against this shifting backdrop.

Notwithstanding the conspicuously technical nature of the medium, questions of film technology and filmic technique did not play the leading role in German debate. This was not, it should be emphasized, for lack of interest in American achievements. It reflects rather the relative ease with which photographic and shooting techniques were exchanged and, above all, the assumption that these did not constitute the determinative factors in competition between Hollywood and Berlin. Informed contemporaries were certainly fascinated with American cinematographic feats and included them in explanations for Hollywood's international dominance. But they also isolated domestic films which were the equal of any from the United States in this respect. Furthermore, they ultimately looked elsewhere to explain the peculiarities of American cinema and the ability of Hollywood to make its product a universal staple of movie entertainment. Trained to think in terms of national cultures, they sought the difference between domestic and American film in mentalities, values and cultural traditions as well as commercial and organizational factors. Their attention focused on national identities expressed through the thematic, stylistic and entrepreneurial characteristics of each cinema.[45]

This preoccupation with national identity made it impossible to avoid the issue of Americanization. By middecade a buzzword in everything from industrial organization to women's hair styles, it represented both promise and peril. Since contemporary reflections on the subject were self-conscious and usually polemical, they present an extremely unreliable gauge of Hollywood's impact. Historical analysis of the problem may escape these two limitations, but confronts other, no less formidable, ones. That the cinema did more than any other medium to bring the United States to Europe, offering the most widely accessible and immediate contact with the land of unlimited possibilities, is undeniable. That the voluminous import of American movies conditioned the tastes, consumption patterns and social ambitions of foreign audiences can likewise hardly be disputed.[46] But if cinema, like the attention drawn by Lindbergh's solo flight to Europe in 1927, "quickened the pace of Americanization," separation of its influence from that of other cultural imports or domestic trends is highly problematic. No tidy formula exists for establishing the quantitative or qualitative influence of American film in Germany.[47]

D. L. LeMahieu, who argues the symbiotic relationship of film and the gramophone in accelerating the "Americanization" of England, points out that Americanization was itself a reciprocal influence and often operated at invisible levels. Changes effected by Hollywood in everything from consumer preferences to sex roles are notoriously difficult to trace to a single source.[48] In his study of interwar Italian film culture James Hay suggests analysis of advertising, dubbing, stereotyping of Americans in Italian movies and film criticism to determine the impact of American cinema on the Italian public consciousness.[49] Apart from the fact that these approaches are of uneven potential—the second and third recycle stereotypes familiar from other sources—they present all the problems of representativeness for national opinion posed by the motion pictures themselves. In the German case they also meet frustrating lack of hard data with which to ascertain to what extent American movies found popular resonance. To the larger question of how audiences perceived and were influenced by American movies contemporary surveys offer only fragmentary answers.[50]

German cinema, like many other sectors of the economy, both competed against and received capital and managerial input from the United States. It contributed directly (in the form of personnel) and indirectly (via its filmic presence on the American market) to Hollywood. In turn American motion picture companies engaged in extensive personal and corporate interaction with their German counterparts and produced a substantial portion of the films consumed in Germany. The case for Weimar's assimilation of filmic Americanisms can be made from contemporary and historical perspectives. Contemporaries, whether opposed to or in favor of the practice, agreed that borrowing was widespread. Using a crude but popular image of American cinema as thematically optimistic, stylistically syncretic, technically imposing and commercially calculated, they detected Hollywood in, for instance, the happy ending of Murnau's *Der letzte Mann* (*The Last Laugh*) or Pabst's *Die Liebe der Jeanne Ney* and in the stylistic eclecticism, technological fetishism and ethical simplification of *Metropolis*.[51] Historically and more systematically, Barry Salt has argued that American cutting rhythms, camera angles and acting styles were deliberately adopted in German production from the mid-1920s. His research suggests that by the final years of silents German filmmakers had appropriated the principal components of American cinematic form.[52]

However normative Hollywood became, hard evidence to demonstrate a simple cause and effect relationship between American and German cinemas is fragmentary and ambiguous. Since production files have perished for the bulk of German motion pictures in the 1920s, and since the films themselves are in good proportion lost or extant only in truncated versions, a general case for American influence must be made with caution.[53] The extant films can, moreover, confuse as much as clarify the issue. To scrutinize them for assimilation of Hollywood misses one essential element of the German-American confrontation to which reference has already been made. Some filmmakers sought independence and marketability by shunning obvious Americanisms. Weimar's most prominent motion picture producer, Erich Pommer, was not alone in arguing that competition with Hollywood, at least in the first half of the 1920s, could best be mounted by a distinctive, national approach rather than imitation. Although Pommer changed his tune after working in Hollywood, it can still be argued that one outcome of American dominance was cultivation of an alternative film discourse.[54]

The American star system, performing styles, flair for publicity and increasing standardization of production elicited enormous attention and imitation in Germany. German filmmakers closely followed the work of the leading American directors and performers. Many took study trips to New York and Hollywood to be schooled in everything from business organization to camera types and lighting. Some worked in Hollywood and so had first-hand experience of American aims and methods. A number, such as Karl Freund, Wilhelm Dieterle and Friedrich Zelnik, found employment with American subsidiaries in Germany. There is also unequivocal as well as circumstantial evidence of deliberate targeting of the American market by the foremost German companies. From all these perspectives Americanization was clearly inescapable. Nevertheless, the larger question of whether American influence ultimately homogenized or diversified domestic film production admits no categorical response. Classical narrative cinema, the studio system and promotional hype may be identified as quintessentially American. The logic behind each was not peculiarly American any more than it pertained only to the motion picture. The challenge of habituating the public to visit the movies, like that of maximizing and stabilizing the demand for pulp fiction or daily newspapers, was inherent in the conditions of production and consumption in a competitive, capitalist system.[55] Weimar took American models of business rationalization and mass marketing seriously precisely because they corresponded to the internal dynamic of German development.[56]

With all these qualifications to facile generalizations about Americanization, what cannot be doubted is that Weimar was intensely engaged in dialogue with Hollywood and made it the primary reference point for domestic achievements. This was true both at the level of informed opinion—filmmakers, theater owners, critics—and among moviegoers. From the period before resumption of import, through the era when American movies became domesticated, to the early phase of the transition from silent to sound film, experts scrutinized, responded to and debated the lessons to be drawn from American cinema. Simultaneously, millions of moviegoers passed judgment on American films and, wittingly or otherwise, on the American way of life. Unfortunately, the latter, apart from voting with their feet (a vote for which we lack aggregate, not to mention more detailed statistics) indulged in applause, laughter, tears or protest which are remembered only insofar as critics and trade experts recorded them. Weimar's encounter with Hollywood is therefore recorded primarily in the discourse of those with a vested interest—cultural, artistic, commercial, educational—in motion picture enterprise. Literary intellectuals represent only one, and not the most numerous, nor necessarily influential or informed, group of commentators. A more essential filter for the historian is the German motion picture establishment. At once more concerned to monitor Hollywood's inroads, editorialize on its achievements and devise means to counter or profit from its presence, the film community also entertained cultural ambitions which shaped its encounter with American cinema.

This extensive and diverse community was comprised of creative personnel (producers, directors, performers and screen authors), entrepreneurs (board directors, distributors and theater owners), and an army of journalists, critics, advertisers and miscellaneous camp followers. While anything but united in perception or purpose, these persons shared immediate concern for motion picture issues. Their collective interests and opinions formed the commercial and ideological matrix for German cinema. More systematically than any other groups they represented Weimar vis-à-vis Hollywood. Critics, less able than moviegoers to vote with their feet, used their public voice to establish the terms on which American imports would be discussed and to urge on filmmakers specific creative responses to Hollywood. Those involved in the production process, as performers, screenwriters or directors, had direct input into competitive strategies and often also publicized their opinions. Through an enormous range of printed material, from advertising brochures, company or fan magazines and a burgeoning trade press to daily papers and highbrow art journals, the critical and creative spokespersons of the industry located American film in Germany and defined domestic objectives by contrast with it. Within this energetic and outspoken community of cognoscenti, dissection of Hollywood was therefore both deeply self-conscious and eminently scrutable.

The following pages examine Weimar's experience of Hollywood from several perspectives. The starting point is to locate the motion picture in Weimar culture. Since the record of contemporaries who wrestled with Hollywood's presence in Germany serves as a principal historical source, this includes an introduction to the character and scope of film commentary in this period. Equally essential—the burden of chapter two—is discussion of industrial relations, particularly of contemporary attitudes toward the infiltration of American financing and methods. Chapter three traces patterns of response to American film entertainment from the beginning of the decade until the relative stabilization of middecade in order to restore the historical contours of a theme usually handled statically. Chapters four and five chronicle and dissect the popular and critical boundaries which American motion pictures encountered in Germany. Subsequent chapters narrow in on specific categories of American film—slapstick, German-American productions and talkies—which raised particular challenges. Throughout, the aim is to contextualize the discourse on American cinema according to shifting German expectations. Comparison of German and American methods inevitably preoccupied contemporaries, but is not itself the primary issue. American motion pictures acted as a foil for more than their German counterparts, giving Hollywood relevance to broader cultural as well as cinematic questions.

1
THE SETTING
Weimar Germany and the Motion Picture

Weimar cinema, like Weimar culture in general, dates not from 1918 but from immediately before the war. Whether one examines the outstanding art films, the debate over the cinema's social and political significance or the varieties of postwar cinema culture, the formative years were the last of the German empire. From about 1910 German film entered an era of rapid commercial, artistic and technical development. Over the next decade the cinema experienced unprecedented growth and acquired a position which would have shocked turn-of-the-century observers. Until shortly before the war most films came from abroad, catered to a predominantly lower class audience and appeared in a relatively few, unimposing theaters. One decade later they were produced in the main in Germany, boasted impressive cinematographic qualities, drew patrons from all social classes and were released in theaters which in number and style far surpassed the standards of pre-1914. By the beginning of the 1920s the cinema was not only *the* mass entertainment medium of the period but a booming industry and a novel art form.[1]

The simplest and most revealing indicator of the cinema's growing public role was a sharp increase in the number of motion picture theaters. In 1910 there were approximately 1,000 theaters in the Reich; two years later, 1,500; in 1914, 2,446; in 1919, 2,836.[2] Although these figures conceal variations in size, luxury and program which mock the attempt to speak of a single cinema culture, they actually understate the extent of expansion. Theaters grew in size as well as number. In 1910 1,000 cinemas accommodated roughly 200,000 patrons; nine years later fewer than three times that number of theaters could seat almost five times as many viewers.[3] Furthermore, among these were a growing number of movie palaces which symbolized the maturity and importance of the cinema in the subsequent decade. Clusters of downtown premiere cinemas appeared in major German cities, foremost among them the group along Berlin's Kurfürstendamm running into the Tauentzienstrasse, where films premiered before Germany's social and political elite.[4]

Central to growth in the exhibition sector was the establishment of a substantial production base. Before 1914 German filmmaking remained relatively modest in scale.[5] Estimates for the period 1905–1910 indicate that French, American, Italian and Scandinavian imports accounted for thirty, twenty-five, twenty and fifteen percent respectively of the movies released in Germany. Domestic output did not exceed ten percent of the home market. Nor did the immediate prewar theater boom find a full parallel in the production sector. In 1912–1913 the native share of the market still reached only thirteen percent.[6] Precisely at this moment German cinema experienced the breakthrough from confectionary trade to art and big business. For historical convenience that transformation is often dated to the appearance in 1913 of two feature literary adaptations (*Autorenfilme*)—*Der Andere* and the original Paul Wegener version of *Der Student von Prag*—as well as the publication by Kurt Pinthus of *Das Kinobuch*, a collection of film treatments by young Expressionist authors. These milestones marked both the technical/industrial potential and the literary/intellectual resources which were to give Weimar cinema its distinctive face.[7]

It was the war which spawned an independent German cinema, partly because it provided existing producers new opportunities, and more essentially because it finally mobilized the financial forces required to sustain large-scale production. In the first instance, declining output in France and Italy gave a crucial fillip to native production. This was accompanied in 1915 by a ban on import of foreign (chiefly French, British and Italian) films made *since* the outbreak of war. Then in February 1916 a comprehensive ban was imposed as part of a general tightening of import/export regulations, leaving import permission to a federal commissioner.[8] By 1916 German films outnumbered imports by somewhat less than 2 : 1. Admittedly, this ratio concealed anomalies. Chief of these was the fact that the foremost "German" producer was still a foreign company. The Danish concern, Nordisk, largely filled the void left by the French and Americans and enjoyed a commanding position on the German market. Nordisk not only distributed in Germany but had its own production facilities and owned the largest chain of German theaters. So powerful was its position that it gained exemption from the import ban. Thus restriction of import provided a precondition but not a guarantee for the ascendancy of domestic producers.[9]

More portentous than the removal of foreign film suppliers was the role of the war in impressing upon business and government leaders the untapped potential of film in propaganda for German cultural and industrial interests. The realization finally dawned that motion picture production could not only be profitable in its own right but was also indispensable to the selling of Germany and German products abroad. The skill with which Allied film propaganda blackened Germany's worldwide reputation drove the lesson home. In the latter half of the war the creation of Deutsche Lichtbild Gesellschaft (DLG) and the better known and more ambitious Universum Film A.G. (UFA), introduced a new era in German film history. DLG owed its establishment to the director of Krupp, Alfred Hugenberg, and other leaders of heavy industry in the Ruhr of which he was the representative. It specialized in the production of short educational and advertising films which were to bolster the image of Germany and German industry.[10] UFA proved the more significant creation, for it was to become the leading concern of the interwar period. It too originally aimed to counter Allied propaganda but very rapidly took the lead in general movie entertainment. Its capital base of twenty-five million marks towered over that of every other German firm. In it were united the interests of the government, of shipping, electrical and banking firms brought together by the director of the Deutsche Bank, Emil Georg von Stauss, and of the heretofore predominant Nordisk. From its inception UFA represented the same type of vertical integration, though on a grander scale, which had characterized the operations of Nordisk. Production, distribution and theater management were combined in one mammoth undertaking. All these features suggest what was made explicit in UFA's initial press statement, namely, that the company saw itself as the advance guard of German film in postwar competition against the foreign firms which had previously dominated the German and international markets.[11]

The third pivotal development in the decade before the founding of the Weimar Republic was the initial collision between the motion picture and interests representing literature, the theater, national virtue and public order. The early *Autorenfilme* and *Das Kinobuch* symbolized the breakthrough of the cinema as a serious art form. Authors, playwrights and performers began to recognize in film a new field of creative endeavor. The acceptance of film roles by such theatrical performers as Paul Wegener and Albert Bassermann lent credibility to the young medium. Simultaneously, however, the movies disturbed entrenched interests. Live theaters, varietés and pubs saw their existence jeopardized by cheap competition and launched petitions to limit the cinema's expansion. More influential was a concerted campaign by the trustees of German *Kultur* to adapt the motion picture to their social and political purposes. Middle-class conservative pedagogues, clerics and jurists, the guardians of German moral and social probity, launched a "film reform movement" to tame this sensationalist, escapist and immoral form of entertainment.[12] For the extremists among them this meant a blanket ban on all but educational films. More generally they sought supervision of the movies through censorship and state ownership. From their efforts emerged a prewar compromise—local censorship and entertainment taxes.[13]

Immediately after 1918 the motion picture experienced a veritable *Gründerzeit*. Another boom in theater construction between 1918 and 1920 pushed the number of cinemas up from 2,299 to 3,731. With this explosion came growing numbers of elegant premiere theaters seating as many as 2,000 viewers, most notably in Berlin's west end, which became institutions of the urban bourgeoisie.[14] After 1920 there were slight setbacks but the long-term trend remained upward so that at the end of the decade Germany boasted over 5,000 movie theaters. Estimates of attendance at middecade vary widely, between slightly fewer than one million and two million persons daily, but even the lower figure implies that on average every German over 18 years of age went to the movies 6.6 times annually.[15]

Domestic film production grew apace. UFA's lead was felt immediately, even though it did not possess a numerically dominant share of German output. In 1918 UFA already controlled roughly one quarter of all the motion pictures distributed in Germany. It employed many leading German performers and directors, among them Henny Porten, Paul Wegener and Ernst Lubitsch, and it operated the largest chain of theaters.[16] Nor did UFA's impact extend only to the motion pictures it produced, distributed and exhibited. Like Nordisk it pioneered film's breakthrough on German capital markets. The immediate post-war period witnessed the founding of the other major concerns which together led the German film industry in the 1920s: Emelka, Terra, Decla-Bioscop, Deulig (a reorganized DLG), and National. The common aim was concentration of capital and resources, which meant that banks were the prime movers behind these creations. At the same time, a host of smaller firms sprang up to exploit the seemingly endless demand for motion picture entertainment. The net result then of UFA's appearance was not the monopoly which trade circles initially feared. In the distribution sector several firms (UFA, Emelka, National) were clearly dominant and in exhibition the large concerns controlled many of the prestigious cinemas, but lesser companies continued to thrive.[17]

So fundamental was the transformation of the German film industry that by 1919 native firms were technically the sole suppliers of the domestic market. Although motion pictures continued to enter Germany from abroad, by any previous standard native producers had a well-sheltered and expanding market at their disposal. Moreover, with the growing and then precipitous decline of the German mark they could dump their output abroad in exchange for hard currency. The promise of fantastic foreign earnings, plus the natural barrier which inflation erected against foreign competition at home, lent this era its distinctive flavor. Hand in hand with commercial expansion went the filmic experimentation responsible for Weimar's cinematic reputation. Expressionist films, chamber dramas which with a limited cast and minimal dialogue gave mimetic form to psychological conflicts, and historical pageants with imposing mass scenes enriched German production and thanks to foreign, not least American, applause, also quickly became Weimar's self-assigned trademark.

Since many of the feature films from the early 1920s have perished, it is difficult to generalize accurately about German production values in this period. But there is no doubt that the hundreds of features produced in the inflationary period exhibited enormous variety. Immediately after the armistice so-called *Aufklärungsfilme*, pretending to warn the population of the dangers of vice and venereal disease while capitalizing on the abolition of censorship, earned notoriety. Detective and adventure films of uneven sophistication, romances and humorous subjects likewise flourished. Isolation from American suppliers even prompted German studios to produce ersatz westerns to quench the screen thirst for Karl May. All in all, despite uneven quality—inflation encouraged quick and inexpensive production for export—German output was both variegated and served a socially diverse and expanding clientele.

On the basis of all this evidence the historian can endorse the contemporary perception that the German cinema came of age at the end of the war. Contemporaries were awed by the whirlwind tempo at which casual amusement for the working classes became serious business and part of the nation's culture.[18] Historians have been impressed primarily by the qualitative achievements of a young industry. Both views are well founded, but neither does full justice to the position of film in Weimar culture. No amount of evidence detailing expansion and popularity can disguise the fact that the *Kulturkampf* over film which raged before the war did not end in 1918. Relations between cinema and various levels of state, cultural and artistic authority (or vested interest) remained unsettled. Moreover, even as rapid development spawned a substantial community of persons bound to the motion picture, it generated internal divisions over the cinema's nature and purpose. For social, economic and political as well as artistic reasons, Weimar cinema displayed greater pluralism than homogeneity. Since external pressure at the point of contact with entrenched interests and internal strain arising from disagreement about the purpose of the medium created the *Sitz im Leben* for reception of American movies, both require elaboration.

State concern for the motion picture dated from its birth as a public medium, initially because it posed an extreme fire hazard. Very rapidly film began to cause anxiety for moral and social reasons. The suggestiveness both of film content and of the atmosphere in which it was shown became a point of complaint among middle-class guardians of German virtue. In the last years before the war the film reform movement sought to focus public attention on the dangers of movies, especially for German youth. While local authorities, usually the police, acted as censors, the reformers sought national measures governing censorship and permitting municipal takeover of movie theaters. Legislation embodying these proposals came before the Reichstag but was set aside under the circumstances of national mobilization. For the duration of hostilities Germany remained under martial law, giving regional military commanders ultimate authority over licensing and censorship. Tightening of control and a ban on imports went hand in hand with growing recognition of the vital propaganda and entertainment role of the cinema, witnessed by the cooperation of government and big business to found UFA.[19]

The fall of the imperial regime and end of martial law seemed to portend a new era in the relationship between government and the cinema. But it very rapidly became apparent that the revolution had not transformed concerns or regulatory mechanisms. The attempt to do away with the Bismarckian state ended, ironically, in a motion picture law whose centralization and consistency fit the authoritarian image of the old regime. Ultimately the movie industry remained in the private sector and was regulated from without by two traditional expedients—taxation and censorship. State supervision throws into sharp relief the blend of respect and dismay with which official, middle-class Germany confronted the cinema.

Just three days after the proclamation of the Republic the temporary Council of People's Representatives abolished all forms of censorship. Initial drafts of the Weimar constitution likewise rejected any infringement on freedom of expression.

Yet as finally adopted the constitution included a rider (article 117) which permitted eventual censorship of film. Less than one year later (May 1920) a Motion Picture Law instituted nationwide censorship. Article 117 of the constitution and the law of May 1920 came from a National Assembly in which socialist and liberal-democratic deputies dominated. Both provisions also passed by overwhelming majorities. The usual explanation for the behavior of an assembly led by parties hostile to restrictions on freedom of expression cites the wave of "enlightenment" films about prostitution and venereal disease which appeared in the aftermath of the war. Ostensibly serving to educate and thus protect the public, these films exploited the subject material for such sensational effect that they prompted public protest.[20] Although the Reichstag debates on the problem substantiate this interpretation—postwar social/moral decline concerned all parties—they also reveal assumptions about the power of the cinema which transcended worries about sexual explicitness.

The decision to include censorship provisions in the constitution was taken almost without debate, particularly on the part of the ruling parties. In the spring and summer of 1919 the National Assembly admittedly had many more pressing matters to settle than a brief clause authorizing some future arrangement for movies. Nonetheless, apparent absence of partisanship is striking. Two weeks before ratification of the constitution, article 117 prompted a brief exchange. The German Democratic Party (DDP) took the stand expected of liberals' descendants, arguing that film censorship represented a throwback to the Metternich era and negated constitutional recognition of adulthood at age twenty. Independent Socialists (USPD), by now seriously disaffected by the use of Republican troops against striking workers, blamed current abuses on the profiteering of big business and demanded state intervention to curb it, advocating censorship only to protect minors. The German Nationalists (DNVP) echoed these sentiments towards capitalist manipulation of the cultural and moral standards of the German people but believed censorship an adequate solution to the problem. While right and left therefore made common cause, Majority Socialists (SPD) and the Catholic Center (Zentrum), the dominant parties in the assembly, silently accepted the reigning consensus.[21]

The parliamentary discussion late in 1919 which preceded introduction of formal legislation underscored near unanimity on the need for action. That a Nationalist deputy who decried movies as a pestilence unleashed by unscrupulous capitalists won the applause of both the Center and the SPD gives a fair indication of the prevailing mood.[22] While members forwarded a number of measures for consideration—licensing or outright communal ownership of cinemas and socialization of film production—the simplest one to agree upon was censorship. Attempts by the USPD and DDP to challenge this approach to the problem made little headway. To defend the cinema as an enormously important cultural advance and to question the practicality of censorship did little to dent the general opinion, prevalent even in their own ranks, that something had to be done, and immediately, to arrest the poisoning of German minds with filth and lies. Censorship not only had the advantage of familiarity, but it also skirted the larger economic and political issues raised by suggestions of socializing the industry or communalizing the cinemas. Following the path of least resistance, Erich Koch, the Democratic Minister of the Interior, adopted the nationalist cry that the issue was not political but moral. He promised a draft censorship law and possible restrictions on the expansion of motion picture theaters.[23]

The sense of inevitability about censorship pervades debate which ensued on second reading of the bill in April 1920. Each party now had its spokesperson and sought to articulate a distinct position, but on essentials the consensus emerged stronger than ever. The DDP launched debate with the open admission that in this case a break with its cherished principle of free speech was unavoidable. Later the SPD followed suit, accepting "with heavy heart" the need for censorship even though it ran contrary to party philosophy. Similarly, while the USPD made another assault on the bill as evasion of socialization measures necessary in the production and exhibition sectors, it too preferred immediate action of some kind to a continuation of present circumstances.[24] The other parties had minor criticisms of the bill but accepted it in principle. Consensus was so overwhelming that the spokesperson for the Center praised the agreement of deputies to limit debate so as to speed the enactment of the bill. Despite some sqabbling over details the Reichstag passed the final version rapidly and with only minor changes.[25]

The National Motion Picture Law thereby enacted created two censorship boards, one in Berlin and one in Munich, and an appeal board located in Berlin. Films were to be reviewed by a five-person committee, a chairperson and four others. Representation was granted the film industry as well as pedagogues and cultural authorities. The appeal procedure was likewise handled by a mixed committee of experts. Although some disagreement surfaced over the composition and jurisdiction of these boards the greatest source of controversy was the crucial clause stipulating the grounds upon which the boards were to cut or ban motion pictures.[26] Examination of this clause indicates that Germany's political leaders were concerned not only with the corrosive influence of sexual explicitness. Any motion picture which would "endanger public order and security, offend religious sensibilities, have a brutalizing or immoral influence or compromise the German reputation or Germany's relations with foreign states" was banned from German theaters. Moreover, persons under eighteen years of age were not to be admitted to any screening from which there was cause to fear a "harmful effect on the moral, spiritual or physical development or overstimulation of the imagination of young people."[27]

In retrospect, the outstanding feature of the final bill, as of the Reichstag debates, was the intense anxiety written between its lines on the part of Germany's political and cultural leadership vis-à-vis the lower classes which constituted the bulk of moviegoers. Although sexual suggestiveness created the immediate offense, the origins of the law must be located in assumptions about the influence of the medium. In fact, the kernel of the motion picture law offers the most eloquent statement of contemporary fears about the persuasive powers of the cinema and the serious challenge it posed to the religious, social, moral and political status quo. To counter this challenge censors received a mandate comprehensive and flexible enough to cover any eventuality.[28] That at the same time they were being handed a double-edged sword did not entirely escape the deputies intent on reforming German cinemas. Not by accident, the SPD spokesperson insisted that in no instance should political, social, religious, ethical or ideological opinions justify a ban. But the inclusion of a clause to this effect and the defeat of a Nationalist motion to ban films "fomenting class hatred" (i.e, advocating socialism!) could still not divorce the review process from politics. If censors had authority to protect public order and security their role could not but be political. As the USPD repeatedly warned, censorship reflected a desire for control rooted in politics and was inevitably susceptible to abuse.[29]

If the heart of censorship legislation was fear of the cinema's enormous power, the social group most threatened was German youth. Here partisan opinion vanished. The left sought a lowering of the age of majority from eighteen to sixteen, but agreed entirely that Germany's young people were to be protected from moral contamination. The very general and universally applicable clause for restricting films did not leave much doubt about government intentions. Nor did the fact that the law overrode central control in this department, allowing local authorities to supercede the central boards to restrict films. Nor finally did censorship practice disappoint the framers of the legislation. Whereas censors banned a negligible number of films in the 1920s, they classified roughly one-third of the total for adults only.[30] In this context it is not at all anomalous that such an unsparing critic of German officialdom as Kurt Tucholsky fully endorsed special protection for German youth. Protests from the film industry against this aspect of state paternalism proved futile.[31]

The upshot then of postwar policy was not the extensive restructuring envisioned since before the war by film reformers. Although for a short period the Damocles sword of socialization and/or communalization hung over the industry, the outcome was a national motion picture law that the industry had considerable cause to welcome. The establishment in Berlin and Munich of central censorship boards spared producers the caprice of state or municipal authorities who, in the absence of federal control, had begun to exercise their own rights to censor movies. Furthermore, the new system provided representation and safeguards for film interests. One-quarter of the committee which classified films was to consist of delegates of the industry and adverse decisions could be appealed to a supreme censorship court. Apart from complaints about unfair scapegoating of the cinema by centering it out for systematic censorship, and notwithstanding a fitful campaign to have the age of majority lowered to sixteen, trade reactions to the new law were not uniformly hostile. Although disliked from opposing sides by advocates of freedom of expression and conservative film reformers, censorship represented a workable compromise.[32]

Less a matter for national politics but equally revealing for the place of cinema in Germany was the second official expedient used to control the movies, the entertainment tax or *Lustbarkeitssteuer*. This, a prewar practice borrowed from regulation of circuses and other public amusements, was a surcharge imposed by the municipality on ticket prices. It fluctuated so widely from one locality to the next that any generalization about its severity is hazardous, but in the early 1920s it ranged in the neighborhood of twenty to thirty percent. In some cities it rose well above these values, however, and was blamed for bankrupting otherwise profitable cinemas.[33] Even if city councils did not aim to strangle motion picture enterprise entirely, as theater owners charged, their taxation policies did reflect residual disdain or distrust for the motion picture paralleling the sentiments of Reichstag deputies.[34] The provision for tax savings of up to fifty percent for films with artistic or educational merit confirmed the bias against dramatic or entertainment films.[35] The motion picture lobby fought a lengthy, uphill battle for standardization and reduction of the entertainment tax. Needless to say, the loss of income—by its own reckoning this amounted in 1925 to roughly thirty-six million marks—rubbed salt in the wound caused by an official attitude for which film's chief virtue lay in the tax revenue it generated.[36]

State control over the cinema through censorship and taxes merits attention not as evidence of outside manipulation of film production but as testimony to a consensus which acted as a powerful internal constraint. Apart from decisions on restricted films, censors made relatively few controversial judgments. If in a handful of notorious rulings they became arbiters of Weimar's

political and social stalemate, they functioned primarily to rein-
force tendencies built into the mass orientation of the medium.
On the matter of taxation, loss of revenue obviously impacted
the industry negatively, but it is idle to speculate about what
German producers would have accomplished with an extra several million marks annually. The point is rather to emphasize
the ambivalent position of cinema within Weimar culture as a
whole. On the one hand, the motion picture had become in the
space of a decade an industry giving work to tens of thousands
and diversion and instruction to millions. Its power to entertain
and influence found almost universal recognition. On the other
hand, there were no guarantees that the diversion and instruction it offered would prove either harmless or beneficial. The
speculative, profit-seeking character of the industry weighed
heavily against it. Official Germany, not entirely certain how to
cope with the new medium, adopted a policy of better safe than
sorry. Fearing the unwashed heritage of the medium, the authorities devised a code which gave them virtually unlimited
power over what German companies could produce or theaters
exhibit and endorsed an entertainment tax which prevented
the cinema from underbidding all other forms of amusement.

Censorship and tax policies indicate clearly what official Germany did not appreciate about the cinema. Their restrictive
functions should not disguise, however, that both used negative
means to forward a positive goal, namely, development of a
cinema consonant with middle-class artistic, educational and
moral standards.[37] Since this purpose had its immediate roots
in the film reform movement it can be judged, with some justification, as socially and politically reactionary, an expression of
visceral hostility toward the plebeian roots and uncultured character of the medium from persons unwilling to enter the twentieth century. A prime case in point was the postwar report by
the Popular Association for the Preservation of Decency and
Good Morals in Cologne which damned ninety percent of all
film releases as worthless or harmful.[38] Behind this judgment,
a match for the sharpest prewar polemics, lay deep-seated social
and cultural bias against the motion picture. But the attitudes
which it betrayed cannot be dismissed as the pettifogging of a
morally fastidious fringe. Although extreme in formulation, it

expressed sentiments which enjoyed wide currency in bourgeois Germany. These did more than is usually acknowledged to shape the contours of Weimar cinema culture.

Moral crusaders and state authorities played no active role in the production process. While the industry had no choice but to cooperate at one remove with the latter, it ridiculed and pretended to ignore the former as exponents of a dying world. Nonetheless, both carried tremendous indirect weight because their aspirations were those of the dominant groups in German society. Their desire to ennoble the movies, to fit them to a middle-class mold of sophistication, virtue and seriousness, impacted German producers in three ways. First, it demanded practical accommodation as a means of broadening and enlarging the domestic cinema audience. Second, it encouraged production eligible for tax relief and other forms of indulgence from local, provincial and national authorities. Third and most crucially, it corresponded to a need for legitimization and self-realization which existed within film circles. The drive to ennoble the cinema was not just imposed from without. Whether through literary adaptations, chamber drama, exploration of myth and legend, Expressionist devices or the later realism of *Neue Sachlichkeit,* Weimar's film artists shared the aspirations of reformers to see the cinema realize possibilities beyond mass escapism. Indeed the unifying feature of that portion of Weimar cinema best remembered today was self-conscious striving for the embourgeoisement of the motion picture—even if in antibourgeois interest.[39] This drive left an indelible mark on the production process and on the whole ambience of Weimar cinema culture, including the practice of film criticism which is crucial to this study.

Efforts by film reformers, censors and champions of film art to preserve bourgeois cultural hegemony and inherited artistic values reinforced the tendency for cinema to fracture along class lines. While Weimar did not entertain a strictly dualistic cinema culture, it did resist the democratic tendencies of the medium. One symptom of the differentiation which resulted, though scarcely unique to Germany, was the wide range of theater types. At one extreme, cinema entertainment rivaled opera or live theater in orchestration and dramatic impact, not to mention in admission price. Gala premieres in palatial theaters boasting big-budget movies, full orchestras and illustrated programs, attended by leading government and business personalities, lent the cinema respectability.[40] At the other extreme, there still existed a moviegoing experience not far removed from the circus and vaudeville, offering a cheap source of laughter, tears and excitement: here pianos took the place of orchestras and luxurious furnishings gave way to a meeting hall decor.

Another indication of the varieties of cinema experience was the range of motion pictures produced in Germany. Historical interest has, of course, been heavily weighted toward a group of artistically pioneering motion pictures. Although informed contemporaries had a natural tendency to identify Weimar cinema with this select group of films, they knew that experimental works and artistic masterpieces did not dominate domestic production. More numerous and generally more popular were the sensationalist films of Harry Piel, light dramas of Helen Richter or the military farces and Rhein-Wein-Gesang films which fed provincial audiences.[41] Equally noteworthy is that the line between high and low cinema culture remained fluid. Fritz Lang was a master of the potboiler, sometimes disguised as art; Henny Porten played in everything from serious chamber drama to sentimental family comedies; Erich Pommer produced a kaleidoscopic array of pretentious and unsophisticated entertainment. In the final analysis it is misleading to designate any one variant of domestic production normative.

Under these circumstances it is no surprise that contemporary opinion on the cinema exhibited multiple purposes and levels of seriousness. In the broadest sense of the term, the film press encompassed everything from advertising to philosophy. Closest to the former were illustrated theater programs, fan magazines, and company papers maintained by larger concerns such as UFA or Südfilm. At one remove, trade papers served the industry with news, film criticism and a forum for representation and debate of issues affecting the industry. Daily newspapers, both national and local, offered commercial news, criticism and feuilleton meditations on the medium. Select journals of art and culture included the motion picture within their purview as both an artistic and commercial phenomenon. In addition, miscellaneous publications ranging from dissertations to technical reports treated the economic, legal or political dimensions of the movies.

All of this material is relevant for what follows, but the most important category for evaluating Hollywood's place in postwar Germany is motion picture criticism. Concentrated in Berlin, where it had the broadest audience and the greatest potential for impacting the production process, criticism became a small industry in its own right.[42] Since it served multiple purposes and assumed diverse forms, and since it belongs to the larger complex of the relationship between film and the press, no brief survey can do it full justice. Institutionalized in the context of the industrialization and embourgeoisement of the cinema outlined above, it inevitably became caught between competing agendas for the cinema. The often bitter struggle to define legitimate criticism paralleled conflict over the balance of commercial and creative impulses appropriate to the medium.

Critical judgment on motion pictures juxtaposed the dominant public voice of the nineteenth century—the press—and the dominant public medium of the twentieth century—the moving picture.[43] By the turn of the century the press served as the forum in which clerics and pedagogues catalogued film's baneful influence on youth and the lower classes. Thereafter, apart from notices announcing movie programs, press treatment of the cinema remained spotty until the establishment of permanent theaters (1905) and the flowering of the film reform movement in the last years before the outbreak of war. Beginning in 1907 the first of the trade papers appeared, giving the branches of the industry a vehicle with which to present their views and counter the publishing crusade of the reformers. At the same time movie ads became part of the growing tie between film and newspapers. Shortly before 1914 film began to receive serious though selective treatment in the daily press and some magazines of art and culture.[44] The apogee of the film reform movement, the appearance of the first *Autorenfilme* and the intense literary confrontation with the cinema documented by Anton Kaes and Heinz Heller placed the movies increasingly in the public eye as entertainment and as art.[45]

Despite the deepening and inevitable tie between cinema and

the press, relations were not altogether harmonious. As the up-start, the motion picture quickly recognized that the press had the power to do it great harm or great good. Film interests knew that without capturing press attention and sympathy there existed little chance of winning a broader audience. As a seminal prewar trade article put it, the press was the field upon which the battle between friends and foes of cinema would be de-cided.[46] During the war, trade journals continued to invite in-formed, unprejudiced reportage of motion picture affairs in the German press and to exhort the industry to exploit opportu-nities for greater coverage. They recommended systematic co-operation in order to enhance the cinema's prestige among the better public, to defend it against malicious attack from unbend-ing opponents, including government, and to refine it as a na-tional resource. Since public recognition represented the first priority of the industry, and since the key to that lay in the hands of the press, close collaboration was highly desirable. To encourage benevolent exposure on the widest possible front film companies began to establish news services and appoint press representatives to improve their public profile.[47]

In the unfolding relationship between the cinema and the press film criticism came to occupy a pivotal role. The motion picture industry welcomed the attention which reviews pro-vided and especially the dignity conferred by critical appraisal. To be ignored meant relegation to casual amusement; serious reviews lent motion pictures status comparable to opera or the-ater. However, the possibility of unsympathetic or uninformed reviews which masqueraded as earnest commentary created considerable ambivalence.[48] Particularly troublesome was the inability of trade circles to pick and choose critical coverage. The right of unfettered criticism, to which even the industry had to pay lip service to maintain its pretensions to cultural worth, boomeranged all too frequently. Unlike statements about the cinema's growing economic significance as an ex-porter or employer, critical commentary opened the field to rival opinions of culture and entertainment.

Although film circles could not monopolize opinion, trade journals provided an inherently friendly and prolific source of film reviews. By the 1920s a handful of trade papers had become firmly established. The oldest, *Kinematograph*, originated in Düsseldorf and was published there until May 1923 when it passed into the hands of Alfred Hugenberg's Scherl Publishers and moved to the capital. The others all were native to Berlin, *Lichtbildbühne* appearing before the war, *Der Film* in the midst of it and *Film-Kurier* and *Reichsfilmblatt* immediately thereafter. Outside Berlin the *Süddeutsche Filmzeitung* (later *Deutsche Filmzeitung*) in Munich and *Film-Journal* of Hamburg enjoyed similar stability, though the latter of these eventually moved to Berlin. Apart from providing commentary on economic, political and artistic issues, technical news, and copious advertising space, they all published film reviews.[49]

Trade reviews varied greatly in nature and quality depending on the specific clientele to which a journal was directed, the commercial ties between the paper and the industry, and, of course, the individuals responsible. While most trade papers professed to serve the entire film business, rather than one of its branches, differences still existed. For most of the decade *Reichsfilmblatt* represented independent cinema owners. *Film-Kurier*, at least in the 1920s, had pretensions to elevated status as a national newspaper serving the public as well as the specialist. *Kinematograph*, part of the Scherl concern from 1923, and after 1927 married through Hugenberg to UFA, had specific economic as well as political interests to defend. *Lichtbildbühne* was published by Karl Wolffsohn, an entrepreneur of enormous energies with wide-ranging film interests and financial ties to Ullstein publishers. It devoted considerable attention to the economic potential and international connections of the German cinema.[50]

Despite their differences, trade papers ostensibly reviewed motion pictures to provide exhibitors a basis for determining which films to book. To this end *Reichsfilmblatt* and, in less systematic ways, other papers included box-office estimates with their critiques of plot, cinematography and acting. While this approach respected the commercial realities of filmmaking, it also betrayed proximity to the industry which was widely held to infringe critical objectivity. The nontrade critics often branded trade reviewers the servants of commercial interests and refused to take them seriously.[51] These outsiders, concentrated

in the second and even more voluminous source of critical opinion on the motion picture, the daily press, were, however, anything but uniformly disinterested.

Many newspapers treated motion pictures casually before the
Weimar period, but it was in the course of the first half of the
1920s that they institutionalized film criticism. Numerous dailies introduced weekly film sections with general news and reviews. Even the stuffier bourgeois press deigned to make some
space for film affairs. Nonetheless, variations in coverage and
perspective were considerable. Some attempted to provide reviews of all new releases; others operated very selectively. A
major premiere which merited a feuilleton article in one could
elicit only a few lines in another. Since two large publishers,
Scherl and Ullstein, had investments in cinema, it is also fanciful
to assume newspaper critics necessarily enjoyed fewer commercial entanglements than their trade colleagues. To the third
group of critics, those who published in independent journals
of art and culture, newspaper reviewers were generally no less
compromised.[52]

This last source of critical opinion, much more select than
the first two, includes the well-known left-wing weeklies, *Das
Tagebuch* and *Die Weltbühne*, as well as more mainstream cultural
journals such as *Freie Deutsche Bühne* (*Das blaue Heft*), *Der Kunstwart, Die literarische Welt* and *Der Kritiker*. Other literary or theatrical journals contributed to one or other aspect of the debate
about cinema, but did not publish regular film reviews. Independent journals devoted to the motion picture—*Der Bildwart*,
which served pedagogues and communal cinema organizations,
Film und Volk, the mouthpiece of the socialist Volksverband für
Filmkunst, and the nationalist *Filmkünstler und Filmkunst*—were
few and generally short-lived.[53] This has made the journals of
art and culture which treated film systematically especially attractive as critical sources.

Paralleling the hierarchy of sources which reviewed motion
pictures was a hierarchy of critics. At its top stood a handful of
persons whose reputations have persisted—Herbert Ihering,
Siegfried Kracauer, Willy Haas, Kurt Pinthus, Rudolf Arnheim,
Lotte Eisner and Béla Balázs.[54] Next to them can be ranged a
group of prolific critics which includes Axel Eggebrecht, Hans

Siemsen, Hans Sahl, Roland Schacht and Hans Pander, as well as the feuilleton scribes of the leading dailies, such as Fred Hildenbrandt (*Berliner Tageblatt*) or Curt Emmerich (*Deutsche Allgemeine Zeitung*), who occasionally pontificated on the most important film releases. Taken together, the majority of these published either in the independent political-cultural journals (Pinthus in *Das Tagebuch*, Eggebrecht and Siemsen in *Die Weltbühne*, Schacht in *Der Kunstwart* and *Das blaue Heft*, Pander in *Der Bildwart*) or in newspapers of national stature (Kracauer in *Frankfurter Zeitung*, Ihering in *Berliner Börsen-Courier*), or frequently in both. There is therefore meaningful correlation between the quality usually assigned the source and the eminence of the individual responsible for reviews.

Within this select group persona and perspective can be related on the basis of substantial collections of critical material.[55] Nonetheless, most of these writers are remembered less for their film reviews than for other pursuits. Herbert Ihering was first and foremost a theater critic; Kracauer was a sociologist and cultural critic of very catholic interests and only much later famous as a film historian and theorist; Willy Haas launched his journalistic career as a critic for *Film-Kurier,* became a screenwriter and then graduated to the editorial chair of the prestigious *Literarische Welt;* Balázs's reputation hinges mainly on his work as a theorist and script writer; Pinthus is remembered as frequently for his association with literary Expressionism as with film. In sum, even the outstanding names of Weimar film criticism rarely derived their incomes and reputations exclusively or predominantly from this pursuit.[56]

Beyond a score of prominent figures, most of whom could afford to treat film criticism as only one facet of their careers, there existed a large pool of critics for whom film was a way of life. Numbering dozens in Berlin alone, these ranged from the trade critics to the regular reviewers for newspapers and popular film magazines. Since keeping pace with the half-dozen or more releases which appeared each week during the premiere season strained the capacity of a single reviewer, trade journals and newspapers alike frequently had a lead critic who handled the most important premieres and a number of assistants to cope with the rest. According to the trade press, newspaper criticism suffered from this state of affairs because the individuals entrusted with reviews often proved woefully ignorant of film basics. Young, bottom-ranking or part-time reporters were assigned to cover premieres regardless of their knowledge of or interest in motion pictures. Fritz Olimsky, principal critic for the *Berliner Börsen-Zeitung*, argued that early in the Weimar period no qualifications were demanded of the film journalist.[57]

At a distance of six decades the more salient problem is that sheer numbers and rapid turnover blur personalities and approaches. Moreover, it is not always possible even to identify reviewers: some hid behind initials or pseudonyms and others provided no identification whatsoever for their work.[58] Any investigation which penetrates beyond the circle of well-known critics therefore encounters either outright anonymity or a host of names whose only historical significance lies in their attachment to specific reviews. It also encounters an endless mass of criticism distinguished only by its lack of distinction. Small wonder that historians have generally ignored this material, considering it worthless except perhaps as testimony to the endless repetition which characterizes movie entertainment. Their indifference is doubly justified if one accepts the view that much of the film criticism from this period was tainted by financial pressure. Yet if the lack of personal profiles for many critics is frustrating, it is not sufficient reason to disregard a large body of opinion whose importance lies as much in its uniformity as in its peculiarities. For the purpose of establishing broad patterns of opinion, anonymity presents no insuperable obstacle.

Although generalizations about the majority of critics must be somewhat tentative, three fairly obvious ones can be ventured. The first is that critics belonged to the same generation as cinematography itself. As a rule they were born in the 1880s or 1890s and grew up alongside, if not in close association with, the movies. The reason for this is not hard to find. As a boom business in the troubled years right after the war, film attracted an assorted band of young employment seekers—writers as well as actors, technicians, extras and theater attendants. Film criticism provided an outlet for an educated stratum unable to find positions in traditional areas. A surprising number of doctorates turned up in a field which enjoyed almost no academic respectability at this point except on the fringes of economics and law.[59] Conversely, for those without academic credentials, writing about motion pictures offered otherwise unobtainable opportunities. Entering a tight job market as the cinema expanded, they found a new avenue by which to enjoy status, however dubious, as writers or journalists.

The second generic feature one may identify follows directly from the first. By affiliating themselves with the movies, even if only in a critical capacity, these persons demonstrated allegiance to a cultural upstart. Certainly their interest in the cinema was mercenary, but there is ample evidence of broader commitment to a novel medium, one not yet encrusted by convention. This youthful, forward-looking dimension of the motion picture made it attractive to a generation in search of new cultural models.[60]

The third point of note is that many critics served the motion picture industry in other capacities. Three prominent ones—Willy Haas, Béla Balázs and Axel Eggebrecht—simultaneously made names for themselves as screen authors. Also active in this dual respect were Bobby Lüthge, Julius Sternheim, Fritz Podehl, Hans Brennert, Ludwig Brauner and Erwin Gepard. Yet another group of critics functioned as press agents for leading firms, among them Fritz Olimsky, Hans Tintner, Kurt Mühsam and Axel Eggebrecht. This overlap of function has the historical advantage that critics were insiders or spokespersons for the industry, a fact of major importance when evaluating critical perceptions of Hollywood. It also, however, raises serious questions about the integrity of the critical process.

The contemporary controversy about film criticism revolved around two basic questions—evaluative paradigms and professional ethics. Both arose in the context of the motion picture's uneasy balance between big business and cultural pretensions, between maximization of profit and pursuit of cultural respectability. Its practice necessarily reflected the tension between these goals. Film criticism had to justify itself against middle-class notions of art as autonomous, individual creation divorced from commerce and profit. To those deeply suspicious of cinema's manipulation by financial interests and alienated by its plebeian roots, serious film criticism dignified the medium with a status it did not deserve.[61] Their cynicism did not prevent the growing professionalization of film criticism, but it did contribute to its aims and principles. Some disagreement about emphasis and purpose was certainly inevitable. Whether reviews should focus on theme, acting and directing, or be preoccupied with cinematography, or address questions of public resonance, commercial prospects and political overtones: these are questions of approach which in any era allow room for debate. However, in Weimar Germany these issues became matters of principle which generated much acrimony. Trade critics charged their counterparts in the daily press and cultural journals with ignorance of the medium, application of lofty and irrelevant criteria and disregard for the commercial risks and responsibilities of the industry. The latter replied with accusations of inconsistency, whitewashing and outright corruption. At the heart of this feud lay not only differences of opinion but also confusion about the nature of the medium and unfair generalization. Although reviews in trade papers, the daily press and independent journals showed significant variations, these did not correspond neatly to stereotype. Trade critics did focus heavily on technical questions and box-office appeal, but they also systematically evaluated acting and directing with the artistic criteria they complained dominated newspaper criticism. The prominent theater critic, Herbert Ihering, identified in this the uncertainty of the industry about its cultural role. Wanting acceptance of cinema as a unique form of expression rather than a poor cousin to literature or theater, film experts demanded recognition of the industrial character of the medium, resisting measurement by critical standards from other media. Wanting simultaneously to impress with the motion picture's sophistication they borrowed, for want of language of their own, categories pertinent to literature, art and live drama. Questions of psychological depth, plot development and dramatic conflict crowded out specifically filmic concerns such as pictorial rhythm or lighting effects. In short, the film industry welcomed the use of literary or theatrical paradigms when these flattered its productions; otherwise it demanded treatment as a commercial and technical medium.[62]

Although the principle that cinema was a case sui generis would have received virtually universal assent, in critical practice, no party applied it consistently. No critic could escape the language and categories of other art forms in attempting to give the motion picture its aesthetic due. Trade critics were by no means the only ones to interchange critical standards to suit their purposes. Ihering himself tried to preserve a traditional understanding of the critical process while infusing it with paradigms appropriate to the motion picture. Just as in commercial concerns the trade press reached outside itself for recognized standards, nontrade critics had to appreciate the industrial character of cinema to write meaningful reviews. Consequently, distinctions between criticism in the trade press, dailies and journals of art and culture were anything but tidy.

Tension between the industrial, public and artistic dimensions of the medium plagued attempts to establish the parameters of motion picture criticism, but it also generated bitter polemics about professional ethics. Confrontation occurred at two levels, corporate and personal. The first of these involved the intimate relationship between publishers and the film industry, especially in the matter of advertising. The trade papers included extensive advertising sections, usually in excess of editorial information. They also received a variety of complimentary promotional material--photos, film synopses, premiere notices or articles on popular performers—from the film companies. Their reliance on income from advertising and the convenience of prepackaged news pressured them to trim reviews to avoid offending major producers and theater chains. Trade reviews therefore tended to be lame or bland, loaded with euphemisms to cover flaws, or indiscriminately effusive in a fashion better suited to advertising than criticism. Neither served the best interests of the industry in the long run, as the trade papers themselves repeatedly warned, but the pressure to temper criticism to safeguard their financial lifeline remained.[63]

Trade papers relied most directly on industrial benevolence, but they were not alone in their commercial entanglements. Newspapers too had more than casual associations with the industry. As noted above, leading publishers had investments in film. More pervasively, movie advertising became a prime source of revenue for the daily press. There can be no doubt that the industry felt it paid for a certain measure of goodwill.

For the marks it invested in advertising it expected critical respect. To what extent this colored the critical process became a subject of rancorous debate.

Although it is difficult to pinpoint editorial pressure on critics, the evidence for conflict and reprisals against the press when reviews failed to meet the expected standard of kindness is incontrovertible. Complaints to publishers from producers disturbed by the treatment of their products occasionally became public issues in which critics had the opportunity to make their opinions heard.[64] Early in the decade critics in Berlin and Munich created professional associations, one of whose purposes was defense against the conflicting pressures of the industry and publishers.[65] The extant UFA documents clearly demonstrate that their complaints were not unfounded. Under Hugenberg's management UFA on several occasions threatened and acted to withdraw advertising contracts from both the trade press (*Lichtbildbühne*) and major newspapers (Ullstein and Mosse dailies) when its films or management came under attack.[66] In early 1928 UFA's board of directors approached the publisher of *Der Film*, Max Mathisson, over a review of Fritz Lang's *Spione* which it believed employed inflated artistic criteria. Later that year, disgruntled with the state of film criticism, UFA decided to publish comparisons of public responses and critical practice in the United States and Germany to expose the subjective, unhelpful character of German film reviews.[67]

Conflict between the industry and the press spilled over into feuds between the trade journals and between critics from the top to the bottom of the hierarchy. Disputes essentially concerned the charge of conflict of interest. Chief culprits were those who mixed critical functions with personal enrichment from the industry, principally trade journalists who wrote reviews with one hand and sold advertising contracts with the other. The most notorious of these was the motion picture mouthpiece of Scherl Publishers, Alfred Rosenthal (Aros), press agent, ad man and critic with outlets in *Kinematograph* and in the Hugenberg dailies. In 1927 he and Max Feige, editor of *Der Film,* were involved in a libel suit with the former editor-in-chief of *Lichtbildbühne*, Kurt Mühsam, over their practice of combining editorial and advertising work. For outsiders this case reinforced the conviction that corruption was rampant in the trade press.[68]

Personal vendettas in the trade press highlighted a search for workable ethical norms which reached to the very top of the critical pyramid and bore directly on the ability of American companies to purchase benevolent treatment with advertising space and gratis promotional information. The nub of the controversy was the propriety of contributing in any fashion to the business of film while continuing to pursue critical activity. The association of critics in Berlin expressly excluded from membership those entertaining financial ties with any branch of the industry. But practice deviated substantially from principle. As already noted, some critics served the industry as press or advertising agents; some combined writing of reviews and editing of foreign films; others mixed authorship of reviews and screenplays.[69] In the last instance, high personal profiles gave disagreements considerable prominence. The prime case in point involved two of Berlin's outstanding critical voices, Willy Haas and Hans Siemsen. Haas, well known as a script writer for *Die freudlose Gasse* (1925), had early in his critical career articulated formal objections to reviews penned by nonexperts with general literary backgrounds. Only those with experience in the industry possessed the know-how to criticize effectively. To illustrate his point he chose the work of Hans Siemsen, an itinerant essayist and sometime film critic for *Die Weltbühne*. In his opinion Siemsen had a brilliant eye for the effects and impact of movies, but little sense for the possibilities of the medium because he lacked familiarity with the craft. His criticism was stillborn rather than creative or productive.[70]

Haas' plea for trained and informed reviewers represented the views of trade circles. But Haas was also vulnerable to charges of conflict of interest. As early as 1923 Ihering took him to task for combining critical work and screen writing.[71] At middecade Siemsen touched off a sharp polemic by laying charges of corruption against the majority of film critics, maintaining that very few escaped compromise caused by overt or covert financial pressure.[72] Siemsen insisted that reputable criticism had to maintain distance from the commercial interests of the cinema; Haas retorted that despite the dangers involved, critics had to be conversant with the technical and commercial interests of film. Failure to reconcile these positions was symptomatic of contemporary disputes about the boundaries of cinema as art, entertainment and big business.[73]

Given undeniable conflicts of interest and possibilities for abuse it is not surprising that historians tend to adopt Siemsen's position that the vast bulk of film criticism was tainted by proximity to the industry and turn to the independent journals as the repositories of disinterested commentary. None of these had advertising commitments which infringed on the freedom of expression allowed reviewers. Some of them printed film reviews despite indifference or antagonism toward the cinema on the part of their editors. Thus quite apart from their accessibility and commitment to film as art, they offer the promise of impartiality.[74] It is not the case, however, that only a handful of financially unaffiliated periodicals in Berlin published serious film commentary. Generally speaking, the criticism of trade papers was conciliatory and not terribly discriminating, but exceptions were frequent and cannot be ignored. It is even more difficult to generalize about criticism in the daily press. It too was susceptible to commercial pressures and blended concern for profit, popular appeal and artistry. Hard evidence for reprisals against publications not sufficiently accommodating in their film reviews must be considered, but it should not lead to wholesale dismissal of criticism in publications which carried advertising. It is noteworthy that some companies continued to advertise even when their products received withering reviews, clear evidence that editorial policy retained its independence.[75] Therefore, although the relationship between economic obligations and critical freedom was a troubled one, no tidy formula separates so-called independent critics, distinct and important as they were, from those subject to fear of editorial reprisal.

Varieties of cinema culture and controversy over film criticism inevitably raise one final consideration—the relationship between film and politics. Germany's first republic is notorious for the acerbity of its political divisions in spheres as diverse as literature, architecture and theater. Evidence for politicization of Weimar cinema is also abundant from several perspectives. The Republic experienced a flood of patriotic military feature films and newsreels, plus nostalgic recreations of prewar German life which were at least implicitly anti-Republican.[76] These were countered by several domestically produced features which pilloried the Republic from the other side, foremost among them Bert Brecht's *Kuhle Wampe* and Piel Jutzi's *Mutter Krausens Fahrt ins Glück,* as well as by release of the outstanding Soviet revolutionary films. Government investments in the motion picture industry were controversial with UFA and provoked major scandal in the later case of Phoebus Film Company. Notorious censorship cases over such releases as *Battleship Potemkin* and *All Quiet on the Western Front* embroiled government and political parties in lengthy battles to control the political influence of the medium.[77]

While the cinema certainly participated in Weimar's political passions, it is crucial to delimit the precise nature of that participation. The takeover of UFA by Alfred Hugenberg and associates in 1927, probably the most notorious example of political infiltration in this period, provides some guidance in this regard. Control of UFA, the country's largest production, distribution and exhibition company, promised the nationalist right a forum from which to lead the anti-Republican campaign in the last years of Weimar. The takeover also coincided with what the most thorough study to date of politics and Weimar film argues was the onset of polarization in the cinema.[78] Whether Hugenberg's production policies can be blamed for these developments remains debatable. The Republican and left-wing press cried foul when the nationalists took over, but UFA had not, of course, been a paragon of Republican virtue, not to mention a friend of socialism, before Hugenberg assumed control. Moreover, anyone with the slightest familiarity with motion picture affairs knew that Hugenberg rescued a company mired in financial woes since 1925. In 1926, after American subventions had been accepted to keep the company afloat, UFA appeared about to become a branch operation of Paramount and Metro-Goldwyn. One did not have to appreciate Hugenberg's politics to gain some satisfaction from seeing the company kept in German hands. The cognoscenti also realized that as the pilot of a salvage operation, Hugenberg had immediate economic concerns to address. He enjoyed little freedom of maneuver to push a political program. None of this meant that Hugenberg could be absolved of political intentions, but it did signify that other considerations intruded.[79]

The economic imperative faced by Alfred Hugenberg confronted the industry as a whole and indicates the principal reason it handled politics very gingerly. The film industry repeatedly proclaimed its political neutrality, insisting that because the movies provided mass entertainment they had no business (literally) taking sides.[80] Although one can scarcely take these protestations at face value, they honestly reflect the commercial pressure to maintain a "neutral" position likely to appeal to the broadest possible audience. Weimar's deep political antagonisms reinforced rather than eroded this pressure. An enterprise devoted to the maximization of profit could not afford to alienate large segments of the population.[81] Walter Laqueur's generalization that film was funded from right of center but made by those left of center, and that films themselves consistently endorsed the socioeconomic status quo, is a roundabout way of saying that the industry generally minimized or camouflaged politics. Incentive to avoid themes or treatments which would limit in advance the audience to which they spoke was reinforced by censorship, the instrument of status quo par excellence. It is possible to identify several dozen feature films with express partisan intent and many more with political overtones. It is also possible to agree with Hans Siemsen's judgment that all motion pictures, indeed all art, are political in the broad sense of assuming positions on fundamental human questions, even if only by refusing to face them. Yet this is a truism, rather than a guide to analysis. Weimar filmmakers were under economic and legal obligation to find that elusive middle ground where shared values camouflaged ever-present class and ideological differences.[82]

What can be said about the production and marketing of motion pictures applies in broad terms to critical opinion. Weimar had a rich and politically diverse press. Although depth of cinema coverage varied somewhat according to political affiliation, publications of all political persuasions—communist, socialist, democratic, catholic and nationalist—treated film to some extent. Political preferences did play a role in determining which movies were reviewed and which ignored, particularly on the extremes of left and right where coverage thinned noticeably. These preferences emerged clearly in collisions over specific motion pictures, nationalist or socially progressive. Moreover, what passed as harmless amusement on the right or among democratic reviewers not infrequently roused the ire of the left for its refusal to deal honestly with socioeconomic reality. Thus reactions to motion pictures from conflicting political sources offer noteworthy and hardly surprising contrasts.[83]

Those looking for political polemics in Weimar film criticism can readily find them. The question is whether political allegiance provides the key to the bulk of critical commentary. The practice of treating film in its technical and aesthetic rather than social-economic or political dimensions predominated in the bourgeois press but did not stop there. Socialist and communist sources also indulged in it. Critics did not shed their political preferences, but nor did they always follow them. Open opponents of the Soviet system acknowledged the provocative power of its motion picture production, while outspoken enemies of capitalism confessed admiration for some works which made romantic lies out of the social question. Anyone seeking hard and fast correspondence between political affiliation and the judgment passed on the broad mass of entertainment films is bound to be disappointed. What can be discerned are patterns of response which characterized political extremes, especially toward select types of films. Therefore while it is certainly impossible to understand the Weimar cinema with the party politics left out, these were not normally the point of departure for critical opinion, at least not until the latter years of the Republic when the cinema became increasingly politicized.[84]

This brief survey of motion picture expansion and film criticism suggests some of the complexities of Weimar cinema. Just to list its generic characteristics is to indicate the paradoxes and tensions which it embodied. It was at once the child of modern technology, the first mode of entertainment to acquire mass appeal, a portentous means of public persuasion, a novel art form, and last, but certainly not least, big business. To this congeries of meanings must be added the paradox that although rooted in a national context, cinema was decidedly international in distribution and impact.

Controversies surrounding motion picture criticism were deeply rooted in contemporary uncertainty about how to accommodate the new medium. Although neither peculiar to Germany nor to that period, they were acute in a society fragmented by cultural differences. Critics belonged to one segment of this society and acted as mediators between the industry and its consumers. In this respect they sat at the center of the Weimar debate over the relationship between art, technology, commerce and society. How they settled accounts with Hollywood was inextricably linked to the broader problem of their cultural role.

2
GERMAN-AMERICAN FILM RELATIONS
Competition and Cooperation

International trade in motion pictures has flourished from the first decade of the century when cinemas settled in urban areas. Since movies were cheap to transport and, while silent, convenient to retitle in other languages, they made obvious export material. France led a field of producing and exporting nations which included Denmark, Italy, Sweden and the United States. French producers therefore initially enjoyed primacy in determining the boundaries of movie entertainment. Major companies, most notably Pathé and Gaumont, also invested in branch operations abroad. The combination of voluminous film exchange and movement of capital and expertise created a truly international cinema culture.[1]

By 1918 French dominance had given way to an unprecedented degree of international market control by American film. The United States produced several times the number of feature films annually as its nearest competitor, Germany, and had almost as many cinema seats as all other countries combined. The ongoing expansion of motion picture enterprise raised the stakes in international competition. By the 1920s motion pictures represented enormous investments in studios, equipment and theaters. In Germany alone they directly employed tens of thousands of persons, from stars to theater attendants and projectionists. Industrial concentration and rising production standards became prerequisites for a role on the international market.

Early in the 1920s Germany momentarily seemed poised to shatter the American monopoly. While the Republic lived in the shadow of inflation until late 1923, Weimar cinema enjoyed primacy at home and growing recognition abroad. German films created an invasion scare in the United States and won respect elsewhere. However, between 1924 and 1929, as Germany enjoyed a period of relative economic and political stability, supported by foreign loans and confirmed by reintegration into the international community, a credit squeeze and large-scale American inroads clearly relegated Germany to a supporting role. American tariffs and resistance to German imports, as well as the departure of leading filmmakers to the United States, threatened to reduce German cinema to an appendage of Hollywood. Only with the introduction of talking pictures at the close of the decade did American influence in Germany recede somewhat, though American international hegemony remained unshakeable.

Thanks to the studies of Siegfried Kracauer and Lotte Eisner the inflationary period is usually seen as Weimar cinema's commercial and artistic golden age. In the cinema, as in other sectors of the German economy, inflation, though ultimately catastrophic in proportions and impact, massively aided the cause of postwar recovery. By sheltering the domestic market from foreign interference and encouraging industrial concentration, it fostered experimentation and growth. UFA's absorption in 1921 of Decla-Bioscop, a company which under the direction of Erich Pommer championed national cinema art, marked the confluence of industrial and creative trends which characterized this period. From the flowering of Expressionism in Robert Wiene's *Das Cabinet des Dr. Caligari*, through the chamber dramas of Lupu Pick and F. W. Murnau, the early thrillers of Fritz Lang, the comic and epic classics scripted by Hans Kraely and directed by Ernst Lubitsch, to the historical and mythical works of Richard Oswald and Paul Wegener, Weimar cinema expanded rapidly and won international prominence. Inflation underwrote a remarkable boom.[2]

By contrast, from the mid-1920s, when relative economic stabilization was achieved, German cinema passed through commercial and creative crises which checked expansion and eroded national identity. Retrenchment and stagnation coincided closely with the rise of American influence. Whereas before 1924 the ailing mark discouraged export to Germany, keeping Hollywood in the background, thereafter American cinema consolidated a place in Germany and threatened to extinguish the independence of the German cinema. Hollywood bit deeply into the domestic market, fairly or otherwise limited German markets abroad and deprived the native industry of its best personnel. Its inroads compelled adoption of American methods, including acceptance by German companies of American funding and direction in the second half of the decade. UFA's alliance with Paramount and Metro-Goldwyn at the end of 1925, better known as Parufamet, was the most prominent of these arrangements. It has been read ever since as a byword for Americanization of the Weimar cinema.[3]

Kracauer and Eisner, both former critics concerned with the peculiarities of Weimar cinema, drew heavily on sentiments prevalent in the second half of the 1920s to distinguish golden age from decline. From 1925 contemporaries began to reflect nostalgically on the dynamism and international success of native accomplishments in the previous five years. Hollywood became the principal villain in accounts of domestic film woes. However, stigmatization of Hollywood to explain German setbacks did not originate with middecade stagnation. It was rooted in earlier perceptions of the American challenge. At the end of the war film experts approached the problem of America's global dominance with sharp antinomies. The dichotomies of "we" and "they" prevalent in wartime elevation of German *Kultur* carried over into postwar film debates. In place of military fronts came filmic ones. Experts foresaw a full-scale confrontation between Hollywood and Berlin to decide ownership of the international market. The persistence of wartime rhetoric meant that the postinflationary American invasion signified the defeat of Germany. That in turn shed a sinister light on the otherwise natural and widely approved internationalization of film which ensued.

The magnitude of the American challenge to Weimar cinema is apparent in censorship data quantifying the proportions of domestic and American movies passed for German theaters. Censorship figures do not, of course, tell an unequivocal tale. They say nothing about the character of the films, the extent of their distribution, or the popular responses which they evoked. Nor do they identify those imports made by outstanding German or other European filmmakers and performers who accepted employment in the United States, on the one hand, or domestic films made by American affiliates, on the other. Nor do they offer a guide to the Americanization of German production. They do, however, reveal the fundamental restructuring of the German film market which took place in the first half of the 1920s.[4] In 1920 the German market belonged essentially to native producers. Between 1921 and 1924 Hollywood's inroads revolutionized the composition of German exhibition.[5]

Market Shares: German and American Films, 1921–1929

	Feature Films		*Shorts*		*Totals*	
	German	*American*	*German*	*American*	*German*	*American*
1921	—	—	—	—	646	136
1922	—	—	—	—	474	202
1923	253	102	94	149	347	251
1924	220	186	51	155	271	341
1925	212	216	16	391	228	607
1926	185	216	4	337	189	553
1927	243	190	3	394	246	584
1928	224	199	8	422	232	621
1929	183	142	5	316	188	458

Breakdowns of short and feature films are not available for 1921 and 1922.

Two patterns deserve highlighting. Most visible is the decimation of domestic entertainment shorts, which, unlike feature production, did not receive quota protection. Native producers did retain a stranglehold on the so-called *Kulturfilm*—industrial, educational and advertising motion pictures—but from 1925 German output of entertainment shorts effectively ended. American slapstick, the bulk of the imports in this category, enjoyed an uncontested place in German cinema programs.

Less immediately apparent, but more crucial, was the quantum leap in Hollywood's contribution of feature films and the simultaneous slump in German output with the end of inflation in 1924. Rough parity was established between the number of American and domestic features on the market, a balance which persisted until the end of the decade.

The broader significance of these figures for Weimar cinema culture is the central theme of the chapters which follow. If it is to be meaningfully assessed, one must emphasize from the beginning that neither film industry was a national institution. Private interests in each country competed against each other as much as against foreign companies. Their commercial and artistic representatives traveled between Hollywood and Berlin, learning from and fêting each other, negotiating mutually advantageous trade deals, and making congratulatory speeches about the benefits of international cooperation.[6] German importers, distributors and exhibitors were eager to handle the American product. American companies which established affiliates in Berlin to distribute their pictures and to produce there had no difficulty finding German performers and directors. German and American companies fought each other for control of national and international markets; they also worked together to best their domestic competitors. No tidy formula distinguishes cooperation from competition. Since, however, the language employed borrowed heavily from high diplomacy, assuming nationally uniform differences of interest and purpose, it is necessary to sketch the main contours of German-American film exchange, indicating the nuances and contradictions it involved.

The first and fundamental fact in the relationship between Hollywood and Berlin was the former's overwhelming primacy. The American film industry so successfully exploited other markets, drawing on official support and the assistance of foreign agents, that its international hegemony was quickly taken for granted.[7] Set against the American achievement, Germany's international ambitions appear unrealistic or farcical. Nonetheless, visions of challenging or duplicating the American achievement touched virtually every aspect of German-American film interaction. They conditioned the extent and nature of German import restrictions, since preservation of domestic production had to be balanced against possibilities for export. They prompted German firms to establish liaisons with American companies, in the interests of access to the latters' exhibition outlets. They also provided incentive to Americanize German film production.

At the beginning of the Weimar period the presupposition of opposing national interests in motion pictures was relatively easily sustained. During the war America became a leader in manufacture of anti-German propaganda. Its declaration of war on Germany in April 1917 coincided with Hollywood's advance to front-runner on the world market. Not surprisingly, patriotic sentiments heavily colored discussions of American motion picture achievements in German trade circles. Despite its wartime isolation, Germany received reports of American takeover of markets in such diverse places as France, Russia, Sweden and South America. From the time of America's entry into the war German trade circles began to ponder the challenges of peace.[8] One commentator's prediction that following the war the leading film-producing nations would battle for a "place in the sun" captured general sentiments. Language favored by Pan Germans and made common coin during the war reflected the prevailing belief that while the nation was at war the motion picture business enjoyed relative international peace; when the war ended the conflict would begin.[9] In this respect the founding of UFA in late 1917 represented the outstanding case of an industry preparing itself for postwar competition. As UFA's production program clearly demonstrated, long-term ambitions on the international market figured more prominently than the short-term demand for propaganda to counter the Entente.[10]

Nationalist rhetoric notwithstanding, from the cessation of hostilities German companies prepared to collaborate with Hollywood in the import trade. January 1919 saw the appearance in leading trade publications of the first advertisements for American movies by would-be importers. Just weeks later isolated American films showed in German theaters, despite the maintenance of the wartime import ban. Since the industry believed that the ban would be lifted with the conclusion of a formal peace, its greater and lesser distributors engaged in a long campaign to best each other in the potentially lucrative import trade.[11] Characteristic once again is that superpatriotic UFA led the chase for American contracts. No sooner was the company founded than it began to exploit its Danish connection (Nordisk), while presuming upon its privileged position with government, to gain import allowances. Following the armistice it opened negotiations with American agents in Copenhagen which led to signature in mid-1919 of an agreement to import more than 900 American features and shorts for the equivalent of twenty million marks.[12] When news of the transaction leaked to the German press there was a loud protest that UFA, a semiofficial company, enjoyed an unfair advantage. At stake was less the prospect of American motion pictures returning to German theaters than the fear that UFA would monopolize the import trade, for other companies were quick to join the race for import agreements.[13] Defensive responses to Hollywood's wartime expansion did not, therefore, preclude internecine struggles over its German spoils. Indeed, this particular case illustrates a pattern which can be observed through much of the subsequent decade. German companies wanted to profit from Hollywood's reputation at the expense of their competitors, but dressed their policy in patriotic phrases. Hollywood, while appearing to present an external threat, almost immediately became enmeshed in domestic rivalries.

Early conflict of interest over American motion pictures inevitably surfaced in the debate over the timing and extent of film import controls. The rationale for the import ban of 1916, denial of currency reserves to nonessential imports, remained powerful in the troubled circumstances of the immediate postwar period when Germany continued to suffer from shortages of basic foodstuffs and raw materials. Given the pressure on reserves of foreign currency, the Reichsbank foresaw at least a two-year ban on motion picture import. Nonetheless, from early 1919 the government initiated a process of consultation with trade representatives on eventual policy. The industry proved badly divided. Broadly speaking, theater owners and distributors were pitted against producers and employees, the former welcoming foreign film as a novelty bound to heighten public interest and as a means to mitigate price increases, the latter opposing more than a token import quota so as not to jeopardize domestic primacy and jobs. Each side lobbied actively in support of its position. Companies with foreign contracts in hand urged speedy restoration of film import and sought exceptional treatment in the interim.[14]

Although American motion pictures were not the only ones affected by the extended import ban, they were clearly the principal concern. Since the scramble to gain contracts for American pictures presupposed early resumption of film exchange, extension of the ban had enormous ramifications for the interested parties. This was especially true of UFA, which in its contract of 1919 agreed to pay dollar equivalents for American pictures from the period 1915–1918. The progressive deterioration of the German mark meant UFA paid installments in increasingly dear hard currency while the pictures depreciated with age. This proved a staggering financial blow to the company. Appeals to Reich authorities for special import permission met blunt refusal. Only with suspension of the agreement in 1920 did the company escape financial suicide.[15]

A full year after the first round of trade negotiations with representatives of the Ministry of Economics the import question had still not been resolved. Only between August and December 1920 was an agreement reached. The import quota for 1921 was set at 180,000 meters of negative film, roughly equivalent to fifteen percent of domestic production in 1919, or 90–120 feature films. A Film Trade Board, comprised of industry representatives and answering to the Ministry of Economics, oversaw distribution of import certificates according to an agreed formula.[16] All parties realized, however, that the ceiling and distribution formula were first steps rather than definitive arrangements. With import restored and a framework for resolving disputes in place, the competition for influence in the import trade could finally begin in earnest. Consensus never emerged on optimal import levels, but subsequent years witnessed a dramatic liberalization of film trade. The ceiling was raised to 250,000 meters annually for 1922 and 1923 and to 260,000 meters for 1924, but in practice proved extremely flexible: actual import exceeded it by twenty percent or more. In

1925 a quota system was instituted which permitted the import of one feature film for each domestic feature distributed.[17]

While a number of factors, fiscal and cultural, determined the level of film import, and although every settlement of this question involved a compromise between conflicting interests, the debate revolved essentially around American pictures. From the start American motion pictures constituted the overwhelming proportion of imports. Thus the liberalization of import restrictions reveals acceptance of Hollywood as a constituent part of Weimar film culture. Despite acute awareness of America's near eradication of French, British, Swedish and Italian production bases, the German trade circles considered collaboration with American companies to be compatible with preservation of a domestic industry. Even later criticism of the import system for encouraging American companies to finance cheap German "quota" pictures to earn import permits testifies to the normalcy of corporate liaisons between Hollywood and Berlin.[18]

Before 1924 the character of relations between Hollywood and Berlin was conditioned largely by the inflation. German interest in American motion pictures rested on relatively meager purchasing power. Yet because import licenses were granted to domestic companies with previous track records, and because American firms initially did not have branch offices in Germany, the first American motion pictures distributed in Germany were handled by German companies. Apart from William Fox, a relative latecomer who in 1923 founded his own German subsidiary, the major American companies chose to market their product through short-term agreements with German distributors. Universal pictures, for instance, were distributed by Oskar Einstein; Metro, Triangle and Mutual releases by UFA (Damra); First National films by Transocean; and Paramount pictures by Phoebus Film.[19] A contract from August 1921 between Decla-Verleih and Goldwyn illustrates the general pattern. Decla purchased distribution rights to eight Goldwyn pictures at a cost of 150,000 marks each plus fifty percent of the net box office exceeding that figure. License to these films for a period of four years was complemented by the exclusive right to represent Goldwyn in Germany until April 1922.

In addition Decla had an option for renewing the contract for 1922–1923 if both parties could agree on the number of pictures to be distributed. Each side clearly desired to benefit from the partnership but was reluctant to make far-reaching arrangements until the market response to American film could be ascertained. Moreover, the erratic and ailing fortunes of the German currency made long-term deals unattractive.[20]

The one exception to the pattern of limited partnerships to distribute American movies in Germany came in response to production opportunities afforded by the German inflation. In late 1920 *Madame Dubarry*, the UFA spectacle directed by Ernst Lubitsch, created a motion picture sensation in the United States as *Passion*. In its wake *Das Cabinet des Dr. Caligari* and Lubitsch's subsequent historical epic, *Anna Boleyn* (*Deception*), confirmed Germany's talent and technical know-how.[21] American film moguls—Arthur Ziehm of Goldwyn and Carl Laemmle, president of Universal—had already visited Berlin to explore ways to exploit the German market and the cheapness in dollars of German production. At the end of 1920 Famous Players (Paramount) staked its German claim by signing contracts with Ernst Lubitsch, Pola Negri and Joe May for employment in both Germany and the United States.[22] It also negotiated with UFA for a comprehensive production and distribution agreement. Although these negotiations proved abortive, apparently because the Americans made agreement conditional on their right to acquire a controlling share of UFA stock, the grandiose ambitions they concealed were almost immediately realized by an independent initiative from Famous Players. In April 1921 it launched, via two German-American agents, Ben Blumenthal and Sam Rachmann, a German holding company, the European Film Alliance (EFA).[23]

EFA acquired the most modern studios in Germany and plundered much of the best UFA talent by offering irresistible dollar contracts to those it believed could make films to the standard set by *Madame Dubarry*. On paper it possessed the very best requisites available in Germany. It embraced production companies formed for Ernst Lubitsch, Pola Negri, Joe May and the outstanding theater director, Max Reinhardt, to name only its most famous contributors. Its technical staff was second to none, as was its directorate. Paul Davidson, Germany's leading production chief, left his post at UFA to work with Lubitsch under the aegis of EFA, and he was joined by Carl Bratz, a member of the board at UFA. EFA could count on the extensive international distribution network maintained by Famous Players as an outlet rivaled by no native company. It seemed destined to become a model of international collaboration between Hollywood and Berlin.[24]

EFA's import ambitions matched the boldness of its production program. Founded when the import quota and allocation for 1921 had already been determined, it quickly sought to translate its financial muscle into import certificates. In a lengthy petition to the Film Trade Board EFA appealed in August 1921 for permission to import 100,000 meters of film negative (that is, over half the total quota) from Famous Players. Its rationale blended the usual phrases about the cultural importance of film for overcoming national barriers with self-congratulations for opening the American market to German film and for funneling dollars into German production. In concrete terms it recommended reciprocity as the basis of film exchange—exporters of German films should receive a corresponding quota of imports—a proposal which, ironically, later became a stick with which German critics beat American firms for inundating the German market with their pictures but refusing to import German films.[25]

In the event, neither the production ambitions nor import hopes were realized. The request for a special quota for Famous Players films met flat refusal from the Film Trade Board. EFA was not eligible under the existing system to acquire import permits; Famous Players would have to work with an established distributor.[26] Deflation of production dreams took place over a longer period but was no less final. After major investments in studios, equipment and personnel—by its own boast over thirty million marks by mid-1921—EFA produced only a handful of motion pictures, notably two works by Lubitsch, *Die Flamme* and *Das Weib des Pharao*, which failed to justify high commercial expectations.[27] To what extent Famous Players planned to help offset these investments through German earnings on previously amortized American pictures is unclear; denial of import permission presumably presented financial complications. Nonetheless, production extravagance, low-quantity output, disappointing box office and above all dissension between American and German management of the company quickly soured the dream. Officially founded in April 1921, EFA ceased production late the following year. Pola Negri, Ernst Lubitsch and Dimitri Buchowetzki accepted contracts to work in America, the first of a stream of German film people who relocated to Hollywood. The other EFA employees had their contracts canceled effective 31 December or received substantial compensation and pursued their own paths within the German film industry.[28]

This early case of collaboration between Hollywood and Berlin provoked extremely ambivalent reactions from German trade circles. EFA offered badly needed international acceptance and prestige for an industry still suffering from international suspicions inflamed by the war. The willingness of Hollywood's largest company to enlist the services of German artists and producers placed a seal of approval on German accomplishments, a seal very high on the list of postwar priorities. Moreover, EFA provided an international distribution network with which to spread the works and reputation of the German cinema abroad. Lubitsch and Davidson put it succinctly: "If German film can only make inroads over there and if it is at all enjoyed, the entire German industry will derive benefit from it as it is attracted more strongly to export to America."[29] Both were pleading in their own defence when they argued that international cooperation would open the American market to German film, but they were also playing skillfully upon general aspirations.

Yet the prospect of American moguls buying up German talent and with it the future of German cinema caused concern. There had already been deep reservations about American financing and control in the company. From its birth EFA raised the specter of Americanization through the co-option of German resources and personnel.[30] Consequently, its demise occasioned little regret. Its brief and troubled history was taken as demonstration that American financial largesse did not automatically generate film successes. American misunderstanding and mismanagement of German talent appeared the root cause of the company's debacle. Dollars had been dispensed so liberally that German creativity had been impaired. Amusement and self-satisfaction greeted the failure, despite dollar investments and favorable circumstances, to realize the American dream in Berlin. According to Fritz Olimsky, EFA taught the Americans for the first time that dollars alone could not bridge the gulf between national tastes and cinematic styles.[31]

EFA's collapse came at a critical moment for the German cinema. Quite apart from the loss of Pola Negri, Ernst Lubitsch and Dimitri Buchowetzki, the industry faced a mounting inflation which was eroding profitability on the domestic market. Whereas at the end of the war the domestic market alone covered 100 percent of production expenses, in the period 1921–1923 its contribution fell from forty to as low as ten percent.[32] Foreign earnings became critical to German producers. It had become virtually mandatory either to produce cheaply, trusting any income from abroad to yield a profit, or, as EFA hoped, to make lavish spectacles like *Madame Dubarry* which were costly but could captivate audiences abroad. As the world's largest and wealthiest film market America occupied a critical place in any export calculation.[33]

While German endeavors to penetrate the American market represent a history of their own, they bear sufficiently on Hollywood's role in Germany to merit brief discussion. It is a history which began with almost unbounded hopes but gave way to disappointment and some bitterness. The sensation created by the American release of *Madame Dubarry* late in 1920 augured very favorably for the future. Critical acclaim for other major releases of this period—*Das Cabinet des Dr. Caligari, Der Golem, wie er in die Welt kam* and *Anna Boleyn*—and EFA's employment of German talent confirmed German excellence and gave substance to reports that Hollywood both feared the German cinema and felt compelled to learn from it.[34] German experts noted proudly that an American compilation of the ten best pictures at the box office in 1921 placed *Madame Dubarry* first, ahead of *Way Down East* and *The Kid*, while *Caligari, Anna Boleyn, Golem* and *Carmen* placed fourth, fifth, seventh and eighth re-

spectively. They concluded that German pictures generally surpassed American in appeal as well as quality.[35]

After these auspicious beginnings came a series of rude
shocks. Even while dependence on foreign earnings continued
to grow, disconcerting news arrived from the United States. In
the summer of 1922 Rudolf Berg, a German distributor just
returned from a seven month American study tour, noted that
the favorable first impression made by outstanding German film
releases had been nullified by the showing of older, inferior
productions. American sympathy for German movies had
abruptly evaporated, leaving the German cinema back at the
beginning, having to overcome American prejudices.[36] The following year Berg's appraisal was corroborated by two other
prominent executives who visited America, Hermann Rosenfeld, head of the National Film Company, and E. H. Correll,
director of Phoebus Film. Rosenfeld still employed the language
of "conquering the American market," but his analysis of present circumstances offered scarce hope for conquest. Correll
confirmed the bitter truth that Americans showed virtually no
interest in German motion pictures and asserted that Germans
had received greatly exaggerated reports of the popular acclaim
and box-office take for the first German movies to succeed in the
United States, *Madame Dubarry* and *Das Cabinet des Dr. Caligari*.[37]

These disappointments coincided with increasing recognition
that inflation was a double-edged sword. While it gave German
films a tremendous edge on foreign markets it not only reduced
the national market to negligible proportions but also played
havoc with production costs and fostered cheap production for
dumping abroad.[38] The far-sighted recognized that producers
could not proceed on the premise of a limitless export market.
Sooner or later monetary madness would end. Native producers
would then have to face competition at home and abroad on
an equal footing. In the meantime, dumping threatened to discredit Germany's cinematic reputation and jeopardize long-
term foreign sales, making future adjustments even more problematic.[39]

Despite these dark clouds on the horizon, the appeal of the
American market was so powerful that German producers
worked with at least one eye on possibilities in the United States.

Even when monetary stabilization restored the earning capacity of domestic exhibition, pressure to gear production to an imagined American audience remained strong. Behind this pressure lay not only the size of America's exhibition circuit but Hollywood's invasion of the German market in late 1923 and 1924. At the same moment that German export ambitions to the United States met frustration, American motion pictures became qualitative and quantitative fixtures in Germany. Qualitatively, the release of the first films starring Jackie Coogan (chief among them Chaplin's *The Kid*), and a number of recent sensationalist and social dramas by Cecil B. De Mille and Maurice Tourneur, generated widespread respect for American filmmaking. Quantitatively, a fresh influx of American movies helped offset a catastrophic decline in domestic production in 1922 and 1923. Since inflation made domestic production costs increasingly unpredictable, German concerns turned increasingly to distribution as the safest branch of film enterprise. Stabilization of the currency in 1924 created a painful adjustment to responsible fiscal behavior which perpetuated the shrinkage in domestic output.[40]

Even before introduction of a new currency experts began to admit that the tables had been turned. In the second half of 1923 they conceded that the battle for position had narrowed to a struggle against Hollywood in Germany. In August Willy Haas looked back on a year of German production and judged it qualitatively incapable of competing abroad. Its export continued only because it underbid all competitors. In October Wolfgang Martini, a leading trade journalist in Munich, conceded that in the public mind American film had already achieved victory in Germany.[41] Under these circumstances, the ambition to sell motion pictures in the United States joined hands with the perception that Hollywood's motion picture formula also worked in Germany to encourage filmmakers to aim their work at an imagined American audience. From UFA's early pledge to challenge the world's leading producers, through the reign of Erich Pommer and the big budget spectacles and art films, to the early sound era when UFA spared no expense to create English versions of its leading pictures, American cinemas exerted irresistible pull. UFA's policy of finding world-renowned, especially American stars, to make its films internationally attractive, was just one symptom of the general ambition.[42] Although UFA was the only firm to establish its own American affiliate, and most systematically committed to creation of motion pictures which that affiliate could distribute in the United States, export hopes continued to shape general responses to Hollywood. These hopes became inextricably linked to distribution contracts for release of American pictures in Germany.

As indicated by the table earlier in this chapter, 1924 witnessed the breakthrough of the American feature film to rough parity with German features on the domestic market. This breakthrough is the principal measure of the fact that in the cinema, as in the economy generally, late 1923 and early 1924 marked a watershed. While the economy came to depend on massive infusions of American capital via the Dawes Plan, German theaters became dependent on American imports for a significant portion of their programs.[43] In addition to exporting its films, Hollywood exported its capital and corporate influence. Although loans to German film companies were modest by the scale of investment in the automobile or shipping industry, they played a pivotal and controversial role. Moreover, at middecade a number of the American majors founded production as well as distribution affiliates in Berlin. None approached the grandiose scale of EFA, but in conjunction with American investments in German firms these ventures revived the specter of Americanization.

From the end of the inflationary period contractual ties between Hollywood and Berlin for distribution of American films in Germany proliferated. For instance, in September 1923 National Film established a partnership with Famous Players which made it the latter's German representative. In July 1924 Trianon negotiated a cooperative arrangement for production and distribution with Selznick Co. Phoebus acquired, with some fanfare, rights to Metro-Goldwyn films, before entering a longterm relationship with United Artists. The subsequent year Bruckmann entered into a distribution compact with Universal and UFA acquired short-term rights to Warner Bros., First National, Paramount and Metro-Goldwyn films.[44] Simultaneously, American corporations founded their own German affiliates or acquired controlling shares in existing firms. First National, after distributing through UFA, created German First National (Defina) in 1927. Universal took over Matador Film, in 1928 changing its name to German Universal. Warner Bros. made Bruckmann its German branch office.

Where the Americans established their own distribution companies they were legally obliged, by quota regulations, to distribute as many German features as imports. Generally this entailed producing as well as distributing in Germany. William Fox, who had created a German office in 1923, launched a production program in 1926 (Deutsche Fox) under the supervision of the eminent cameraman, Karl Freund. Fox also acquired a premiere theater in Berlin to showcase his product. Carl Laemmle's Deutsche Universal also chose to manufacture its quota of German pictures to earn import permits. First National likewise incorporated a production subsidiary (German Film Union—Defu), acquiring for a time the services of Friedrich Zelnik, arguably Germany's most successful director at the box office.[45]

Since in retrospect the various forms of Hollywood's commercial penetration have been linked to the loss of artistic and cultural independence, thus the waning of a distinctive Weimar cinema, it cannot be too strongly stressed that German-American collaboration was a commonplace and generally accepted feature of Weimar film culture in the second half of the 1920s. It must also be emphasized that this collaboration served both parties. Although the fine print of collaborative contracts was rarely divulged, the general thrust of them was clear. Direct affiliation with leading German companies offered American firms import certificates, distribution networks and theater chains for exploitation of their product. Subsidiaries obliged them to distribute the products of domestic filmmakers or to produce in Germany in order to earn import permits. Since they employed German performers, directors, producers and administrative personnel, their presence was not merely self-serving. German partners received a selection of Hollywood's motion pictures, financial support to produce pictures for import permits, and in some instances, a measure of reciprocal access to the American market. Although the exchange was anything but equal, it cannot be described as altogether one-sided. Whether Hollywood bypassed or associated with existing German companies, its penetration served German as well as American interests.[46]

This much being said, it is nonetheless true that Hollywood's infiltration of the German film industry did not meet universal approval. The speed and volume of its middecade onslaught seriously threatened extinction of independent German cinema. Defensive reactions surfaced on a number of levels. Coincident with the proliferation of German-American alliances there emerged a sharp indictment of Hollywood's product and complaints about the declining market value of American film for German theaters, a theme explored in detail in chapter four. With that indictment went a campaign to halve the import quota, a maneuver frustrated by the fact that sufficient domestic firms had contractual ties with American companies to have a vested interest in preservation of an open door. But the chief target of anti-American sentiment was not, significantly, the series of newly established American production companies in Berlin staffed by German personnel. Rather it was the outstanding collaborative venture of middecade, the partnership of UFA, Paramount and Metro-Goldwyn known as Parufamet, which became the cynosure of critical reaction against Hollywood's role in Germany. As Germany's leading motion picture conglomerate, initially supported by public funds, UFA encountered criticism for policies which could be tolerated from lesser firms. Since documentation pertaining to the agreement has been preserved, it is possible to examine this particular liaison between Hollywood and Berlin against the backdrop of the public responses it provoked.

UFA's commitment to Paramount and Metro-Goldwyn was the product both of long-term interaction with Hollywood and of short-term pressures. The negotiations which led to the agreement actually began with Universal, which was then preempted by aggressive action by Paramount and Metro-Goldwyn.[47] But the roots of the deal can be traced back to the beginning of the decade, when the formation of EFA followed upon UFA's refusal to accept American terms for direct collaboration. Hollywood's interest in UFA's distribution and theater network did not evaporate. The opportunity to access it appeared once again with the financial difficulties which German cinema experienced in the aftermath of the inflation. The conjunction of tight credit, pressure from American competition in Germany and the failure of German films to obtain a foothold in the United States created growing deficits for native producers. The consequences were especially fateful for UFA, whose size gave substance to the ambition to rival Hollywood.

More than any other producer, UFA staked its reputation, and ultimately its existence, on gaining entry to the American market. In the first half of the decade it embarked on a bold program to challenge Hollywood. Although its own production output was a fraction of that of the largest American companies, it distributed a disproportionate share of German motion pictures. In 1924 it opened a branch office in New York to supervise distribution rights in America and launched an impressive drive to expand its theater holdings in Germany.[48] Furthermore, under Erich Pommer it produced a number of art and/or big budget spectacles—*Die Nibelungen, Der letzte Mann, Tartüff, Faust* and *Metropolis*—which were intended as Germany's answer to Hollywood. When these pictures failed to justify the expense with substantial American earnings, UFA encountered severe financial difficulties. Already at the beginning of 1925 it borrowed fifteen million marks to remain solvent. At the end of the year the Deutsche Bank, the principal investor in the company, recalled its loan and UFA accepted slightly more than this sum again from Paramount and Metro-Goldwyn.[49]

As the visible consequence of financial mismanagement and foiled ambitions the accord quite understandably came in for unfriendly commentary. But the criticism did not stop there, for the agreement had potentially far-reaching consequences for UFA and with it German cinema as a whole. According to the studiously vague press release from UFA the loan of $4 million was accompanied by terms for 1) the establishment in Germany of a joint distribution agency (Parufamet) to handle the best productions of all three companies, 2) joint production in Germany, "under the direction of UFA," and cooperative theater management, again with "full protection" of UFA's interests, and 3) the export to the United States of a "substantial portion" of UFA's film output.[50] UFA received fifty percent ownership of the new distribution company (the other half being split between Paramount and Metro) to which each of the three contracting parties agreed to contribute its twenty best feature pictures annually. Paramount and Metro-Goldwyn each contracted to release five UFA films annually in the United States.[51]

Contemporaries had good reason to question what specific terms lay behind the ambiguous official communiqué, especially since UFA's financial woes, no secret at the time, received absolutely no mention.[52] As an exhibitor UFA had its hands tied. It had obligations to its two contracting partners to release forty feature films annually, plus by separate arrangement a commitment to Universal for another ten pictures each year. Together these meant reserving the majority of UFA theater bookings for American films. In the distribution sector UFA likewise surrendered many of its prerogatives. Its twenty best productions would be handled by a joint company, giving the American firms not only equal voice in distribution arrangements but also an equal share of the profits. Since in early 1926 American movies were dubious box-office value in Germany, the right of Paramount and Metro-Goldwyn to profit from UFA's productions constituted a major concession.[53]

In light of these disparities, projected cooperation in theater management and production raised further questions. Although no joint companies were created comparable to the distributor Parufamet, UFA's protestations that its sovereignty had not been infringed only sharpened suspicions to the contrary. In the fall of 1925 moviegoers had already received a foretaste of Americanized theater programs. UFA's show theater, UFA-Palast am Zoo, had been renovated under the direction of Sam Rachmann and reopened with a tremendous fanfare, boasting a program of jazz and stage shows as well as motion pictures. Wholesale importation of methods not necessarily appropriate in Germany stirred as much or more resentment as inundation with American movies. Even more threatening was American influence in the production sector. Paramount and Metro-Goldwyn provided capital to help produce or otherwise finance the acquisition of the forty German movies which, according to the quota law, UFA had to distribute to obtain import licenses for an equal number of American films. In the face of growing concern that the quota system was encouraging German firms to produce cheaply and in quantity just to acquire import certificates, UFA's agreement raised the possibility of forced Americanization.[54]

Although the accord naturally made no reference to the Americanization of UFA's production, it contained unpublished clauses which confirmed the gloomier speculations of contemporaries about Hollywood's influence. In the contract governing export of UFA films Paramount and Metro-Goldwyn received supervisory rights over UFA productions destined for America. Both firms could intervene at the preliminary production stage to insure that UFA films would be acceptable for American release.

> The Licensor [UFA] will submit from time to time copy of story, continuity, cast and proposed director for such pictures as they believe suitable for the American market and will carry out such criticism, suggestions, alterations and changes made by the Licensee [Paramount or Metro-Goldwyn] with respect to such proposed picture[s].[55]

Intervention of this type provided an apparently guaranteed means to realize the long-standing ambition to make motion pictures suitable for American audiences. But this external jurisdiction assumed embarrassingly comprehensive form, extending to the right to "re-edit, cut and title" UFA productions, subject only to the condition that nothing be done to discredit UFA or Germany.[56] The clause authorizing American input at the production stage had no counterpart in the agreement governing American production for Germany. A counterpart to the stipulation regarding editing of finished films did appear, flatly denying UFA the liberty to rework American features.

> Licensee [UFA] agrees to exhibit or cause said productions [of Paramount or Metro-Goldwyn] to be exhibited under such titles as shall be requested by Licensor, and in their original continuity of subject and in identically the same form as delivered to Licensee, and that no changes, interpolations, additions or eliminations shall be made therein without the written consent of Licensor first obtained, ex-

cept insofar as may be necessary to conform to the requirements or laws of the said territory.[57]

Apart from revealing Hollywood's boundless confidence in the superiority of its motion pictures, this paragraph hamstrung Parufamet at a moment when, as will be seen in chapter four, the call for careful editing of American films became a panacea for overcoming audience dissatisfaction with American imports.

Although contemporaries lacked details to substantiate their suspicions regarding Hollywood's influence, the more acute among them identified the implications of UFA's financial dependence—artistic restrictions and conformity to American expectations. The reactions of three prominent critics, whose views, to be heard frequently in this study, were anything but uniformly hostile toward American movies, indicate the tenor of opinion. Kurt Pinthus protested even before the UFA-Paramount/Metro-Goldwyn agreement at the prospect of a comparable arrangement with Universal. After seeing what had happened to the UFA-Palast under Sam Rachmann, Pinthus became convinced that distribution and production under American supervision would spell catastrophe for the German cinema as an independent artistic and public force.[58] Herbert Ihering shared the fear that American corporations would eliminate the German cinema as a distinct cultural and artistic entity. In a graphic metaphor he labeled the American cinema the new international breed of militarism, subjugating whole nations with insipid, sugary, standardized films and dictating American uniformity of tastes around the globe.[59] Roland Schacht adopted a less apocalyptic tone but was equally concerned with the dual threat of vanishing German independence and saturation with American movies. Although he professed disinterest in the origins of valuable motion pictures, he expressed dismay that front-ranking German artists would have to submit to American production methods. To cooperate with Hollywood apparently meant dictation of the ingredients which made up an acceptable German motion picture. Schacht also refused to accept as beneficent the import of numerous nondescript American movies to the exclusion of high quality European productions.[60]

Pinthus, Ihering and Schacht all rebelled at the prospect that German artists would be compelled to make American films and underwrite Americanized cinema culture. By itself this is hardly surprising, particularly coming from critics independent of the industry. It is striking, nonetheless, that trade perspectives on collaboration with Hollywood also underwent a shift. In the first half of the decade UFA's ambitions to rival Hollywood met considerable praise, even insofar as they involved American partnerships.[61] As late as the summer of 1925 UFA was credited with a major coup when it secured agreements with First National, Warner Bros., Metro-Goldwyn and Paramount to corner the American import trade. One estimate put the pool from which it could draw at 150 feature films. Since quota restrictions prevented import of more than a portion of this total, UFA appeared to be able to promise a selection of the very best American pictures for German distribution.[62] Trade papers treated this arrangement as a welcome check on American ambitions to establish their own distribution firms in Germany and acquire their own theaters. The decision of Paramount in particular to work with UFA rather than independently, as elsewhere in Europe, testified gratifyingly to UFA's commanding position. Without UFA the largest American concerns would have achieved absolute control.[63] Moreover, UFA's function as a bulwark for the whole German industry was enhanced by the apparent freedom of German experts to determine the selection and timing of American releases. UFA could prevent imports from overshadowing or displacing its own products and could choose only the outstanding Hollywood pictures for German theaters. In addition, although no promise that the general demand for reciprocity in film trade between Germany and the United States was forthcoming, critics expressed hope that the cooperation implied by distribution arrangements for Germany would spill over into entry for German films into America.[64]

Less than six months later UFA's deal with Metro-Goldwyn and Paramount met a very different response pattern. The existence of the loan clearly set off alarm signals. Also significant was the ten-year duration of the contract, the fact that American companies were granted a share in domestic profits from UFA's pictures and the prospect of American influence in joint production. Less visible but no less real was the general perception of sharply declining interest among German moviegoers in American motion pictures. Ultimately, however, the suspicions raised by Parufamet reflected long-standing fears of American takeover of German cinema. From the nationalist and later National Socialist perspective Parufamet epitomized national betrayal, a sellout redeemed only by the intervention of Alfred Hugenberg and associates in 1927.[65] For other analysts Parufamet represented the end of the golden age of the German cinema, for with it began the great exodus of German talent to Hollywood, led by Erich Pommer, F. W. Murnau and Emil Jannings. For many contemporaries, even those resentful of the fact, UFA was the German cinema in the sense that as *primus inter pares* its fortunes determined those of the industry as a whole. Once it fell under American influence the fate of the remainder was only a matter of time. UFA therefore became a lightning rod for sentiments about Hollywood.[66]

If the general tenor of opinion on Parufamet was sceptical, the great hope in the arrangement was that German motion pictures would finally have access to American theaters. In 1925 German-American film exchange still occurred overwhelmingly in one direction, the hopes of 1920–1921 no closer to fulfillment. Some measure of the disappointment and bitterness this engendered can be gained from the reflections of Georg Herzberg, columnist and critic for *Film-Kurier*, on a rerun in August 1925 of the famous Lubitsch work, *Madame Dubarry*. Herzberg took this picture as the embodiment of German postwar expertise responsible for breaking the boycott against German films abroad. But its challenge to American hegemony was of short duration, partly for economic reasons, partly because the German industry had become complacent and far too friendly toward Hollywood and, not least, because of American duplicity:

> The Americans were laughing up their sleeve. They were by no means of the opinion that the sale of film abroad must be based on reciprocity. We Germans had sold a few films to America and spoke of reciprocity; today American film controls half the German market; and America is making every conceivable effort to counter the import of German films.[67]

Although the Parufamet arrangement did not even approximate reciprocity, it contained fresh promise. Galling though it was that only one UFA film was to reach America for every four Metro-Goldwyn or Paramount pictures released in Germany, the fact that UFA movies gained entry to the American market at all was perceived as a major step forward. The ratio of four imports to one export left much to be desired, but it was a thousand times better than the ratio of 100:0, especially given that the United States had roughly six times the number of theaters as Germany. Even an open detractor of the whole transaction judged this its one ray of light, for the simple reason that to date no American firm of importance had committed itself to distribute an annual quota of German motion pictures.[68] Under these circumstances it is no surprise that UFA defended the pact before the public and its shareholders as a ticket to the American market. What UFA did not immediately reveal, but emerged when the Hugenberg group acquired the company, was that the American obligation to accept ten UFA features carried the proviso that these first be judged suitable for release in the United States. Despite securing the authorization to oversee UFA's output, Paramount and Metro-Goldwyn reserved the right to reject the finished product. Although UFA's records show that a fair portion of its films did see American release, and generated a substantial portion of its overall distribution revenue, the discrimination apparent in this escape clause caused further resentment toward the agreement.[69]

In one respect the debate about Parufamet proved much fuss about nothing, for contrary to initial projections it operated for scarcely two years. Shortly after Hugenberg acquired a ruling share in UFA in 1927 the distribution agreement underwent substantial revision and the American loan was paid off by sale of the real estate set as collateral against it. By 1928 differences in the distribution sector led UFA to withdraw its films from the joint company and Parufamet essentially distributed the movies only of the two American firms. Collaborative production resulted in only one feature film before being indefinitely scotched. Not long afterwards the appearance of talking pictures undermined Parufamet's *raison d'être* and it was scrapped altogether.[70]

In another respect, however, the debate which ensued over the agreement exposes the fundamental dilemma of Germany's ties with Hollywood in the era of relative stability. Central to it was the problem of selling Hollywood to German audiences, an issue which had polarized trade circles before signature of Parufamet and continued to plague it thereafter. As early as 1924 some film experts began to allege that overexposure to American motion pictures was diminishing their commercial value.[71] In response to these allegations, *Reichsfilmblatt*, the trade paper representing the interests of independent exhibitors (i.e., those outside the large theater chains like UFA), detected a plot among German producers to discredit Hollywood. The editor of the journal, Dr. Rudolf Beissel, claimed that domestic producers, threatened by their inability to make popular films, were trying to gain reduction of the import ceiling on the grounds that American pictures did not appeal to German moviegoers. Beissel believed a systematic campaign had been launched by sections of the German press to denigrate American movies and extend special consideration to domestic productions. In his opinion, moviegoers preferred Hollywood.[72]

The ulterior motive which *Reichsfilmblatt* attributed to producers had a thinly veiled counterpart among theater owners. In late 1924, when the paper commented on charges by the Emelka Company of corruption and pro-American bias among critics in Munich, it admitted that German cinemas had become so dependent on American imports that if the public were persuaded of their unattractiveness, a serious exhibition crisis could ensue.

> The fairy tale of declining appeal of American films will be recited to the public until it believes it and begins more and more to avoid American film. And what will happen once the prejudice has taken root? *In the long term we are absolutely dependent on American film in our programs.*[73] (my emphasis)

Theater owners therefore had a stake in public appreciation of Hollywood to offset the catastrophic decline in domestic production and to encourage competition.

Hollywood's instrumentalization in the dispute between the independent exhibitors and the large concerns provides one illustration of the way in which American motion pictures had been domesticated in Germany by 1924. What makes it particularly noteworthy in the present context is that in the course of 1925 attitudes vis-à-vis Hollywood underwent a fundamental reversal. From late 1924 *Reichsfilmblatt* began to report incidents of public dissatisfaction with American movies. By early 1925 it advocated an end to the mass import of American films. In July, Beissel, clearly anxious that the Americans could become seriously interested in German theater operations, argued that cheap American mass production was no longer profitable for German theaters. In September the journal decried the exorbitant prices demanded for American motion pictures which repelled German viewers. The combined fear that Hollywood could dictate rental prices for unpopular pictures and buy up financially ailing German theaters occasioned a dramatic shift of opinion.[74]

News of UFA's pact with Paramount and Metro-Goldwyn hit a raw nerve. Criticism of American movies in *Reichsfilmblatt* now became venomous. In the early months of 1926 editorials espoused bitter anti-American sentiment: they wrote UFA off as an American company and charged the Americans with a systematic attempt to destroy German cultural independence. Between German and American sensibilities there existed no possibility of reconciliation. Felix Henseleit, lead critic for the paper, went so far as to blame the Americans for ruining theater business in Germany with mediocre motion pictures! Thus in the space of slightly more than a year Hollywood's staunchest German ally was publishing chauvinistic tirades against America.[75]

In contrast to *Reichsfilmblatt*'s vocal anti-American campaign, the other leading trade papers—*Der Film, Film-Kurier, Kinematograph* and *Lichtbildbühne*—adopted a policy of appeasement. Rather than frontal attack on Hollywood they challenged the manner and form of American releases. In the spring of 1926 *Der Film* repeatedly suggested that the American features shown in Berlin's foremost UFA theaters failed to match the quality of domestic films premiered in lesser theaters. UFA was shortsighted or bound to a self-defeating policy by commitments to American partners.[76] A parallel tack gained currency in *Film-*

Kurier and *Lichtbildbühne* and to a somewhat lesser extent in *Kinematograph*. In addition to urging greater discrimination in the selection and theater placement of American imports these recommended careful revision and titling of American imports by editors conversant with German sensibilities. Skillful editing could eliminate elements offensive to German audiences.[77]

In sum, the exhibitors, erstwhile champions of American motion pictures, now railed against the weakness of all but a handful of them and against the exorbitant rental fees they commanded, declined participation in a banquet given in honor of the visiting American celebrities, Douglas Fairbanks and Mary Pickford, and even slapped a boycott on Metro productions to protest the release abroad of the hate film *Mare Nostrum*.[78] Meanwhile, those concerned for the welfare of German production, formerly opposed to extensive import, now grasped for ways and means, such as more intelligent theater placement and publicity, or clever editing, to bolster sagging interest in American movies. While theater owners became increasingly anxious about public resistance to American film and about the imminent threat of American investments in German theater operations, producers encouraged peaceful ties with American capital. Parufamet thus completed an exchange of positions.[79]

In this general backlash against Hollywood all branches of the German cinema faced a dilemma. As formulated by Alfred Rosenthal, film expert for Scherl Publishers, its crux was domestic need of American production capital. Rosenthal argued that so long as native companies retained managerial independence and German artists enjoyed sufficient freedom to create motion pictures suited to German tastes, the sources of capital were irrelevant. He therefore welcomed the recent spate of alliances between American and German companies, of which Parufamet was chief. Quota films financed through these agreements could, he admitted, undermine the quality and reputation of the German cinema, but this danger had to be weighed against the more fundamental consideration that without American capital German production would be relegated to insignificance in any case.[80]

Inseparable from the need for funding was the compulsion to import American films. Again Rosenthal was among the outspoken advocates of realism.[81] Consequently, he found the anti-American offensive of the theater owners, especially their plans to boycott American film, irrational. Native production had been quantitatively inadequate for several years running. If this were not problem enough, an honest appraisal of present circumstances showed that "at least seventy-five percent of the so-called German films were financed with American money." Most importantly, "the import of a corresponding number of American films [was] a *conditio sine qua non* for this German production." The conclusion was inescapable: if theater owners sincerely desired more German movies they were obliged to screen American film. Refusal to face the reality that the German industry functioned only with American subventions was suicidal.[82] That in turn gave considerable priority to polishing Hollywood's German image. As *Lichtbildbühne* baldly argued:

> We who not so very long ago were still frightened by the word 'Americanization' are presently in the paradoxical position of having to ponder means to procure for American film domestic rights in Germany. That this product, 'American film,' becomes a marketable article of trade in Germany—in this alone lies the key to the whole problem Germany-America as far as we film people are concerned.[83]

In this light Parufamet appears less as the source of German woes than as a symptom of them. As a business transaction it followed logically from earlier arrangements which linked German and American firms.[84] Furthermore, UFA's behavior was perfectly consistent with the general pattern at middecade: Germany drew on American resources for projects for which domestic support was inadequate or lacking.[85] Responses were as mixed here as in other sectors of the economy. On the one hand, it seemed pointless to bite the hand feeding German production by refusing the American movies which thanks to the quota law encouraged American investment in German production. On the other hand, it appeared fatal to theater owners to acquiesce in the onslaught of what they considered unpopular and costly American films. All had reservations about mass import of American film and sought preservation of native production. But while the one stressed the indissoluble link between

German and American firms and downplayed the negative elements in this arrangement, the other lashed out at Hollywood. The clash of interests indicates the parameters within which American motion pictures were assigned a place in German culture. Caught between Hollywood's alleged foreignness to German sensibilities and its highly prized dowry, namely, production capital, German commentators had extremely limited freedom to maneuvre.

Depending then upon the particular interests and inclinations of the observer Parufamet became analogous either to the Versailles Treaty or to the Dawes Plan. Versailles, to Germans a dictated, vengeful peace, signified Germany's defeat, war guilt and obligation to pay reparations. The Dawes Plan of 1924, while perpetuating the Versailles system, provided massive foreign loans to Germany, chiefly from the United States, to stabilize the economy. It thereby facilitated Germany's readmission to the international community through the multilateral Treaty of Locarno (1925) and membership in the League of Nations. Against this backdrop Herbert Ihering noted with bitter irony that a company established to propagandize Germanness abroad now served the interests of *Amerikanismus* in Germany. Instead of fruitful cross-fertilization, German-American film ties resulted in the triumph of one national type. Parufamet symbolized not Locarno but Versailles, the imposition by one cinema culture of its values and methods on another.[86] By contrast, the business editor of *Berliner Tageblatt* assumed UFA had been fortunate to gain a partnership with two leading American companies and endorsed the pact, artistically as well as commercially, for insuring Hollywood's participation in UFA's production. Parufamet resembled the Dawes Plan more than Versailles.[87]

With hindsight it is possible to appreciate the logic in both perspectives. The former parallel is apt inasmuch as UFA's recourse to American aid was equivalent to surrender in the film war projected early in the decade. Like Versailles, Parufamet outlined the meaning of defeat. At the same time Parufamet resembled the Dawes Plan in its extension of funding to a capital-hungry sector of the German economy. As a business transaction it exhibited advantages and disadvantages which could be isolated and discussed. Between the extremes of UFA's platitudes about cooperation and the cultural pessimism about Americanization lay a realism appropriate to the new sobriety of the period. Yet Parufamet also symbolized the American phase in postwar German cinema. Like the Dawes Plan it stood for more than the sum of its individual parts, namely, German dependence on the United States and American influence in German affairs.[88]

The attention drawn by Parufamet has obscured, both then and since, the extent to which alliances with American companies became the norm. At the beginning of 1925 National Film concluded a pact with Paramount to distribute American films in Germany and made no secret of plans to establish cooperative production or the appointment of an American representative to the board of directors.[89] Later that year Bruckmann entered a distribution partnership with Universal, albeit with sharp denials that the latter had acquired any corporate control. The following year it signed a cooperative agreement with Warner Bros. covering production and distribution which effectively made it an American branch office.[90] In 1926 Fox-Europa released its first productions, among them *Der Trödler von Amsterdam* and *Die Mühle von Sanssouci*, and later produced Walter Ruttmann's *Berlin, Sinfonie der Großstadt* as well as Béla Balázs's *Die Abenteuer eines Zehnmarkscheins*.[91] United Artists extended its field of operations first with Phoebus-Film—here cooperation included appointment of Joseph Schenck to the Phoebus board—and then with Rex-Film under the directorship of Lupu Pick.[92] First National enlisted prominent German personnel, initially Friedrich Zelnik and then Wilhelm Dieterle, for its production company. Deutsche Universal began to produce in Germany in 1927. Warner Bros. also signed an agreement with National Film for joint production.[93] In all of these the trade press generally continued to find the promise of both respectable domestic production and export to America. Hollywood's funding of German artistic, technical and business talent was preferable to paralysis of it through lack of domestic capital or loss of it altogether to the emigration.[94]

Despite mixed responses to the Parufamet agreement, UFA

also openly hitched its fortunes to the American market. Its new director, Ferdinand Bausback, appointed in the aftermath of Parufamet to restore financial accountability, announced that the age of expansion and bold experiments was over. That did not, however, mean eschewing the American market. Bausback publicly endorsed a policy of courting America, declaring that henceforth all UFA features would be suited for release in the United States. Even his assurance that the company would produce German rather than American motion pictures was qualified by the need to take "the mentality of the American public" into account.[95] His plan was clearly to introduce rational business calculation on behalf of American sales. Hugenberg's UFA followed a similar strategy. With eyes fixed squarely on the American market, in 1927 it rehired Erich Pommer, who had left the company and the country for Hollywood in 1926, as head of its world-class production team. Pommer was on contract from an American firm (Producers' Service Corporation) with a specific mandate to create UFA films suitable for American release.[96] Having demonstrated in the United States his skill at creation of "international" features, he was hired to duplicate the feat in Germany. His round trip from Berlin to Hollywood and back again parallels the larger circle of competition, defeat and cooperation experienced by Weimar cinema as a whole.

In the second half of the 1920s not only did America's motion picture and corporate presence become the norm, but experts also favored, albeit with some reservations, Americanization of domestic production and promotional techniques in the interests of sales to the United States. German artists, technicians and executives routinely served the American market, if not American-backed domestic companies, and despite all the stigma attached to Hollywood generally congratulated each other for doing so. Without achieving full reciprocity they also had the satisfaction of seeing an increasing number of German features released in the United States. Thus a *modus vivendi* was reached—regularization of German-American film relations analogous to the relative stabilization of the period.

None of this denies the multiple grievances aired against American films or business methods. Theater owners repeatedly lamented not only the quality of the American product but the unfair practices by which it was foisted on them, particularly the blind and block booking system which obliged them to accept numerous unknown and unpopular pictures at inflated prices. Nor does it suggest that the American presence did not have other deleterious side effects. The most notorious of these was the temptation to produce cheaply in order to earn import certificates, thus depressing domestic standards while opening the market further to American imports.[97] The more pervasive pressure, one met with considerable ambivalence, was to Americanize production to suit the American moviegoer.

Nevertheless, a one-dimensional model of outrage at American industrial inroads is clearly inadequate. The American phase in the German cinema, particularly the period of crisis following signing of Parufamet, also had positive features. UFA's liaison with Paramount and Metro-Goldwyn meant American influence over the type of movies Germans would produce and consume but also a breathing space for Germany's most important film concern. The desire to gain a foothold in the United States, the most potent single factor in Americanization of German production, recommended collaboration with American counterparts. Therefore, despite multiple sources of friction, partnerships with Hollywood were accepted as a fact of German cinematic life. On balance, the 1920s witnessed as much or more cooperation as competition between parties in opposite national camps.

3
HOLLYWOOD IN BERLIN
The Initiation, 1921–1923

Commercial realities constituted one facet of the relationship between Hollywood and Berlin in the Weimar period. On balance they favored collaboration. But they were not neatly separable from filmic, aesthetic or broader cultural considerations. The *modus vivendi* which came into being between Hollywood and Berlin generated protracted resistance as well as accommodation. G. W. Pabst's lament in 1927 that producers, bowing to commercial realities, were compelling filmmakers to adopt "the American style" is only the best known of many allegations that pressure to conform to American standards and sell in the United States perverted German cinematic development.[1] Persuasive arguments for preserving cultural independence clashed head on with economic imperatives. Although cultural historians have tended to measure Americanization by the volume of anti-American discourse, Weimar's experience of Hollywood did not begin in 1924, the year that American films flooded the market and provoked a backlash. Between 1921 and the complete collapse of the currency in late 1923 Germany was reintroduced gradually to American film culture. This process of rediscovery, an historical narrative in its own right, reveals Weimar's experience of Hollywood as more than rationalization of vested interests or articulation of prejudices rooted in long-standing images of American culture.

Unlike the dramatic advent of Soviet film in Germany in 1926 with the premiere of Sergei Eisenstein's *Battleship Potemkin*, Hollywood's return to Germany in 1921 is a forgotten chapter in Weimar cinema history. In one sense this is justified, for the event made headlines neither in the press at large nor in trade papers. In fact, the first American releases were little more than curiosities. Until 1923 quantitatively insufficient to provoke trade concern, they stood qualitatively in the shadow of domestic features and did not command broad respect. Nor did they initially compel revision of prewar stereotypes applied both to Hollywood and American culture. Action-packed, violent, superficial and ethically naive, they confirmed visions of the United States as a prosperous, optimistic and technologically sophisticated but culturally adolescent country.[2] While Hollywood's return does not, therefore, make compelling drama, it had much more than casual significance for Weimar cinema and popular culture. The enormous expansion of American cultural export since the outbreak of World War I, in conjunction with cinema's rise to prominence in Germany, gave familiar images and approaches a new edge. Postwar Germany could no longer smugly assume general cultural superiority vis-à-vis the New World. Weimar cinema could not avoid comparison and competition with Hollywood.[3]

Until the restoration of legal import in 1921 Weimar's dialogue with Hollywood was muted and derivative. Since Germany was isolated from the international market, both information and interest in the subject were slight.[4] Attempts to characterize Hollywood fell back on received wisdom, reinforced by modes of cultural stereotyping popularized during the war. Limitations of evidence encouraged extrapolation from general visions of American culture to Hollywood. Reports from abroad and isolated showings in Germany quickly established a contrast between Hollywood's strengths in acting, directing and technical work and feebleness in selection and structure of subject matter. At the root of the contrast was the discrepancy between talent for tempo, suspense and sensationalism and American ineptidude in creating logical, original screenplays.[5] Scenarios contained, at best, some interesting ideas; more commonly they were labeled thin or elementary; at worst they were roasted for intellectual superficiality and classified with the cheap novels upon which the cinema had fed in its infancy.[6]

None of this, any more than the sketchy character of the sources on which it was based, prevented the postwar rush by importers to secure stocks of American motion pictures: since

Hollywood had entertained the world, it would also presumably entertain Germans. And although the stereotypes were generalized to the point of being analytically unrewarding, they served a discernible purpose. German sources made repeated reference to incoherent or inconsequential screenplays to expose the incommensurability between Hollywood as industry and Hollywood as producer of cultural values. In what critics dubbed characteristically American fashion, magnitude served as surrogate for substance. It followed that Hollywood's international ascendancy rested on a hollow and challengeable base.[7]

While critics jumped at the opportunity to identify a competitor's Achilles heel, they also rapidly adopted Hollywood as a source of cinematic prescriptions. Immediately after the war, reviews and advertisements involving domestic pictures began to compare German and American quality. A German work applauded for pictorial grandeur became a model on the grounds that this was a key to the international success of American motion pictures. It became increasingly common to congratulate a native film for demonstrating German ability to match or even outdo foreign, above all American, competition.[8] German commentators at least in part used American film as their reference standard, even though they were as yet scarcely conversant with it. Brainwashed, as one of them admitted, by tales of American movie expertise, they claimed, despite very little opportunity to make comparisons, that Germany's best works equaled or even surpassed America's.[9]

Hollywood's shadow also lengthened rapidly in explicit attempts to predict or program the evolution of the German cinema. Shortly after the armistice a poll was conducted among German screenwriters to ascertain their views on the evolution of German film production. Opinions varied tremendously. One author felt that America would profoundly influence the plans of German film producers and compel the foremost directors to rival Hollywood by making more sensational, expensive pictures. Another believed German filmmakers would pursue an independent path, although he conceded that some would attempt unsuccessfully to imitate French and American styles. If there was a unifying theme in this prophetic mélange, other than concern for international competitiveness, it was the attempt to make the logical structure and psychological depth of German dramaturgy Germany's answer to Hollywood.[10] Karl Figdor, script author and lead copy writer for *Film Welt*, argued that domestic pictures were unique on the grounds of their psychological perceptiveness and coherence. In substance, English, American and Italian films were all superficial.[11] Most emphatic was the prominent Danish author and director, Urban Gad, who in early 1919 identified monumentalism, brutality and sentimentality as America's dominant film traits and advised German producers to focus on internal consistency and substance.[12]

Even when allowance is made for self-advertising on the part of script writers, these opinions confirm that the contradictory impulses of Americanization emerged even before American movies were familiar to experts or audiences. On the one hand, German filmmakers wished to match American accomplishments; on the other hand, they played German strengths off against American weaknesses and advocated pursuit of an independent path. Although this ambivalence was rooted in domestic uncertainty about the public function of cinema, it was also inseparable from perceptions of the American challenge and the formulation of strategies to counter it.[13]

A general appraisal of Hollywood from mid-1919 illustrates how early analysis was typecast to serve a national agenda. A sometime correspondent for *Kinematograph*, R. Genenncher, sorted American film production into three categories: westerns, social dramas and comedies. To each film type he assigned a national identity. The first he labeled quintessentially American, the second quite the reverse and the last a no-man's-land in between. Westerns epitomized American film culture because they exploited a native environment and motifs, honestly captured American moral sentiments and drew on unique performing and cinematographic qualities. Social dramas exhibited excellent acting, directing and set work, but were plagued by unsatisfactory plot composition. The psychological subtleties, upon whose skillful handling the interest and success of such films depended, were lacking in American screenplays and inadequately camouflaged by lively tempo, moralizing or sensationalism. American film comedy fell between these two extremes, blending unrivaled inventiveness and unbearable repetitiveness.[14]

The rationale for these characterizations is sufficiently transparent to require little elaboration. Westerns were uniquely American because Germany produced nothing to rival them. American social dramas, by contrast, failed to match their European, especially German, counterparts because Hollywood lacked sophisticated screenplays. American film humor assumed an intermediate position because it boasted achievements which Germans could not attain yet did not always prove digestible abroad. Thus, all three categories provided ideal types against which to program domestic production. Genenncher believed domestic filmmakers had yet to consolidate a characteristic style, but clearly intimated that the social drama offered the greatest potential for success.

Genennecher's approach, apart from graphically confirming the truism that criticism of a foreign culture cannot be divorced from self-appraisal, indicates the primary role of Hollywood in the formative period of Weimar cinema. During the war some of Germany's best minds cast about for cultural virtues which justified the uneven struggle against east and west. Postwar identification of cinematic qualities worth cultivating followed a similar research method, scrutinizing American cinema to locate the areas in which Hollywood was vulnerable to foreign rivals. Arguing that Hollywood's weakness was Germany's strength, experts, among them screenwriters and directors, invented a formula which promised success against America. Although Hollywood had conquered the world, native cinema still enjoyed a "monopoly on intellect and logic which even the Treaty of Versailles was unable to take from the 'nation of poets and philosophers.'"[15] Description of American film therefore served a blatantly prescriptive function, being conceived from the start as a guide to national advance.

Hollywood's function as touchstone for domestic endeavors applied whether it was perceived in flattering or critical terms. Two commentators with experience abroad who rejected the conventional wisdom that American motion pictures lacked substance were still intent on securing for German cinema a place in the sun. Both urged acceptance of the American model for German filmmaking. This essentially meant that German filmmakers should create more heroic lead roles, accommodate the viewer's desire for emotional identification with screen characters, devise morally edifying plots with happy endings and inject a judicious element of humor into serious scenes.[16] This stereotypical contrast of German and American cinemas really amounted to a value judgment on two types of filmmaking, one geared to a general, undiscriminating audience and the other with pretensions to innovation and aimed at sophisticated viewers. In this respect, whether selected as a positive or negative model, Hollywood became a reference point in the debate about evolution of Weimar cinema.

In the first half of the 1920s that debate revolved mainly around whether to pursue a national or international motion picture identity. Before the war film reformers had lamented German subjection to foreign movies and urged the foundation of a German cinema.[17] By 1918, when domestic producers controlled the market, the industrial prerequisites for national identity were in place. But the contours of German cinema remained indistinct. Within trade circles the matter revolved less around whether to target foreign markets—economic considerations decided that in the affirmative—than around how best to succeed there. Should producers attempt to create a distinctly German cinema (whatever that might be) or should they assimilate the best of foreign trends to yield a hybrid offering something to all viewers? For artistic and economic reasons, majority opinion plumped for the former. However, in practice, lack of consensus on what constituted German cinema and the inevitable urge to share some of Hollywood's international profits meant that choices were rarely so clear-cut.[18]

Even before American movies gained legal re-entry to the German market contemporaries identified domestic trends conditioned by Hollywood. The emergence of the star system, the growing numbers of monumental films and the manufacture of serial films, such as those by Fritz Lang and Joe May, suggested that German producers were attuned to American precedents. As one expert put it: "America is currently in style. We imitate it in order to steal a march on it and would like if possible to be more American than the Americans." Given the ambition to break America's international hegemony Hollywood served both to rationalize a national motion picture orientation and as a model to emulate.[19]

The problem which Hollywood posed for German film-makers was a special case of a dilemma increasingly to confront Weimar industry and culture in general. Was it possible to challenge America without adopting American methods, without becoming Americanized? More precisely, was a revolt against Hollywood tantamount to a revolt against cinema, or were there alternative cinematic forms of equal potency which had yet to be discovered?[20] These queries applied as much for Hollywood enthusiasts as for cultural nationalists. Moreover, they had consequences well beyond the confines of the cinema. The observer who divided the world into American/Anglo-Saxon and German/Latin cinematic spheres which would duel to decide global hegemony demonstrated the persistence of wartime thought patterns, indicated the possibilities and dangers imagined by the postwar film community and captured the dilemma of German cinema vis-à-vis Hollywood in the 1920s. Since motion pictures disseminated more effectively than any other medium the essence of a national culture, the loser in the film war would be bombarded by foreign influence. Still worse, the vanquished would be forced to tolerate representation by the victor to the rest of the world. If Hollywood were to squeeze the German film industry at home, other countries would eventually be exposed to an image of Germany made in America.[21]

From all these perspectives it became increasingly impossible to define the German cinema without reference to Hollywood. Ironically, it mattered little, indeed it proved advantageous, that American motion pictures remained generally unfamiliar. They functioned admirably as symbol, as the "other," precisely because from a comfortable distance they could be summarily classified and defined. Hollywood became a slogan derived from commonplaces about American culture—exciting, lavishly staged and technically polished but lacking substance. Although virtually no one outside trade circles showed interest in the coming film war, because German cinema was engaged in carving out artistic and cultural space for itself, its spokespersons approached Hollywood with language appropriate to cultural struggle. Trying to consolidate a domestic position they employed stereotypes which highlighted differences between German and American film cultures. While convenient so long as American film remained a distant specter, this proved problematic once American motion pictures began to appear again in German theaters. The long-awaited film war then became a confrontation of cultures as well as industries.

The wider domestic context for this confrontation dated to before the war when writers, artists and critics began to debate the distinctiveness of film vis-à-vis other modes of communication. Broadly speaking, two currents of thought collided. Reformation and ennoblement of the cinema through borrowing from established art forms promised respectability; the *Autorenfilm*, the marriage of film and literature, was the industry's answer to criticisms that the movies failed to speak to the educated middle class.[22] Simultaneously, a younger generation of Expressionist leanings sought to use film to explode respectable bourgeois cultural norms. Though unable to shed its literary heritage, this generation in revolt contended that the motion picture was a case sui generis which did not answer to a literary muse.[23] While neither approach proved successful in capturing the mainstream of film production, together they set the parameters for the initial reception of American motion pictures in Germany.

America's incorporation into the discussion of the cinema's nature and purpose became explicit and general in 1921 on the eve of restored import. A debate on cinematic principles, launched in the radical political-cultural weekly, *Die Weltbühne*, evolved with first exposure to Hollywood into a full-scale confrontation over the relative merits of German and American motion pictures. Its instigator, Hans Siemsen, an essayist who directed his considerable energies to denunciation of capitalism, militarism and nationalism, was an outsider to the trade with a passion for cinema fed by his loathing of bourgeois cultural pretensions.[24] His socialist convictions meant that he deeply distrusted the capitalist structure of the motion picture industry. In 1919 he had savaged an article by Rudolf Kurtz, scenarist for UFA, film advisor for the Chancellory, later editor of *Lichtbildbühne* and author of a study of Expressionist cinema, for suggesting that artistic maturation of the cinema was simply a matter of time. Siemsen believed motion picture production would remain regressive so long as it was ruled by the profit motive. Only socialization could redeem it.[25]

Early in 1921 Siemsen resumed his polemic against German production. The immediate target for his criticism was the confidence with which the domestic industry assessed its own accomplishments. Despite breakthroughs in the United States it did not, in his opinion, face a bright future. The problem lay this time less in capitalism than in German cultural presuppositions. Against the pundits who proclaimed German superiority in matters of substance, Siemsen argued that domestic production failed to grasp the fundamentals of the medium. The essence of film was not grandeur, glitter and exoticism, three popular devices in early Weimar filmmaking, but naturalism. By virtue of its intrinsic tie to the real world, the cinema relied primarily on simplicity, naiveté and human spontaneity. Screenplays were not to be complex, psychologically subtle constructs, but frameworks within which a cast of human beings, as opposed to performers, enjoyed freedom to be innovative.[26]

Siemsen's rudimentary theory of film had little claim to originality, building as it did upon conceptions of the naturalist impulse behind the medium that circulated widely both within and outside trade circles.[27] It was the timing and application of the theory which distinguished his polemic. Not only did he direct it squarely against German filmmakers, but he also indicated direct indebtedness to Hollywood. On the basis of experience abroad he used American examples (primarily Charlie Chaplin) to confirm his arguments, despite his undiminished opposition to capitalism in American or German incarnation.[28] Others, such as French avant-garde authors like Guillaume Apollinaire, had earlier responded enthusiastically to American comedy and westerns, above all the films of Charlie Chaplin.[29] Claire and Yvan Goll directly anticipated Siemsen in mid-1920 by arguing that America had rightly comprehended the moving picture as a medium impervious to the canons of literature or theater and the social distinctions which these presupposed.[30] But because Siemsen aimed his polemic directly against the domestic industry on the eve of German reacquaintance with Hollywood, he precipitated a major debate on the relative merits of German and American motion pictures.

The first to take up Siemsen's challenge in the pages of *Die Weltbühne* was Rudolf Kurtz. In an angry outburst which reads more as a rebuttal to Siemsen's article of 1919, Kurtz styled Siemsen an outsider to the film trade unable to fathom the financial realities of motion picture production. Without adequate capital and respect for commercial considerations Siemsen's demands on the medium were noble but fanciful. Before Siemsen could reply to these charges, the famous satirist, Kurt Tucholsky, joined the debate, endorsing Siemsen's opinions on the character of the medium and the nefarious character of capitalist production. From the other side, *Film-Kurier* reprinted Kurtz's article, appending editorial support for his opinions, and then published a reply from Willy Haas to Tucholsky's insinuations that the capitalist system had corrupted film criticism.[31]

As the controversy began to form along the line separating trade critics from "outsiders" Siemsen rebounded in a manner which brought Hollywood closer to center stage. In reply to Kurtz he dissected and then damned five current German releases as demonstration that deplorable films could result despite ample financing. Over against these he set American models, principally the westerns of W. S. Hart, to illustrate the laws of the medium. Unlike the German cinema, which had a disastrous penchant for forcing performers into pretentious but boring milieus, or ignoring them altogether to emphasize settings or literary relevance, Hollywood achieved unity of personality and setting, thus naturalness. One shot of Hart rolling himself a cigarette therefore carried greater filmic weight than all five German pictures under review.[32] This characteristically provocative assertion prompted a sharp response from one of the script writers and directors whose work Siemsen had blasted. Ludwig Wolff took aim at what he read as endorsement of the emerging and very controversial star system. Insofar as films were scripted to suit the performer(s) Wolff judged both screenplay and finished film weak.[33] To this charge Siemsen retorted by citing first the achievements of two giants of the German cinema, Paul Wegener and Asta Nielsen, as proof that

films conceived and produced for unique personalities were valuable. He then lauded Charlie Chaplin, W. S. Hart and Douglas
Fairbanks for never playing roles other than those designed
and tailored to fit them. The only problem with the star system
was the quality of the star. He admitted that American scripts
were frequently rather stupid concoctions, but they at least permitted the star to perform and generated much better motion
pictures than the literary and logical masterpieces made in
Germany.[34]

The final round of the debate addressed the contrast between
Hollywood and Berlin most directly. Another respondent, Hans
Glenk, attempted to turn the theory of the "primacy of the
performer" against Siemsen by establishing a subtle link between film content and performance. He conceded American
expertise in making westerns but asked patronisingly whether
movies existed merely to provide a forum for boxing. American
motion pictures amounted to displays of physical prowess.
Siemsen's favorite model, Charlie Chaplin, was overrated and
overpaid. Among Hollywood stars only Mary Pickford merited
closer attention, yet despite performing genius her motion pictures were miserable productions because of the incoherence,
silliness and sentimentality of their screenplays. Though the
very best in foreign film, they were only average by German
standards. In short, Glenk revived the centrality of screenplays:
without textual substance acting could not be highly rated.[35]

Noteworthy here, and indicative of the broader cultural issues at stake, is the fact that both parties perceived Hollywood
in essentially identical terms. Like Siemsen, Glenk commended
the western for its naturalness and excitement, and he applauded Mary Pickford's artistry in words which echoed Siemsen's theory that naiveté and naturalness were cinematic virtues.
What he could not accept was Siemsen's valorization of these
traits and his corresponding toleration of American screenplays. The same divergence is evident in the much more elegantly formulated opinions of Willy Haas. As a participant in
the early stage of the debate, Haas took the occasion of a press
showing in February 1921 of Mary Pickford's *Daddy-Long-Legs*
to explore the relationship between Hollywood and American
culture.[36] Anticipating the Siemsen-Glenk argument, he evalu-

ated *Daddy-Long-Legs* qua film and qua culture. On the first test he gave it high marks: it boasted marvelously straightforward directing and comprehension of visual effect, a storehouse of admirable acting techniques, and simply inimitable photography. On the second count, however, it scored miserably. Its screenplay, which related the rise of an orphaned girl to wealth and happiness, was such absolute kitsch that Haas claimed the least of German producers would have tossed its author out of his office. As content it was not only silly and sentimental, as Glenk was later to assert, but it betrayed infatuation with social conventions and prejudices borrowed from Old Europe. With a medium which epitomized the youthfulness and modernity of the New World, Hollywood advertised archaic values.[37]

In restating the tension between form and content thematized in the *Weltbühne* debate, Haas indicated that the challenge which Hollywood posed for German cinema was how to learn from one without absorbing the other. In a slightly later article which explicitly endorsed Siemsen's film theory, Haas commissioned domestic filmmakers to exploit the childlikeness and naturalness of American film to develop an art form which Hollywood lacked the other prerequisites to discover.[38] However, even Haas had doubts that his dream would be fulfilled. His concluding comments on *Daddy-Long-Legs* hinted that the appeal of this film to every social class and national audience could frustrate the progression of film art. So long as polished kitsch captivated international audiences there was scant incentive to pursue a higher cinematic form.

As the *Weltbühne* debate reveals, on the eve of Hollywood's return to the German market three interlocking questions preoccupied experts: the character of American cinema vis-à-vis its German counterpart, the feasibility of borrowing from it to enhance native production, and the potential responses of German audiences. As yet, given isolation from American motion pictures, answers to all three questions were highly speculative. Willingness to engage them in the absence of extensive filmic evidence testifies to ambitions to program the cinema's development. Siemsen's parting shot to his interlocutors that American motion pictures would quickly demonstrate their su-

periority in Germany passed judgment on what he saw as a set
of moribund cinematic paradigms.

When American motion pictures returned to the German market in 1921 they came in quantities and types determined as
much by the miserable state of the German economy and currency as by legal restrictions. Since German importers wielded
little buying power and American exporters gained limited
profit, it paid both parties to deal in older, cheaper motion pictures. First and most numerous were what Germans knew as
Sensationsfilme, in the main serialized westerns of five or six feature-length installments, released at the rate of one or two per
week.[39] Amidst the deluge with serials, social dramas also began
to appear, though they became familiar only in 1922 and 1923.
Likewise, slapstick comedies, on the market in late 1921, first
generated considerable attention in the subsequent two years.
Here, as with the westerns, Germans saw mainly older works.
While Charlie Chaplin and Harold Lloyd, for example, had
graduated to feature-length production, Germans viewed
shorts made during or just following the war.

If German importers had conspired to tar the American cinema with the brush used by Siemsen's opponents they could
not have devised a better plot than purchase of rights to a hefty
quota of sensationalist pictures. So readily did these fit what for
most was an unflattering stereotype that experts appeared to
have their expectations confirmed. Nonetheless, these early imports became such an integral part of Weimar film culture that
their public role generated controversy. Critics encountered the
novel task of finding words with which to enliven appraisals of
a genre characterized to their eyes by endless repetition, while
struggling to fathom the reactions of German audiences. For
censors these films presented not only the first but also the outstanding challenge from Hollywood.

Critics lost no time reducing American sensationalism to a
tidy formula. Three months after first exposure to the genre a
critic for *Der Film* captured general opinion with the declaration
that the style and structure of American sensationalist movies
were so consistent that to review one was to review them all.
The components of the formula were: an elementary plot, truly

phenomenal physical stunts, abundant brawls, dynamic camera work, breath-taking tempos and performers intent less on acting than on showing courage and agility.[40] Critical typecasting went beyond the films to embrace Hollywood and American culture. Ludwig Brauner, chief critic for *Kinematograph,* contended in his very first review of an American film that stunts and brawls slaked the American thirst for sports and were typical of "almost every American film"! Another critic used an early version of Tarzan to deduce the religious and social values of America's middle class, claiming its tastes were marked by "infantile coarseness and lack of intellectual elasticity." Others highlighted the value Americans placed on athletic as opposed to intellectual achievements, noting the equation of muscle and moral rectitude to the exclusion of emotional development.[41]

All of these commonplaces were meant as pejoratively as earlier judgments about American screenplays. Incessant violence and unshakable faith in the triumph of good over evil did not make a favorable first impression. The critic who gloated that if *Elmo, The Mighty,* the most notorious of the early serialized imports, faithfully represented Hollywood, Germany could look forward to international motion picture primacy, voiced the general consensus. That sensationalism, not least in serial form, flourished in postwar German motion picture production was conveniently forgotten, for whereas German thrillers were viewed in the context of other domestic film styles, America's initially appeared in isolation. The peculiar type and polish of the American variant also encouraged equation of sensationalism with Hollywood. American superiority in this genre led German commentators to believe that sensationalism had to be America's strong suit.[42]

Although easily categorized, American thrillers raised questions of public impact to which censors as well as critics proved sensitive. The latter plied their trade on the fashionable strip in Berlin's west end among middle-class audiences which could scarcely be expected to revel in violence. Nevertheless, there is evidence that Hans Siemsen's prediction of popular interest was not entirely self-serving. Critics found themselves in an uncomfortable position. Fritz Podehl, a screen writer and critic for *Der Film,* warned almost from first encounter with these imports

that despite deviation in certain respects from German counterparts they would become just as tiresome to the public. But in
subsequent reviews he reported unmistakably favorable audience response to them, a fact he admitted was doubly significant
given the well-to-do and discriminating public of the Kurfürstendamm. Since he considered the pictures in question devoid
of dramatic moment, he could only conclude that German audiences did not take them seriously: they were simply captivated
by the furious action and fantastic stunts.[43] Ludwig Brauner
initially betrayed considerable awe and admiration for American sensationalism, but even when he began to write scorching
reviews of major American thrillers he continued to acknowledge popular enjoyment of them. To his amazement the moviegoers of Berlin's west end, who normally preferred the very
antithesis of adventure, the "chamber drama" made memorable
by the films of Lupu Pick, Paul Leni and F. W. Murnau, enjoyed
the "dizzying riding, alternating ups and downs of the action
and forcibly concocted chase scenes," without worrying about
plot coherence. In striking parallel to Podehl he assessed the
viewers' mood as "oscillating between sporting enthusiasm and
an ironic smile."[44]

While signs of interest in American serials among the better
public raised critical eyebrows, appreciation of them among the
lower classes provoked alarmed responses from German censors. As guardians of public welfare, censors were empowered
to protect Germans from depictions of criminal, brutal or immoral behavior which adversely affected the average viewer.
Competence to judge in this matter presupposed familiarity
with the mentality and behavior of the German public. The
conspicuous feature of the official reception of American thrillers was the vacillation, duplicating almost to perfection the ambivalence of critics, between dismissing them as harmless because they were too naive for Germans to take seriously and
admitting concern because German watched them eagerly. Censors found themselves defining the similarities and differences
between German and American culture. Ultimately they defended a worldview against America which their very role suggested had limited popular support. American films exposed
their isolation from the broader public.

When censors first encountered American sensationalist movies they exhibited considerable confidence in national resilience. In September 1921 the Censorship Appeal Board overturned the ban imposed on the first installment of the serial, *King of the Circus,* for violence which in the first instance had been judged brutalizing. In its decision the higher authority conceded the prevalence of violence but chose to place it in cultural perspective. What was more typical of Hollywood than chase scenes, disasters and wild brawls? Criminal behavior belonged organically to the milieu, the American frontier, in which this picture was set, however incredible its plot line. There was, therefore, no reason to fear that it would incite Germans to crime and violence. Europe was so much more civilized than the American West that Germans would at worst be repelled and disgusted by the brutality of this film.[45]

The extremely smug assumptions about the distance which separated German and American civilization quickly found a check in growing levels of domestic criminal violence. Several weeks after the decision to pass part one of *King of the Circus* the censors banned part six of the same. Although they judged its chaotic plot line humorous for "serious" viewers they decided that in light of current circumstances it constituted a source of brutalization for an "average" audience. The Appeal Board both upheld the ban and concurred with its justification, labeling this picture a "serious social menace for the lower part of the populace."[46]

Following the assassination in June 1922 of the Republic's foreign minister, Walther Rathenau, the crackdown continued. The day before Rathenau was shot the censors banned an American criminal thriller, *Outside the Law,* for its detailed depiction of violence and death.[47] Two weeks later the Appeal Board upheld the ban with the argument that the lead role in the film was played by the revolver. Circumstances in Germany made this impermissible.

> There is no doubt that in recent years crime has increased in Germany at a frightening rate. Robbery, manslaughter [and] murder are more and more frequent. A depiction of such American gunslingers has to have a provocative effect and rouse the imitative instinct.[48]

While conceding that Hollywood's imagination fitted German reality to an uncomfortable extent, censors also concerned themselves with the cultural implications of exposing Germans to pure sensationalism. Preservation of social control was compatible with release of motion pictures focused so heavily on stunts and acrobatic feats that the events portrayed lacked the menace of realism, but sensationalism for its own sake, if preferable to thrills of the sort that might encourage criminal behavior, found little favor with the censors.[49] A convoluted case from the height of the inflationary spiral in the fall of 1923 lays bare their presuppositions.

The case opened with a ban on the first episode of a pirate adventure which the censors judged brutalizing. One week later the Appeal Board reversed the decision on the grounds that because worthless as drama and cinema, the picture presented no dangerous influence: the only effect of such juvenile adventure on adults was to produce boredom. Thus part one was passed for adults only.[50] Here the matter would have been resolved had not the lower tribunal banned the subsequent episodes. Once again the charge was brutality, but the judgment sustaining it concentrated less on its impact on German viewers than on the failure of the film to provide anything but sensations. The board evidently valued sensationalism negatively and believed movies devoted to it merited screening in Germany only when offset by what was called a "compensating factor."[51] This rating scheme had nothing to do with the censorship laws but everything to do, as the above discussion of critical opinions makes clear, with the prejudices of cultural spokespersons in Germany. These had, of course, to be given legally binding form. The Appeal Board, already sympathetic, as its aside on the "worthlessness" of part one indicates, to the argument of the lower board, followed it when faced with the three subsequent installments. This time the initial decision was upheld. Incessant raids, beatings and violence characterized these pictures, but did not in themselves justify the ban. More disturbing were signs of audience enthrallment by such characteristics.

> The Board is aware that precisely American films of such inferior subject matter are greatly enjoyed by the German populace. This

enjoyment presupposes growing attenuation of healthy emotion
and thereby proves [the existence of] a corrupting influence according to the Motion Picture Law. That precisely these films . . . had
the prospect of being screened in Germany with particular success
becomes apparent from the plaintiff's statements, according to
which the plaintiff succeeded in acquiring these films only with
great effort and at unusually high expense, in strong competition
with other buyers.[52]

In addition, the censors made public appreciation of the American thrillers both the symptom and the cause of the German
malaise:

This enjoyment has . . . the prerequisite and likewise the consequence that a healthy moral perception on the part of the populace
is flattened and deadened by such films, that, therefore, according
to the Motion Picture Law, a corrupting influence is exerted on
the populace.[53]

Liberated from official jargon, American sensationalism was
trash which, because it was appreciated by German moviegoers,
had to be kept off the German market.

As the sequel to the Appeal Board's handling of this serial
reveals, American sensationalist films landed German censors
in a dilemma. It will be recalled that part one passed on appeal
because it was judged childishly romantic and harmless for
grown-ups. Subsequent episodes were banned, at the initial and
appeal levels, for the same reason that the first installment was
passed. What changed were censors' presuppositions about the
consequences for German viewers. The company affected by
these decisions recognized their incongruity and tried yet again
to have a revised version of the third installment passed. When
this too was promptly banned by the lower board as violent and
without compensatory features to mitigate its impact on viewers,
the firm launched an appeal which chose to confront the board
with its own inconsistency. The company claimed disingenu-
ously that the film was of such exceptionally poor quality that
its content would have no effect at all on the viewer, apart perhaps from seeming ridiculous and generating apathy. The Appeal Board was doubtless tempted to accept this curious admis-

sion, but must also have realized that there were then precedents of its own making to pass the film. Caught somewhat by its own vagaries, but refusing to be cowed, the Appeal Board upheld the ban:

> The events portrayed [here] consist of brutality and repulsiveness emanating from the basest instincts, [events] whose overall impact on a large portion of the populace is certainly not to seem ridiculous or produce apathy, but which in the striking character of their brutality satisfy the need for thrills of a large portion of the populace.[54]

The early American serials therefore provoked from censors an inconsistent blend of condescension toward Hollywood, confidence in German cultural resilience and deep unease about public susceptibility to the content and form of American motion pictures. Like critics, censors therefore experienced considerable tension between their roles as spokespersons for and spokespersons to broader opinion. Unable to ignore audience receptivity to movies they considered worthless, they fought a rearguard action to impose their values on the public. Admittedly, their concern about the impact of screen violence predated the resumption of American import. It is also the case that domestic motion pictures of similar nature—the infamous enlightenment films for instance—had already caused serious alarm: bifurcation of critical and audience opinion occurred not only in response to American motion pictures. Nevertheless, American films drove each point home, both because they were intruders from abroad and because they appeared capable of triumphing in Germany as they had done elsewhere. Censors inadvertently paid tribute to what seemed an ineluctable force behind Hollywood's penetration of foreign markets, even when spearheaded by inferior or downright harmful entertainment. With critics, they reluctantly admitted that German viewers were spellbound by the amount of action Americans crammed onto a strip of celluloid. This spell demanded explanation. Why American motion pictures pleased viewers across the globe, a question which until this juncture had had only international dimensions, now became applicable to German audiences.

In the controversy unleashed by Hans Siemsen, explanations

for Hollywood's international ascendancy remained largely implicit. Siemsen himself believed American movies more attuned to the laws of the medium than German films and accordingly judged them superior. His opponents presumed domestic motion pictures to be competitive in terms of directing and technical expertise and superior in the screenwriting and performing arts. Yet even in the period before Hollywood's economic clout was so strongly felt that it shaped explanations for American dominance, straightforward equation of excellence and public success could not be sustained. Despite the unmistakably plebeian, commercial history of the medium, German experts tended to blame Hollywood for seducing viewers with inferior pictures. Willy Haas feared the seduction of *Daddy-Long-Legs* but at least granted qualities which attracted audiences. Other prominent voices, among them the producer Paul Davidson and Fritz Engel, literary and theater critic for *Berliner Tageblatt,* characterized American cinema as an endless chain of chase scenes and brutality without deeper purpose, implying that public appreciation was an inverse function of quality.[55] The eminent director, Urban Gad, concurred, rationalizing Hollywood's success, despite the relative weakness of its set work, performing, directing and screenwriting, in terms of American wealth. Thanks to the strength of the dollar Hollywood cranked out a glossy product which avoided all serious issues and portrayed life as beautiful and carefree. This assured its popularity in less fortunate parts of the world, not least in postwar Europe: "The world, the poor old impoverished world needs a smile, [yet] it can no longer muster one itself and therefore must import it preserved on celluloid. That is why American film triumphs."[56]

Such concessions of popularity despite allegations of inferior quality are strongly reminiscent of the opinions entertained by German censors. Behind them lay prejudices about public tastes which were the stock-in-trade of film reformers, namely, that the masses could be corrupted by primitive entertainment. Hollywood was cast in the role of servant to the lowest common denominator and made the antipode to domestic production, which had allegedly demonstrated ambition to raise cinema above its plebeian roots. Even though the American product was inferior and more expensive, German motion pictures could not compete in playing down to the audience.[57]

With American cinema cast as the villain, but nonetheless popular, trade experts found themselves in an equivocal position vis-à-vis German moviegoers. Audiences either deserved castigating along with Hollywood, or needed to be pried loose from a momentary failure of judgment. In late 1921 *Film-Kurier* published a piece by Dr. Paul Meißner which tried to do both. Meißner presented the usual stereotype of Hollywood as the home of sensational stunts and intellectual immaturity, but his main agenda was to account for and counteract the appreciation of American sensationalism in Germany. Much to Meißner's chagrin, German producers had begun to ape American methods and audiences had condescended to devour a recipe they should have rejected. Meißner could make sense of German susceptibility only by recourse to the proverbial German interest in things novel or foreign which had been sharpened by the isolation of wartime. He appealed plaintively to producers and viewers not to abandon their roots. Instead of copying America, filmmakers should make "good German films . . . from which the public benefits." Audiences should avoid American screenings and thus force their banishment from German theaters.[58] In the words of another expert, German and American expectations were fundamentally incompatible.

> It is unquestionably true that America is still as ever superior to us in stunning film feats. It would, however, be unjust not to recognize that the German moviegoer will always object to the modesty of American requirements in respect to logic and structure, and does not approve of a film merely on the basis of its sensationalism. . . . The German cinema will always, even in this area, have a complexion different from the American. Thank God![59]

Against this attempt to assert distance between German and American viewers, those who accepted audience behavior as authentic showed willingness to reconsider domestic cinematic agendas. Representative is the position taken by Hans Siemsen. In September 1921 Siemsen took up the thread of his earlier argument, armed now not only with further personal exposure to Hollywood, but also with evidence of public responses. What he had seen of the American thrillers confirmed his earlier observations. One movie of this type differed only superficially from another. Screenplays, if such had ever existed, were essentially identical and never more sophisticated than the most childish tale of cowboys and Indians. To this extent he agreed with Hollywood's denigrators. Nevertheless, Siemsen judged these films superior to those made in Germany for the simple reason that they were entertaining instead of boring. These straightforward terms, already juxtaposed in the earlier debate, now became loaded by correlation with two distinct types of German response. From his experience the cultivated segment of German film audiences rejected entertainment not legitimized by literary or psychological accoutrements. These viewers responded in the spirit of one highly cultivated academic who remarked that an American western was more entertaining than German movies but had "no intellectual value whatsoever." The average viewer, by contrast, was indifferent to the benefits conferred by entertainment and preferred the uncultured American picture to the cultured German one. Good-looking performers, magnificent natural settings, abundant action and technical brilliance—features virtually all critics ascribed to American adventure movies—assured their value as entertainment.[60]

Siemsen's appeal to popular tastes appeared to align his interests with those of the industry which he otherwise so soundly abused. But if his demand for film-specific approaches freed cinema from theatrical or literary paradigms, his opinions did not endear him to the industry. His selection of Hollywood as the relevant model for domestic filmmakers went not only almost without echo in 1921, but also represented an offense to critics, who generally viewed the early American imports with a mixture of condescension, boredom and exasperation. The closest Siemsen's perspective came to programmatic formulation was in a review of a Tarzan film which reflects culture shock, amusement and fascination at the peculiarities of Hollywood's motion picture practice. Its argument deserves quoting at length.

> With this film we must throw overboard all our previous experience, perceptions, convictions, as well as demands on the cinema,

and create a new foundation. In other words: in order to adjust to this film we must relinquish everything we have always striven for, are fighting for and what we are demanding programmatically. "Tarzan" is something completely new, something completely different, and in any case something which sets itself with sovereign self-glorification above probability, truthfulness, logic and other such modest criteria of modern thought. The greatest thing about it, however, is that one does not notice or even sense this flaw as long as the film is showing; one only becomes aware of the inner incoherence and improbabilities when on the way home one smokes a cigarette and tries to rework intellectually what has been seen. Then one suddenly confronts closed doors, then the strange accidents stand out all the more conspicuously, and one—smiles. For despite all this the film is a masterpiece of modern technique, is extremely suspenseful, adventurous, interesting and attractive in the abundance of its happenings. Individual scenes are of simply exquisite fineness; here and there is a flash of something which creates artistic impact.[61]

Instead of intellectual gratification this film offered captivation by technical finesse. Rather than encouraging contemplation it frustrated it. In place of permanence—art as reference to lasting values—the viewer found diversion in transitory sensory perceptions. Yet as the concluding observations suggest, this did not preclude the attainment of a still vaguely conceived notion of cinematic art. The binary pairs of this analysis—probability or adventure, truth or attractiveness, logic or suspense—exploited conventional wisdom about domestic and American cinema to encourage a fresh perspective. In short, this review worked with the peculiarities of American sensationalist film enumerated by its enemies, but reversed their point. Hollywood became the basis from which to urge on critics and filmmakers a veritable revolution in domestic motion picture agendas.

Although the early debate on Hollywood was loaded heavily in favor of those who resisted this revolution, the next two years were to witness some measure of revisionism in informed opinion. Initially, denial of Hollywood's ability to fulfill the artistic and entertainment requirements of cinema meant some contradiction between perceived and prescribed reality. The incongruity lamented between visual grandeur and spiritual emptiness, repeated complaints about chaotic screenplays and superficial acting and, finally, puzzlement at apparent public enthusiasm, reflected tensions which were largely inherited from the period prior to resumption of import.[62] In the course of 1922 and 1923, broader exposure to American film revised its image while simultaneously deepening the challenge it posed. In three overlapping phases American imports qualified and sharpened generalizations drawn from the sensationalist films and compelled reconsideration of Hollywood's importance.

Phase one saw destruction of the belief that American cinema excelled only in sensationalism. Though in retrospect a mundane development, some contemporaries evidenced considerable surprise that westerns and adventure films were not the dominant or necessarily most popular films produced in the United States. Hollywood made society dramas which omitted the customary thrills and spills without reversion to tear-jerking sentimentality. Furthermore, Americans showed competence, even excellence, in a genre allegedly more suited to German capabilities. One of the earliest American society dramas released in Germany, *Madame X* (starring Pauline Frederick), sparked this revisionism. A tragic story of a woman rejected by her husband and separated from her son, *Madame X* drew particular attention for an extended courtroom scene in which the son, in the presence of his father, defends on a murder charge a vagabond woman who, unknown to both, is mother and wife to them respectively. Those able to see past its sentimentality and moralizing shared the surprise of Paul Ickes, the editor of *Film-Kurier*, that American film was not pure sensationalism, incapable of transmitting "soul" or "emotion." Contrary to the German shibboleth, Americans could act, that is, succeed in dramatically respectable roles. Ickes had the extreme audacity to place Pauline Frederick on par with the dramatic goddess of the German cinema, Asta Nielsen, and he prophesied a conceivable victory of American film in Germany in a genre on which Germans prided themselves. The fulfillment in an American motion picture of ideals previously realized only in native

and Scandinavian chamber dramas demonstrated that Hollywood could meet German critical requirements.[63]

Phase two in the revision process added a twist to phase one:
Hollywood did not need to employ German formulas to match
Berlin in dramatic intensity. Whereas the charges of shallowness, incoherence and improbability had previously sufficed to
damn American motion pictures, a number of films, among
them *Madame X,* showed that content was not decisive. Despite
naive, improbable and sentimental screenplays, dramatic intensity could be communicated through sensitive directing, superb
photography and gripping acting. It appeared that in this
genre, as in sensationalist pictures, the form or "how" counted
more than substance or "what." A review by Dr. Max Prels of
Forbidden Fruit, the first of Cecil B. De Mille's satirical society
dramas released in Germany, which labeled it a wonderful
rather than a significant film, vividly communicates the disproportion of form and content with a series of mixed metaphors.

> The innovative twist dominates, the blossoms exhale their fragrance
> in an unattractive field, the ornament sparkles out of the surface.
> So it goes in film-America. Delicacies on an earthernware dish.
> Story: very simple. Cinderella motif transposed into the world of
> oil trusts.[64]

This admiring discrimination is particularly noticeable in
commentary on the motion pictures of Viola Dana. Although
Dana does not belong to the foremost rank of American silent
stars, she won an oversized critical reputation in Weimar Germany, not least because a series of her dramas and comedies
appeared before those of other American film idols. Neither
the roles in which she was cast nor the films in which she starred
drew praise. Those concerned with content found almost nothing pleasing in her films.[65] Those enthralled by her were indifferent to content. The only other American actress to receive
comparable praise was Pauline Frederick, who although a surprise, could be classified with Asta Nielsen. Dana, however, was
a novelty in the stricter sense that she was a type for which
Germany had no counterpart. What astounded critics was the
range of Dana's expressiveness, especially given the inanities of
the roles she filled and her disregard for accepted means of

maximizing impact. Rejecting the contemplative or "inner" approach, she succeeded, paradoxically, in communicating "soul." Naiveté, the instinctive capturing of moods and emotions which performers normally approached with extreme deliberation, meant subtlety rather than the exaggerated mimicry usual in silent cinema.[66]

These traits contrasted so obviously with those on which German film prided itself that their enumeration alone was a tacit reprimand to native producers. Several experts pointed the barb more openly, recommending Dana as a female type needed by the German cinema to lend it vitality and fluidity and as a revelation about the nature of the medium. Paul Ickes indulged in paeans of praise which he recognized were self-contradictory. He raved about her artistry precisely because there was no artistry involved in it. Dana demonstrated to German directors and production heads that film acting was less about performing than about naturalness.[67] Ickes's conclusion thus closely approximated Siemsen's and implied what Siemsen stated polemically: German production operated on mistaken premises. It was underscored by a *Tagebuch* critic who saw Dana as a palpable threat to German cinema. Her acting style so outclassed that cultivated in Germany that the failure to emulate it would take German pictures out of the running on the international market. It also provided the key to elevation of film to an independent art form.[68]

Familiarity with Dana's talents marked the transition from the second to third phase of Hollywood's initial challenge to Berlin. In this last stage, broad exposure to American imports yielded revised generalizations. Having experienced Hollywood's diversity, experts sought the unifying thread which characterized the specifically American grasp of the medium. Crucial to this stage was the proliferation of slapstick films and a trade show staged by William Fox in 1922. Slapstick, which struck at the heart of the attempt to ennoble the cinema with sophisticated subject matter, presented a special case which will be analyzed closely in a later chapter. The Fox trade show, since it included slapstick shorts, provides a convenient locus for summation of discourse in the period of initiation.

In July 1922 William Fox staged three consecutive days of

promotional showings in Berlin to introduce his products to German trade circles. His belated but grand German open house offered critics a timely smorgasbord. Society dramas, slapsticks, westerns and historical pageants were all on the table, giving commentators the opportunity to rank one against another and reach interim conclusions about Hollywood. The rank assigned each genre tells much about German understanding of American cinema at this particular juncture. Slapstick stood at the top of the list; historical films sat at the very bottom; westerns and society dramas fell between them. The basis for these designations remained essentially as it had been before resumption of import. Slapstick won recognition as an American specialty while the historical film, for which Germany was renowned in 1922, encountered some of the most caustic criticism yet directed at Hollywood because it betrayed America's almost total lack of historical consciousness.[69] Superficially, little had changed. Critics still defined and ranked American film by reference to domestic achievements. However, despite vast differences in rank, experts paid attention to a generic quality of these films, namely, the nature and breadth of their public appeal. The Fox showings focused attention on the source of Hollywood's popularity.

Previous explanations for Hollywood's public appeal, as outlined above, hardly rose above the level of cliché. Denigrators of American thrillers implied that viewers either tolerated these pictures as novelties after a period of isolation or were seduced by the tempo and titillation they offered. They also implied that Hollywood was unscrupulous enough to capture audiences with inferior motion pictures, principally by tapping darker instincts and passions. The gap which this opened between critical and popular opinion could be blamed on America's indifference to cinematic art. Simple, down-to-earth screenplays combined with technical brilliance scored at the box office. Alfred Rosenthal summed up conventional wisdom in response to the Fox films with the phrase that the American "adapts himself completely to the audience and lets art be art."[70]

Rosenthal's restatement of received wisdom did not, however, find universal assent. A number of critics noted that even the historical epics, *Nero* and *The Queen of Sheba*, shared in what

Max Prels called an "undefinable magic" which overwhelmed an appalling ahistoricity. Prels pinpointed this ineffable magic in his review of the latter picture.

> They captivate one precisely by virtue of their inner, certainly not always admirable rhythm. They drag one along, although one senses plainly: here the machinery runs itself, here the pose is exhibitionist. Everything is very deliberate here, nothing originates from the heart; it is cold but fired-up machinery; anyone who sees a glow has an illusion of getting warm. Unbiblically conceived, unbiblical in the style of acting, unbiblical where it pleads naiveté and primitiveness. It challenges our European taste [and] it does not satisfy it, provokes contradictions; and this critical European taste still lets itself be conquered by the élan of the whole affair. One disapproves and is—enchanted, inundated, drawn into the pull of the Fox films.[71]

What stands out here is not alone the refusal to play content off against form, but both the admission that even discriminating viewers could be captivated by an approach which disturbed them and the implicit surrender of standard critical canons. Very few trade reviews escaped the categories of plot, acting, directing and cinematography. Prel's substitution of "inner rhythm" for these conventions challenged both standard critical categories and production values.

Although no paradigm shift occurred in response to the Fox show, there is evidence of strikingly parallel arguments from other quarters. A prominent trade critic in Munich, Wolfgang Martini, discovered in the Fox films the key to cinema's unique place in current culture. Every other art form had its origins in a nonurban, nonindustrial environment, whose elemental driving force had been human muscle. Film, however, was the offspring of the modern metropolis, industrial development and global communication. The motive power of this new world was no longer human muscle, but human nerves. These determined the tempo of life and in turn the character of the moving picture. From this perspective the Fox films demonstrated that the cinematic muse prescribed a distinctive rhythm or dynamic.

> These films definitely have an artistic style. It does not, however, lie in the pictorially static where it is often still sought in Germany.

It lies purely in the rhythm which acquires expression through tempo and dynamic force. This rhythm corresponds to the laws of reaction of the nervous system and functions in a purely artistically-symbolic fashion, completely independent of naturalistic or historical logic. Into its place steps a new artistic film logic whose secrets the true film artist must partly instinctively and partly consciously master, like every artist his art.[72]

Although more arcanely phrased, Martini's analysis dovetailed with rationalizations used with respect to the screen version of Tarzan. It also shared the explicit demand for fundamental revision of German attitudes toward the medium. Finally, it cast serious doubt on the value of debating the artistic properties of cinema with the categories usually applied in German film circles.[73] The Fox films underscored the kinetic character of cinema, demonstrating the primacy of pictorial rhythm over lighting, acting and innovative *mise-en-scène* which earmarked classical Weimar cinema. As another critic reflected, employing even while aiming to overthrow cultural stereotypes:

In the course of its intellectual development the nation of ponderers and thinkers has buried itself too deeply in the underground labyrinth beneath matter to find its way easily back to the illuminated surface of all forms and shapes whose colourful, kaleidoscopic diversity can alone give to film what belongs to it. . . . German film development is suffering from an excess of intellectual culture as a racial characteristic: In the beginning was the word. In its films as well. The beginning of all filmic matters is, however, illuminated, moving shapes.[74]

The point here is not the commonplace that American culture was less literary and more democratic than German. Rather it is that discourse within the film community on the nature of the American challenge underwent substantial revision after 1921. Even though association of film with the pace of urban life and dissociation of it from older cultural forms predated reintroduction to Hollywood, direct and sustained confrontation with the American alternative drove these lessons home. While domestic filmmakers were experimenting with Expressionist stylization, chamber plays and historical spectacles, Hollywood appeared able to place a generic, filmically defensible and commercially viable stamp on a variety of motion pictures. Given its global hegemony and rapid inroads into Germany, contemporaries could no longer treat it dismissively as primitive and uncultured.

In the aftermath of the Fox series, as the period of initiation drew to a close, the reputation of American cinema reached an all-time high. Family drama, comedy, society films and sensationalism made a powerful impression on critics and audiences. The first films starring Jackie Coogan, *My Boy* and *The Kid*, the former released before, though made after the latter, created a veritable Coogan cult. Audiences wept and critics spoke in reverent awe of this childhood wonder.[75] Two social satires by Cecil B. De Mille, *Saturday Night* and *The Affairs of Anatol*, drew praise for their cinematic fluidity and human charm. Critics confessed shock that a potboiler by Maurice Tourneur, *The Isle of Lost Ships*, could be so consummately filmed as to overwhelm all objections. It now appeared that Hollywood had earned its international standing more honestly than initially believed.[76]

Viewed as a whole the extended period of initiation into American movies both confirmed and overthrew much accepted wisdom. First exposure, overwhelmingly to sensationalist films, vindicated the prevailing opinion that Hollywood was a hothouse for action and adventure. The only cause for concern, and one which could be rationalized in terms of previous isolation from American motion pictures, was popular interest in these imports. Acquaintance with American society dramas partially confirmed established belief—Hollywood stumbled in the scenario department and had an irritating bent for sentimentality and moralizing—yet caused some serious rethinking of conventional assumptions. Hollywood could achieve dramatic impact comparable to Berlin. The fact that it did so without adoption of German methods intimated what became increasingly evident in contact with the films of Viola Dana and the series presented by Fox. America posed a threat because it displayed a confidence and consistency in its exploitation of the medium which the German cinema had not matched.

Acknowledgment of this aptitude was by no means universal, nor did it necessarily reconcile critics to all Hollywood's quirks.

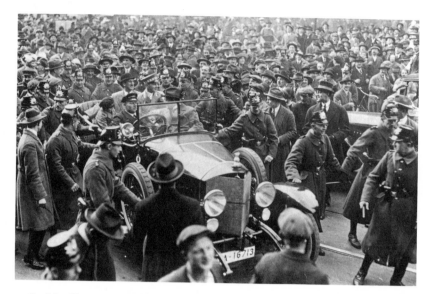

Jackie Coogan, Hollywood's boy wonder, accompanied by his father, greeted by Berlin crowds, 1924. (Photo courtesy Ullstein Bilderdienst)

Mary Pickford with Emil Jannings at the Babelsberg studios, 1924. (Photo courtesy Ullstein Bilderdienst)

Douglas Fairbanks and Mary Pickford in Hotel Adlon at the Brandenburg Gate, 1926. (Photo courtesy Ullstein Bilderdienst)

Harold Lloyd at the six-day races, 1925. (Photo courtesy Landesbildstelle Berlin)

It did, however, in its elaboration on ideas espoused early in 1921 by Hans Siemsen, suggest that the American cinema was a more dangerous competitor than it had originally appeared. Behind the apparent inconsequence of Hollywood's output lay both generic forces—industrialization, urbanization and mechanization of life—which were also systemic in Germany, and filmic principles consistent with the technological and kinetic character of the medium.[77] German cinema had impressed discriminating viewers in Europe and America but by the admission of its own spokespersons had yet to establish an unequivocal public role. The period from 1921 to 1923 therefore witnessed growing recognition that Hollywood had tapped the intrinsic and public dimensions of the medium at their point of mutual reinforcement.

4

THE HOLLYWOOD INVASION
Amerikanismus and *Amerikamüdigkeit*

Beginning in 1924 Germany experienced a cultural invasion
without parallel since the age of Napoleon. In the wake of the
Dawes Plan and other American loans Germans encountered
a wave of what they styled *Amerikanismus*, the cultural essence
of a nation which worshiped technology, efficiency, and commercial success. Much of this invasion was mediated through
German travelers and scholars, who responded to the explosion
of interest in America with books and articles on the subject.[1]
A large portion of German contact with the United States was
also immediate, provided by imported American culture. In late
1923 the release of Henry Ford's autobiography did more than
any other single work to put America and *Amerikanismus* in the
spotlight, quickly becoming a best-selling and controversial
blueprint for a free enterprise utopia.[2] While Ford sparked
lively debate about the social and economic structures which
promised prosperity, jazz broke through in Germany with a
musical rhythm appropriate to the industrial pulse of the modern metropolis. American literature and theater also became
increasingly ubiquitous. Weimar culture became preoccupied
with American models and achievements.[3]

The American invasion coincided with the advent of what is
traditionally known as the era of *Neue Sachlichkeit*. Although no
more applicable to Weimar culture as a whole than Expressionism in the previous period, new objectivity highlights the urge
to forget the chaotic social and political circumstances of the
postwar years, bury the anguished passions of Expressionism
and come to terms with technological advance. It portended
Germany's adjustment to postwar realities. Among these was
the extent of American involvement in German affairs. Indeed,

new sobriety and the American phase in Weimar's history were not casual correlates. The United States modeled *Neue Sachlichkeit* in social, industrial and cultural patterns shorn of tradition and ideological schisms. Those enthused about modern technology, industrial rationalization and mass culture made America the object of a secular cult. Those enraged by the same developments attacked it as the source of cultural degeneracy. Attitudes toward American and domestic cultural trends became heavily interdependent.[4]

German cinema participated in both inundation by American motion pictures and the adjustments characteristic of the post-inflationary years. Currency stabilization finally decided the film war projected at the start of the decade in Hollywood's favor. Germany became a primary outlet for American motion pictures, a recipient of American financing, a borrower of cinematic expertise and a major source of talent for American studios. As demonstrated in chapter two, Weimar cinema hitched its fortunes irrevocably to Hollywood, allowing American motion pictures to win a prominent if not commanding position in Germany. However, Weimar cinema did not simply capitulate. If this phase owed more to America than any in the past, it also witnessed shifts of emphasis in production agendas. In reaction against the fantastic, exaggerated and stylized films of the earlier period and in partial modification of the romanticized versions of prewar society and the military, it encouraged realistic portrayal of contemporary circumstances or problems. Again it is easy to dramatize the contrast with postwar production, yet films such as adaptations of Heinrich Zille sketches (*Die Verrufenen, Die da unten*), Walter Ruttmann's *Berlin*, G. W. Pabst's *Die Liebe der Jeanne Ney*, and later socially critical works such as *Cyankali, Mädchen in Uniform, Mutter Krausens Fahrt ins Glück* and *Kuhle Wampe*, exemplify a noticeable trend. Growing politicization of production and reception was one dimension of this trend. Realistic filmmaking also promised, however, to revive the slumping fortunes of German production. The German industry, squeezed first by the assembly-line entertainment of Hollywood and then by Soviet cinema, felt mounting pressure to discover a domestic counterpart, namely, production anchored in German circumstances. From middecade there was growing correlation between critical approbation and films which scored highly on the test of realism.[5]

The irony in these developments is that even as Hollywood became a fixture in Weimar film culture, saturation with *Amerikanismus* provoked a backlash. As the most visible outpost of American culture in Germany, and as a constant reminder of economic dependence, motion pictures began to generate hostile reactions. From 1924 the prevailing tide of earlier years began to ebb. Quantity and industrial interference help explain counterrevisionism, but most contemporaries blamed it directly on the nature of the American films released in Germany. Explanations for what they alleged was German "weariness of America" focused on Hollywood's standardization, mediocrity and foreignness to German sensibilities. By late 1925 critical and public opinion appeared to coalesce in a new anti-American consensus which denied the suitability of most American imports for German theaters. Film experts found themselves obliged to interpret popular distaste as well as their own disdain for Hollywood.[6]

Recoil from the American film invasion took place on two levels. Among cultural conservatives it was grafted onto the general cry, *Los von Amerika*. A glance at their aversion to Hollywood reveals that it differed only in degree from that toward the cinema in general. Symptomatic is the case of Adolf Halfeld, author of an exhaustive *völkisch* diatribe against *Amerikanismus*. In the preface to his book Halfeld attributed the Americanization of Germany principally to Hollywood's world monopoly and invasion of Germany rather than to direct political or economic influences. Yet while he acknowledged the profound influence of the cinema he felt no obligation to deal with it seriously. Claiming thorough acquaintance with American film, he disposed of it in a single paragraph.[7] What Halfeld did for America in general, an ideological cousin, Hans Buchner, did for Hollywood in particular. Buchner presented an extended critique of film affairs and showed familiarity with specific American movies. But his judgments were those of a reactionary film reformer: Charlie Chaplin was a Bolshevist, American social dramas were the epitome of moral degeneracy, and American film as a whole substituted technology and materialism for art and life.[8]

At this level of resistance to Americanization, Hollywood became a scapegoat for the sins of the motion picture. Intrinsic to that resistance was hostility toward a medium whose technological, commercial and public components jeopardized a nineteenth century notion of art remote from the masses and the marketplace. While important in the larger context of anti-American opinion, such views scarcely bore on the problems facing German film culture in the 1920s. Not only did American cinema occupy such a prominent place in Weimar that its presence could not be exorcised with thunderous denunciations, but the medium also obeyed imperatives which obtained in Germany as well as the United States. Flight from the financial and political dimensions of film to the ivory tower of art or *Kultur* was flight from reality. Consequently, the impassioned assault on *Amerikanismus* offers only superficial insight into the meaning of Hollywood for Weimar cinema.

Reaction against Hollywood was no less prominent within the German film community, but it arose out of an established and more informed discourse about cinema and society. For the motion picture, *Amerikanismus* and *Amerikanisierung,* the slogans of middecade cultural reaction, represented the culmination of challenges which had begun shortly after the war. Many experts shared sentiments expressed by anti-American cultural crusaders, but they responded to American inroads with considerable discrimination, recognizing the need to rethink certain assumptions even as others were affirmed. They took seriously the task of identifying the fundamental flaws in American cinema (thereby explaining the perceived alienation of German viewers) while simultaneously accounting for Hollywood's ability to gain a stranglehold on the domestic market.[9]

As this dual obligation suggests, making sense of Hollywood's role in Germany at middecade proved at least as problematic as it had before 1924. Tension again existed not only between the image of Hollywood and the extent of its inroads, but also between the receptivity of German audiences and the rationalizations of German experts. In both cases it was overlaid with considerable disregard for separation of image and reality or perception and fact. In retrospect it is difficult to disentangle popular anti-American sentiment from the backlash in critical perspectives. In the absence of comprehensive box office statistics or independent public opinion surveys, experts enjoyed the rare but dubious privilege of extrapolating from personal impressions, hearsay and partial statistical information. The question of Hollywood's popularity thus became a polemical as much as a statistical one. Since perception was at least as important as fact, and often outran it, it deserves first treatment. A subsequent chapter will examine more closely the evidence for public disenchantment.

The shift in trade opinion on Hollywood was marked by a new periodization in assessments of its role in Germany. By 1925 the first three years of contact with American motion pictures appeared a honeymoon, an era in which Hollywood courted and captured the German imagination, when "every purchase of an American film was *celebrated as a cultural achievement in which the German purchasing firm could take pride.*"[10] With the honeymoon over, experts looked back and questioned whether they had let themselves be deceived. Had they been brainwashed into believing American superiority and contributed to the Hollywood invasion by idolizing its product? Two prominent commentators replied in the negative, but affirmed that times had changed. The screenwriter and critic, Willy Haas, and the director of Deulig-Film, David Melamerson, agreed that initially Hollywood had boasted, in addition to novelty-value, superior acting, directing and technical accomplishments. However, in the interim German cinema had closed the technical gap, and intellectual and moral objections had arisen to the growing number of American films shown in Germany. Overexposure to average American films, coupled with improvements in native production, created aversion to Hollywood.[11]

The belief that evolving circumstances within Germany and Hollywood had transformed the relationship between the two enjoyed wider currency. Kurt Pinthus, for instance, interpreted changing public sentiments as a result of growing powers of discrimination. Having become familiar with the full range of American films, Germans found the bulk of what Hollywood offered unacceptable.[12] A Munich critic, Hans Spielhofer, and one of Berlin's leading theater managers, Hanns Brodnitz, related the revolution in opinion to socioeconomic as well as cinematic developments.

> It's the fashionable thing to do today to grumble about America after having for years proclaimed American film the ultimate revelation. When in 1923 the American motion picture conquered the German public with one bold stroke the key factor was the contrast between our dog's life in inflation and America's booming existence. Sick people took refreshment from the healthiness of a stronger stranger.

Germans had found the optimism and naiveté of American film a "narcotic and refresher," "a greeting from a fantastically carefree land." Now the novelty was dead, the American cinema had experienced a creative crisis and Germans had lost interest in the American formula.[13]

Such reflective comments capture the general tenor of the perceptual shift which took place at middecade, but they represent at best the tip of the critical iceberg. A more systematically articulated and penetrating guide to changing attitudes is the critical work of Roland Schacht. One of the most prolific and literate critics of the 1920s, Schacht wrote both for highbrow theatrical and cultural journals (*Das blaue Heft* and *Der Kunstwart*) and for the popular tabloid *B.Z. am Mittag*. As a doctor of German literature and critic of contemporary art, he belonged to the cultural elite whose prevailing scepticism toward cinema represented a persisting challenge to the German industry. Since he had a passionate commitment to the motion picture as mass entertainment, believing that the measure of cinema culture was not the occasional art film but run-of-the-mill production, he reprimanded both the sceptics and the businesspeople for failure to give serious attention to the film fare swallowed by one to two million Germans daily. From this perspective his weekly or bimonthly review essays in *Kunstwart* and *Das blaue Heft* frequently contrasted the distinctive features of American and German productions.[14]

In the course of 1922 and 1923 Schacht had encouraged German filmmakers to learn from the American cinema, calling like Siemsen for more emphasis on performers and declining to dismiss American sensationalism as mere kitsch.[15] From early 1924 his enthusiasm began to wane. He did not abandon the critical insights of the preceding year, nor did he cease selecting specific American pictures as object lessons for the German producer. Yet he increasingly drew a line between the few American films which merited discussion and the mass which did not, and he cautioned against irresponsible overestimation of Hollywood.

> The fame of the foreigners is generally beginning to fade slowly as a consequence of mass import. The average is still better than our average but the number of great masterpieces is seemingly exhausted. . . . One-sided worship of the foreign over the best German films cannot be opposed strongly enough, not for national but for artistic reasons.[16]

Schacht still refused to laud native achievements to spite Hollywood, but he became increasingly critical of American imports. Henceforth his critical corpus can be read as a microcosm of German reaction patterns over the next three years: a blend of denunciation of the species and plaudits for its exceptional members.

As Schacht's distaste for Hollywood grew so did the directness of his criticism. Following the contingent of American features which appeared through the summer of 1924 his tone sharpened perceptibly. On the eve of the new film season he labeled a series of American works, all social dramas, garbage not worth discussion except to illustrate the heavy feminist tinge in American film plots and the repetition and abundance of lesser talents in Hollywood movies. Prefiguring sentiments which in 1925 and 1926 were to coalesce into the slogan "no more American average," he questioned the need to import the work of Hollywood's novices and epigones. What particularly irritated him was the way these pictures were being released in Germany. Though appropriate only for inexpensive theaters they were being "artificially whipped up into 'premieres' in places where their intellectual primitiveness, their inner foolishness and empty window dressing [were] doubly painful." For the moment, extravagant, American-style publicity campaigns were drawing customers, but the Americans were sabotaging their own future by duping the public into attending mediocre pictures. Once Germans saw through the advertising ruse they would disbelieve every word from Hollywood.[17]

The interplay of antipathy toward Hollywood's intellectual backwardness, a standard complaint about American film, and efforts to camouflage it with publicity and pomp, techniques for which the Americans were equally renowned, became fully apparent in Schacht's response to two major American releases of the new season, *The Ten Commandments* and *The Hunchback of Notre Dame*. On filmic grounds he damned the first of these, Cecil B. De Mille's epic, for focus on technical achievement at the expense of character portrayal.[18] But he also expressed irritation at the mammoth advertising campaign and extravagant premiere which Paramount staged. Schacht suspected efforts to take German intellectuals by storm with ceremony and an air of literary seriousness. The effect was rather to disappoint high hopes and provoke anger by the claim of cultural significance for a film which lacked it.[19] The American rendition of Victor Hugo's *The Hunchback of Notre Dame*, starring Lon Chaney, likewise appeared in a festive setting. Wreaths and flowers filled the foyer of the theater, the organist played Handel and P. E. Bach as part of the prelude to the film, and the management offered complimentary carnations to the ladies and matches to the men. But Schacht claimed the audience was alienated by the feature film itself. What Americans looked for in the cinema did not comprise motion picture virtues in Germany:

> The American white-collar worker may be impressed to hear that the facade of Notre Dame was replicated in original size; this collection of many medieval buildings, the historical authenticity of the costumes, this incomprehensible mélange of kings and beggars, knights and monsters may attract and amuse him. For us it's all dull and, despite the mass scenes, boringly made film-theater, with totally impossible or quite superficial performers, in which neither the Middle Ages nor the best of Victor Hugo nor anything at all comes alive.[20]

Given earlier distaste for American historical epics these reactions could be read as genre-specific. In Schacht's opinion, however, much more was at stake than Hollywood's handling of history. The timing of these two releases made them turning points in German attitudes toward American film. Coming on top of many nondescript American pictures which filled the void in German theaters in the summer of 1924, they failed, despite vast budgets, assiduous press agents and gala premieres, to restore German appreciation for American movies. Since both pictures were of major proportions, they compelled him, and he believed they would compel others, to reassess American capabilities. *The Ten Commandments* in particular was seen as such a representative picture that Schacht judged its failure to satisfy German demands a heavy blow to Hollywood's reputation in Germany.

In subsequent commentary Schacht confirmed that disenchantment with Hollywood did not begin and end with historical pageants. He also claimed increasing authority, evident already in response to *The Ten Commandments* and *The Hunchback of Notre Dame,* to speak on behalf of German moviegoers. In the summer of 1925 he asserted that all major American releases since De Mille's epic had met with cool receptions. Incompatible mentalities, especially relevant for non-Berliners, accounted for displeasure. Generally speaking, German viewers were less naive and in greater need of cinematic variety than their American counterparts.[21] Shortly thereafter, outspoken audience hostility to a Raymond Griffith comedy, *Never Say Die,* permitted him to focus his judgment. In this instance the Kurfürstendamm premiere met a chorus of derisory whistles from the audience which the German distributor of the movie, Phoebus, tried to pin on the machinations of an unspecified competitor. Schacht, although admitting the picture was no worse than many other American films which had been greeted with applause or indifference, lent little credence to this version of the affair:

> It was not the competition which brought about the downfall of the film, but a dull hostility of the German public, to be sure hard to explain but nonetheless very real, toward the American style; toward this brisk, smooth routine which in a coldly, commercially calculating manner makes variations on the same motif over and over again. . . . The rejection of *Never Say Die* was the revenge of a public served too many American films which were poor or insuf-

ficiently geared to our mentality. The feeling was that the winter
season had begun and there was no desire to have it opened with
an average American film.[22]

The real problem then was accumulated grudges against the
formula Hollywood presented to German moviegoers.

Schacht was among the first to note and interpret the swing
in critical and public mood which occurred in 1924 and 1925.[23]
A glance at commentary in other sources confirms the essential
points of his assessment. Critical reception of *The Ten Commandments*, for example, exhibited the blend of condescension and
irritation which characterized Schacht's response to Hollywood.
Almost without exception reviewers complained that, however
this film fared in the United States, it could never engage German viewers intensely. Despite grandiose dimensions and technical sophistication it failed to do justice to the monumentality
of its theme.[24] Schacht's predictions were also confirmed in the
growing number of cases in which motion picture audiences
gave vocal expression to their distaste for American features.
Particularly in the early months of 1926, the first-run theaters in
Berlin experienced "whistle concerts" in response to American
premieres. Public Hollywood-bashing became fashionable.[25]

Schacht's explanation for German reactions combined rather
conventional criticisms of the American product and reference
to considerations of the quantity and timing of its release. Mutually reinforcing factors, both intrinsic to the films and circumstantial in nature, transformed appreciation into latent resistance or active opposition to Hollywood. Cinematic tendencies
once viewed with indulgence became sharp irritants. Schacht's
perceptions in this regard can again be taken as generally representative of broader opinion. By middecade the notion of incompatible national tastes or mentalities assumed axiomatic
character. Strictly speaking, the idea that Germans had cinematic expectations not met by American film dated to the period
prior to resumption of import. It surfaced in reviews of the
early imports and found explicit formulation from a number
of specialists who warned that only certain types of pictures
would wear well beyond their place of origin.[26] Yet prior to
1924 the taste barrier applied most frequently to discussions

of Germany's failure to win a share of the American market: American experts repeatedly reminded German filmmakers that their product was too ponderous and taxing for American viewers. Beginning in 1924 German trade circles inverted this argument, claiming that the taste barrier cited by the Americans functioned also to restrict the popularity of American film in Germany. Whatever the quality of American imports, German viewers possessed an inherently limited capacity to appreciate them.

Appeal to nationally conditioned taste differences resuscitated many of the stereotypes applied at the beginning of the decade. Hollywood became the repository of national character and values which distinguished the United States from Germany. It embodied America's childishness, emotional coldness and naked lust for profit. American cinema represented merely entertainment and dollar chasing, not artistic refinement and cultural enrichment.[27]

The filmic point of departure for application of these stereotypes was the screenplay. Notwithstanding the intervening lesson that these were not decisive, the old complaints about naiveté, improbability, false characterization and resort to sensationalism and sentimentality to resolve conflicts multiplied, even from observers as indulgent in these matters as Roland Schacht. Moreover, on the basis of extensive observation critics could now charge that Hollywood followed a predictable routine which made its scenarios especially unpalatable, even when otherwise attractive as film. To take just one example: the drama, *Kentucky Derby,* released in mid-1924, met the kind of generic dissection reminiscent of 1921. According to a trade critic, this was "an authentically American film! Pluses: steady directing, tempo, excellent acting, flawless photography, good popular appeal. Minuses: a very routine plot with an overabundance of gross inconsistencies in characterization of types, false sentimentality spread finger thick." In the reductionist formula of Erna Büsing in the socialist daily, *Vorwärts,* this picture was "an average American film made according to pattern," with a screenplay which was "one-third sentimentality, one-third improbability and one-third muscle flexing."[28]

Middecade reaction against American cinema culture therefore built on traditional foundations. What was novel, at least in emphasis, was protest against the manner in which American motion pictures were promoted in Germany and rebellion against American ethical or moral norms. Publicity campaigns were a specialty, if hardly a preserve, of American companies which trade circles admitted German distributors and exhibitors could afford to learn from. The news and advertising service provided by the larger concerns to enhance the public profile of their products was recognized as a key to Hollywood's international success. Yet at middecade experts proved extremely sensitive to the incommensurability of advertising and product. American historical pageants remained the cardinal offenders. Never critical successes in Germany, these invited particular hostility because they came with inflated reputations. The release of Fred Niblo's *Ben Hur* and De Mille's other biblical colossus, *King of Kings*, generated, like the appearance of the earlier historical epics, admiration for visual effects but condemnation for lack of heart and soul.[29] Advertising campaigns and elaborate premieres continued to mislead and alienate. *Ben Hur*, a picture whose sensationalist and cinematic qualities made it a smash hit in Germany, elicited much the same sentiment of disappointment and irritation expressed two years earlier by Schacht. A lead article in *Film-Kurier* complained sharply that advertising cast in superlatives and orchestration of the premiere as a society event attended by government officials, leading figures of the theater and even the American ambassador, falsely assumed that Berlin was New York: "Even at the movies the German looks for more than entertainment, even when it is the most breathtaking, gigantic and powerful in the world."[30]

Importation of American promotional and staging practices became most conspicuous in mid-1925 when UFA hired Sam Rachmann to revamp its show theater, UFA-Palast am Zoo. Redecoration of the interior in purple and gold and installation of multicolored spotlights provided a Broadway ambience. The renovated cinema opened with three hours of uninterrupted entertainment, ranging from the Tannhäuser overture and jazz under the baton of Ernö Rappé, enhanced by light shows, to dancing girls, cartoons, newsreels and an American feature comedy starring Sydney Chaplin. This potpourri of music, stage show and film apparently entranced the audience but left critics stunned and somewhat sceptical. Hats came off to Rappé, an acknowledged master of jazz, but critical response to such wholesale Americanization of the theater program was decidedly mixed. Crowding out of the motion picture in favor of music and varieté numbers defeated the purpose of motion picture exhibition.[31]

Resistance to American methods of film exhibition aimed essentially at the trend to treat Berlin and New York interchangeably. German objections to Hollywood's ethical perspectives arose in opposition to the same trend. That these objections became prominent in 1924 rather than 1921 or 1922 has less to do with trends in America than with disillusionment with Hollywood in Germany.[32] German observers began to castigate American moral prudery and idolization of the female sex because both became conspicuous impositions of the period in which American movies saturated the German market. The general drift of critical commentary remained the same, but it became more explicit and was framed in ironic and acerbic language which served as the last wall of defence against ideological subjugation by Hollywood.

Schematic handling of the conflict between good and evil had drawn scoffing remarks in response to the early serial films. But it was in the second half of 1924, as American features gained ground in German theaters, that a series of society dramas brought caustic reactions to the fore. Two films starring Gloria Swanson precipitated the hardening of attitudes. *Prodigal Daughters* betrayed its content in its title: two young sisters from an affluent family leave home, embark on a life of sin, eventually recognize the error of their ways and return penitently to the family fold. The moral, as one critic put it, amounted to the "banal bit of wisdom that home is still the best place to be and children would always do well to return to their parents."[33] Worse, the pretext for moral concern was what Georg Mendel called "a good subject for the Salvation Army."

The 'lostness' of both these charming millionaire's daughters is so mild (they smoke cigarettes—outrageous—they dance and drive cars and have fun and dress elegantly and enchantingly . . .) that

the conversion and return home and automatically ensuing engagement to the moral and 'respectable' airplane engineer seems by
German standards rather awfully primitive, tame and musty.[34]

According to the socialist paper *Vorwärts* the whole affair was
simply a lesson in virtue aimed at the lower classes using an
upper class milieu to provide titillation.[35]

The other Swanson vehicle, *Beyond the Rocks*, paired her with
Rudolph Valentino. Its German title, *Thou shalt not covet thy
neighbour's wife*, gave a blatantly moralizing tone to a story of a
young woman whose unhappy marriage to an older man ended
with his timely death, permitting her to marry without moral
trespass the young aristocrat she loved. Again its portrayal of
virtue and vice appeared so juvenile to Germans that it could
not be taken seriously. Hollywood wanted both to enjoy the
spice of immoral behavior and to uphold moral codes:

> A film of the erotic almost, of the I would like to but I can't. Ameri-
> can decency requires that the unwanted husband goes to Africa
> and gets himself shot by a Beduin, but the filmmaker still manages
> to have the dying man expire in the arms of his wife who is called
> in hurriedly.[36]

Sarcasm became the only serviceable critical mode for this
"American morally trite story" about lust for a married woman:

> Have no fear! Lust means: to chat fashionably at costume balls
> and romantic stage plays. Covetousness means: to dress well and
> preserve one's dignity. Any deeper impulse does not develop in the
> six-act movie; thin cliché, most externalized format. A superlative
> degree of innocence.[37]

The revelation of these reviews is not that Hollywood shied
from confronting conventional moral precepts, itself a cliché,
but that critics could no longer tolerate or take seriously the
combination of cant and superficiality they ascribed to American drama. A critic for *Reichsfilmblatt* put it bluntly: "The manu-
facturing of such a screenplay is to feed the hillbillies in Arizona,
not an educated audience."[38]

Critical rebellion against portrayal of humans either as para-
gons of virtue or masters of vice was part of the more general

distaste for the "naive Old Testament retributive law of guilt and atonement which the American [made] the basis for his film plots." Nothing elicited more caustic commentary than the simplistic, primitive ethical maxim that good was invariably rewarded and evil punished.[39] Once again, criticism dated from the very first sensationalist imports but turned to revulsion during the anti-American reaction of middecade. Here too disgust at American moral obtuseness found an outlet in ironic humor: if critics could not be edified or impressed, they could at least be amused. The classic among their mocking responses was a review of *The Ten Commandments* by Kurt Pinthus cast as ten commandments to the German viewer. Other critics expressed contempt for American efforts to parallel the Mosaic account and a contemporary story of two brothers, one God-fearing and the other, a contractor, disdainful of divine legislation.[40] Pinthus used the parallel to encapsulate and ridicule the moral lesson of the film.

> If you, as a contractor, mix too much sand in the cement for building a church it will fall on none other than your mother whom you did not honour; your wife will fall from the steeple into the arms of your righteous brother who did not dare to covet her. But the commandment-breaker will contract leprosy, which we contemporaries call syphilis, through adultery with an adventuress, and in flight from earthly justice will be smashed to pieces on the rocks by the sea.[41]

The problem, according to Pinthus, was the "emotionally deadening and dollar-chasing life" of the average American. As compensation Americans looked for more "kitsch, sentimentality, moralizing and all kinds of falsehood" than Germans in matters of art and entertainment. Since, however, this otherwise unpalatable brew encouraged sympathy for Germany's economic plight, Germans were advised to be cautiously indulgent.

> You shall not despise this kitsch, even when it is only barely tolerable for you; for it is impressive and made with all finesse, and every evening for a year it stirred the entire nation of Yankees to tears of soul-searching and reformation so that they intend to give their poor German brothers a large loan.
>
> But do not desire to imitate such films, which deliver us a little

treatise and want to lead us into the past. For we belong to the future, which we should serve, since it is our promised land.[42]

In short, Germans could smile at American childishness, grateful that it fostered financial support through the Dawes Plan, but they were not to be snared by it morally or intellectually.

Next to Hollywood's moral sermonizing the most irritating facet of America's value system was the so-called girl cult. Virtually all female stars were stereotyped to a standard which made one indistinguishable from the next. Beauty became the mark of moral purity to the extent that faces and figures overwhelmed character—females became dolls.[43] Their supreme virtue was innocence, but of a sort which repelled German critics. Its mainstay, sexual continence, simultaneously a pillar of social respectability, had to be preserved at all emotional and intellectual costs. Its corollary was a flirtatious approach to romantic involvement, particularly obnoxious because the deference paid feminine virtue spilled over into a more general idolization of the female sex which made men slaves of female whims. German film critics, overwhelmingly male, and not unmoved by the attractiveness of American actresses, found this last the most repugnant facet of the "feminist" cast of Hollywood films.[44]

Since ethical norms are deeply woven into the fabric of any society, and since German opinion drew on long-standing images of the United States, critics did not normally systematize their objections. These constituted unspoken assumptions which surfaced mainly in ironic sniping at American film plots. However, in late 1925 Willy Haas compiled a list of ten theses under the heading "What we find alien about American motion picture morality" which addressed the question of national mentalities directly. Two of his ten theses concerned the female image in American film, and a third related to it by critiquing American sexual prudery. Haas maintained that a woman's innocence was not, contrary to what was taught by American movies, "the sole and highest criterion of her worth as a human being," and he interpreted the brutality and sadism displayed in American movies as sublimation of sexual drives prevented from finding normal outlets by false moral codes. Haas also

challenged head-on the schematic way in which Hollywood ap-
portioned good and evil in its films:

> We know that every person is a mix of good and evil. We know
> that real evil, fundamental evil, does not originate from the intent
> of an evil person to do evil; but that it is a product of a historical
> mechanism; that sincere, subjectively innocent people play a part
> in it. The American does not know this, or he does not (at least in
> the cinema) want to know it.

Haas's other theses elaborated on America's hostility to reality
and tendency to bend life to serve morality. America took pride
in its refusal to face the facts of life, as its insistence on happy
endings demonstrated. Ultimately, Germans and Americans approached life from fundamentally opposed perspectives.

> We derive morality from life, from nature. The American im-
> poses one on the other. . . . We love truth. Even our mendacious-
> ness is still unconscious deferral to the truth. For us the innocent
> lie is more despicable than the guilty one. This is particularly true
> in sexual matters. The Americans base their entire film morality
> on the supreme value of the innocent lie.[45]

Haas's catalogue of American moral peculiarities, exceptional
for explicitness, was entirely unexceptional in general drift and
point of departure. Its unifying element was Hollywood's refusal or inability to face the real world. American filmmakers
simplified and prettified, falsifying life to force its correspondence to moral requirements. Although the United States provided inspiration for *Neue Sachlichkeit* in its pragmatism and efficiency, its motion pictures continued to revel in sentimentality,
falsehood and artificial happy endings.[46] In making this judgment, Haas, much like the dealers in cultural stereotypes of the
early 1920s, made Hollywood the alter ego of an hypostatized
German mentality rather than of the German cinema. Critical
opinion generally followed him in presupposing a standard of
native production honored more in the breach than the observ-
ance. Equally striking is that experts, like censors reacting to
American sensationalist serials, established themselves as arbiters of German opinion. Quite apart from the fact that the accu-
racy with which they gauged and interpreted audience senti-

ment remains debatable, their assault on American moral kitsch amounted to an indirect swipe at successful domestic counterparts. Isolation of Hollywood's moral peculiarities permitted critics to vent their spleen as much at, as on behalf of, German moviegoers. In short, however convenient the argument of incompatible national tastes proved for explaining middecade aversion to Hollywood, it rested on problematic assumptions about the unity of critical and audience opinion. A celebrated case of public protest against an American premiere, Erich Stroheim's *Greed* (1924), reveals that claims about opposing national mentalities could be badly dented by divergent responses among experts and between experts and moviegoers.

In the history of film, Erich Stroheim is a byword for controversy.[47] Notorious for his rebellion against the Hollywood studio system, he won the distinction in Germany of provoking a minor theater riot which was to be remembered until the storm unleashed by the National Socialists against *All Quiet on the Western Front* in 1930. The source of the riot, *Greed*, like virtually everything Stroheim touched in Hollywood, had a checkered history. The studio wars which accompanied its production had, however, no direct bearing on its reception in Germany. *Greed*, or to translate its German title, *Lust for Money*, appears to have prompted violent responses in Berlin both on its own merits, as an experiment in gritty naturalism, and because of Stroheim's wartime reputation for fouling his own nest in anti-German propaganda films. In one respect it illustrates the depth of anti-American feeling in Germany in 1926. Yet the film scarcely fitted the model pilloried by critics and tiresome to audiences. Both found *Greed* distasteful, but not primarily for the reasons otherwise adduced against American film.

A story of human relationships fractured by avarice and consummated in hate and murder, *Greed* related the climb to petty bourgeois respectability of a miner, first via employment as a dentist and then through marriage to the former sweetheart of his closest friend. Pursuit of the American dream turned into a nightmare when his bride began to focus her passions on $5,000 earlier won in a lottery. She became so obsessed with hoarding the coins that she drove her husband to destitution, until finally in blind rage he strangled her. Hunted down and captured in the desert by the erstwhile boyfriend, the husband murdered him as well, despite handcuffs which insured that neither would escape the desert unless both did. In the closing scene the "hero" is thus shown, no less than his wife and friend, as a victim of all-consuming greed.[48]

The German premiere of *Greed* came in mid-May 1926 in UFA's newly renovated Palast am Zoo. The uproar began almost immediately. At the first showing on opening night the audience hissed but endured the film. The second showing met an unprecedented chorus of hooting, whistling and foot stamping. Part way through the show, to cries that the Americans could keep their filth, the performance was interrupted and not resumed. Patrons demanded, and received, a refund on their admission. UFA's surrender to the mob in refunding tickets turned out to be only the first stage of total surrender, for the picture was immediately withdrawn and never rescheduled. In its place UFA recycled the Emil Jannings vehicle, *Varieté*, which had been successful the previous year. *Greed* was subsequently to appear in repertoire cinemas but never saw general circulation in Germany.[49]

UFA understandably sought to bury the incident quickly, informing the press that the uproar had been caused by "systematic agitation." But it offered no enlightenment about who had mounted the protest or what these agitators may have wished to prove. That remained the task of critics, who in contrast to UFA, refused to let the matter die quietly. They could not gloss over the affair as though it were an everyday occurrence in German cinemas. Even amidst general discontent with Hollywood and specific instances of vocal rebellion, cancellation of a show, refund of tickets and termination of an engagement, all apparently thanks to what one observer called a revolution in the audience, constituted a spectacular event. *Greed* took its place among a tiny group of motion pictures which struck a raw nerve in the German public. The problem was to identify that nerve.[50]

Since many reviews of *Greed* were written in response to a preview or the first public showing, they offer relatively unprejudiced insights into the source of the public rebellion which followed. Used in conjunction with retrospective appraisals of the second showing, they paint a picture which in its very contradictions mirrors the tensions already seen in German responses to Hollywood. The main element of continuity lies in the tendency to blame audience rejection on ethical and dramatic peculiarities of the screenplay which were offensive to German sensibilities. Roland Schacht and Fritz Olimsky, for instance, argued that *Greed* flopped because it contained enough typically American sentimentality and crass moralizing to enrage German viewers. A review in *Vorwärts* went so far as to label the film "average" and explain audience reaction as ventilation of disgust with Hollywood's standardization. Alfred Rosenthal concurred with this last judgment, claiming that whatever might be said about the original full-length film, the truncated and miserably titled German edition deserved the furor which it provoked.[51]

To compare *Greed* with the bulk of American production is curious by any standard, though least so perhaps against the backdrop of anti-American sentiment in German film circles. Even under these circumstances, however, some experts approached the picture quite differently, recognizing in Stroheim's work a major departure for Hollywood, albeit one which went awry. Their reactions focussed on *Greed*'s deviation from American type. In this they inadvertently followed an advertising lead given by UFA in the week before the premiere. In a rather unusual style of salesmanship UFA drew attention to *Greed*'s "un-American" qualities to try to exploit anti-American sentiment on its behalf. In a prerelease press notice the company hailed the film as a pioneering work which promised to defuse undeniable and at times warranted resistance to Hollywood. *Greed* would "cause the convictions of even the most inveterate opponent of the American cinema to waver."[52] Although this press statement offered scant rationale for such confidence, other than to label the film a superproduct in respect of content, acting and technique, a further newspaper advertisement placed by UFA supplied the missing motivation. Here *Greed* was characterized in a single phrase as a masterpiece made "in the spirit and with the technique of *German* production." In other words, it belonged neither among the "average" American imports nor among those alien to German sensibilities.[53]

Greed's reception dealt a rude blow to UFA's hope that it would overcome anti-American sentiment, especially since critical opinion generally sympathized with the protest of the premiere audience. However, critics did not uniformly mock UFA's analysis of the film. Whether or not prompted by the advertising campaign, some drew parallels between *Greed* and specific German film conventions. Of these, a few grudgingly conceded *Greed* a place among the select group of art films, even though they showed slight appreciation for Stroheim's staging and handling of characters.[54] Others noted affinities with German filmic practice but challenged UFA's assumption that these flattered Stroheim's work. Hollywood's imitation of German stylistic devices exposed these rather as dated and flawed. Ernst Blass, poet and lead critic for *Berliner Tageblatt,* argued that Stroheim had copied the chief *faults* of the German cinema, "the penchant for exaggerated theatrical conflicts and the taste for pictorial allegory."[55] According to a review in *Lichtbildbühne*, in the second half of the film Stroheim had attempted to stage a motion picture chamber drama in the German tradition. Focusing attention on the emotional confrontation of three persons, he adopted the technique discovered by Ernst Lubitsch of depicting emotional states and suggesting plot developments by parallels with nature or inanimate objects. But his ambition to do for the cinema what Dostoyevsky had done for the novel—explore in infinite detail every facet of a mood or situation—demonstrated the inherent limitations of the medium. Symbolism carried to excess robbed *Greed* of tempo and pushed the viewer's tolerance of morbid content beyond the breaking point. Film could not borrow literary ambitions or styles.[56]

If the approximation between German practice and Stroheim's style constituted one recurring theme in commentary on *Greed,* an element of excess or fanaticism was the other. In this critics confirmed that UFA had correctly sensed, though falsely understood, the deviation of *Greed* from American motion picture convention. Stroheim made a noteworthy departure but lacked a sense of proportion. Wanting to get to the heart of an issue, he flogged it so unremittingly that it lost meaning. After a lengthy introduction which portrayed in striking realism the petty bourgeois society of America, the film plunged into a tale

Advertisments for *Greed*. In the first instance both sketch and script completely romanticize the film. The second offers a clue, albeit still muted, to the unsuspecting viewer. (*Lichtbildbühne*, 15 May 1926, p. 17; *Kinematograph*, 16 May 1926, p. 30.)

Gier nach Geld

REGIE: ERICH von STROHEIM

METRO.GOLDWYN.FILM DER UFA
DECLA-BIOSCOP.VERLEIH G.M.B.H. VERLEIHBETRIEB DER
UNIVERSUM-FILM AKTIENGESELLSCHAFT

of fanatical lust for money whose naturalism strained the limits of credibility. The plot centred on a "borderline case" and left the viewer with a feeling of "oppressive torment."

> Nowhere is there a humanly conciliatory ray of light. In this film everything is bitterness and torment right to an end which withers performers and audience. Here art is poisoned by philosophy, all life is ridiculous or horrifying madness.[57]

Willy Haas welded these ideas into a blistering denunciation of the picture and its director.

> A frightful film; the most frightful, the most horrific film ever made. An orgy of hatred; a symphony of nausea; cold, hoarse, devilish laughter. Three thousand meters of indigestion at human meanness.
>
> This Erich von Stroheim is a sick man. . . . If he had made any run-of-the-mill film he would have almost seemed brilliant; but with the diseased craving of the hysteric he takes everything to the heights and depths of a fundamental analysis of life.[58]

Needless to say, none of these indictments applied to the mainstream of Hollywood's production. As the critic for *Montag Morgen* argued, Stroheim had become addicted to an excess of *Un-Amerikanismus:* "He made a gloomy, over-psychological, morose-cranky chamber play which could have more likely been devised in Germany."[59] Several weeks after the ill-fated premiere Ernst Blass underscored this point and suggested that Stroheim's brand of naturalism fell between two stools. Popular and critical distaste were both understandable:

> If the all too normalized character of the American average production is boring in the long run, the abnormal is still no refinement. Protest was made against this film because it was all too un-American. Without being art it was all too unpopular. The downfall of the average is, however, being all too popular for Europe.[60]

Significant here are the underlying value judgments. American motion pictures were repeatedly mocked for idealizing life, for evasion of touchy subjects or refusal to treat these realistically and consistently and, of course, for the happy endings which symbolized all these tendencies. In these respects they were too popular; they conceded too much to the instincts of the American masses. By contrast, *Greed* had taken upon itself the portrayal of human misery and death, had relentlessly pursued the pernicious consequences of lust for money (and in a land which allegedly worshiped the almighty dollar) and had distinguished itself with the very opposite of a happy ending. Yet Blass, and many other critics, refused to assign it artistic worth because it flew from one extreme to the other. Its affinities with German art films failed to redeem it.

Initial responses to *Greed* blended recognition of Stroheim's Germanic tendencies and chagrin that his fanaticism resulted in a caricature of the chamber dramas for which the German cinema was famous. Only in isolated cases did the picture win unqualified endorsement as an artistic achievement.[61] But the case on *Greed* did not close in May 1926. Although the film never shook its reputation as a box office disaster, it did gain critical rehabilitation. Panned in 1926, it became almost a cult film among cognoscenti in the subsequent two years. Ironically, the cult focused on the features which had earlier provoked such sharp rejection.[62]

Rehabilitation came in conjunction with the realistic impulses of *Neue Sachlichkeit,* particularly amidst acclaim for Soviet cinema. Critics had as many reservations about the political message of Russian motion pictures as they had about Stroheim's quite different fanaticism, but their respect for the stylistic innovativeness and impact of the former spilled over into reassessment of *Greed.*[63] One reviewer, later reminded of Stroheim's film by Sergei Eisenstein's *Strike,* maintained that common to both films was celebration of hatred—in the Russian film, of capitalists and police; in *Greed,* of mankind as a whole, including the movie audience, which sensed it and reciprocated with a chorus of whistles. *Greed* thus deserved the riot it provoked. But it also deserved applause for adopting an independent artistic line. Its unsparing naturalist style linked it with Soviet experimentation.[64]

Revival of *Greed* in special showings in 1927 and 1928 prompted more explicit revisionism. Looking back from 1927 Helmut Brandis summarized earlier critical opinion as a blend of respect for Stroheim's brilliance and horror at his poisoned outlook on life. Brandis argued that the personality types depicted in the film belonged in asylums, but they functioned as mirrors to expose a submerged segment of human character. In blatant contrast to the vast majority of motion pictures with their candied, false moralizing, *Greed* attained extraordinary realism. For this reason it deserved appellation as "an unprecedented accomplishment artistically and morally."[65] In the parallel formulation of another critic, the departure of this film from conventional approaches comprised its chief plus: in place of mendacious, beautified kitsch and the sensations dreamed up by script writers the reviewer encountered "unadorned truth, life as it is."[66]

Without always stating why *Greed* had stirred audience feeling in May 1926, these later analyses made it self-evident: the public had no appetite for a glimpse of life without the conventional filmic cosmetic. At stake was not just popular resistance to an unusual motion picture formula. Harry Kahn, a critic for *Die Weltbühne*, spelled out in mid-1928 the root cause of audience outrage, even as he articulated the immensity of Stroheim's achievement. Like critics of the premiere, Kahn found Stroheim guilty of exaggeration and distortion in his zeal to paint the perverse side of life. The extremism of the contrasts he drew between human types and milieus exceeded even that of Russian directors. By the same token, however, he became the lone non-Russian director to give film a content worthy of its technical sophistication; to escape conventional sentimentality and fantasizing in pursuit of uncompromising naturalism. The facet of life he chose to confront, and the method he used to portray it, predestined *Greed* to public rejection:

> A person is happy to pay several marks to sit two hours in a comfortable theater seat horrified at the sight of fates which can never touch him. But to have the horror of the emptiness of his own existence driven home to him is something which the average man scarcely tolerates in theater; in film he still today rebels against it.[67]

In short, *Greed* struck a chord in viewers which they simply refused to hear.

In retrospect *Greed*'s reception stands out for conflicting reasons. Strictly speaking, it presents a case with neither precedents nor sequels. Other motion pictures, such as *Fridericus Rex, Battleship Potemkin* or *All Quiet on the Western Front*, which triggered more violent responses (involving politicians and censors), did so on generally recognizable grounds. *Greed*'s rejection was much more problematic. Attempts were made to politicize the incident, beginning with UFA's vague allegations about premeditated, organized opposition. Stroheim already enjoyed notoriety as a self-proclaimed renegade Austrian officer who had made a name in America during the war in anti-German hate pictures. Some suggested that the protest was at least partially directed against him. (Much later a leftist film journal claimed that for this reason UFA had itself orchestrated the demonstration in order to sabotage the premiere.) At the same time, however, there was a substantial body of opinion which pinned the uproar on the film, though again for diverse reasons. Critics found much internal evidence to support the theory that *Greed* was doomed to failure whatever the specifics of protest at the premiere. Popular resistance was thus at once part of the general aversion to American film and a reflection of *Greed*'s nonconformist approach.[68]

The timing of *Greed*'s release made its rejection the epitome of German rebellion against Hollywood. Ernö Rapée, the prominent Hungarian-American music director with UFA, argued that the scandal originated with shock and disappointment that UFA had been compelled to link its fortunes with those of Paramount and Metro-Goldwyn: protest aimed squarely at the Americanization of German cinema.[69] However, those who identified *Greed* as un-American, or at least more German than American, questioned so simple a reading of the affair. Their interpretation of audience response raised the possibility that Hollywood enjoyed greater acceptance in 1926 than complaints about moral and dramatic quirks implied: if "un-American" motion pictures provoked more protest than Hollywood's assembly-line production, the latter had conceivably become more normative than experts wished to acknowledge. At a moment when domestic production was troubled by emigration of leading artists to the United States and was struggling financially and artistically to find a distinct identity, *Greed* called into question prevailing judgments about Hollywood's place in Germany. *Greed*'s posthumous rehabilitation underscored the fact that Hollywood was not a spent force. It also threw into sharp relief the disjunction between critical and popular attitudes concealed by recourse to national taste differences. The *Los von Amerika* movement which has been traced in this chapter allegedly embraced all levels of German opinion. *Greed* initially appeared to confirm this, but its deviance from the Hollywood mainstream and later rehabilitation exposed the disharmony of critical and popular sensibilities. In sum, while spotlighting Hollywood's middecade troubles in Germany, *Greed*'s reception also exposed unresolved domestic film dilemmas.

5

EXCURSUS
Popular Culture and American
Hegemony

For Weimar cinema the era of *Neue Sachlichkeit* has conventionally been related to thematic and stylistic adjustments which
anchored film in real-life problems. It is symbolized by the aban-
donment of the mythical/historical or fantastic world of *Caligari,*
Der müde Tod, Die Nibelungen or *Faust* for the asphalt and moral
jungle of *Dirnentragödie, Die freudlose Gasse* and *Die Büchse der*
Pandora. More fundamental to the new sobriety, however, than
partly nominal shifts in production priorities was the process
of coming to terms with Hollywood's international dominance
and presence in Germany. One practical form of this process,
discussed in chapter two, was collaboration in production and
distribution. The other was clinical assessment of the reasons
for American hegemony, of Hollywood's meaning for German
culture and of the possibilities for resisting Americanization. In
search of means by which to restore the fortunes of domestic
filmmaking, experts retraced the origins of national defeat and
reappraised the relationship between popular expectations and
the American formula.

Hollywood's domination of the global film market appears
so much a natural right that its origins have received surprisingly little historical attention. Only recently, with research into
the consolidation of the star system, studio production and Hollywood's narrative tradition has the American achievement
been historicized sufficiently to be seen as contingent rather
than predestined. As this filmic achievement is anchored in
changing American values and life-styles, the second and third
decades of this century have become increasingly pivotal for

readings of modern mass culture.[1] This era witnessed the first large-scale influx of American culture into Europe and the triumph of Hollywood's products on European movie screens. In retrospect it holds the key to the enduring ascendancy of American popular culture. Broadly speaking, two mutually reinforcing explanations for American hegemony may be identified. The first emphasizes correspondence between the nature of the American product and popular demand, seeing the source of public interest in the combination of American narrative structures, cutting rhythms and cinematographic polish, on the one hand, and possibilities for audience identification provided by the relative openness of American society and the accessibility of American screen personalities, on the other hand. The second cites the substantial edge offered Hollywood by a large domestic market, wartime difficulties in European production and American exploitation of favorable circumstances through everything from rationalization of production to advertising.[2]

In essentials these explanations were first formulated in the 1920s. In a decade when for the first time Europe met three-quarters or more of its film demand from American supply, contemporaries could scarcely evade trying to rationalize Hollywood's inroads. German film experts devised an explanation which combined American financial clout, havoc wreaked by inflation and overextension of resources in Germany with characteristic features of American motion pictures. In a nutshell: America was a prosperous, populous nation very fond of movies (this movie-mania was often attributed to the absence of alternate forms of entertainment, such as theater, and to the constraints imposed by prohibition). Producers could therefore afford the best talent and the most refined technical apparatus, sparing no expense to please moviegoers. Motion pictures enjoyed such public esteem that they received benevolent treatment by governmental authority through tariff protection and lenient taxation policies. Since production costs were covered by the return from the large and well-to-do domestic market, American corporations could underbid any competitor abroad.[3]

Immediately striking about this rationale was its point-by-point and often explicit contrast with circumstances prevailing in Germany. In a smaller, financially troubled country, with many fewer theaters, the investment required for major pictures could not be recovered on the domestic market. Cinema had to compete against long-established cultural traditions and overcome the suspicion of the cultural elite. In addition it faced hostility and exploitative taxation policies from the various levels of government.[4]

Although this explanation of Hollywood's supremacy in no way denied the appeal of the American product, it tended to subordinate popularity to a set of commercial preconditions. As a result, though powerful and persuasive, it proved extremely problematic. Its very attractiveness as an interpretive paradigm made it almost useless for prescribing solutions, for on the basis of circumstantial factors it conceded dominance to the American cinema. By treating the motion picture as an industrial commodity whose distribution depended on considerations of investment capital, market size, and tariff protection, it minimized the relevance of national mentalities otherwise so eagerly cited and reduced the issue of competition to one of cost-effectiveness and government regulation. It also proceeded unhistorically in assuming Hollywood's wealth was the cause rather than result of success. If, as it implied, the respective fortunes of German and American cinemas were determined by factors beyond their immediate control, there was scant possibility of creating a cinematic alternative to Hollywood which would simultaneously be remunerative.[5]

All this fit awkwardly with what experts interpreted as audience rebellion against Hollywood. Alone among major European states, Germany managed to retain close to half of its own feature film market. That accomplishment was backed by substantial indication that German audiences did not, as a rule, prefer the American product. Germany therefore had less reason than other states to accept American invincibility. By that token, the apparently persuasive case for Hollywood's dominance could not stand unchallenged. Without disregarding Hollywood's undeniable advantages, German experts clearly believed that improvements at home were in order and would enhance Germany's competitive position. If that meant taking lessons from Hollywood, most of all in coordinating production strategies with the market, the prospect of Americanization could not be dismissed as altogether objectionable.

Identifying the areas in which Hollywood had a positive contribution to make to German cinema was a controversial enterprise in all phases of the Weimar period, but especially so at middecade. If, as trade circles generally argued, American motion pictures had exhausted their welcome, there seemed little point adopting Hollywood as a model. Remarkably, however, not all experts denied Hollywood's ongoing relevance. Moreover, a number significantly qualified the reigning orthodoxy that German moviegoers had lost interest in American film. Situated mainly outside trade circles, thus lacking the commercial interests which had encouraged exhibitors to defend Hollywood's reputation in 1924, they still found in American cinema qualities which German filmmakers needed to emulate.

Probably the most outspoken defender of Hollywood at a moment when prevailing opinion turned against it was Hans Pander. As a regular columnist and reviewer for *Der Bildwart*, a journal devoted to educational motion pictures, Pander would normally have been an unlikely candidate to champion American movie entertainment against the domestic industry. However, his interests reached well beyond educational film to include the relationship between motion picture production and public consumption. Writing for an independent journal, Pander established an independent line. In the aftermath of the Parufamet agreement he wrote a lengthy polemic against current wisdom on the significance of national differences and Hollywood's economic advantages. He denied the national origins of a film more than a peripheral role in audience response. Moviegoers sought captivation and entertainment and would accept these from whichever nation best obliged them. He also indicated that America remained the leading source of such pictures for Germany as for all other countries. But he did not believe that Hollywood had a birthright to hegemony. It admittedly enjoyed an edge over Berlin because of the sums it could invest and the benevolent treatment it received from government. But these two givens could not be taken as decisive without abjectly surrendering to Hollywood.[6]

Pander's rationalization of American superiority, to be pursued at greater length below, presupposed a level of popularity for American film which flew in the face of prevailing opinion. By late 1925 popular reaction against Hollywood appeared so ubiquitous that most experts simply took for granted that American films alienated German viewers. *Reichsfilmblatt's* assault on American imports in 1925 initially appeared peculiar to that journal, but closer examination shows that trade opinion proved divided more about tactics than fundamentals. While *Reichsfilmblatt* heaped abuse directly on American producers, other journals, without exonerating Hollywood, tended to shift the responsibility to German importers and distributors. *Film-Kurier*, for example, urged more serious attention to the editing of American works since the form in which some were released raised suspicions that those responsible were covertly trying to discredit Hollywood. But it even more vehemently repudiated the suggestion that American movies had become victims of German chauvinism or deliberate smear tactics: public displeasure was genuine and rooted in the lesser quality or unsuitability of many American imports.[7] *Lichtbildbühne* offered similar double-talk. It judged theater owners' complaints about American features exaggerated and misguided inasmuch as most American imports were potential popular successes if wisely edited. Yet Karl Wolffsohn, publisher of the journal, still insisted that even lesser native works filled theaters which better American pictures could not. Indirectly, he advised exhibitors to make the best of their unfortunate dependence upon Hollywood.[8]

It is striking, given the signs of anti-American sentiment, that Pander developed an argument for the supremacy of American motion pictures without questioning whether that supremacy actually obtained at the German box office. He simply deduced from Hollywood's worldwide hegemony and his own impression of audience reactions the existence of a typical moviegoer whose demands were best met by American film. This disregard for empirical evidence makes his conclusion suspect, but not altogether unlike that of Hollywood's detractors. For they too, in the absence of hard, comprehensive statistics, often resorted to educated guesswork.[9] Since the fairly impressive compendia of film facts and figures in the Weimar era did not include sure guides to the market results of motion pictures, contemporaries, like historians, had to try to piece this information together. German distributors and exhibitors had the raw material from which to derive box-office earnings, but unlike the Americans did not compile and publish them. Irmalotte Guttmann, a doctoral student whose thesis of 1927 represents one of the few attempts to ascertain box office results at middecade, found that many theater owners kept no accounts or only fragmentary records of ticket sales and receipts. Alexander Jason, another contemporary scholar who labored prodigiously to construct a comprehensive statistical picture of the German cinema, lamented that the trade tended to treat the relation between supply and demand more emotionally than scientifically. It had yet to grasp the supreme importance of complete, accurate data on theater attendance.[10]

Although it is safe to assume that trade generalizations about Hollywood's unpopularity partially drew on inside information about the success or failure of specific pictures, hard published data to support trade opinion was in short supply. Much testimony to moviegoers' disenchantment came from film critics and cannot be considered disinterested. The tendency to conflate signs of waning enthusiasm for American movies and analyses of its causes makes it extremely difficult to disentangle fact and interpretation. What follows presents tentative conclusions from the limited and somewhat conflicting evidence available.

It was Hollywood which in a twofold sense encouraged the first systematic attempts to determine audience preferences. American models of business operation suggested the importance of such information and Hollywood's presence in Germany provided the principal ax to grind in determination of German tastes. The only broad survey of moviegoing trends in this period was pioneered at middecade and was largely preoccupied with the issue of domestic versus foreign successes on the German feature film market. Beginning in late 1925 *Film-Kurier* invited theater owners to submit a list of their five best and three worst pictures at the box office. The results of this annual poll, for 1925 and each subsequent year, overwhelmingly endorsed prevailing opinion—German viewers preferred the native product.[11] How much this result can be trusted is quite another matter. Here, as in other statistical endeavors, the aversion to rigor apparent in neglect of accurate bookkeeping is still very much in evidence. Among numerous distorting factors were the unrepresentative number of replies in the first two years of the survey, the failure to correlate votes for a film and seating capacity of the theater (which ranged broadly from 300 to 2000) and the seasonal nature of the voting, which severely disadvantaged pictures whose exploitation began late or was spread across more than one season.[12] More serious inconsistencies followed from failure to ask exhibitors to rank their replies. Every mention of a title therefore received equal weight, obscuring a potentially enormous gap between the top five pictures. Finally, the very basis of the replies remains unclear: in some cases they presumably reflected box-office records; in others simply impressions and general recollections. In sum, as a rough guide to audience preferences, the *Film-Kurier* poll is valuable, especially since it was one of a kind in Weimar Germany, but it should not be confused with box-office precision.[13]

A primary agenda of the *Film-Kurier* poll—to determine Hollywood's place in German cinemas—dominated every other attempt from this period to determine the popularity of feature films. That agenda surfaces most blatantly in statistical evidence presented by Ludwig Scheer, president of the National Association of German Exhibitors, to the Association's annual conference in Düsseldorf in 1926. In defense of the independent exhibitors' crusade against Hollywood, Scheer cited attendance figures from his own operations in six provincial cities to argue that American films were ruining German cinemas. Comparing total attendance for "average" motion pictures, six German and six American, he claimed the former attracted 33,645 patrons in one week while the latter drew only 19,196. If one grants that the films and thus the week in question can be taken as representative, the relative weakness of American film in Germany seems difficult to deny. But Scheer was not content with this conclusion. Rather than qualifying his evidence he tried to construct from it an airtight case against Hollywood. Estimating that in the previous year 3,000 German cinemas had given half their playing time to American features, he extrapolated from his own figures to conclude that in 1925 Hollywood had cost

Jackie Coogan in *A Boy of Flanders*, set here amidst Berlin's daily press, 1925. (Photo courtesy Landesbildstelle Berlin)

The Son of the Sheik, with Rudolph Valentino and Vilma Banky, at the Capitol Theater, 1926. (Photo courtesy Ullstein Bilderdienst)

German theaters a grand total of 187,837,000 patrons—more than half again of the actual number.[14]

Such cavalier treatment of statistics from a leading business figure testifies to the emotion generated by Hollywood's inroads. In the absence of any more trustworthy and comprehensive data Scheer created his own patently self-serving calculations. As Alfred Rosenthal retorted, too many variables came into play to permit such sweeping conclusions from a handful of cases. A different set of figures could prove precisely the opposite argument.[15] Nonetheless, there is corroborative evidence—albeit still limited in scope—to suggest that the case Scheer tried to establish had some foundation in fact. In its middecade crisis UFA carried out a confidential audit in the distribution sector to compare the company's fortunes with domestic and American feature films. The report paints a picture

The Thief of Bagdad, with Douglas Fairbanks, at the Capitol Theater, 1925. (Photo courtesy Ullstein Bilderdienst)

Charley's Aunt, with Sydney Chaplin, at the Albert Schumann Theater, 1925. (Photo courtesy Landesbildstelle Berlin)

of crushing financial loss through pre-Parufamet commitments
to handle American film. In the crucial season 1925–1926 ten
of eleven pictures from Paramount, twelve of fifteen from Goldwyn, ten of fifteen from First National, and seven of twelve from
Warner Bros. each entailed losses of 10,000 marks or more for
UFA. Fully three-quarters of UFA's American releases fell into
this category, for losses totalling 1,283,796 marks! Only three
American pictures (Rin Tin Tin in *Lighthouse by the Sea,* Buster
Keaton's *The Navigator* and Victor Sjöström's *He Who Gets
Slapped*) showed significant profits. By contrast a mere four to
six percent of the remaining, mostly domestic, movies distrib-
uted by UFA caused losses greater than 10,000 marks.[16]

The UFA audit confirms the findings of *Film-Kurier* and the
very limited evidence offered by Ludwig Scheer. However, it

Barbed Wire, Erich Pommer's second Paramount production, starring Pola Negri, in its sixth week at UFA's Kurfürstendamm Theater, 1927. (*Kinematograph*, 16 October 1927, p. 22.)

Facade of UFA-Palast am Zoo for the premiere of the war picture, *Wings*, 1929. (Photo courtesy Ullstein Bilderdienst)

stands in considerable contrast to the most sophisticated analysis of moviegoers' preferences from this period, the dissertation by Irmalotte Guttmann to which reference has already been made. It too was preoccupied with German-American rivalry, seeking to explain and erect barriers against American inroads. It drew, moreover, on a combination of the sources used by UFA, *Film-Kurier* and Scheer. Guttmann questioned theater owners in Cologne and Danzig for specific case studies and gained access to the distribution records of Parufamet (1926–1927) as the basis for national conclusions. In the first instance she distinguished three grades of movie theaters—premiere, middle class and working class—to relate the types and origins of feature films to the social background of the audience.

Replies to the poll indicated that the best American films were popular at both extremes—in the movie palaces and among workers—while middling native productions best suited the petty bourgeoisie. Guttmann concluded that German producers were being displaced in two of three market categories, though she conceded that these results did not necessarily apply nation-wide.[17]

In the second section of her research she then checked these results over a larger area. On the basis of Parufamet's books she selected theaters from twenty-five cities with more than 200,000 inhabitants as test cases. Receipts from eighty theaters of all types showed that the least profitable German features drew much better than their American counterparts, but that the four most successful American movies outdrew German box office hits by more than 2:1.[18] These figures spoke for themselves, but Guttmann, like Scheer, had greater ambitions—to prove that Hollywood provided more of these successful pictures than did native producers. Abandoning empirical investigation she appealed to the opinions of experts to argue that in the previous season four times as many American as native features were hits on the German market. Her conclusion therefore had two aspects. American movies attracted a broader public—though less so the petty bourgeoisie—and Hollywood provided a much higher proportion of successful films.[19]

Since portions of Parufamet's books have been preserved in extant UFA files it is possible to exercise some historical control over Guttmann's conclusions. UFA, stung already by the audit of the season 1925–1926, had reason to monitor Parufamet's performance very carefully. After the new management under Alfred Hugenberg took charge in the spring of 1927, Parufamet's first season came under thorough review. The result was a picture of profit and loss from American pictures which corresponds closely to the perceptions of experts about the discrepancy between run-of-the-mill and outstanding Hollywood pictures. In terms of gross revenue, the fact that the combined income of Parufamet and UFA's own distribution agency equaled projections for the latter had Parufamet not been created intimated that UFA's own productions largely carried the company in 1926–1927.[20] A comparison of revenue from the feature films contributed by each company initially overturns that conclusion. In total rental receipts Metro-Goldwyn pictures easily topped those of UFA and Paramount. However, the source of this discrepancy was one motion picture, *Ben Hur*, which grossed over one-third of Parufamet's total revenue; alone more than all UFA pictures released by Parufamet and almost twice as much as all those from Paramount! Without *Ben Hur*, the income from eighteen UFA pictures roughly equaled that from thirty-one features of Paramount and Metro-Goldwyn, substantiating UFA's estimate that an average UFA release was worth twice as much as an average American film. Moreover, apart from *Ben Hur*, Metro-Goldwyn's performance on the German market was almost entirely disappointing.[21]

The rental records Parufamet forwarded weekly to UFA did not, unfortunately, include breakdowns by city. It is therefore impossible to comment directly on Guttmann's assertions about the superior performance of the best American pictures in the largest urban areas. Cumulative totals indicate that UFA produced at least as many winners at the box office as the American companies combined. There is also some evidence that UFA's exhibition division had to cope with the backlash caused by American motion pictures which alienated German moviegoers.[22]

What can one conclude from this rather fragmentary, uneven and at times contradictory evidence about the popularity of American feature films in Germany? Although no formula can reconcile Guttmann's research, the *Film-Kurier* poll, Ludwig Scheer's findings and UFA's records, with proper qualifiers several generalizations can be made. Given the shifting terms of reference of these sources, extrapolation from any one of them without controlling dependent variables through the others is perilous. Guttmann's dissertation is both unique and invaluable, not least for its attention to the moviegoing habits of different social groups. By focusing on box-office hits it directly challenges the broader findings of the *Film-Kurier* poll. However, by the same token it sidestepped a crucial issue, namely, whether run-of-the-mill American pictures were hurting theater business.[23] Since no one, including Ludwig Scheer, denied the appeal of select American films, this constituted a serious evasion. Moreover, Guttmann's research did not cast much light on trends outside the purview of Parufamet, the largest but by no means a monopolistic distributor. What her results do indicate is that a single season, 1926–1927, does not make a trend. UFA's experience with American features in 1925–1926 proved singularly unhappy. By contrast, interim results for Parufamet's second year, 1927–1928, indicate that although Metro-Goldwyn pictures continued to perform miserably, Paramount films outdrew those from UFA by a substantial margin.[24]

What stands out on the basis of distribution records is the enormous range of responses to Hollywood. At one extreme, *Ben Hur* represented a phenomenon probably without equal in the 1920s. At the other extreme, numerous American features failed to do more than cover their rental costs. Here then appears confirmation of trade opinion that German viewers had grown tired of American *Durchschnitt* but still enjoyed the outstanding imports. However, to argue that Hollywood's average movies flopped begs further definition. In terms of production cost *Ben Hur*, for instance, certainly ranked as an outstanding motion picture, yet to disgruntled critics it typified much of what was wrong with Hollywood. Conversely, what was standard fare for the American market, such as a Rin Tin Tin picture or a feature slapstick, could qualify as a special attraction for German moviegoers. Insofar as the receipts for Parufamet pictures are a guide, the least attractive of Hollywood's products were society dramas. Nonetheless, no fixed set of criteria distinguished American pictures which won popular approval. In some instances star value appears determinative: *La Bohème* with Lillian Gish and Harold Lloyd's *The Freshman* were hits of 1926–1927. In other cases, such as the war picture *Hotel Imperial* and a film about the foreign legion, *Beau Geste*, subject matter and dramatic treatment probably weighed more heavily. *Ben Hur*'s phenomenal success presumably was rooted in its sensational mass scenes. Although in each of these cases budgets exceeded all but the most extravagant in Germany, and production values were correspondingly of the first rank, this is no demonstration that the most popular American pictures were uniformly the most expensive to produce.

By the same token, despite some hard data to support impressionistic evidence of sagging public interest in American movies, it is misleading to assume a uniform public. As Guttmann's study indicates, popular appeal varied according to the social background of the audience as well as film type and nationality. The relatively homogenous public which experts tended to assume did not exist. Distinctions between the working class and the petty bourgeoisie, although insignificant economically, continued to shape status perceptions and motion picture preferences.[25]

With all these qualifications to accepted wisdom it is clear that Hollywood was anything but synonymous with motion picture entertainment in Germany by the mid-1920s. American motion pictures encountered a somewhat jaundiced public and did not command respect on the basis of their origins alone. Some types enjoyed more appreciation than others, depending in part on the social composition of the audience. Otherwise it is difficult to generalize. UFA's pre-Parufamet audit probably came closest to summarizing the very uneven popular appreciation for Hollywood when it concluded laconically that further unpleasant consequences would ensue if in the future Paramount and Metro-Goldwyn pictures were not chosen with greater caution. This warning, ironic given that it came after signature of the Parufamet agreement, and doubly ironic in light of the box-office success of *Ben Hur,* indicates that American motion pictures could be both bane and blessing in the German context.[26]

Against this backdrop, Hans Pander's defense of Hollywood must be read with a critical eye, but nonetheless taken seriously. For although Pander's case was predicated on American popularity, it ultimately aimed to challenge the economic argument for Hollywood's international hegemony at its weakest point, namely, its fatalism. As indicated above, no one serious about German film culture counseled selling out to America on the grounds that competition had become hopeless. But many compartmentalized their thinking to locate the source of German problems in exogenous factors by treating the motion picture as an article of trade.[27] Pander adopted this treatment, but turned conventional wisdom against itself by asking why Germans refused to be consistent in their approach. If the Americans suc-

ceeded essentially because they respected the industrial nature
of the medium and followed sound marketing practices, why
did German producers not copy them? Hollywood was an industry whose primary task was "to produce such a commodity
as the market either demands or as it can at least absorb." Consequently, it subordinated technical possibilities or the personal
preferences of the director or performers to the tastes and de-
sires of moviegoers. Since sound business practices counted
more than national tastes or artistic innovation, Pander concluded Hollywood earned its hegemony.

> Whoever sees German and American films regularly simply can-
> not fail to notice that on the average the Americans are better, i.e.
> not better made, but better calculated from the start, with a more
> confident psychology of the consumer.[28]

Without denying America's enviable financial preconditions or
its seemingly inborn cinematic sense, Pander indicated that
American producers prospered by virtue of organizational and
marketing techniques which were well within the grasp of German filmmakers.

Although one does not have to search very far to discover
other commentators critical of unremunerative aestheticism,
Pander's outspoken admiration for Hollywood's orientation was
not typical, especially at middecade. The previous chapter
noted critical and public rebellion against the very practice Pander seemed to applaud, that is, mathematically precise calculation by American producers of the relative proportions of good,
evil, romance, sensationalism and emotion blended in every
movie. Apart from the fact that the specific American blend
offended German sensibilities, its very calculatedness and predictability created distaste. Pander claimed not to believe this,
rejecting orthodox opinion on national taste differences and
Hollywood's unpopularity. Nonetheless, he was not alone in
suggesting that even now Hollywood had lessons to teach.
Whether schoolmaster or outcast it encouraged perception of
German problems through American lenses. Even critics disgruntled with its films interpreted its hegemony in terms which
implicitly endorsed partial Americanization of German culture.
Roland Schacht, whose account of Hollywood's waning popu-

larity has already been examined, offers a prime illustration of the critic's dilemma. As early as 1923 Schacht had insisted that the crisis in the German film industry which opened the door to Hollywood could not be written off to economic difficulties: it flowed from failures in management, imagination and dedication. At middecade he took up this theme with a vengeance, stressing the importance of efficient business methods and need for a consistent production rationale.[29] Anticipating Pander, Schacht argued that Germany had no lack of talent, the best of which surpassed America's frontrunners, but failed to organize and exploit its strength with the dedication characteristic of Hollywood. The domestic film industry did not adhere to the "simple business rule that customers must be offered real value for their money if one wants to make a profit."[30] Schacht denigrated the schematicism of Hollywood, yet he believed the German cinema could profit from its example. Like Pander he approved American commitment to popular impact or entertainment and compared it favorably with the German aspiration to create film art.

> The German who makes art is unconcerned about whether the company financing him is thereby economically ruined. The American says to himself: how can it be art and what use is it if no one wants it, if people don't even want to lay out the price of admission voluntarily to see it? And who will give me money any longer so that I can make art if I ruin one company after another?
> The German either makes art for himself in a vacuum, at best for his class, to which he occasionally condescends to be willing to elevate even the "lower" people, without giving a thought to the economic basis of his production, or unscrupulously and bent on nothing more than quick profit he makes trash for the mob.[31]

Against what he called artistic "contempt for the masses" in Germany, Schacht set the "democratic worldview" of America which understood culture as a consensual phenomenon rather than the preserve of an educated elite. He concluded that "in the final analysis film production is thus a social problem. It demands connectedness, community with the people."[32]

Schacht's dissection of American film culture isolates characteristics which in one respect had already become platitudes. It was a commonplace that Hollywood reflected the New World's democratic traditions and social leveling. Its ability to appeal to the lowest common denominator, recognized from the beginning of the decade, was initially related primarily to filmic ingredients such as shot rhythms, acting styles, or narrative tempos. By middecade, terms of reference had shifted to approximate those familiar to subsequent scholarship, namely, rationalization of production, star value, advertising strategies and audience identification with screen characters. This shift in emphasis from technical-artistic impulses to the organizational and public dimensions of the medium brought experts face to face with tensions in their own visions for motion picture development.[33]

Since 1918 German interest in foreign markets had dictated respect for America's motion picture mentality. Postinflationary reaction against Hollywood challenged that respect. Viable competitive strategies against American cinema remained elusive. Roland Schacht, while making Hollywood's agenda inescapable for domestic development even as he resisted mass American import, groped towards a third way between national solipsism and international (i.e., American) homogeneity which would supply a radical cure for domestic production and exhibition woes. By explicitly anchoring the cinema in sociocultural context Schacht made domestic problems the symptoms of broader developments. His focus fell not on economic or legal questions, but on the dualism between art and popular culture, particularly on filmmakers whose artistic consciences caused disdain for commercial considerations. Even when they sought to create popular, commercially successful motion pictures, their awareness of condescending to mass sensibilities robbed their work of conviction and impact. To create in bad faith inevitably resulted in inconsistent pictures which failed to grip broad audiences.[34]

The remedy Schacht suggested was obvious enough: re-education or replacement of filmmakers who believed art and popular culture to be incompatible. But by the inexorable logic of his own argument it could only be implemented in conjunction with a cultural revolution. The source and nature of that revolution could hardly be in doubt. Americanization of German assumptions about the relationship between culture and society, if not of society itself, was necessary to permit native filmmakers to rival their American counterparts. Schacht declined, given his aversion to aspects of the American model, to state the case so plainly, but his arguments pointed unmistakably in this direction.[35]

The unspoken conclusion yielded by Schacht's analysis of domestic cinema problems emerges from the arguments of others dedicated to preservation of a distinct German cinema. Herbert Ihering, even more strongly opposed to Hollywood's breed of cultural imperialism, came independently to equally ambivalent conclusions. Like Pander and Schacht, he too rejected one-track economic explanations for the misfortunes of native production. He also cited a fundamental distinction between American and German approaches to film production which was rooted in different understandings of the relationship between art and popular culture and between culture and technology. Whereas the German cinema, uncertain of its public role, oscillated between artistic experiments and popularizing, Hollywood knew no such bifurcation. The link between cinema and society emerges once again as the critical issue.

> In America the cinema is immediate because the producers are themselves the public. In Germany they either consider themselves better: literati and intellectuals; or they are worse: speculators and dealers. . . . Perhaps the cinema requires an impersonal, a nonisolated public—America—and not an individualized one—Germany. In America the film public is there from the beginning. In Germany it has to be created by each film.[36]

Since the problem lay as much with the consumer as the producer, its solution clearly lay beyond tinkering with German cinematic technique or borrowing from Hollywood. American dramatic devices derived authenticity and impact from the indivisibility of filmmaker and public. What for the German producer would be deliberate falsification—in Schacht's terminology, conscious condescension to popular taste—and thus unconvincing, succeeded in Hollywood because there was no concession or compromise born of the gulf separating producer and consumer. Ihering therefore expressly warned against the superficial, futile exercise of copying dramatic devices indigenous to Hollywood. Instead, like Schacht, he covertly advised the need for cultural Americanization. This he understood as a process of reconciliation between technology and preindustrial cultural norms. What in Germany remained a proverbial gap between culture and technology had been bridged in the United States.[37] Until Germany paralleled this achievement Ihering believed native film production would be poorly synchronized with its audience.

> When a generation has grown up in Germany which has risen with the inventions [of modern society], which does not know a world without the telephone, radio, cinema and the automobile; when therefore technology has also become a matter of course for us, . . . when there is experience and intellect again beyond technology, then there will also be a public in Germany again, then the German cinema and even the German theater will exist.[38]

Thus although Ihering welcomed Americanization of German culture even less than Schacht, his prescription for establishing the cinema's popular relevance included it.

Schacht and Ihering followed a logical sequence in arriving at reluctant approval of the American model. The first step was rejection of a purely economic rationale for American film supremacy. Its corollary was refusal to accept German misfortune as predetermined. This brought solutions into the realm of the possible but also forced a search for mistakes and misconceptions. This search identified characteristics within German culture which militated against competitive film production. Without absolving native filmmakers, Schacht and Ihering decided that cultural preconditions required modification to place domestic production on a sound footing. The United States provided the obvious source of inspiration for this task not only because of Hollywood's current hegemony but because American culture as a whole exhibited many features thought to be signposts of the future for industrial societies. Neither critic advocated blind or wholesale adoption of Hollywood's methods, yet both intimated the need for Americanization.[39]

The reflections of Pander, Schacht and Ihering contextualize a better known and direct debate on German misfortune conducted by another prominent critical trio. In early 1928 Kurt

Pinthus, Willy Haas and Béla Balázs locked horns over the origins of the domestic film malaise. Pinthus opened the debate with a wide-ranging lament about current circumstances. From the opaque assertion that the German predicament followed less from economic factors than from the "miserable quality" of German film, he developed an indictment not only of shoddy workmanship in German production but of the import legislation and American capital which encouraged cheap, third-rate "quota films." A stinging rebuke, worthy of Schacht at his most vehement, of the complacency, carelessness and incapability of German producers, Pinthus's argument simultaneously supported trade opinion that the German cinema was fulfilling the role to which American supremacy relegated it.[40]

The replies to Pinthus from Haas and Balázs approached the German problem quite differently, but in each case the American cinema formed the essential reference point. Pinthus had openly admitted the superiority of American motion pictures. Haas made Hollywood's industrial and financial hegemony, more precisely its dependence on Wall Street, the overriding factor in contemporary motion picture development. Balázs focused directly on the theme elaborated by Schacht, the fusion in American culture of art and popularity. Significantly, neither Haas nor Pinthus could avoid reference to this theme even though they emphasized other issues. Haas continued to entertain visions of a third cinematic way fusing American technology and German creativity. He refused to concede that the American model was the only one possible for overcoming the antithesis between art and popular culture. The "decisive battle" over whether film would serve or command the human race remained to be fought.[41] While Haas clearly aspired to command, Pinthus decided the motion picture could only serve: he advised domestic filmmakers to surrender considerations of quality in order to achieve popular appeal. Balázs challenged this last opinion directly, without endorsing Haas. In language reminiscent of Pander he rephrased the dualism as that between "good" art and "popular" art. Against Pinthus he argued that Hollywood made allies of these categories while German filmmakers treated them as antagonists. Like Schacht, Balázs thought the problem not unique to the cinema, but a symptom of cultural standards inbred in the educated middle class. What Pinthus dubbed the film crisis therefore represented one aspect of a general crisis in German culture which had to be overcome to establish domestic production on a sound footing.[42]

To Haas, Balázs and Pinthus America represented financial power, a cultural model and a cinematic model respectively. The latter two implied the need for Americanization, though neither welcomed the prospect any more than Schacht or Ihering. In another context (see chapter seven below) Haas came to very similar conclusions, though no more willingly than his critical colleagues. Ultimately none of these very acute observers of German cultural trends was prepared to recommend Americanization. Too discriminating and realistic to accept as satisfactory standard explanations for Hollywood's global preponderance, they remained too disturbed by features of American culture to advocate its general adoption for German purposes. Unlike the dramatists in Hollywood, they could not introduce some *deus ex machina* to rescue them from the impasse. What they required was a formula which while giving due recognition to Hollywood also gave domestic filmmakers clear direction. Blanket anti-Americanism could not stand close scrutiny, yet the German cinema still needed to distinguish itself from Hollywood.

The dilemma faced by German cinema was that of any culture threatened by displacement or extinction, namely, whether borrowing presents a viable method of preserving independence. To enter into competition with Hollywood implied accepting American terms of reference. It simultaneously stiffened resistance to American methods and mentalities. As noted in chapter two, debate revolved around whether native filmmakers could best compete internationally by cultivating a national or cosmopolitan style. Preference for the former coexisted with vagueness about what constituted "German" cinema. By middecade sentiment hardened that native talent should not try to imitate American models, not least because these had become so pervasive in Germany. But against sentiment had to be set the uncomfortable reality of American hegemony and the size of its market, the vital context for UFA's decision to collaborate with Hollywood and orient production to American consumers. Not surprisingly then, the search continued for a third way.

In terms of critical discourse, a vague filmic application of *Neue Sachlichkeit* became the formula by which some experts hoped to discover new terrain. The quest for a comprehensive solution to German problems necessitated demolition of the barrier between commercial and aesthetic categories. So long as Hollywood dominated cinema screens, laments about its character and alleged unpopularity confused the search for a national alternative. Reluctance to advocate the outright Americanization of German culture pushed some experts to seek the foundation for a national cinema in another sphere. *Neue Sachlichkeit*, a cultural mode lifted partly from the American socio-economic example, became a device for distinguishing German motion pictures from Hollywood, reaffirming the possibility of a popular national cinema and avoiding Americanization.[43] Since realism stood at the pole opposite American untruthfulness in respect of characterization, emotional content and causality, it formed the obvious antidote to Hollywood. Pundits counseled filmmakers to borrow business and stylistic matter-of-factness from Hollywood but treat subjects of current national interest. This counsel also conformed to what was perceived as the drift of public tastes away from pomp and cheap emotionalism.

> Sentiment is no longer in order. The world of traffic lights, of radio transmission of dance music and of technological autocracy doesn't like lovers who walk hand in hand into the setting sun. It smiles at mystical gentlemen from the criminal underworld. There are no more Casanovas, no Cagliostros, no robbers. The big adventurer is anonymous. [The world] hails the more palpable heroism of the Tunneys, the oceanic intoxication of the Chamberlains and the Kohls, the six-day racers and fashion queens.[44]

Yet if German experts employed realism as the acid test of a motion picture's excellence, Hollywood's hegemony could not be broken with a trendy formula, particularly one as ambiguous as realism. Its attraction is understandable enough: it appeared to promise both intellectual respectability and popularity. Contemporary, down-to-earth themes could broaden the appeal of the native cinema without requiring it to bow openly to Hollywood.[45] Yet as the case of *Greed* illustrates, it was not a cureall. Béla Balázs responded sharply to the "fashionable slogan of the realist dogmatists" because he saw in it the same intellectual tendencies—abstractness and doctrinairism—which traditionally hampered German film creativity. A new slogan would not bring salvation to German cinema. Adducing the recent works of Charlie Chaplin, the most highly respected of American film personalities, Balázs maintained that success could not be ascribed to realism. In reaction against kitschy romanticism, critics missed the point:

> The opposite of false is not real but genuine, the opposite of mendacious is not real but truthful, the opposite of lifeless and empty is not real but alive, striking, graphic. Even a fairy tale can be genuine, truthfully striking, graphic. Just as a Chaplin fairy tale is. . . . For there is no reality without the human being, without his feelings, moods and dreams.[46]

By this definition realism had nothing to do with Erich Stroheim's naturalism. It referred rather to that ability to capture common human sentiments which Schacht and Pander credited to Hollywood. Balázs's enlistment of Chaplin, rather than domestic achievements, to substantiate his argument, pointed back to Hollywood even as it sought to refocus the German cinema agenda. The next chapter documents how Chaplin and the entire slapstick tradition were enlisted to address discontinuities perceived in German film culture.

6

COMIC REDEMPTION
The Slapstick Synthesis[1]

People argue about the good, the best, the artistic and the "most popular" film and forget that there is a genre which I dare say always pleases the tastes of all classes of public most: those irrepressible American slapsticks in which the goings-on are so delightfully unsentimental, so tremendously reckless . . . and whose overflowing humor is simply based on a completely unadorned and open depiction of grotesque, bizarre everyday reality and its very abundant melancholy-amusing "side" effects.[2]

The dissatisfaction with American film which pervaded the entire spectrum of trade and nonspecialist publications, if general, was neither universal nor entirely consistent. As reaction against Hollywood became the rule, exceptions to it were explicitly admitted by pleas that German screens show only the best of Hollywood. "Outstanding" films should be imported; "average" pictures should remain in America. Each category presupposed the existence of the other. However, the line between them fluctuated widely depending on the ebb or flow of the import tide and individual preferences. Thanks to sheer enormity and diversity, Hollywood's output repeatedly shattered stereotypes imposed on it. Even in the period when Hollywood became a byword for kitsch and predictability, select American films or film types drew attention as filmically innovative and humanly valuable.

By middecade contemporaries rarely identified these pictures on anything but a film-by-film basis. In the period of initiation classification according to genre had seemed both satisfactory and convenient. Society dramas, slapstick, westerns, and historical pictures were identified and ranked by type and polish. But these categories became increasingly inadequate guides to German opinion. Growing familiarity with Hollywood introduced such kaleidoscopic variety into German movie programs and punctured so many commonplaces that a catalogue of noteworthy motion pictures defied summary classification and treatment. Numerous performers acquired German profiles. One could devote individual attention to those like Mary Pickford, Lillian Gish, Douglas Fairbanks or Jackie Coogan, whose representative role in American culture bestowed significance beyond star attraction. Imaginative and cinematographic achievements which intrigued German experts, such as the cartoon, could likewise receive detailed consideration. Yet no simple criteria entirely distinguished motion pictures of average from those of outstanding qualities.

None of this is terribly surprising, except insofar as the swell of anti-American sentiment creates an impression of consistency which did not obtain. It is not the case, however, that no discernible patterns emerge from the crosscurrents of opinion. Just as specific characteristics of American pictures proved particularly irritating, so others commanded appreciation and interest. This chapter and the one that follows it examine two generic types, within which critics or audiences discovered traits deserving attention and approbation. Each in its own way lacked direct German parallels. Motion pictures made by German émigrés to the United States constituted by definition a unique Hollywood product, whose relationship to previous German production drew immediate attention. Slapstick comedy was identified almost from first exposure as a specialty for which Germany had scant counterpart. While winning recognition as a genre which embodied America's motion picture peculiarities, it proved less vulnerable to critical or popular demolition than other American genres. Although archetypically American, thus un-German in mentality, style and tempo, it earned a place in German theaters and repeatedly compelled critics to qualify damning judgments of Hollywood.

Slapstick movies came to Germany in two distinct forms. One or two act shorts, normally used as program fillers, became familiar during the era of inflation. Because they were exempt from import restrictions, by 1925 they had virtually wiped out domestic production of short entertainment pictures. Feature length slapstick films arrived on the German market relatively late—1923–1924—and remained a relatively small portion of all American features released. However, they drew attention disproportionate to their numbers. Together with the shorts they did much to create and define laughter for Weimar movie-goers.

The first impression made by the shorts which appeared in 1921 and 1922 did not augur well for slapstick's critical reputation. Even the work of Charlie Chaplin, the king of the genre and a living legend, provoked limited and not always friendly commentary. Elsewhere, especially in France, he had already been elevated by artists and intellectuals from an entertainer to a universal principle.[3] In Germany he met neither immediate nor unanimous acclaim. With the other films in the first wave of slapstick imports, his usually received only passing attention. Worship of Chaplin amounted to sectarianism, as the first high priest of the cult, Hans Siemsen, was later to boast.

In the autumn of 1921 Chaplin had made a triumphal return (his first) to England and had also visited the continent. The British received him almost as royalty. He was wined and dined by the élite and overwhelmed by a flood of letters and petitions from movie fans. The French accorded him a similar reception, crowning it with decoration by the state. But in Berlin he was essentially ignored. According to his own account he went unrecognized until spotted by a former prisoner of war held in England who became so excited he embraced and kissed the famous tramp.[4] Despite subsequent contact with film circles in the German capital, Chaplin rightly portrayed his stay in Berlin in stark contrast to those in Paris and London. The fact that the first of his older shorts (*The Rink*, made in 1916) had finally just been shown in Berlin theaters weighed little against the wartime exposure to his work in Britain and France which had generated such a massive, enthusiastic following.[5]

Siemsen took critical reserve to Chaplin as a measure of German national isolation after the war. While everywhere else on the globe Chaplin was publicly idolized, Germans continued to worship their erstwhile war heroes.[6] Delayed exposure to his work certainly conditioned the way in which it was received.

Apart from the fact that the initial releases were already well aged when they appeared in German cinemas, as shorts they did not typically merit more than passing notice from German critics. However, other factors also came into play. Although critics admitted that German audiences laughed hysterically, they simultaneously trivialized or dismissed the source of laughter. The parallel with attitudes toward the sensationalist serials is striking, not least in critical distance from public responses and in predictions that the genre would wear poorly. The tongue-in-cheek remark that animals in the zoo adjoining the UFA-Palast planned legal suits against moviegoers for infringement of patent on roars, shrieks and bellows emitted in response to Charlie's antics inferred mutual lack of sophistication on the part of film and audience.

> If Charlie Chaplin currently dominates German movie theaters that means little or nothing for the future or the value of German comedy. . . . A briskly acted, action-packed German comedy has a much higher value than the essentially silly American clown tricks! The audience may well be laughing for the moment at Chaplin's incredible nonsense, but is neither amused in the sense of that word nor satisfied.[7]

It was the combination of primitiveness and silliness which offended critical sensibilities. Childishness, coarseness and disproportion between form and content headed the list of complaints. Even when comic value could not be disputed, critics referred to the "perfect nonsense" or "nothingness" of Chaplin's scripts and expressed distaste for the juvenile and excessively brutal character of his comedy.[8] The underlying theme was the irreconcilability of the German and American sense of humor. Such discord provoked intensely personal reactions.

> He remains a splendid joker in a mediocre field. However filmic, however filmoid he may be; however much he may conform to the a priori of film, however much he moves in keeping with the laws of the camera—it does not especially move me. I speak German—not American. I'm not a child on the potty with a thick cigar in my mouth. Much may seem very humorous—I'm not fond of jokes based on mechanical things, on machines and objects. He is brilliant

in his own style, but this style has so far not been very rich in content.[9]

Willy Haas, later an outspoken Chaplin enthusiast, accused the comedian of drawing laughter from contradictory human impulses. At one moment Chaplin primed audiences to laugh at acts of treacherous cruelty. The next moment amusement sprang from expressions of human sympathy. This created emotional schizophrenia, scrambling the logic of human relationships and preventing full identification with his humor.[10]

While critics carped, audiences responded with gales of laughter which by all accounts were without precedent in German cinemas.[11] Slapstick shorts, led primarily by the works of Chaplin, Fatty Arbuckle and Harold Lloyd, captured the popular imagination to the point that in 1922 exhibitors began to book whole programs of them in place of feature films. More than ever, critics now had occasion to evaluate both the films and their public reception. The disgruntled continued to predict that, like the serialized sensationalist films dumped on the market in 1921–1922, slapstick would eventually wear out its welcome among German viewers. Endless repetition promised to nullify the attraction of its momentarily fascinating tempos and stunts.[12] Those, by contrast, who began to recognize in the genre, particularly the dated Chaplin shorts, comic value for which Germany had scant counterpart, sided with the public. Even before they discovered metaphysical principles or political messages in slapstick, they joined moviegoers in gratitude for the sidesplitting laughter.[13]

To the extent that dissatisfaction with this genre persisted through middecade, it adopted arguments used to deprecate Hollywood in general. Defensiveness about Germany's cultural orientation generated resistance to this facet of the American invasion as well. It remained rooted in the assumption that American comic formulae did not match or satisfy German requirements. Applying criteria appropriate to other media and styles, some critics denigrated slapstick as unsubstantial, repetitive and unsuited to German tastes. Hand in hand with charges of vacuous screenplays went disparagement of the acting as really nothing more than schematized clowning.[14] More broadly, slapstick, like the serialized westerns, functioned as the embodiment of American primitiveness and a corrosive influence in Germany. Paul Sorgenfrei argued that although audiences were spellbound and laughed hysterically at American slapstick, public tastes were being totally corrupted by overexposure. He rationalized this judgment with a well-worn contrast: Germans treated film as art or culture while Americans baptized it as commercial enterprise. American slapstick did not deserve classification as comedy as Germans understood the term.[15]

The leap from comic styles to national mentalities served, as in the past, to put forward a cinematic agenda. Maxim Ziese, lead critic for *Deutsche Allgemeine Zeitung,* articulated this emphatically in response to Buster Keaton's *The Navigator.* Although Ziese conceded that the audience of UFA-Palast thoroughly enjoyed Keaton's peculiar blend of comic ingredients, he took pains to point out that slapstick was not art because it involved neither thought nor human feeling. It amounted only to a technologically mediated way of seeing the world.[16] Ziese thereby smuggled into his review a barely disguised version of a rationale popular among intransigent opponents of the cinema: a medium dependent on mechanical means of reproduction could not produce art. That someone who took film seriously enough to criticize it should borrow this argument suggests that slapstick occasioned a hostile reflex by drawing attention to the technological dimensions of the medium.[17] Although that reflex did not dominate critical opinion, it had more than curiosity value, for it is detectable in less blatant forms even among those who endorsed Hollywood's comic formula. The latter differed in gleaning from these films a much-needed corrective to domestic approaches, but their admiration was still largely rooted in presuppositions shared by slapstick's opponents. Ironically, slapstick was enlisted to affirm very traditional artistic standards.

As already noted, initial critical approval of slapstick shorts presupposed willingness to laugh along with German audiences. As described by Kurt Pinthus, that willingness came from a conversion experience in which tears of laughter suspended scepticism and critical impulses.[18] Common to it was appreciation for comic moments which domestic producers did not offer. Heinz Pol, chief critic for the *Vossische Zeitung*, related his own and audience enthusiasm to Hollywood's ability to provide truly funny entertainment in the midst of Germany's depressing postwar circumstances.[19] Others tied enjoyment less to slapstick's therapeutic benefits in difficult times than to its compensation for deficiencies in the German sense of humor. Paul Medina interpreted the slapstick craze as a sign of an undeveloped and thus almost insatiable national appetite for comedy. "From a very uncultivated disposition toward humor extremely greedy for it, we cannot get enough of it. We want a ton of whipping cream immediately. Thus it happens that we overstuff ourselves earlier than is necessary."[20] Exploring these assumptions Paul Ickes and Joseph Aubinger confronted the apparent inability of domestic filmmakers to satisfy the national appetite. The key to slapstick was a playful attitude toward a hostile world. Germans lacked that key, for despite numerous reasons to feel tricked and cheated, they perceived their situation so fatalistically that they failed to capitalize on its comic possibilities. American slapstick exposed Germans' inability to see themselves and find laughter in the less admirable of their national foibles.

> We are too self-tormenting, too learned, too conscientious, too fussy, too much in need of censorship and mothering. We are passable cobblers of drama, masterminds of all possible and impossible areas; jacks-of-all-trades but masters of none; we don't know how to laugh at our own folly.[21]

Betrayed politically, cheated by the Treaty of Versailles and the victim of an unstable currency, Germans desperately needed laughter but seemed incapable of creating it. Slapstick movies therefore did for Germany what it could not do for itself.

Praise for the capacity of slapstick to satisfy moviegoers and provide a filmic recipe for which German producers had scant counterpart parallels closely the more appreciative evaluations of the early serialized imports. Just as the American frontier offered a venue for chases, fights and daredevilry that domestic filmmakers could not duplicate, so Hollywood provided a home for gags and stunts matched by no other film industry. Yet here the parallel ends. Critics acknowledged the demand for westerns, but they showed relatively little interest in exploring its social or cultural relevance. Slapstick, by contrast, provoked critical attention and with it a striking metamorphosis of opinion. By middecade it had become the source of searching reflections on man, machine and the modern age. It offered heuristic as well as entertainment value, material for rumination as well as diversion, interest for cultured as well as general audiences. More by accident than design, American film humor promised redemption from a number of interlocking cultural impasses.

The outstanding exception to the generalization that slapstick initially merited only brief asides or applause for generating laughter was the critical response of Hans Siemsen. Even before the slapstick shorts appeared in German cinemas, Siemsen indicated acquaintance with Chaplin from travel abroad and began to use him as a model for German filmmakers. In 1922 he wrote a series of articles on Chaplin in *Die Weltbühne* which subsequently appeared as a slim monograph.[22] One of these was dedicated to the political dimension of his work and laid the foundation for his later reputation as a friend of the working classes. Without fixing a party political label on him Siemsen insisted that he was a revolutionary because he consistently challenged the established social order. In his role as a social outcast he exposed as hollow and inhuman the values defended by his betters.[23] The bulk of Siemsen's commentary on Chaplin focused, however, on his personal discovery and exploitation of the laws of the medium. As author, performer and director, Chaplin reunited creative roles which had become fragmented by the specialization and rationalization of the motion picture industry. He therefore earned the title of the first authentic artist of the cinema. Both on these grounds, and because Chaplin championed universal human values, Siemsen assigned his work epochal significance.[24]

Siemsen's fulsome praise of Chaplin, while derivative in an international context, pioneered philosophical reflections on the man and his work in Germany.[25] Simultaneously, slapstick moved into the mainstream of German debates on the artistic boundaries of cinema and the role of Hollywood in domestic culture. Its assimilation reflected, on the one hand, the stylistic refinement and growing sophistication of the genre as feature film and, on the other hand, evolution in the conditions of its German reception. Until late 1923 German moviegoers' experience of slapstick was restricted to shorts made during or immediately following the war. Only from the end of the great inflation, with the release of *The Kid,* did feature-length comedies by the outstanding trio of Charlie Chaplin, Harold Lloyd and Buster Keaton appear on the market. While the import of shorts continued unabated, as did the practice of using them to create entire theater programs, the release of the comic features proved timely. Just as Hollywood's reputation suffered a relapse, its comic specialty assumed characteristics that encouraged serious treatment from German critics.[26] The feature-length works smoothed some of the coarser features of the genre and boasted narrational and compositional sophistication which gave them prominence disproportionate to their numbers. In retrospect it could be argued that the mature feature films transcended the boundaries of slapstick, becoming less frenetic in tempo, less chaotic in organization and more reflective in style. Granted these differences, however, contemporaries generally treated the feature films as extensions of the early shorts.[27]

Maturation from *Beiprogramm* to feature marked a timely shift in orientation, but one met more than halfway by an independent pursuit on the side of its recipients to make sense out of nonsense. As the quintessentially American, un-German form of humor became a fixture in cinema programs, the challenge to critics to decipher its relevance for the German condition became sharper.[28] In the first encounter, German commentators puzzled over how to read creative works indifferent to the usual canons of narrative structure and causality. Attention focused primarily on two distinctive features of the genre: meticulous precision in execution and filmic fantasy. On more than one occasion Roland Schacht isolated the discrepancy between the American and German work ethic as the primary reason for the international appeal of slapstick and the relatively limited interest in German film humor. He judged Harold Lloyd, for example, a second- or third-rate performer, but believed he came by his fame honestly because he outworked his competitors in Germany. Lloyd and other American comedians expended incalculable effort on each scene for just a few seconds of laughter.[29] Inseparable from devotion to the craft was imaginative richness. In some instances this left German experts stunned or overwhelmed. Their stupefaction is nicely captured in a comment by Kurt Pinthus on Harold Lloyds's *A Sailor-Made Man:* it contained such an abundance of gags that ten German companies could each make ten comedies from them, any one of which would be funnier than any ten German comedies put together.[30]

While diligence and creativity prompted widespread admiration, narrative substance and structure were relegated to subordinate status. More clearly than in any other genre the "how" took precedence over the "what." Meager or completely chaotic plots proved no obstacle to captivating and successful motion pictures. Taken to the extreme this meant that total absence of conventional plot development was no obstacle to excellence.[31] Yet consistent though it was to de-emphasize narrational qualities when praising slapstick for other virtues, the broader significance of this American comic specialty was not so conveniently settled. By presenting the extreme case of form over content, of the "how" outweighing the "what," of technique and the technical overpowering logic or coherence, of the optical dominating the cerebral, slapstick challenged ingrained beliefs. After years of effort to elevate the movies from a purely technical, juvenile amusement to an art form, experts encountered comic nonsense which inferred that film obeyed other imperatives. In this way slapstick invited reordering of cinematic priorities.[32]

Discourse on the slapstick challenge fractured in three main directions. The first, already examined, rebelled against its purely optical, technical impulse and dismissed it as symptomatic of motion picture immaturity. This meant consigning it to motion picture history. The second, its mirror image, discarded traditional standards and deduced from slapstick new motion picture laws, thereby making it a signpost to the future. Rudolf Arnheim, like Hans Siemsen, embraced slapstick as proof that the cinema respected an optical rather than a discursive or narrational logic. With remarkable consistency he argued that in revealing the priority of visual impressions over psychological connectedness, slapstick led the field in the race to create film art.[33] The final direction paralleled the search for a third way to meet the overall threat of Americanization. It sought a blend of traditional ends and innovative means, thus borrowing from slapstick without acceptance of all its ramifications.

Pursuit of this third path meant rationalizing personal and public enjoyment of slapstick while preserving critical distance from its broader challenge. Here refusal to see the optical, technical impulse of the motion picture as a characteristic only of its infantile stage did not equal endorsement of knockabout comedy as a general cinematic model. As Rudolf Arnheim observed, despite effusive praise for Hollywood's unique brand of humor, most filmmakers sought the realization of cinematic art via other paths. Early in the decade Hans Siemsen had asked whether viewers and experts could enjoy American sensationalism without subsequently becoming disgruntled.[34] A similar query now applied to slapstick imports. Could Germans laugh at nonsense without claiming *ex post facto* dissatisfaction? Siemsen and Arnheim implied affirmative answers to this question. Their colleagues, many of whom ranked slapstick highly in the cinematic hierarchy, did so only with qualifications. Careful examination reveals that their enthusiasm rested on more than captivation by "optical miracles." Apparent conversion by American tricks and acrobatics fell far short of complete. Consistent with the criteria employed to evaluate other film types critics prized the latter too for achieving supraoptical significance. Ironically, the same impulse which initially led to slapstick's rapid dismissal later stimulated critical reflections which allowed critics to embrace it.

Following the release of *The Kid* in 1923 critics began both to take slapstick seriously and to reflect self-consciously on the paradox of doing so. Kurt Pinthus began to philosophize against his will on the grounds that slapstick begged reading on more than one level: "Precisely these artistic performances, which the average person terms nonsense to begin with, ultimately lead into the greatest human and metaphysical depths."[35] Pinthus's discovery marked a trend which by middecade permitted Hans Siemsen to joke that his critical colleagues could disclaim their

earlier obtuseness by blaming a printing error for their description of Chaplin's work as nonsense (*Unsinn*) rather than profundity (*Tiefsinn*).[36] The same trend provoked Alfred Polgar,
theater critic for *Die Weltbühne*, to appeal to the literati who led
the Chaplin craze to drop their pretensions. Charlie had become
an "attorney of the oppressed," a "symbolic fighter" against the
malice of the objective world, a "protester against global injustice." Even his shoes and his characteristic waddle served as
clues to ethical and philosophical principles. Polgar denounced
the hunt for profundity in Chaplin's films as pointless and one-
sided, but he, like Pinthus, could not resist it. By denying philosophical depth to Chaplin's dress and behavior with the argument that "their meaning lies in their meaninglessness," he attributed broader significance to Chaplin's suspension of
conventional logic and morality.[37]

Chaplin's apotheosis, despite the strictures of Polgar, as sav-
ior and brother to the proletariat symptomized a search for
values and meaning which was not unique to the cinema. It
reflected the grasping after straws of a generation convinced
by war of the death of God and humankind's inhumanity to
itself. Chaplin symbolized the possibility of meaning in a world
which had lost its sense of direction.[38] Yet Polgar rightly pointed
to the fact that Chaplin remained a popular artist of the cinema
rather than a philosopher. However exalted his position in
twentieth century culture, and however much he defied classification by genre, he belonged first and foremost to the American slapstick tradition. Moreover, as Pinthus suggested, Chaplin
was not the lone slapstick artist to address fundamental human
issues through humor. While undoubtedly a special case, he
represented a way of viewing the world which was characteristic
of American film comedy. His place in Weimar culture must
therefore be anchored within discourse about American cinema
in general.

Set against middecade reactions to Hollywood documented
in chapter four, slapstick initially won applause for what it was
not. Though unique to Hollywood, it gained a grateful critical
following because it differed in crucial respects from the other
imports from America. Not only was the heroic posturing, moralizing and sentimentality which characterized American film

dramas absent. Filmmakers mocked these otherwise obligatory dramatic devices. Favorites in this respect were takeoffs on well-known western or adventure themes or films in which animals mimed human performers (including a spoof on Douglas Fairbank's *The Thief of Bagdad* performed by monkeys).[39] Most consistently praised were the pictures of Buster Keaton. Rudolf Arnheim found in Keaton's *Sherlock, Jr.* a corrosive parody on movie mysteries and adventure kitsch. Roland Schacht praised *Our Hospitality* for hilarious mimicry of the conventional murder film. And Herbert Ihering located the laughter in *Three Ages* not only in the disjunction between modern customs and those of previous eras but also in Keaton's caricature of pompous historical pictures. Critical appreciation for slapstick therefore rested on its neutralization of many offensive traits of Hollywood's mass production.[40]

Appreciation for mockery of Hollywood's conventions applied more broadly to slapstick's glosses on American society and culture, or more precisely, those features of modern culture commonly associated with the United States. The vagaries of modern technology and gadgetry, current fads such as the sports craze or even movie mania, or the stifling conformism of American society appeared in slapstick films as objects of satirical dissection. Keaton's *College* poked fun at the current obsession with sports; *Our Hospitality* destroyed the romanticism often associated with the past and mocked humankind's worship of technology. Harold Lloyd's *For Heaven's Sake* and Keaton's *Seven Chances* attacked such sacred cows as moral convention and the police.[41] In countless cases slapstick explored humankind's ambivalent relationship to the technological marvels of their own making. In a number of instances Hollywood also engaged in the delicate exercise of satirically dissecting military heroism or war. Slapstick tore the mask off contemporary values, institutions and accepted codes of behavior.[42]

As these examples suggest, critical enthusiasm for American film comedy rested largely on its ability to mirror, if in distorted fashion, the vagaries of the real world. Bizarre though its presuppositions might be, slapstick took its point of departure from concrete, current issues, everything from the human ramifications of the postwar housing shortage to the animal-like qualities of humanity released by a large department store sale.[43] It demonstrated unparalleled facility for illuminating the human condition, particularly man's interaction with nature or his own inventions. Roland Schacht's apposition of American and German practice in film comedy isolated precisely this facility as the kernel of Hollywood's success.

> The Americans work from what everyone knows, the Germans from what they contrive. The Americans aren't afraid to show their hero in truly ludicrous situations which arise in daily life rather than plundering old funny papers like the Germans. . . . Germans consider comedy a Sunday state of emergency. An otherwise sensible human being isn't allowed to be funny. The Americans on the other hand know that comedy is only the flip side of seriousness and belongs to it organically.[44]

In this context the particular virtue of slapstick lay in its eye for fraud and insanity in inventions, institutions and morals which constituted America's contribution to civilization. Not only did this mean that slapstick dared to explore the disjunction between life as it was and life as moral codes prescribed it, but it permitted the audience to laugh through identification with the weaknesses and sufferings of the character on the screen. To quote Schacht once again, generalizing from the comic persona of Buster Keaton:

> The American, a poor dear fellow, a complete simpleton in the hubbub of modern life, embodies suffering humanity; the German shouts in all he does: look here, how funny, how terribly funny I am. The public laughs away its sorrows at the American comedians; with the German it laughs at an individual simpleton, a freak.[45]

The dialectical relationship between nonsense and reality exercised considerable fascination for interpreters of slapstick. On the one hand these films subverted standard notions of logic, causality and probability, conjuring up a world bound only by the limits of imagination. On the other hand they offered a powerful commentary on the arbitrariness of the real world, man's alienation from technological culture and the mentality of American society and the so-called realistic film. Critics alternately emphasized one or the other dialectical pole. Axel Egge-brecht, a leftist critic and screen author, praised Chaplin as an "insistent exposer of the real, unromantic course of life." Felix Henseleit labeled Keaton's short, *One Week*—a hilarious jab at the wonders of modern consumer-oriented enterprise (in this case a prefab home for do-it-yourselfers whose sections had become jumbled)—"a contribution to the sociology of Ameri-can institutions." The editor of *Lichtbildbühne*, Georg Mendel, fully conscious of the paradox of gleaning pedagogical insights from slapstick, rated Keaton's *Go West* an educational film be-cause it truthfully captured human feeling.[46]

At the opposite dialectical pole slapstick was a vehicle for escaping reality. Its function in this regard frequently found expression through parallels with the fairy tale. Alfred Polgar employed that parallel to underwrite refusal to make Chaplin the propagator of a social creed. Béla Balázs used it to explain Chaplin's public appeal. Kurt Pinthus and Siegfried Kracauer hailed slapstick for suspending the weight of routinized, techno-logical culture and demolishing piece by piece the unbearably regimented structure of American society. Laughter proved lib-erating because humankind's ability to identify its enslavement to the machine and extrapolate ad absurdum from mechanical laws confirmed human sovereignty.[47] Buster Keaton proved the primary illustration of the dialectical relationship between oth-er-worldliness and the modern, technologically determined imagination. As a wanderer from another realm into the real world, American-style, he created a modern fairy tale in which fact and fantasy served each other.[48]

Slapstick's unrivaled power of illuminating the human condi-tion made it a source of political statements congenial to the political left. Chaplin's pictures provided the obvious quarry in this regard, not least because they offered a bridge by which leftists overcame their suspicion of the cinema as an instrument of bourgeois ideology and big business.[49] Early in the 1920s Chaplin attracted attention for his role as the conscience of an unjust society. In 1922 Kurt Tucholsky introduced Chaplin in an article which ventured beyond the physical virtuosity and tangle of stunts to social commentary. Chaplin's work testified to the existence of a worldview and human identity radically different from that fostered by the regimented culture and society of Germany. Not least of his merits was the instruction he offered in laughter for a nation which took itself and its position far too seriously.[50] The same year Hans Siemsen explored the significance of Chaplin's chosen persona—a vagabond struggling against an oppressive social system and state institutions. In *The Immigrant* Chaplin debunked the myth of personal liberty worshiped by Americans and in *The Bank* he desecrated the modern holy place, the vault. Siemsen read Chaplin's iconoclasm as a much-needed corrosive to German prostration before social status and political authority.

> As harmless as all these Chaplinades appear, in reality they are nothing other than a constant undermining of everything which today has reputation, office and dignity—they are a single battle against the contemporary social order. . . . He teaches that nothing should be taken seriously, nothing but the most straightforward human things; and that nothing should be feared. . . . He teaches complete, radical disrespect. God bless him! He is a revolutionary.[51]

From middecade the left acknowledged Chaplin as a political comedian, as a "friend of the working class" and thus a phenomenon which the bourgeoisie could only superficially appreciate.[52] Socialist and communist intellectuals admitted he could not be labeled to fit their specific purposes but made him an opponent of many injustices they too combated. At the very least Chaplin exposed the hypocrisy and inconsistencies of the bourgeois social order and indicated sympathy with the disadvantaged and oppressed. To some he was a "proletarian artist" if not an "artist of the proletariat," or partisan toward the proletarian struggle even though not a party man.[53] In the socialist journal *Film und Volk* Gerhart Pohl expanded the scope of the discussion to include films by Keaton and Lloyd, arguing that slapstick as a genre, while not revolutionary by profession, was revolutionary by implication because it revealed apparent social absolutes to be relative values which could be changed.[54]

The left-wing tendency to politicize slapstick is a noteworthy facet of discourse on this genre, but it cannot be divorced from other levels of criticism. Slapstick could not be poured into a partisan mold because it did not belong to one social class. As leftist critics had to concede, the bourgeoisie derived as many laughs as the proletariat from these pictures and indirectly much more profit, even if it missed their social significance. Furthermore, intellectuals of differing persuasions found in slapstick artistic values which overrode political categories. While Chaplin provided ammunition for the political left, he also supplied grist for the mill of those dedicated to art as autonomous creation. These too discovered deeper meaning in comic fairy tales. What serious drama conveyed inadequately, Chaplin and his leading rivals managed to capture. Precisely in the synthesis of the fairy tale and the down-to-earth, slapstick broke through the barrier between entertainment and art.

The outstanding representative of this synthesis was Charlie Chaplin. Despite the warning from Alfred Polgar in 1924 not to fabricate momentous principles from his clowning or outfit, artists and intellectuals created a Chaplin cult, indulging otherwise frustrated hopes in paeans to his work. If these homages to Chaplin offered a common theme it was that Chaplin, more than any other contemporary filmmaker or artist, represented and championed the cause of humanity. His pictures excelled by virtue of what Hans Pander called their "human content." Some identified this human content as his support for the mass of downtrodden and oppressed; others as his exploitation of the underlying link between the tragic and the comic; others as his transcendence of the mechanical world. All derived from this profoundly human dimension the right to label his work art. All also made Chaplin the exemplar of artistic values which antedated the motion picture, indeed which belonged by and large to a world which interwar Germans felt had been lost. Chaplin's humanity consisted in upholding traditional values in a nontraditional world.[55]

The most striking illustration of attitudes came in response to *The Gold Rush*. At once pinnacle of the genre and of Chaplin's accomplishments, *The Gold Rush* provoked such superlatives that critical faculties were temporarily suspended. To the extent that critics rationalized their rapture, they focused attention on Chaplin's handling of human emotions. Herbert Ihering, whose concern for the growing discrepancy between the technical means at the filmmaker's disposal and the goals which informed

them has already been discussed, saw in *The Gold Rush* the creation of a human and artistic genius not enslaved by mechanical
progress but able to perfect a human type with the aid of modern technology.[56] A critic for *Süddeutsche Filmzeitung*, R. Pabst,
argued similarly that the ultimate worth of *The Gold Rush* re-
sided neither in its plot, nor in its technical approach, nor in
its masterful directing, but in the gripping human base on which
it was conceived. Here a technical art form had captured a creative, emotional dream.[57]

Nowhere did the power of this picture to synthesize cultural
currents become more apparent than in its ability to forge unity
between experts otherwise at loggerheads. Hans Siemsen and
Willy Haas clashed sharply over critical practice but used *The
Gold Rush* for very similar purposes. Siemsen, a long-time Chaplin fan, chased the film through Italy and Switzerland in 1925.
By the Berlin premiere of February 1926 he had already seen
it a dozen times. Although his enthusiasm remained undimmed,
he felt it unnecessary to rehearse everything he had said in
1922, particularly now that his colleagues were echoing his sentiments. He did, however, reassert Chaplin's epochal significance, insisting that his contribution to cinema and human development would still live long after the world war had been
forgotten.[58] Willy Haas's lengthy and equally ecstatic review of
The Gold Rush used variant language to articulate very similar
views. Haas had earlier, of course, entertained misgivings about
Chaplin's style.[59] With *The Gold Rush* he jettisoned these. Chaplin's "strange, godless faith . . . in absurd fate," his depiction of
humankind's inability to know or understand its fellow human
beings, captured the essence of modern tragedy just as his exploration of the senseless or absurd led to discovery of comic
meaning. Haas argued that this motion picture marked a historical watershed in the development of the cinema and the dawn-
ing of a new era in human history. On the first count it swept
aside once and for all the controversy over whether film would
ever rank as an art form. With *The Gold Rush* Chaplin earned
the title of "the most brilliant artist alive," challenging literature,
the traditional repository of cultural leadership, to demonstrate
its artistic worth. On the second and related count, *The Gold
Rush* vaulted the cinema into the place long envisioned for it

Buster Keaton in *Go West*, the modern antihero's spoof on heroism
in the wild west, 1926. (Photo courtesy Landesbildstelle Berlin)

Charlie Chaplin in *The Gold Rush,* symbol of an age, 1926. (Photo courtesy Bundesarchiv-Filmarchiv Berlin)

"Recognizable Features." In this illustration of typecasting and identifiability, Hollywood's three great clowns and its leading swashbuckler crowd Germany's screen personification of Frederick the Great, Otto Gebühr. Phoebus brochure, February 1926. (Photo courtesy Bundesarchiv-Filmarchiv Berlin)

by Haas as the art form destined to overcome national boundaries and unite humankind on a global level.

> We have always stated and hoped: the cinema is the great *Volkskunst* of a future, united world; just as the individual nation created its national anthem, its national mythology at the historical moment when it became a nation . . . so one day united humanity would create a completely silent and multilingual national anthem, and this national anthem could only be the cinema.
>
> And now all at once it exists. The silent national anthem of tomorrow's universal nation of united humans, the wordless legend of tomorrow's modern humanity. No, more: the only art which can legitimately call itself "modern," film art.[60]

As these grandiose projections suggest, Chaplin worship served private visions of both human and cinematic progress. For Willy Haas, Chaplin symbolized the emergence of a new world order.[61] For others, such as Kurt Tucholsky and Hans Siemsen, who were outspoken opponents of social injustices perpetuated under the Weimar Republic, his comedy was a scourge to flog the system. Tucholsky set Chaplin's humanity over against the oppressive regimentation and callousness of contemporary Germany. Siemsen lamented the relative infrequency with which Germany received Chaplin films because his works made life bearable in a country with stultifying judicial, educational and political institutions.[62] Other critics preferred to avoid the politicization of their trade and so isolated the "endlessly human" or "truly human" quality of his films, that is, his ability to give visual form to human joy and sorrow and simultaneously produce laughter. Chaplin became all things to all people.[63]

Amidst adulation and universalizing of Chaplin's humanity the ability of his and other slapstick films to create laughter was so much taken for granted that it tended to be forgotten. Yet diverse agendas for cultural and cinematic progress remained anchored in unrestrained amusement. It was laughter which provided the common denominator in acclaim for slapstick's madness and sanity, fantasy and realism, melancholy and hilarity, devotion to man and exploration of machine. Hans Feld presented a useful reminder of this fact when he dismissed the questions which dominated the slapstick debate—"is it the pleasant way these slapsticks are made; is it the disarming innocence, is it a deeper instinct which recognizes and exploits human schadenfreude, or is it the confidence with which absurdity is made a principle?"—as irrelevant: "one cares less about the answer and laughs, laughs, laughs."[64] His restatement of the position initially adopted by Kurt Pinthus points to a fundamental component of what critics called slapstick's human content.

The burden of this chapter has been to contextualize discourse along lines suggested by Feld's questions rather than to accept his answer uncritically. But the fact that after middecade audiences and critics continued to laugh as they had in 1921–1922 is of more than casual significance. Without enjoyment, the need to comprehend would have been much less urgent, particularly insofar as slapstick evoked responses which surprised experts. Probing for deeper meaning presupposed laughter. Rationalization of laughter was, in turn, crucial to slapstick's appreciation by critics. A number of trade reviewers, accustomed to assessing box-office value, hinted that slapstick therefore possessed a unique advantage. Felix Henseleit groped towards a formula for salvaging artistic conventions while still endorsing Buster Keaton's humor when he assigned Keaton's films "intellectual class even though they [were] superb achievements technically."[65] After viewing *The General*, the classic Civil War comedy, Henseleit ranked Keaton next to Chaplin for his ability to capture the "human and the all too human." Technology had not excised the human dimension. Moreover, the fact that "everybody laughed, laughed heartily and amid tears" led Henseleit to conclude that *The General* appeared a "rare case where intellectuals and less intellectual persons" would see eye to eye. Both sophisticated and undemanding viewers found their expectations fulfilled.[66] Max Feige and Hans-Walther Betz drew comparable conclusions, relating the externally primitive but philosophically profound features of Keaton's films to unusually wide box-office appeal. Keaton's work was "perfectly gratifying for the literate as for the naive person."[67]

Slapstick's ability to engage viewers on both sides of the cultural divide, an achievement impressive enough to draw critical attention, underscored its contribution to human development.[68] In his review of *The Gold Rush* Willy Haas argued that Chaplin had perfected a universal language and indicated a basis for international understanding. In a general article which appeared several weeks later Haas developed a program based on *The Gold Rush* whose essence was the breakdown of the barrier between high and low cinema culture: Chaplin exploded the myth of the intrinsic incompatibility of art and business or cultivated and mass tastes.[69] Hans Siemsen developed this point even more insistently. Chaplin enthused the intellectual and artistically spoiled élite while speaking a language understood and loved by the simplest, most uncultivated workers. He also shrank the distance between them. Siemsen cited an incident in which an artist encountered his housemaid outside the cinema after seeing a Chaplin comedy. Without quite understanding why, master and maid approached one another, and though not able to converse, experienced a momentary sense of comradeship. This, in Siemsen's opinion, was Chaplin's ultimate achievement.

> He destroys barriers. He makes human beings what they really always should be: human beings. He demolishes everything which prevents them from being human beings: barriers of social standing, of education, of upbringing, barriers of title, vanity, power and ignorance. This funny little clown is the greatest thing a man can be: a world improver. God bless him![70]

In sum, slapstick did more than offer intellectuals something to ponder while attracting a mass audience looking for laughter. It actually forged bonds between them.

Siemsen, like many others, distilled from Chaplin's screen image the meaning he hoped to find. His promotion of Chaplin from clown to world improver did not receive universal assent. Indeed, as suggested earlier in this chapter, transfiguration of Chaplin invited artistic, philosophical or political debunking. The more emphatically Chaplin, or any other slapstick artist, was made the protagonist of larger causes, even that of humanity, the more vulnerable his image became to competing agendas. This became especially apparent when Chaplin made his second visit to Berlin in 1931. Arriving in the midst of the depression, this time to popular acclaim, he became drawn into a contest of hostile cultural and political factions which no comedian or philosopher could have negotiated successfully. In a country as fragmented as Germany in the early 1930s, the synthesis he appeared to offer proved more wishful thinking than reality.[71]

This being said, critical adulation of slapstick cannot be dismissed as mere intellectual pathos. Desire to discover the secret of a successful formula, fascination with the power of anarchy in images, and obligation to account for personal captivation by "optical miracles" yielded paradoxical statements on the meaning of an apparently make-believe, nonsensical comic style. In one respect these were rationalizations of personal enjoyment born of a cultural tradition which, as Siemsen argued in respect to sensationalist films, could not approve enjoyment unless it entailed intellectual enrichment. Intellectuals did not suspend critical thought readily, especially when they appreciated stunts which should not have interested them.[72]

In slapstick critics discovered material for rumination, they received reassurance that the highly rationalized, mechanical world had not eliminated the possibility of individual creativity, and they gained relief from the miles of kitsch which otherwise crossed movie screens. Their faith in the autonomy of art, in nonutilitarian, preindustrial cultural values was reaffirmed.[73] But Chaplin and company also helped bridge the awkward divide between the ideal and the real. As a popular genre slapstick provided ammunition against artistic snobbery and unwillingness to address the public. In the formulation of Ernst Blass, it had "more to do with genuine art than many a stylish product of literature."[74] Most significantly, it functioned as a meeting ground for the articulate and the mute masses. The latter were surely indifferent to the integrative function of these films, but the former were not. Central to the affirmation slapstick offered intellectuals was a sense of belonging to the *Volk*. Without daring for the most part to admit this, critics appreciated American comedy because it indicated that intellectuals could preserve their integrity and still speak to the masses. While satisfying in inimitable fashion the demands of the "realist dogmatists" discussed in the previous chapter, slapstick eased the descent of sophisticated viewers to communion with the masses. Herein lay its ultimate human value. Universal appeal meant incorporation of discriminating viewers into the broader public. As one paean to Harold Lloyd concluded: "We're grateful to him for the laughter; he reduces us brain snobs to human beings—who has greater merit?"[75]

7

GERMAN-AMERICAN
PRODUCTION IN HOLLYWOOD
AND THE MEANING OF
NATIONAL CINEMA

Somewhere in the film ruins of Neubabelsberg we store the seal of superior film art; such a secret is not exportable. The great directors and performers must leave it here when they go to America and go after the dollar. Certainly we don't intend to cry over them because Hollywood has changed them, made their works and achievements more marketable. But we will admit that they were different here, that they were better here—even if they create more profit over there.[1]

Weimar culture owes much of its nimbus and retrospective coherence to the exodus of German artists and intellectuals in 1933. As refugees from National Socialism, scientists, novelists, film or theater directors and performers enriched other cultures and in many cases gained impressive profiles in exile.[2] Yet for the cinema, the large-scale exodus occasioned by Hitler's assumption of power represented the second wave of emigration rather than a revolutionary departure. Well before Nazi coordination of German film production a substantial group of outstanding film artists accepted employment in America. Beginning with Ernst Lubitsch, Pola Negri and Dimitri Buchowetzki after EFA's collapse, reaching almost epidemic proportions at middecade and concluding in 1930 with the departure of Marlene Dietrich, the German emigration made a formidable contribution to Hollywood.

Although the American careers of several émigrés—F. W. Murnau, Ernst Lubitsch and Marlene Dietrich—have received attention, the collective story of this first motion picture exodus has never been fully told.[3] In part this omission reflects the evanescence of the original German colony. For a variety of reasons the first contingent of emigrants was no longer active in American cinema when the second group arrived. In fact, by 1930 the only really prominent ones among them were Lubitsch, Dietrich and Wilhelm Dieterle. But transitory though the initial colony proved, it played a role in American production transcending the personal experiences of the individuals involved. Moreover, the emigration had far-reaching implications for Weimar cinema. In this respect it assumes importance here. At issue is not Berlin in Hollywood (eminently deserving of independent study though it is) but the reading of émigré work in Germany. From this vantage point the emigration meant obvious losses to domestic production but also the opportunity to evaluate the impact of Hollywood norms and expectations on German personnel. It presented, in short, a microcosm of German cinema under the influence of America. Analysis of American films by these artists served to pinpoint the meaning of Hollywood for Weimar cinema.

American companies showed such discrimination in their choice of German personnel that the list of émigrés reads almost as a who's who of Weimar production. From the mid-1920s they included the producer Erich Pommer, the directors F. W. Murnau, Paul Leni, E. A. Dupont, Ludwig Berger, and Wilhelm Dieterle, actors Emil Jannings and Conrad Veidt and actresses Lya de Putti, Camilla Horn and Vilma Banky.[4] To these can be added the eminent screenwriter Hans Kraely and the directors Dimitri Buchowetzki, Paul Ludwig Stein, Lothar Mendes and Berthold Viertel. While representative rather than exhaustive, this list includes no one, apart perhaps from Vilma Banky, insignificant to Weimar cinema. Lubitsch, Leni, Berger and Dupont were all enticed to leave when they ranked among the very best directors in the country. Erich Pommer, in his role as production chief at Decla-Bioscop and UFA, represented as no other individual the blend of artistic experimentation and entrepreneurial boldness which generated the classics of the early 1920s. Negri, though of Polish descent, achieved stardom in Germany under Lubitsch.[5] Both Jannings and Veidt were performers without peers in their dramatic specialties, as was the screenwriter Hans Kraely.[6] The departure of Berthold Viertel or Lya de Putti constituted an only marginally less significant talent drain. All in all, even if the majority failed to establish themselves permanently in American cinema, their absence left gaping holes in domestic production programs.

The caliber of the German emigration made the exodus a serious issue to all those concerned with the welfare of the German cinema, especially because it coincided with the critical years in which German production appeared in constant danger of becoming an extension of Hollywood. While it would be a futile exercise to calculate the creative and commercial loss to German cinema, the emigration has rightly figured in its middecade troubles. Not surprisingly, some contemporaries interpreted Hollywood's buying up of German talent as a plot to destroy the German cinema, even suggesting that American producers cared less about utilizing European artists than depriving other nations of their cinematic footings.[7] Broadly speaking, however, upset at the immediate loss quickly translated into interest in the creative yield of this German-American partnership. American motion pictures in which German producers, directors, performers or script writers played key roles provided a laboratory for the theories of conflicting cinematic styles which circulated widely in the German film community. They also offered test cases for the possibility or desirability of one film culture fertilizing the other, both in the short and long term. The mix of German personnel and the American production system offered a rare opportunity to identify the corrosive or beneficial influence of America on German culture.

News that a prominent director or performer had a contract to work in America had the immediate effect of reminding German trade circles that in scale and financial backing Berlin remained a distant second to Hollywood. American moguls could pay more attractive salaries and finance more adventuresome projects. The talent drain, like the EFA episode or Parufamet, therefore deflated ambitions of meeting Hollywood on an equal footing. However, in a manner reminiscent of EFA, the reminder of economic inferiority did not necessarily entail pessimism or belief that departure of leading film artists meant a crippling blow to German production. Just as the internal migration caused by the founding of EFA confirmed German artistic excellence and created hope that motion pictures made by Germans with American funding would see worldwide distribution, so employment of Germans in Hollywood certified German excellence and could enhance the international reputation of German cinema.[8] Moreover, some read American hiring policy less as an act of sabotage than as a means by which Hollywood could rejuvenate its own stagnating production. As Felix Henseleit suggested, American interest in German talent in 1925 and 1926 followed directly from Hollywood's realization of European resistance to its movies. The recruitment campaign aimed to regain the favor of disgruntled European moviegoers. German personnel represented an artistic force which Hollywood desperately required. And to the extent that American hiring policy was a plot to destroy German cinema, it demonstrated Hollywood's fear of competition from superior filmmakers.[9]

There was, however, another side to the problem. EFA's enlistment of talent for production in Germany had promised to give creative opportunities and international exposure to German cinema after its wartime isolation. Yet even under these circumstances not all observers had agreed that its films really counted as domestic products. Pictures made by Germans in Hollywood presented more complex problems of nationality. Frank admission that projects of sufficient ambition to interest a Murnau or a Jannings were beyond domestic means, and that these artists were better employed in Hollywood than not at all, did not make their work overseas redound to the credit of German cinema any more than pride in their abilities nullified the loss or outweighed anxiety over their fate.[10] Whether benefits accrued to German cinema from the presence of these artists in Hollywood remained debatable. Did they, in the sharp formulation of Robert Ramin, represent "colony or competition" for their former homeland? Ramin argued that what appeared an outpost of Germans in Hollywood presented serious competition for the German cinema. Pride was misplaced because the émigrés did not deserve consideration as German representatives abroad.[11] In economic terms he was clearly correct. In broader cultural terms most observers saw the case as less clear-cut. They gauged Berlin's loss and Hollywood's gain by assessing the degree to which the motion pictures made by émigrés exhibited German or American characteristics. Their interest focused on the question whether Germans in Hollywood could preserve artistic links with the homeland and in this regard act as apostles of German film abroad.

The first, most long-standing and sharpest test of German fates in Hollywood was the American work of Ernst Lubitsch. When Lubitsch left Germany in late 1922, to return only briefly before settling in Hollywood in 1923, he was Germany's most celebrated and versatile film director. Already attuned to the American production system from financing through EFA on his last German pictures, and by inclination arguably the most "American" of German directors, he became a permanent fixture in Hollywood.[12] While other equally famous German film artists worked in Hollywood for certain periods of the twenties and early thirties, his American career alone spanned virtually the entire era on which this study focuses (unlike most of his compatriots he survived the transition to sound in the late 1920s). In his early years with Warner Bros. he also enjoyed artistic license within the budgets assigned him. Working frequently in conjunction with Hans Kraely he directed more than a dozen feature films in the decade 1923–1932.[13]

If in retrospect Lubitsch appears a natural transplant to the American motion picture world, his compatriots saw him as a German director tackling the leviathan of the Hollywood system. Precisely because of his exalted reputation, his fate in Hollywood appeared pivotal for the prospects of German cinema on the world market. Whether he could maintain the level of excellence set in Germany amidst the standardization of Hollywood sat at the forefront of critical concern. Would he be true to his German roots, would he be thoroughly Americanized, or would he land somewhere between these cultural poles? Full answers to these queries required familiarity with American film practice which Germans experts were only beginning to acquire through study trips to New York and Hollywood. Yet paucity of information presented little discouragement to commentators anxious to categorize his work. His first two American pictures, a Carmen film (*Rosita*) starring Mary Pickford and a society comedy (*The Marriage Circle*), his first film for Warner Bros., were both produced in 1923. They premiered in Germany almost simultaneously in the late summer of 1924, giving experts hard evidence upon which to base an evaluation of cultural hybridization.

A frequent contributor to *Kinematograph*, Dr. Ernst Ulitzsch, went straight to the central issue in a joint review entitled "The German and the American Lubitsch." As this title suggests, the point was to classify the national character of Lubitsch's achievement. In his opinion, *Rosita*, a work scripted by a German writer, Norbert Falk, on a theme previously filmed by Lubitsch in Germany, lay very much in Lubitsch's German tradition. It confirmed that Lubitsch could attain those cinematic feats—discipline of performers individually and corporately—for which the Americans had hired him. *The Marriage Circle*, a light comedy of tangled marital relationships set in Vienna, did not classify so readily. Ulitzsch claimed that it represented a departure from anything previously done by the Americans in film humor. Without direct German forerunners, it drew upon German achievements in comedy and the chamber drama. On these grounds Ulitzsch affirmed that despite relocation to Hollywood Lubitsch remained a "German master" whose work strengthened the international prestige of the German cinema.[14]

A parallel case from another trade paper illuminates both the representativeness and analytical softness of such a nationally determined approach. The editor of *Der Film,* Dr. W. Theile, generalized from *Rosita* that "the style of our outstanding German directors does not change when they have a task to accomplish under different conditions than in Germany." Like Ulitzsch, however, he floundered trying to establish a German pedigree for both pictures. Although he conceded that Lubitsch's approach in *Rosita* had altered since his last German works, he still traced these unspecified developments to the "German element of filmic art which remained his directorial style." But in the next breath he credited American input for the success of the picture and expressed unease about Lubitsch's future development.[15] With *The Marriage Circle* Theile reiterated that Lubitsch remained true to form, but again contradicted himself attempting to determine what that meant. Granting that Lubitsch had learned from Hollywood in precision of camera work, he still insisted that an unnamed German influence set the overall tone. In an abrupt disavowal of the whole analytical project he then momentarily decided there was no point debating whether Lubitsch proved himself more German or American, only to renege immediately by describing Lubitsch's personal touch as essentially German.[16]

The discourse adopted by Ulitzsch and Theile indicates that Lubitsch's first American releases in Germany became test cases for national cinematic survival as Hollywood began to flood the German market. It also illustrates how preoccupation with national characteristics programmed critical analysis in terms that produced more passion than precision.[17] Whether or not critics applauded *Rosita*, they measured it with a national yardstick. *Lichtbildbühne* described the film as less than "authentically Lubitsch" precisely because its subject matter, though scripted by a German, was "a little too shallow, a little too much Americanized." "Consciously or unconsciously American sensitivities were obviously allowed to have an influence." Although Lubitsch represented a major asset in Hollywood, full realization of his abilities required freedom from "dilutive American influences." As these characterizations suggest, Lubitsch was expected to resist watering down his films to please the American public. Degeneration in Lubitsch's work, loosely defined as shallowness, was blamed on Hollywood. Regeneration presupposed freedom to make German motion pictures with American financing and resources.[18]

In the case of *The Marriage Circle*, which premiered just four days after *Rosita*, Lubitsch gained credit for preserving his individuality. By general consensus *The Marriage Circle* was an outstanding achievement. All commentators were impressed and many ecstatic, largely because they saw in it a significant departure in motion picture history. Lacking familiarity with Charlie Chaplin's *A Woman of Paris* (1923), a picture of fundamental importance for Lubitsch's development (released in Germany only in 1926), they attributed that departure to Lubitsch's German heritage. While Ulitzsch and Theile intimated this, Heinrich Fraenkel stated it categorically.

Lubitsch's last American-made work is without a doubt one of the finest, most tasteful, technically most successful, most entertaining and—most un-American films ever created. It is an encouraging sign of the fact that this German artistic personality is strong enough not to let himself be "Americanized" and conform to his new home, but again and again to place on his work his own unmistakable stamp.[19]

Not the least of the "un-American" features of the film was its refusal to be bound by moral prudery. Heinz Michaelis surmised that a director of Lubitsch's artistic authority was required "to lead American film comedy out of the constraints of Sunday school into the realm of superior comic genius," confirming once again that German influence had proven determinative.[20]

Beyond the confines of the trade press reactions to Lubitsch's first American pictures showed similar interest in the relative strength of German and American ingredients and comparable problems of distinguishing between them. Frank Warschauer, for example, interpreted the uniqueness of *The Marriage Circle* in terms of three variables—its German setting, its essentially American treatment and an extra un-American intonation which by implication came via Lubitsch from Germany. This last quality was evident in the steady yet comfortable pace at which the picture unfolded and in the balance found in comic style; without refinement to the point of becoming bland, humor remained subtle. Warschauer recognized the novelty produced by the hybridization of the American and German cinemas, but perceived Lubitsch as the principal influence in the birth of a uniquely accented filmic style.[21]

Although preoccupation with Lubitsch's contribution to Hollywood meant that the deviation of *The Marriage Circle* from German type went largely unexplored, two commentators inverted prevailing perspectives. Hans Siemsen maintained that *Rosita* and *The Marriage Circle* belonged to two radically opposed traditions. The former represented the heavy-handedness, pathos and pomposity of the German Lubitsch; the latter revealed a reborn American Lubitsch characterized by dramatic reserve, lightness of touch and ability to create authentic human types.[22]

Similarly, Kurt Pinthus, who was wildly enthusiastic about *The Marriage Circle* as a demonstration that properly conceived and executed film sequences, though silent, could attain an eloquence superior to that of the spoken word, found it no coincidence that Lubitsch made it in Hollywood. Lubitsch succeeded through marriage of the subtlety and refinement of the German chamber drama to the lightness and knack for popular subjects for which the Americans were noted: "Here the chamber drama and popular play are successfully fused. Here is the first and only perfect comedy ever produced by a German hand—tragicomically in America."[23]

Pinthus's reference to the harmonious union of sophistication and slickness in *The Marriage Circle* made explicit what other critics had been reluctant to state outright: American and German cinematic approaches could be welded successfully into a unity greater than the sum of their parts. At a time when German critics were becoming sceptical about the suitability of many American movies for German theaters, this work indicated that crossbreeding could produce films attractive to demanding and less discriminating audiences. However, sequels were to show, for Lubitsch and later émigrés, that the union was anything but consistently happy. What critical spirits sought in American motion pictures involving German artists coincided irregularly with the demands of the American production system and German moviegoers. The line between German and American traditions proved a fine one indeed. As in the days of EFA, critics disturbed by the blend of German and American approaches usually blamed an excess of American ingredients.

The danger of Hollywood for Lubitsch, and by inference for future émigrés, surfaced in his very next release in Germany, *Three Women*. This picture transposed the romantic entanglements of *The Marriage Circle* from a playfully harmless to a more serious mode involving murder and acquittal before happy ending. The timing of its release—September 1925—contributed to the coolness with which it was treated, since critics claimed it contained liberal quantities of what were increasingly objectionable Americanisms. But the discursive framework within which it was evaluated had not significantly changed. The common theme in reviews of *Three Women* was the discrepancy between American and German worldviews and Lubitsch's accommodation to the former at the cost of his appeal in Germany. Concessions to American tastes were identified in Hans Kraely's script, which ran from comedy and sensationalism to a theatrical climax with a sentimental American denouement.[24] The conservative daily, *Deutsche Allgemeine Zeitung*, went so far as to charge Lubitsch with having become an American and directing a purely American average film. The chief problem was Kraely's script, American kitsch which neither Kraely nor Lubitsch would ever have contemplated shooting in Germany. Lubitsch was advised to stick to his specialty, the light comedy, and warned not to allow himself to become further Americanized.[25]

The distinct sense of disappointment characteristic of these evaluations of *Three Women* was related more or less explicitly to the willingness on the part of Lubitsch and Kraely to put their talents at the service of American tastes, particularly in toleration of stylistic pluralism in the screenplay. This disappointment clearly implied disapproval of those qualities which spelled popularity. Kurt Pinthus had acclaimed *The Marriage Circle* for finding the middle way between artistic seriousness and lightness. Commentary on *Three Women* suggests that in the backlash of middecade experts recoiled from a work by two German masters which compromised artistic purity. Alienated by mass import, they proved hypersensitive to indications Lubitsch was becoming a popular director on American terms.

Willy Haas put his finger directly on the sore spot with a massive review conceived along lines later developed by Béla Balázs in reflection on the German film crisis. As a script writer Haas concurred with those who judged Kraely's screenplay "un-German," but he was fascinated by its originality and vitality. How had Kraely managed to shed his German skin? Haas believed that by careful study of English stage dramas Kraely had struck the balance of convention and originality absent in German drama. In the German tradition conventionality was almost invariably confused with banality, and originality with eccentricity. As Haas later argued, whereas the Anglo-American hero was an "ideal average man," the German hero was by definition above convention, the supreme individualist.[26] Taken together these characterizations suggested that artistic significance demanded disregard for popular tastes. In the case of *Three Women*, Haas perceived a bridge by which to unite the alienated categories of art and popular culture. Precisely what other commentators viewed as undesirable concessions to the public, he singled out as the principal lesson that German film people needed to learn from the film—the absolutely assured popularity of its theme and the momentum with which it was delivered cinematically.

Notwithstanding Haas's opinion, the touchstone of critical approbation for Lubitsch's American work remained its Germanness. Following mixed reviews of *Three Women* and *Forbidden Paradise,* (in the latter case ranging from praise to allegations that Lubitsch had fouled his own nest in depicting European culture), his standing in Germany was restored in early 1926 with *Kiss Me Again.*[27] Here, as if heeding the advice of German experts, he reverted to the thematic and stylistic pattern of *The Marriage Circle,* the light domestic comedy. Drawing accolades comparable to those used for that picture, *Kiss Me Again* likewise won respect for its exploitation of devices from the German chamber drama. It was judged a creation of the German, or at least European, rather than the American Lubitsch because its intellectual pedigree, subtlety and acting style were un-American.[28] Willy Haas took *Kiss Me Again* as proof that the German chamber drama could have international relevance and bewailed domestic preoccupation with satisfying an invented notion of world tastes while Hollywood learned from Germany.

> If for years we hadn't succumbed to the inflated idea of finding 'suitable subjects' for inhabitants of the South Sea islands, if we had concerned ourselves more with our own tastes than with the tastes of Massachusetts, New Orleans, Mexico . . . we would today be the foremost film country in the world. As always with us we fertilize the entire world and don't gain a thing from it because we don't believe in ourselves. We only discover ourselves in Hollywood.[29]

Haas's conclusion affirmed the potential for fruitful collaboration between Hollywood and Berlin, but like virtually all other tributes to the German element in Lubitsch's American films it displayed remarkably little concern for popular appeal or box office. This is particularly striking insofar as it came from trade papers, otherwise sensitive to commercial prospects. Only rarely did experts say openly what Warner Bros. and American theaters soon discovered: like the German chamber drama, Lubitsch's films were for viewers of refined tastes.[30] Since his German reputation rested on box office as well as cinematic adeptness, he may well have encountered less friendly criticism had he made such films in Germany. Given, however, that the German industry stood to gain only indirectly from his work, considerations of prestige overrode those of profit. The principal ambition was to maintain national profile at a moment when American inroads threatened to obscure or erase it.

This brief survey of discourse on Lubitsch's early American films exposes the concerns which dominated subsequent discussion on the work of German artists in Hollywood. Foremost among these was the balance of American and German ingredients struck by the émigrés. Next to it was the tendency to trace creative flaws to Americanisms. That tendency gained momentum with the growing reaction against Hollywood in Germany. By the middecade emigration experts had become very doubtful about the benefits of transplanting German talent to Hollywood. When generalizing, they judged the work of German émigrés as failing to measure up to, not to mention surpass, standards earlier set in Germany. Even before the main wave of émigré films which began to appear in 1927, they reached sweeping conclusions by extrapolating from the fates of Lubitsch and Pola Negri. In early 1926 Georg Mendel decided that émigrés either failed to adapt to the Hollywood system or became, like Lubitsch, thoroughly American. Either way their work was bound to be disappointing.[31] Later the same year lead articles in *Kinematograph* and *Film-Kurier* blankly stated that none of those who had moved to Hollywood had enhanced their reputations. Rather, they had been rapidly Americanized. Instead of reciprocal enrichment the emigration had produced a "dangerous blend of styles." Lubitsch in particular directed one pioneering film, *The Marriage Circle*, before settling down to become "Lubitsch in a circle," making reruns rather than venturing into new territory as he had in Germany. Drawing the logical conclusion, Fritz Olimsky warned that the return of

Americanized émigrés would threaten further Americanization of domestic production.[32]

Probably the most insistent, reasoned evaluation of the detrimental influence of the Hollywood environment on German artists came from Herbert Ihering in response to the Parufamet agreement. It too prophesied as much as analyzed. Reflecting in light of Parufamet on earlier American-Swedish "cooperation," which had cost that country two outstanding directors, Victor Sjöström and Mauritz Stiller, Ihering saw an ominous parallel with current attempts to rescue the drowning UFA. The balance sheet of German achievement in Hollywood was not promising. Of Lubitsch's works, only *The Marriage Circle* demonstrated constructive American input—the remainder showed America's standardizing influence. Pola Negri's performances likewise betrayed the absence of artistic development. Looking ahead following the news that Emil Jannings was bound for Hollywood, Ihering forecast that he too would be "absorbed" by the American system. What was the subtle trap set by Hollywood? For Ihering it was erasure of the distinction between filmic adeptness and artistic devotion which characterized the German cinema.

> The development of inspiration, the enrichment of a personal approach has not kept pace with the necessary increase of ability in the filmic craft. For the American mastery of the craft and filmic inventiveness are identical. For Germans this is not so at present. They conform technically and thereby lose their personal imagination.[33]

In one respect Ihering was simply warning against the excess routine for which American production was infamous. At another level, however, he was trying to articulate a distinction between Hollywood and Berlin which revisits that suggested by Haas's review of *Three Women*. Where Haas noted the irreconcilability of conventionality and originality in German screenplays and their successful marriage in America, Ihering believed that a balance rather than a fusion of artistic and filmic impulses distinguished the German cinema from its American counterpart. Any upset of this balance portended extinction of what was unique to the German cinema. In thereby suggesting that

German artists were not yet ready for Hollywood, Ihering defended the peculiarity of the German cinema which weakened
it in international competition with American motion pictures.[34]

Ihering's dissatisfaction with German-American motion pictures focused on the incompatibility of American screenplays
and German artists. Here he was not alone. Critics generally
faulted films by émigrés, even those otherwise applauded, for
just this weakness. Pola Negri's American fate, a long and fascinating tale in its own right, can be summarized from the German perspective almost exclusively in these terms. With very
few exceptions, notably one film directed by Lubitsch and two
produced by Erich Pommer discussed below, her American
work found little critical favor because it was felt she was saddled
with unfortunate and inappropriate screenplays.[35] Similarly,
Emil Jannings, though winner of an Academy Award for his
performance in Joseph von Sternberg's *The Last Command*, became partner to sufficiently sentimental and moralizing screenplays to fulfill Ihering's prophecy. E. A. Dupont, the famed
director of *Varieté*, received some sympathy for being compelled
to shoot an impossible script in his one American work.[36] Similar sympathy was extended to Conrad Veidt for both roles he
played in Hollywood. Although in all these cases the German
artist was usually held less responsible than the dictates of the
American production system, their subjection to that system was
clearly not welcomed.[37]

Unflattering assessments of German-American collaboration
drew on prejudices which predated the main wave of emigration at middecade. These prejudices, reinforced by the backlash
against Hollywood in Germany, growing disenchantment with
Lubitsch's output and apparent assembly-line exploitation of
Pola Negri, spawned disparaging generalizations about émigré
work in Hollywood even before the majority of them had a
chance to prove themselves. Only in 1927 did the release of the
maiden works of the most prominent producer, director and
actor to depart in the wake of the UFA debacle—Erich Pommer, F. W. Murnau and Emil Jannings—offer a broader foundation for evaluating Hollywood's meaning for German film
artists. By then the main lines of critical discussion had already
been established: concern for artistic purity in tension with pop-

ular appeal, fear that the liaison with America sapped German talent of its unique genius, and preoccupation with the screenplay as the beginning of Hollywood's evil. Within these parameters the American debuts of Murnau, Jannings and Pommer assumed paramount significance for evaluations of German-American production. Murnau's maiden work for Fox, *Sunrise*, based on a novel by Hermann Sudermann which was adapted by Carl Mayer, was the first of three features made over the next three years. Jannings's *The Way of All Flesh* opened an American career spanning six films (one directed by Lubitsch) over three years. Pommer's only two American productions, *Hotel Imperial* and *Barbed Wire*, starred Pola Negri and were set in the Great War. All four pictures presented German (Austrian) characters; three of them had European settings. Together they marked the zenith and limitations of German production in Hollywood.

Erich Pommer's American work can easily be passed over as a minor interruption in a career marked by extraordinary achievements after World War I and again in the early phase of sound films. As production chief with Decla-Bioscop and UFA, Pommer made a substantial contribution to the flowering of German cinema and served as patron to a wide range of outstanding German film talent. Powerful, but increasingly at the center of controversy over UFA's strategies when the credit crunch came in the midtwenties, he departed for the United States and found employment with Paramount. Returning to Germany in 1927 he served once again as UFA's foremost production chief and supervised several of the most commercially successful early German talkies until forced to flee by the Nazi takeover.[38] While his reputation therefore rests on two stages of German production, the hiatus in America presented an important transition. As contemporaries recognized, Hollywood schooled Pommer in production strategies appropriate to the international market.[39]

Hotel Imperial and *Barbed Wire* chose motifs interwoven with the war yet at one remove from the front. The former, set in the Polish town of Lemberg under Russian occupation, chronicled romance between a wounded Austrian officer and a hotel maid. The latter, set behind the French lines, presented a tale of love and national reconciliation between a German prisoner of war and a French peasant girl. Both blended suspense, romance, feminine virtue, the struggle between good and evil and happy ending—in short, the stock-in-trade of Hollywood which critics usually lamented. Nevertheless, reaction to Pommer's work was generally positive. Despite sharp hostility to American scripting conventions, critics admired these pictures not least for the relevance and human accessibility of their subject matter. They also recognized the cleverness with which Pommer selected setting and theme to avoid giving offense and to invest potentially divisive subjects with broad appeal. In several instances they expressed regret that Pommer had not produced movies of this stamp in Germany, thereby conceding that Hollywood had contributed positively to reorientation in his approach.[40] His last German features, *Faust, Tartüff* and *Metropolis,* had been costly prestige pictures (in the case of *Metropolis* outrageously so) and an enormous burden to UFA when not sufficiently popular in the United States. Now the advocate of national cinema art as the key to international success supervised pictures whose subject matter and filmic polish had truly international appeal. The gap between artistic and box-office value had been overcome.[41]

General approval for Pommer's two American productions for combining cinematic sophistication and broad appeal suggests a shift in critical perspective since the release of the early Lubitsch imports. These, whose trademark was cultivation and subtlety, usually met criticism insofar as concessions were made to popular tastes. By contrast, Pommer received congratulations for satisfying them. The explanation for this apparent inconsistency lies in the circumstances under which each emigrated as well as in the evolution of critical expectations. In Germany Lubitsch had directed polished and popular motion pictures which paved the way to his employment in the United States. Pommer's name was associated with a wide variety of motion pictures, but latterly with big-budget projects of dubious value to the industry at home or abroad. Although it would be an exaggeration to say he left Germany under a cloud, he certainly exited with the jury still out on whether he had been bane or blessing for postwar German cinema. Given this distinction in German profile, Pommer was under some pressure to redeem his reputation as a producer of remunerative entertainment.

At first glance this appears a countervailing pressure to that exerted by the shift in critical attitudes toward Hollywood since Lubitsch emigrated. In fact, however, sharpening discrimination toward the American product rested primarily on its inappropriateness for German audiences. By 1927 considerations of prestige so evident in discussion of Lubitsch's early American work had given way to more pragmatic concerns. Germany could no longer afford costly experiments which might or might not pay their way. Solid, smooth entertainment of the sort offered by *Hotel Imperial* and *Barbed Wire* deserved emulation, just as it caused some retrospective chagrin that UFA had pursued unremunerative policies. Once more an outstanding German talent found his stride in Hollywood, to the benefit of the American industry.[42]

While endorsing the two Pommer productions, experts proved much less eager than in response to Lubitsch's work to distinguish between "German" and "American" influences. They did not, therefore, explicitly deduce that Hollywood deserved credit for modifying Pommer's approach. Nor did they draw the rather obvious conclusion that these two films testified to the feasibility of mixed marriages that Lubitsch's fate denied. Nonetheless, their commentary left little doubt that in this case Hollywood had provided a much needed corrective to domestic tendencies. By inference, they also conceded the Americanization of their own standards of motion-picture excellence: if Pommer's work upon return to Germany can be taken as a guide, they would have had difficulty denying the importance of the lessons he learned in Hollywood.

While judgments passed on Pommer's American output implied a bright future for joint German-American production, *Sunrise* and *The Way of All Flesh* reactivated controversy on this subject. *Sunrise*, in particular, provoked the most contradictory responses. Once again the earlier German career of Murnau set the stage for critical evaluation. If Pommer was the doyen of the German art film, Murnau was his foremost protégé. From *Phantom* and *Nosferatu* to *Der letzte Mann*, *Faust* and *Tartüff*, Murnau demonstrated an intensity of poetic vision and commitment to cinematic advance which marked him for special attention from the discriminating critic and viewer. Diverse, fantastic and potentially sensational though his film subjects proved, his thematic, rhythmic and photographic sensibilities were quite unlike those conventionally ascribed to Hollywood. It was these which William Fox purchased as artistic augmentation for his studio. From the German perspective, however, Murnau faced the formidable challenge of straddling the cultural divide between Hollywood and Berlin.[43]

As a narrative *Sunrise* follows a peasant, bewitched by a seductress into attempting to murder his wife, from country to city and back again; from lust and attempted murder to remorse, reconciliation and happy end. Given that it was scripted by Carl Mayer, considered by many Germany's foremost author of film, from a tale by Hermann Sudermann, and that its director and set designer (Rochus Gliese) were also Germans, it is understandable that *Sunrise* appeared "extraordinarily German," despite American financing and production initiative.[44] It was no secret, furthermore, that William Fox had given Murnau creative and financial license to create an artistic showpiece surpassing his German productions. American provision of monetary and technical support for German creative genius was an ideal balance of inputs. German artists therefore could create a picture of truly international significance to bridge the proverbial gap between national mentalities.

These extremely favorable preconditions notwithstanding, Murnau's first American film did not live up to all expectations. *Sunrise* did, to be sure, elicit superlatives for overcoming deeply entrenched beliefs about the discrepancy between the artistic potential of cinema and the other creative arts. Attaining for serious drama what Chaplin had accomplished for comedy, Murnau synthesized the artistically valuable and commercially successful motion picture. Yet even the most ecstatic reviews registered caveats with regard to the screenplay. Despite the essential Germanness of the picture, Sudermann's novel had been "Americanized" for the screen. Chief concessions to American tastes were the blatant contrast of character types and dramatic settings and the bending of Sudermann's denouement to create marital bliss for the peasant and his wife. Critics complained that by rescuing the husband from the death he deserved Mayer did Sudermann an injustice, violated his own dramatic code and created psychological inconsistencies in the plot. Hans Pander captured critical ambivalence toward the picture when he remarked that the cooperation of Murnau and Carl Mayer was bound to result in an intriguing motion picture, but being *American* the film was equally bound to leave the viewer divided.[45]

Thematic concessions were highlighted by Murnau's fantastic cinematographic achievements, above all his facility at capturing ambience with light, lens and rhythm. Murnau had crafted an absolutely stunning work of cinematic art. Such awesome technical mastery in the service of "A Song of Two Humans" (the film's subtitle) had critics groping for superlatives. But this same mastery intensified regret that *Sunrise* exhibited flaws of characterization and motivation. Here appeared confirmation of Ihering's prophecy that German émigrés, especially the most artistically sophisticated of them, would find their creative capacities overwhelmed by Hollywood's cinematic genius. Synchronization between *Geist* and *Technik* was lost. As one reviewer concluded, *Sunrise* was a superb motion picture, grandly conceived, but marked by unnerving concessions.[46]

The discontinuities identified in *Sunrise* parallel discrepancies in critical standards applied to Murnau and Pommer, and not unlike those between Pommer and Lubitsch. Given the association of Pommer and Murnau prior to their respective departures for the United States, it is not immediately apparent why one should have been congratulated for concessions to public tastes while the other fell afoul of German opinion for the same. Critical practice arguably had vague auteurist tendencies, attributing greater weight to director and script writer than to producer: Murnau and Mayer were artists whereas Pommer was a businessman. Since, however, outstanding artists were applauded for overcoming the dualism of creativity and commerce, to reaffirm this dualism meant upholding critical paradigms which condemned cinema to second-class citizenship. The problem was not *Sunrise,* but latent resistance to the kind of synthesis otherwise so eagerly sought. As that synthesis came closer to realization in German-American production, experts resorted to conceptual structures which denied its possibility. The dividedness of *Sunrise* was essentially of their own making.

The incongruence between *Geist* and *Technik* critics identified in *Sunrise* surfaced even more glaringly in *The Way of All Flesh*. An outstanding character actor, Emil Jannings, served an enormous, well-oiled, technical apparatus to squeeze saline solution from the tear ducts of viewers. In Germany Jannings had starred in numerous pictures under the leading directors of the time—Lubitsch, Murnau, E. A. Dupont and Joe May. Rivaled as a character actor perhaps only by Werner Krauss and Conrad Veidt, he had excelled in such diverse dramatic roles—historical, mythical and contemporary—that he increasingly became the cynosure of the pictures in which he played. By middecade prominent and self-possessed enough not to be a pawn of any interests but his own, he was an obvious if expensive recruit for Hollywood.[47] Given his enormous and multifarious talents, it was fitting that whatever film included him should be crafted to capitalize on these talents. *The Way of All Flesh* did not disappoint in this regard. Critics gave Paramount full marks for recognizing and exploiting Jannings's talents. He was the excuse for making the movie and was given a role designed to parade his capabilities.[48]

If Jannings fully merited a starring role, the subject in which Paramount showcased his talents provoked much distaste and ironic criticism. Through division of *The Way of All Flesh* into a first half which objectively and masterfully recreated the lifestyle of a German-American family with Jannings at its head, and a second half which depicted his descent, via alcohol and seduction, to disgrace and destitution, critics pinpointed the objectionable elements of the American formula. That the second half offered no miraculous restoration of the outcast father did not redeem the film. The tragic ending proved as forced and fanciful as the fairy-tale ending of *Der letzte Mann*. The thick sentimentality in which it was wrapped overwhelmed any respect for what otherwise may have qualified as narrative consistency.[49] Hollywood had calculated the tear-jerking effect and in the process abused Jannings's great talents. According to Willy Haas, the last half of the film was pure melodrama which could "bring tears to the eyes of a wooden trunk." With a touch of ironic humor mustered by few others, he refrained from detailed criticism of Jannings's virtuoso performance by claiming visual impairment by tears.[50]

Very mixed responses to the blend of Jannings and Hollywood militated against approval of German-American collaboration. However, despite major flaws in the screenplay from a German point of view, reports of audience reaction suggest that *The Way of All Flesh* had the intended effect on German as well as American tear glands. Haas's eyes were not the only wet ones in German theaters.[51] Hollywood therefore deserved credit both for placing Jannings in the spotlight and for devising a popular subject and treatment with a German ambience—the same facility identified in Pommer's American works. Hans Wollenberg, editor of *Lichtbildbühne,* isolated Hollywood's contribution to the mix by contrasting German and American utilization of a talent like Jannings. The former searched literary works for a motif suited to a psychological chamber drama. The latter found a popular subject calculated to grip hearts and dampen eyes. From this perspective a synthesis of Jannings and Hollywood was fruitful, even though *The Way of All Flesh* qualified as a world-class motion picture solely thanks to Jannings.[52]

Even though in 1926–1927 Murnau and Jannings, not to mention compatriots like Paul Leni, Ludwig Berger, Conrad Veidt and Lya de Putti, were just launching American careers, with *The Way of All Flesh* the thematic cycle of German interest in émigré production in the United States was essentially complete. From first anxious inquiries about the shape of Lubitsch's American films to assessments of maiden works by Pommer, Jannings and Murnau, critics revisited the cultural divisions assumed to exist between Germany and the United States. The permutations possible in answer to the question whether Germany's best would remain German and unsurpassed in Hollywood mark the points on a preset circle of opinion. In Lubitsch's first works experts addressed the threat of deterioration in national film identity. Open exultation in the triumph of German artistry alternated with regret or recrimination at émigré transgression of boundaries set in Germany. Oscillation followed a discernible pattern. First came elation at the breakthrough of native talent overseas and confidence that it made a unique contribution to Hollywood. Close on its heels came hairsplitting over the Germanness of the final product. At mid-decade, when the main exodus took place, experts still waffled on whether to judge by criteria of art or accessibility, prestige or profit. Depending upon the prior record of the émigré and predilection of the reviewer, émigré work could be welcomed for its universal appeal (Pommer), greeted as a cinematic milestone but criticized for compromise (Murnau) or given both treatments simultaneously (Jannings).

In parallel with this critical trimming experts developed a two-track scheme for apportioning responsibility for the finished work. The mainline approach, presaged already in analysis of EFA, was to credit German personnel with the laudable features of a given production, blame American meddling or mentalities for concessions and pity German artists condemned to second-class status by the Hollywood system. Fault belonged to the Americans primarily because they imposed unbearably formulaic screenplays on German directors and forced performers into schematic roles. Even when the end result was box-office value which experts urged for domestic production, approbation remained qualified and quality was credited to German input. Fear of losing German filmic traditions curbed gratitude that German artists were finally gaining international popularity via Hollywood. In all of this there obtained enormous confidence that Germans overseas enhanced American production values, that Hollywood desperately needed German talent to inject art and culture into its factory system. Regressive or unproductive influence worked in one direction—from California to Berlin.

Against this mainstream there flowed, however, currents of opinion both more favorable to Hollywood and explicitly critical of Germany's contribution to American cinema. Appreciation for Pommer's achievement, and with qualifications for the American work of Lubitsch, Murnau and Jannings, included respect for Hollywood's input and for further German-American collaboration. In select cases it went further to question whether German personnel were slaves of the American system or necessarily positive contributors to it. Contemporaries did not always exonerate the émigrés as helpless victims. Rudolf

Arnheim castigated Jannings for doing no more in *The Way of All Flesh*—at a very high salary—than had been expected of him, and Herbert Ihering accused him of going "the way of Hollywood," that is, allowing himself to be partner to cheap melodrama.[53] Kurt Pinthus took criticism a step farther, inverting the usual concern for Americanisms which polluted German artistry to consider Germanisms which misled Hollywood. Using *Sunrise* and *The Way of All Flesh* as test cases, he argued that Hollywood had incorporated features characteristic of the German chamber drama to the detriment of its own cinematic excellence. Already superior to the German cinema in comedy, adventure and society films, the Americans chose to play catch-up in a German specialty. The result, however momentarily novel to American audiences, was anachronistic for German eyes. The incongruity he noted in *Sunrise* was not that between form and content but between state-of-the-art American cinematography and antiquated acting styles. The American performers, George O'Brien and Janet Gaynor, had abandoned sparse mimicry for dramatic effect but achieved quite the opposite. Exaggerated, ponderous acting was not only dated, but also, ironically, out of place because it had long since been superseded in Germany by a style gleaned from America. In *The Way of All Flesh* the Americans deserved credit for curbing Jannings's tendency to overact. But if first-rate as a solo performance, the very role and its filmic rendering were essentially atavistic. According to Pinthus, the character types depicted here were reminiscent of motion picture practice twenty years earlier.[54]

The moral of the story has a familiar ring. In the era of initiation Herbert Ihering had suggested that by some perverse logic the exchange of national film identities resulted in the adoption by each country of precisely those traits of the other which were least fruitful or desirable. Pinthus arrived at much the same conclusion. Though differing from those who feared loss of German purity in the American film capital, he too cast doubt on the advisability of cooperative production. He also joined majority opinion on *Sunrise* and *The Way of All Flesh* in the tacit judgment that while both represented progress for Murnau and Jannings in certain respects, they also revealed the breakdown of the overall consistency for which these artists were celebrated in Germany. Gains impressive in isolation were no compensation for loss of rootedness and consistency. In this context it was no longer necessary to denounce Hollywood or defend the Germans who worked there. Germany's best were still supreme, but not in America. In sum, working from a generally high opinion of the American cinema, Pinthus joined with other critics to judge German endeavors in Hollywood artistic misfits. To use the language employed by Harry Kahn in reference to *The Way of All Flesh,* the combination of German and American ingredients resulted in motion pictures which were "not meat and not fish, not Hollywood and not Babelsberg, but a sugary, schmaltzy mixture of both."[55]

Subsequent American pictures by Jannings confirmed that over time mixed marriages had decreasing chance of success. Like Lubitsch, Jannings was seen as too talented to be ruined entirely by Hollywood's commercialism. But also like Lubitsch, he appeared suspended between cultural poles, leaning first one way and then the next, but increasingly tending to surrender to the American side. When teamed with European directors on European themes—as in *The Patriot* (Lubitsch) and *The Last Command* (Joseph von Sternberg)—he came closest to meeting German expectations.[56] When employed to revisit the depths of Anglo-America moralizing or family schmaltz, as in *The King of Soho* or *Sins of the Fathers,* he prostituted his enormous abilities.[57] In sum, despite important exceptions, attitudes toward German production in the United States, both before and after the middecade exodus, were sceptical. Generalizations made in 1926 did not lose their force. The path from curiosity and anxiety to ambivalence and scepticism proved a one-way street. The lesson taught by the American careers of Lubitsch, Murnau et al. was that the longer the sojourn in Hollywood, the less possibility there appeared for fulfillment of artistic promise shown in Germany.

The original emigration to Hollywood proved a short-lived phenomenon. Apart from the inability of some émigrés to find their niche in America, the sound revolution altered the whole foundation of their existence abroad. Emil Jannings, Conrad Veidt and Pola Negri all abandoned Hollywood late in the decade. Erich Pommer began work again for UFA in late 1927. Paul Leni died suddenly, still a young man, in 1929. F. W. Murnau came under studio constraints after the poor box-office showing of *Sunrise* and made only two further pictures, *City Girl* and *Four Devils*, neither of which lived up to his German reputation. Thoroughly disenchanted with Hollywood, he shot a film about life in the South Seas, *Tabu*, before an automobile accident claimed his life in 1931. At the start of a new decade only two really prominent Germans, the original émigré, Ernst Lubitsch, and the most recent one, Marlene Dietrich, were active in Hollywood. Those Hollywood otherwise enlisted to produce German talkies were of lesser fame and their output elicited neither great interest nor great enthusiasm.

In retrospect it is arguable that the émigrés had so many conflicting standards to meet that they were all but condemned in the long run. In the silent era their efforts met with intense scrutiny, both because of their lofty reputations and out of preoccupation with the consequences of blending German and American approaches. For the same reasons critical opinion was seldom unequivocal. Had the artists in question remained at home, their endeavors would still have been measured by a very strict rule, particularly beyond the confines of the trade press. The fact that they worked in Hollywood simultaneously blunted and sharpened criticism. Shortcomings in their films were blamed on Hollywood, yet they were expected, as representatives of the German cinema, to meet the highest qualitative standard. In a number of cases initial joint productions met with acclaim, relief that the given German artist had not been absorbed by Hollywood, or even admiration for the amalgamation of American finance and German *Geist*. The long-term prospects for Germans in Hollywood were, however, dimly viewed. American inroads into German independence seemed inevitable. Sooner or later the American system extracted concessions from German artists which compromised their talents.

8

THE COMING OF SOUND AND
THE WANING OF AMERICA

For most of the 1920s the United States enjoyed a level of prosperity and stability which made it the envy of German observers. Hollywood shared this good fortune and enviable reputation. As a mirror of American culture in everything from its success and wealth to its ethical ideals, the American cinema projected the economic and ideological invincibility of "God's own country." Germans might carp about the facile moral lessons, the almost unshakable optimism and the will to happiness of American movies. They could not dispute America's or Hollywood's world power; not at least until the great depression shattered the image of American invincibility and the coincident introduction of sound films temporarily shook American domination of the international market.

Like the world economic crisis, the overthrow of silent film began in the United States. But Germans could no more escape the consequences of the sound revolution than they could hope for immunity from the effects of the American stock-market crash. Indeed, nothing illustrates the symbiosis of Hollywood and Berlin in the Weimar era more graphically than the upheaval accompanying the demise of silent film and advent of talking motion pictures. American primacy was initially incontestable. Although the technical know-how of sound reproduction originated in large measure with European inventors, Hollywood, and Warner Bros. in particular, perfected the invention and demonstrated its market potential. The American cinema had a jump on its German counterpart and presented it with a *fait accompli*. German producers had no option but to follow

221

suit. Once sound film had proven its drawing power in the United States, the threatened loss of this market alone, quite apart from fears of being upstaged at home and in Europe, compelled German producers to adopt American practice. Essentially two years behind Hollywood—the first domestic sound pictures premiered only in the autumn of 1929—the German film industry worked feverishly from roughly mid-1929 to mid-1930 to establish competitive sound reproduction.[1]

While the German cinema displayed tremendous dependence on Hollywood's leadership, sound also provided it a new level of independence. The market protection enjoyed during the war, and by virtue of currency differences in the inflationary period, was partially restored in the form of the language barrier. In fact, the sound revolution allowed the German cinema to become master in its own house as it had not been since the American invasion of 1923–1924. Over the years 1926–1928 the average German share of the feature film market was 42.5 percent as against 39.5 percent for Hollywood and eighteen percent for all other countries combined. The corresponding figures averaged over the period 1929–1931, including silent and sound pictures, were Germany—48.4 percent, America—31.3 percent and all others—20.3 percent.[2] These figures show an increase in the German share of the domestic market to almost half, and a drop of the American share from virtual parity with the native contribution to two-thirds of it. However, the inclusion of silent pictures camouflages the full extent of the restructuring of the market. In 1929, a transition year in which silent pictures still predominated, distortion is minimal. Thereafter, inclusion of silent movies in the totals yields overrepresentation for Hollywood. Silents did continue to circulate in 1930 and 1931 for the simple reason that smaller, provincial theaters were initially reluctant or unable to invest in sound projection equipment, but by mid-1930 the leading theaters had converted wholesale to sound. A breakdown of feature releases in Germany in the years 1928–1931 into silents and sound pictures makes glaringly apparent German dominance in the category which really counted, the talkie.[3]

Market Shares: German and American Films, 1928–1931

	German Features			American Features		
	Silent	*Sound*	*Total*	*Silent*	*Sound*	*Total*
1928	224	—	224	199	—	199
1929	175	8	183	132	10	142
1930	46	100	146	50	30	80
1931	2	142	144	26	58	84

Several observations can be drawn from these figures. The dramatic drop in absolute numbers of feature releases, native or American, indicates the technical and financial strains imposed by the changeover to sound. Equally noteworthy is the rapidity of this conversion: in one season (1929–1930) sound became supreme; by 1931 silents were reduced to insignificance. Most important, however, is a comparison of entries in the sound columns. For both 1930 and 1931 Hollywood's market share rested well below half of Germany's and far from the two-thirds yielded when the silent pictures of 1929 are included in the computation. The sound revolution therefore precipitated a revolution of comparable dimensions in American-German competition on the German motion picture market, paralleling in uncanny fashion the trend to national autarky fostered by the depression.

Rapid and momentous as the changeover to talking pictures appears statistically, it did not occur instantaneously, nor were its ramifications immediately apparent to contemporaries. Like its political counterparts, this revolution also evinced considerable confusion in its intermediate stages. In the early months a bewildering array of "sound films" competed for audience approval. These ranged from silent films to which a sound track (music or sound effects or both) had subsequently been added, or pictures conceived with such sound tracks, to musicals like the epochal *The Jazz Singer* which combined synchronized music and song, bits of dialogue and conventional titles, to the so-called one hundred percent talkie. Import of this last variant presented an obvious complication. Since dialogue and, where applicable, song, were in English, titles or subtitles were required to translate at least the most critical phrases for German viewers. The only other options, both tried but not well received in the early sound era, were to produce multilingual versions with native actors or to dub pictures after completion into German.[4]

In the initial stages of the sound revolution confusion was heightened by patent wars over the equipment for producing and reproducing dialogue and music. The electrical trusts in the United States and Germany which controlled the rights to this equipment refused to permit interchangeability: movies made with one company's equipment could not be screened on any other reproduction systems. The German patent holder, Tobis-Klangfilm, prevented the screening in Germany of American movies with American sound systems and the Americans boycotted the German market to try to compel Tobis-Klangfilm to back down. Consequently, in the critical period when Hollywood enjoyed a head start, few American sound films reached German theaters.[5]

Even before the boycott there was considerable delay in export of the novelty to Germany. *The Jazz Singer*, the Warner Bros. picture starring Al Jolson which took audiences by storm in New York in October 1927, did not appear in Berlin until September 1928, and was then shown as a silent. In January 1929 *Wings*, a film of air combat in World War I, offered a first taste of sound but of a highly hybrid sort: along with live orchestral accompaniment and the usual titles went a synchronized sound track which provided motor noise to heighten the effect of the aerial scenes.[6] Not until June 1929 did Berlin experience the sensation of sound as New York had in 1927—a premiere boasting dialogue and song, Al Jolson's second picture for the Warner studios, *The Singing Fool*. Yet even then it retained a characteristic trait of silent film in that it used titles (not subtitles) to translate the dialogue. Furthermore, after a very successful run of almost seven weeks its premiere was canceled by a legal injunction against the use of Western Electric equipment in German theaters. The same court order postponed release of Stroheim's *The Wedding March*, a film with music and sound effects but without dialogue.[7] Other upcoming sound releases were either canceled or shown with conventional orchestral accompaniment. *Noah's Ark,* for example, a monumental epic from Warner reminiscent of D. W. Griffith's *Intolerance* in its parallel of the Great War and the Old Testament deluge, first appeared as a silent film.

Although initial exposure to Hollywood's sound pictures (1929–1930) coincided with Germany's transition to sound production, America still enjoyed enough of an edge that for an interim period sound appeared unique to Hollywood. Discourse on the talkie revolution therefore was tantamount to commentary on the American cinema. Substantial initial scepticism about the coordination of sound with motion pictures existed apart from Hollywood's role in the process. Nonetheless, America's lead in this innovation appeared more than coincidental and fostered particular resistance.

The Berlin premiere of *The Singing Fool* in June 1929 marked the breakthrough of talking film on the German market. It was both a society event and the occasion for full-scale debate on the possibilities and significance of the new medium. As already noted, Berliners had waited an extremely long time for this moment. A previously scheduled premiere of the picture had been scuttled at the very last moment by court order. This one was confirmed only at noon on the premiere date, but could still have been canceled at the last minute. Consequently, there was a late scramble for tickets, some critics going empty-handed for the premiere and having to compete against heavy public demand to gain admission to subsequent performances.[8]

Critical discussion of *The Singing Fool* yielded two general observations about the marriage of sound and the moving picture. To the immediate question whether that marriage was technically feasible the answer was a solid yes. Doubtful at the outset that the illusion of sound coming from the lips of screen characters could be established and maintained, critics were overwhelmed by the naturalness with which the optical and audio blended. This single test case demonstrated that the talkie was sufficiently developed to convince viewers and pay for itself.[9] To the broader question of whether sound represented a filmic advance the answer was an almost equally resounding no. Admiration for the technical achievement and for Al Jolson's voice could not erase dismay at the lachrymose subject matter and stage-bound presentation of the film. *The Singing Fool* confirmed pessimists in the fear that thematically and stylistically sound would set film culture back decades to its theatrical roots. Less motion picture than photographed theater, it resurrected the unpalatable falsifications of cheap melodrama and sentimental music. In the words of an indignant Wolfgang Petzet, it nullified thirty years of silent film culture and reverted as feared to the "barbarism of 1900."[10]

Although the early sound releases were not exclusively tearjerking musicals, the criticisms leveled against *The Singing Fool* were symptomatic.[11] In addition to reflecting resentment about erosion of a highly refined filmic tradition, they signified rejection of tendencies seen as inherent in American culture. The particular character of early sound pictures fueled the perception that in the land of unlimited possibilities technological innovation outran and displaced artistic values. Even before the premiere of *The Singing Fool* Maxim Ziese deprecated the American approach to the problem of declining box office receipts.

> In the search for a flaw in its production method for silent film, movie-America hit upon the brilliant way out not of seeking the shortcoming in its intellectual approach, but of finding it in the technical imperfection of the medium. At the moment America is trying to remedy the deficiencies in its worldview, which carried over into its films, by expanding filmic technology.[12]

Other commentators confirmed that the innovation of sound not only typified Hollywood's shallowness but corresponded to America's cultural immaturity. The poverty of theatrical traditions and intellectual pursuits made talking film an ideal surrogate. So long as the talkie possessed sensational or curiosity value the American public would digest it.[13]

Such rhetoric typified the conservative culture critique but in this particular case was not confined to conservatives. Commentators of all persuasions had strong reservations about the sound revolution. Rudolf Arnheim, for example, protested bitterly against the strangulation of silents for purely commercial reasons and denounced sound film as the triumph of bluff over quality.[14] The democratic *Deutsche Republik* took the third major American sound release, *Noah's Ark,* as demonstration that Hollywood employed technological distractions to protect itself against superior German and Russian imports and to lull American audiences "back into the slumber of mental inertia."

> Millions were invested in the play toy, sound film, and when the harmless mental babies enjoyed the noise, when this record player nation was captivated by musical hits, the movie moguls of Hollywood went back unscrupulously with regard to screenplays to the primitive beginnings of 1905. . . . For the present they calculate only in dollars. But one day they will have to reinsert the notion of film art into their calculation.[15]

This resistance to American talking pictures betrays a surprising debt to older blanket condemnations of film as the antithesis of art because it relied on mechanical means of reproduction. Once the status quo was disturbed and the technological nature of the medium was highlighted by the addition of sound, critics became sensitive to a dimension of film they otherwise took for granted.[16] Their reaction against the introduction of sound also drew on latent aversion to the cultural might of big business. That the leap into talkies was a desperate bid on the part of the American film industry to rekindle public interest in the movies and boost profits made sound an advertisement for the industrial character of film enterprise. The same profit motive had, of course, raised the silent cinema from a curiosity to a cultural force of the first rank, but this fact was conveniently overlooked. Sound pictures provided an unpleasant reminder that the movies were a mechanical and commercial proposition before they acquired artistic and cultural standing.[17] They therefore became symbols of cultural primitiveness. In remarkable parallel with stereotyping popular a decade earlier, talking and musical pictures were perceived as mesmerizing for Americans but unsatisfactory for Germans. Sound film thus appeared a typically American solution to a chronic state of national cultural backwardness.[18]

In the hands of nationalist and völkisch commentators such cultural stereotyping acquired the overtones of the postwar film war. Wolfgang Ertel-Breithaupt of *Filmkünstler und Filmkunst*

classified the embryonic talkie as the latest stage in the surrender by Europe to America of its most prized artistic convictions:
America tried something new and Europe adopted it shame-
lessly. In the course of the 1920s the German cinema had already degenerated from a highly dedicated, artistic force to a
factory system borrowed from America. Hollywood's way of
escape from artistic stagnation was invention of sound, what
Ertel-Breithaupt called the "triumph of the international surrogate of American civilization." To the extent that German cinema followed suit, he believed catastrophe would follow. Preoccupation with commercial, technical and patent issues signaled
abdication by German cinema of its mission. American em-
phases were crowding out "character" and "conviction," the two
qualities he dwelt on *ad nauseam* as the distinguishing marks of
German culture.[19]

As in the early 1920s, the discourse of national differences
had unmistakable economic subtexts. In the critical months of
1929 and 1930 the specter of renewed American inroads
loomed once again. At the beginning of 1929 UFA sent a team
to the United States to study sound production. On the basis
of its findings UFA decided to proceed at maximum speed to
make the switch. The language barrier and patent war notwithstanding, the substantial lag of German development behind
Hollywood posed a recognized threat.[20] In addition, American
companies began to hire German talent in an attempt to circum-
vent the language barrier. While the sound revolution brought
the repatriation of Conrad Veidt and Emil Jannings, both of
whom figured prominently in pioneering German talkies (*Die
letzte Kompagnie* and *Der blaue Engel*), it also revived suspicions
that Hollywood would launch another recruitment drive and
plunder the German industry.[21] Moreover, the backstage manipulation of the enormous American electrical trusts which
controlled sound patents and had unrivaled buying power
posed the threat of economic and cultural subservience.[22]

In the event, none of these specters materialized. German
producers made astonishingly rapid progress with the talkie.
American-made German language films generally failed to impress, largely because they featured second-rate performers.
Apart from Marlene Dietrich, Hollywood stole no prominent

German film artist in this period. The patent war and the threat of American monopoly were quickly forgotten, a new *modus operandi* emerging between the patent holders for international interchange and royalties. Nonetheless, short-lived concerns triggered defensive responses familiar from the early 1920s. As at that time, the selection of up-to-date American motion pictures was minimal. Film pundits therefore speculated about the future as much or more as they analyzed the present, groping again to define Germany's place in an unsettled but American-dominated film world. Once more they betrayed uncertainty in taking refuge behind the shield of cultural types. The discourse of national distinctiveness aimed again to erect barriers to Americanization.

Although this discourse served a primarily defensive function, it also fostered hopes of national cinematic renewal through the adoption of sound. Again the correspondence with attitudes in the immediate postwar years is striking. Two commentators who drew attention to the parallel between circumstances right after the war and in 1929 illustrate the dialectic of fear and hope. Franz Schulz used the analogy between the two eras to underscore the danger inherent in German isolation from international, particularly American, developments. In 1929 as in 1919, remoteness from world trends meant jeopardizing Germany's competitive position. Schulz intimated that on the purely technical level German producers could only survive internationally by learning from America.[23] By contrast, Willy Haas acknowledged the need for Germany to catch up with Hollywood but warned, as he had in the past, against indiscriminate borrowing. In the early and midtwenties German filmmakers had erred by taking their thematic cues from, and endeavoring to cater to, America. Now, as ten years previously, the German cinema should rather exploit its isolation, draw upon its own roots (its lengthy, sophisticated stage tradition evidenced the resources waiting to be tapped), and create uniquely German sound pictures which would shake the world and Hollywood's reign over it. Haas therefore challenged native producers not to presume that America would be ultimate master or beneficiary of the revolution it had instigated.[24]

Experts therefore drew hope for cinematic rejuvenation

from the possibilities offered by a fresh start in the new medium
and the belief that Germany was ideally situated to exploit it.
Commercial preponderance and a technical headstart did not
guarantee Hollywood would be most successful in synthesizing
the audio and optical elements of the motion picture.[25] In this
context Haas's plea for cultivation of a distinctly German talking
film, a fresh salvo in the decade-old debate over the national
or international film, found resonance not only in nationalistic
circles. With it came resurrection of artistic expectations which
had been disappointed in the course of the 1920s.[26] Hans
Spielhofer, columnist and critic for a conservative trade journal,
but like Haas anything but narrowly chauvinistic, reasoned that
European culture sought consummation precisely in the combination of speech and picture possible in the talkie. Unlike re-
gions of lesser education and closer proximity to nature (America), Europe was never completely satisfied with reliance on the
more primitive mimic dialogue. With the acquisition by speech
of equality with mimicry, writers and poets could be expected
to show renewed interest in the cinema. In short, what in the
United States represented a technical toy and commercial gim-
mick was pregnant with cultural significance when transposed
to a European setting.[27]

     Haas and Spielhofer wrote in 1929, when the German or
European talkie was barely in embryo. By 1930 their prophecies
had begun to see fulfillment and their confidence appeared vindicated. By the time of the patent truce in July 1930 the uncer-
tainties of the talkie revolution were effectively removed. Sound
had demonstrated its staying power; silents were all but dead.
The release of *Der blaue Engel* and *Westfront 1918* in April and
May respectively demonstrated German technical equality and
proved that sound was not the source of artistic inhibition indicated by the early musicals. Also by mid-1930 the market revolution documented above began to make itself felt. There were
grounds for believing that Hollywood's innovation eroded its
international dominance and served German interests. The pattern of the previous decade appeared broken.

     The resurgence of domestic hopes can be followed in the
editorials of the trade papers. In February 1930 *Lichtbildbühne*
published a lead article under the pretentious title, "Transvalu-

ation of all Values," celebrating the displacement of American silent film by talking pictures, mainly German in origin, in the foremost premiere theaters of Berlin's west end. The triumph of sound was diminishing the American presence in the most representative German theaters.[28] Early in March a second lead article reviewed recent developments and concluded that a corner had been turned.

> Even if there were no patent problems there would no longer be a broad basis for the American talkie in Germany. On the other hand, American silent film is fading into the background with the boom in German language sound films. It poses no more threat to the existence of German silent film and even less to German language sound film.[29]

Several months later *Film-Kurier* corroborated this break with the past in its annual poll of the most successful pictures at the box office. Since inauguration of the poll in 1925 domestic features had regularly accounted for roughly two-thirds of those submitted as commercial successes even though they represented less than half the total releases. By contrast, Hollywood consistently garnered about one-fifth of the total votes despite holding a two-fifths market share. The remaining ten to fifteen percent of the ballots went to productions from other European countries, corresponding approximately to their representation in Germany. In 1929–1930, however, America's share of the vote dropped to less than one-sixth, to the benefit of imports from European filmmakers. *Film-Kurier* noted that for the first time in the history of the poll, the commercial worth of European imports outstripped that of American films.[30] One year later *Film-Kurier* cited recently published censorship data to proclaim a "Market Revolution through Sound Film." The ongoing erosion of Hollywood's presence had quantitative and qualitative dimensions, both favoring further domestic recovery.

> The Americans, who forced sound film to such an outrageous extent, have deprived themselves of their earlier paramount position on the European market. The conversion to sound film has an especially great impact on the German market, since because of the relatively numerous and qualitatively high-ranking sound films in

the vernacular here, the public has already quickly rejected—apart from rather few exceptions—films with foreign dialogue.[31]

Apart from editorializing on the changing ratios of American and domestic releases, the trade press registered the market revolution by disregarding Hollywood and lavishing attention on native achievements. In fact the outstanding characteristic of the trade press in the early thirties is less preoccupation with Hollywood's demise than indulgence for domestic motion pictures. Once the novelty in domestic ascendancy wore off the basic fact remained: the German market no longer relied on American imports any more than it needed protection from a flood of them. The dialectic of dependency and antipathy characteristic of the mid-1920s gave way to relative indifference. Only the exhibitors, who by 1932 realized that national independence left them at the mercy of native producers, called for loosening of import restrictions. Commercially, Hollywood was an issue only insofar as its absence raised the fear of domestic monopoly.[32]

While the commercial consequences of the sound revolution were relatively straightforward, the artistic and national dimensions raised by Haas and Spielhofer proved controversial. Hollywood's diminishing influence was generally accepted as a natural consequence of the language barrier, but opinion was divided on the broader ramifications for German cinema. Some critics detected a logic in changing market shares which conformed to developments in other spheres and to earlier demands for restriction of American import to a minimum of top-grade features. Fritz Olimsky concluded, without any sense of regret, that the language barrier would occasion new approaches. "We'll have to become more and more accustomed to the idea that *sound film is the pacemaker of a predominantly nationally oriented film production*."[33] *Kinematograph* took as its point of departure for this "national shift" the interplay of commercial and cultural determinants. Language restrictions dictated concentration on the domestic market, which in turn meant fewer extravagant productions financed by foreign earnings and more down-to-earth, domestically relevant themes. Reinforcement for the same trend came from a public tired of conventional spectacle. Widespread disenchantment with America and the "soulless worship of the mechanical" it represented provided the opportunity for German filmmakers to captivate Europe. National orientation would serve expansion into markets once dominated by Hollywood.[34]

Other conservative sources detected an inherent link between sound pictures and national introversion. Various attempts to overcome the language barrier confirmed what they took as self-evident: forms of speech belonged to the very essence of a cultural type and could not be interchanged without loss of substance. Speech divided mankind and accentuated national differences in thought and feeling. Language represented the "basic element of national uniqueness" and transferred motion pictures from the realm of "international civilization" to the plateau of "volkhaft-national culture." Talking film thus not only proved a barrier to import of American movies, but highlighted otherwise inexpressible elements of German culture.[35]

Apart from these references to the cultural significance of language, attempts to identify the peculiarly German over against the typically American fell back on clichés. Antitheses popular after the war—culture and civilization, art and entertainment, authenticity and falsification, *Geist* and *Technik*—served to justify Hollywood's relative decline in Germany. The ultimate triumph of the German (European) worldview became the logical outcome of a decade-old *Kulturkampf*.[36] Even when Hollywood was not depicted as an enemy of German culture, the prospect of motion picture autarky acquired broader significance. A lead article in *Deutsche Filmzeitung* deduced from the restoration of domestic primacy that Germany enjoyed sufficient cultural resilience to assimilate foreign influence. Oblivious to the commercial and technical impulses which had spawned talking film, it maintained that legal exclusion of foreign motion pictures was no longer required because a national awakening had stimulated popular demand for patriotic subject matter. Developments in the cinema reflected deeper currents in contemporary Germany.[37]

Against the heralds of national awakening who welcomed Hollywood's declining role in Germany were grouped a number of critics who warned about the dangers of cultural introversion.

Despite reservations about American cinema, they found growing isolation from international markets both constricting and
perilous. Particularly ominous was the tightening of import regulations, at the very moment, ironically, that trade papers
judged such restrictions superfluous given the recovery of domestic independence. Beginning in 1930 the quota system was
indirectly tightened by legal redefinition of a "German" film.
Previously, a feature film had been classified German so long
as it was made in Germany in no less than fourteen studio days
and was at least 1500 meters long. Effective 1 July 1930 the
production company had to be German; the script writer, com-
poser, director and majority of personnel in each production
area had to be German speaking residents; all studio work and,
if feasible, all outdoor scenes had to be shot in Germany. In
1932 these stipulations were considerably sharpened: the producer and seventy-five percent of all production personnel had
to be German, and, most importantly, a German was redefined
as a legal citizen of the Reich.[38]

No one quarreled with the intent of these changes to encourage employment of native over foreign personnel when the
economy was depressed. Insofar, however, as the legislation
jeopardized investment by foreign firms in Germany, affecting
both output and cost of native production, it met a more mixed
response. As in the immediate postwar period, some experts
questioned whether it might lead to retaliatory legislation from
the United States. They also feared its impact on the number
and nature of American films Germans would be permitted to
see. Narrowing the definition of a German film, thereby enlarging the category of imports without expanding their numbers,
appeared counterproductive for ensuring that Germany would
receive the optimal selection of foreign pictures. The smaller
the quantity of American imports, the greater pressure there
would be for distributors to handle the commercially predictable ones to the exclusion of unusual or pioneering works.[39]

Most disturbing to proponents of liberal film trade were the
assumptions behind tightening restrictions. Legal reinforcement for the declining marketability of American film in Germany seemed unnecessary and suggested unhealthy ethnocen-
trism. Its unspoken assumption was the inferiority or lack of

culture of non-German, especially American, motion pictures. Despite the production of many inferior German pictures, the domestic industry was tacitly being awarded a patent for outstanding and cultivated filmmaking. The effect of the modified legislation would be to restrict competition on the German film market and thus foster lesser productions which would otherwise be marginalized.[40]

Stephan Ehrenzweig related this growing cinematic chauvinism to a wider current of national opinion. Attitudes prevalent in film circles paralleled those expressed in response to the recent summer Olympics in Los Angeles. Following the defeat of German runners by black athletes, the National Socialists demanded the exclusion of the latter as competitors in the Games slated for Germany in 1936. In similar fashion, if less stridently, the German cinema was working to eliminate competition and would, as Ehrenzweig sardonically noted, soon be unbeatable. Nationalist appeals to the Prussian tradition and its military glory sufficed to earn accolades for a filmmaker. Already the critic bold enough to criticize a native picture risked denunciation as a cultural Bolshevik or traitor. In the cinema, as in other fields, Germany was retreating to a position beyond critical reach.

> Negroes run faster? Well then we'll run without them. Americans, Frenchmen make better films? We'll just show more of our own. If the word "Prussian" appears three times in them, then they are good. If it appears ten times, then they are important.[41]

Although Ehrenzweig's critique was overdrawn for dramatic effect, it comes very close to capturing the mood of trade reviews in the dying phase of the Weimar Republic. Critics searched the language for superlatives adequate to capture their enthusiasm for the latest German talkie, but exhibited relative coolness toward American imports. What makes this double standard particularly remarkable is the fact that for the first time the popular demand among experts for import only of select, outstanding Hollywood products approached fulfillment. Apart from imports from American firms using German performers in Hollywood or Paris, the imports of 1930–1932 featured top-ranking American casts and directors. Numerical

primacy went to films of Greta Garbo and those directed by
Josef von Sternberg, of *The Blue Angel* fame (usually paired, as
in that picture, with Marlene Dietrich). Next in line came the
features of Ernst Lubitsch, essentially musical comedies featur-
ing Maurice Chevalier, but including his melodramatic excur-
sion into war and personal guilt entitled *Broken Lullaby*. Other
leading figures of the American cinema represented by early
sound imports were Harold Lloyd, Buster Keaton, Charlie
Chaplin, George Bancroft, Erich Stroheim and Rouben Ma-
moulian. German moviegoers did not encounter the complete
list of Hollywood's best, but they saw very little of the so-called
average work dumped on the market in the previous decade.[42]

Contemporary indifference to Hollywood despite quantitative reduction and careful selection of American imports reflects not only growing national introversion but also reliance
on well-entrenched critical paradigms. With rare exceptions,
critics continued to flog the romantic and dramatic products of
Hollywood for disproportion between form and content.
Though hackneyed, this specific flaw of American moviemak-
ing proved particularly apposite for discussion of pictures from
leading Hollywood artists, whose cinematic prowess was indisputable. By itself, however, it does not account for coolness toward the slickest entertainment Hollywood could offer when
the German cinema was outdoing itself with light amusement
capable of diverting popular attention from the deepening socioeconomic and political crisis. Did the fact that American movies made up such a token share of the German market permit
critics to indulge previously suppressed antipathies? Or was
there, as some critics had long argued, an insuperable taste barrier beyond that of language?

A balanced response to these questions must first concede
that critics often acknowledged the entertainment value of
American pictures they otherwise faulted. Ernst Lubitsch, for
example, whose almost exclusive preoccupation with light comedies and operettas began to exasperate even some of his long-
time admirers, was still generally recognized as a master of
filmic amusement.[43] Greta Garbo, pitied for the directors and
screenplays assigned to her, still commanded a reputation for
captivating the viewer like no other screen personality.[44] Even

von Sternberg and Dietrich, whose propensity for screen kitsch outraged critics and audiences, still received plaudits for creating unrivaled thrillers.[45]

This concession made, critics still detected a compound of flaws familiar from the mid-1920s. Ruthless exploitation of star value produced endless, boring remakes of successful pictures. Sensationalism and sentimentalism became calculated devices which might correspond to American tastes but alienated German viewers. Consequently, scenes intended to create drama provoked disbelief and laughter, even when handled by Hollywood's foremost talents.[46] Above all, Hollywood's screenplays were both improbable and unrelated to real life. Characters and plot development lacked both internal consistency and connectedness to contemporary issues. Hermann Sinsheimer, for instance, repeatedly excoriated von Sternberg as a prisoner of the studio incapable of presenting life rather than a lie.[47] Almost as guilty in this regard was Ernst Lubitsch, for whom conformity to the Hollywood production system had meant losing touch with the real world. Even such a long-time Lubitsch fan as Kurt Pinthus suggested that with his stream of musicals set in never-never land he had become averse to life as though it were a disease.[48]

Unwillingness to gloss over shortcomings in content for the sake of technical polish had particular significance in a period in which Hollywood's leading talents were represented in German cinemas. While conceding entertainment value, critics increasingly regretted that such extraordinary talent was squandered on irrelevant or unpalatable subject matter. The main target of their displeasure was von Sternberg, the Austrian émigré, whose undeniable genius still suffered tasteless, pulp-fiction film plots. Much as in Murnau's *Sunrise,* the very brilliance of staging and camera work underscored the vacuity of von Sternberg's thematic repertoire. Grandiose artistry coexisted with the most pathetic and schematic motifs known to the cinema. This appalling gap between form and content again betrayed Hollywood's isolation from reality. In the unequivocal language of Rudolf Arnheim, von Sternberg needed forcing back to life. If he were in Russia instead of Hollywood, he would create the world's greatest motion pictures.[49]

Against this backdrop it is no surprise that the two American motion pictures which garnered most critical acclaim in this period brought slices of real life to the screen. King Vidor's dramatized documentary of life among American blacks, *Hallelujah*, and Josef von Sternberg's screen adaptation of the Theodore Dreiser novel, *An American Tragedy*, stood out as bold departures from studio convention. The former ventured into territory traditionally off-limits for Hollywood and the latter tackled a theme worthy of von Sternberg's genius: the moral pressures and corruption of American society. Despite admission that neither possessed outstanding box office potential, the champions of realism had opportunity to become enthusiastic about Hollywood. In its concern for a touchy subject *Hallelujah* appeared an unparalleled sound document, a masterpiece of folklore and artistic justification for talking pictures. Its breathtaking authenticity was surpassed only by Soviet cinema.[50] *An American Tragedy* peeled the layers of cosmetic off American values familiar from countless American society dramas. Von Sternberg discarded the pictorial poetry of his other films for reportage and cool realism. Manfred Georg read from it Hollywood's adjustment to shifting American self-perceptions. The self-satisfaction typified by designation of America as "God's own country" was dead. Even if Hollywood had yet to explore the causes of real-life problems, it was at least pursuing the facts.[51]

Enthusiasm for these two departures from American film convention confirms the relative marginalization of Hollywood in Weimar film culture. It also hints that mainstream domestic cinema so much resembled Hollywood that any deviation from type was welcome. As in the early 1920s, when critics denigrated the sensationalist imports as un-German even while German directors made potboilers to challenge Hollywood, so now they took exception to American entertainment without confessing that German studios produced sufficient kitsch to make Hollywood's redundant. In other words, Hollywood became a scapegoat for a domestic industry proficient at manufacture of inconsequential, escapist entertainment. For apart from a select group of socially realistic pictures—*Menschen am Sonntag, Mädchen in Uniform, Kuhle Wampe, Kameradschaft, Cyankali*—the German industry created settings and themes as socially and intellectually vacuous as any attributed to Hollywood. Whether historical or contemporary, smash hits such as *Der Kongress tanzt, Die drei von der Tankstelle, Bomben auf Monte Carlo* or *Quick* portrayed characters and circumstances as fantastic in their own way as the postwar Expressionist or serial pictures. Next to them the much despised American features of the 1920s appeared almost down-to-earth. This flight from socioeconomic chaos and political disintegration into wish-dreams, fueled by the increasingly reactionary behavior of the censors, encouraged critics to seek artistic stimulus from foreign pictures. Movies which, like *An American Tragedy*, confronted contemporary issues confirmed that cinema was more than a vehicle for mass escapism.[52]

Since foreign duplication of mainstream domestic production was excess baggage, Hollywood's last offensive in coproductions was abortive. Some dozen German language talkies, produced either in the United States or at a studio outside Paris, provoked little interest even though released within a relatively short time span from late 1930 through 1931. Casts and production values were almost uniformly second-class. Contrary to earlier practice, Hollywood employed lesser directors and performers whose departure meant scant loss to the German industry. Their achievements received correspondingly limited attention. The high-profile critics outside trade circles simply ignored them.[53] Trade critics reviewed these coproductions but seldom judged them more than adequate. The greatest compliment they paid such a film, and rarely at that, was equality with its American prototype or with a comparable German production.[54] This implied that Hollywood's effort to establish German-language production offered nothing not supplied by either cinema working independently. Germany could manufacture sufficient talkies of the caliber of German versions produced in Paris or in the United States. Commercially and artistically these pictures created no synthesis of Hollywood and Berlin, any more than they posed a serious challenge to the dominant trend to national independence.[55]

This chapter has chronicled, in fact and in perception, the demise of American film in Germany following the sound revolution. No longer was the German cinema fated, as one observer had commented ruefully in 1926, to be spice in the American soup.[56] On the contrary, America seemed destined, insofar as the German market was concerned, to offer only occasional diversion from a fundamentally homegrown film diet. This destiny became apparent not only in the volume of American imports, but in the general indifference toward American efforts to produce German talkies. While some critics obviously showed more sensitivity than others to the box-office value of any motion picture, the dwindling commercial importance of American imports made it increasingly possible to downplay their role as entertainment which had to fill theaters. Run-of-the-mill American movies, including those made by Germans, became superfluous. By 1932 at the latest, native producers manufactured sufficient and sufficiently engaging amusement to satisfy the public and satiate the average critic's appetite for pictures with broad popular appeal.

There is therefore a distinct sense of anticlimax in German-American motion picture interaction during the last years of Weimar. Hollywood was as conspicuous by its relative absence as it earlier had been by its presence. Apart from the famous clash provoked by *All Quiet on the Western Front* in late 1930, American films no longer elicited great concern, and that irrespective of whether they met enthusiastic or cool receptions. Nothing illustrates this better than Universal's attempt in 1932 to turn the release of *Frankenstein* into a public spectacle. Bloodcurdling advertising, including the promise of medical assistance to those overcome by horror, boomeranged even more sharply than in the case of *The Ten Commandments* in 1924. The publicity campaign turned against itself when its object created as much laughter as horror.[57] The Hollywood mystique suffered one more puncture and could not be repaired, as in 1924, by the threat of imminent domination. America had debuted a decade earlier with sensationalist serials which created amusement as well as excitement. It saw the curtain come down on a picture which drew laughter though designed to awe and frighten.

CONCLUSION

Telescoped into clear-cut stages Weimar's experience of Hollywood can be formulated very simply: America came, provoked both applause and controversy, and then faded. At the close, as at the opening of the Weimar era, the American cinema sat on the periphery of German cultural concerns. Only in the middle years of the Republic did Americanization, in the cinema as in other spheres, generate sustained discourse. In this sense the first American phase in German history was an interlude, a harbinger of developments after 1945.

Once the stages of Weimar's encounter with Hollywood are dissected, it is clear that history did not come full circle. Despite striking parallels between circumstances and attitudes in the early and late years of the Republic, Hollywood's relative remoteness from Berlin in 1933 had different implications than after 1918. For moviegoers and for the film community, the expectations and apprehensions of the early 1920s gave way to a more distanced and dispassionate appreciation of American imports. Moreover, at any given moment in the intervening years, Hollywood possessed a multiplicity of meanings. By turns a much sought after novelty, an imposition, a scapegoat for domestic film difficulties, a model for cinematic development, a cause of moral outrage, a window on the American soul, or a mirror for German identity: Hollywood served multiple purposes and was integrated into a multitude of discourses. Indeed the measure of its domestication in Germany was the variety of issues it could be enlisted to address.

Domestication did not necessarily presuppose the popularity of American motion pictures. In fact, it is arguable that the layers of discourse on Hollywood were richest when American motion pictures encountered growing box-office difficulties.

Nevertheless, Hollywood's popular appeal was a crucial issue. Film historians have claimed both that American feature films were popular as elsewhere and that German viewers preferred domestic films. Neither generalization is convincing.[1] Impressionistic evidence from critics and theater owners suggests that American cinema initially received a warm welcome. It is possible, ironically, that the dated and largely sensationalist pictures of the first years of import enjoyed greater collective appreciation than any other body of American pictures which followed. At middecade a combination of limited hard evidence and editorial opinion indicates that tastes had become much more selective. Individual pictures, such as *Ben Hur* or slapsticks starring Harold Lloyd, did very well at the German box office. Numerous other imports failed to generate much interest. Whether German viewers were *amerikamüde,* as the pundits maintained, or simply more discriminating than American moviegoers, or increasingly wedded to an Americanized domestic product, as consumers they took what they wanted and left the rest. For the balance of the Weimar period, particularly once talkies were introduced, American imports remained regular features of theater programs but by all accounts less popular as a whole than their German counterparts.

Among trade experts, critics and outside commentators, questions of popularity were overlaid with a complex pattern of commercial and cultural agendas. For literary intellectuals the fascination with America and Hollywood, which has often been noted, vied with indigestion and disdain.[2] On balance it is safe to say that a number of those with leftist leanings found in specific imports justification for domestic causes. Trade experts and critics were likewise both fascinated and repulsed by American motion pictures. Increasingly they distinguished suitable from inappropriate imports, primarily on the grounds of incompatible national tastes. In the middecade reaction against American imports, however, commercial pressures cut across judgments of quality and appeal. Trade circles made efforts to rehabilitate Hollywood in order to safeguard commitments to American companies.

From within the German film industry, discourse on American cinema was heavily conditioned by competitive and expansionist ambitions. Immediately following the war Hollywood was a distant, unknown quantity with an imposing international record. Initial interest, overwhelmingly commercial, was expressed frequently with wartime rhetoric. Lines formed for the battle to decide whether Hollywood or Berlin would rule the motion picture world. Although in retrospect German defeat appears inevitable, the clash was not without a rationale.[3] By 1918 the German cinema was a major industry with visions of expansion abroad, where its principal competitor was the United States. Like other industrial interests the cinema sought to identify its welfare with that of the nation and German *Kultur*. Consequently, discourse drew both on stereotypical images of America as soulless, technologically precocious, artistically childish and uncritical, and on assumptions of cultural collision engendered by the war.

By middecade discourse on Hollywood had shifted somewhat to accommodate the general debate unleashed by the onslaught of *Amerikanismus*. In response to the latter, forward-looking circles adopted the United States as a model of efficiency, rationalization and technological modernity. With the cultural avant garde they revised the traditional, negative judgment on American culture. Sports, jazz, film—in a word, mass culture, with its commercial, social and supranational ramifications—gained acceptance as progressive, democratic and dynamic.[4] Against these enthusiasts for American accomplishments, by no means of a single political persuasion, was ranged a coalition of interests determined to defend German culture against adulteration or sabotage. Gathered in good measure on the nationalist right, but including intellectuals of virtually all political persuasions, this coalition saw America as the embodiment of precisely those tendencies most feared at home.[5] Erosion of national identity, the overwhelming of *Kultur* by American civilization, meant loss of privileged intellectual status. America had room for engineers, technocrats and entertainers but not for the formulators of higher values. American mass culture and rationalization represented the threat of cultural proletarianization.[6]

Although framed in this wider debate, informed discourse on American cinema at middecade cannot be adequately understood in such schematic terms. By this point Hollywood was no longer a legend or abstraction, but a source of inspiration, funding for domestic production and extremely diverse movie entertainment. With respect to the films themselves, the rhetoric of "average" and "outstanding" or "suitable" and "inappropriate," while reasserting differences of taste and culture between Hollywood and Berlin, could not disguise that American film was domesticated both as product and point of reference. Exchange of technology, personnel, promotional techniques and finished products had become so extensive that interests and opinions could no longer be separated. Clear-cut choices for or against Hollywood were an illusion. At stake was rather selection for assimilation of what seemed relevant from the American model for domestic development.[7]

In this context Hollywood did much more than encroach on an important industry or provide a storehouse of filmic techniques. By modeling a successful formula, however unevenly received in German theaters, it created an identity crisis for Weimar cinema, encouraging both imitation and the search for alternative filmic discourses. Moreover, by spotlighting problems in the dualism of high and low culture it challenged the very categories applied to analyze the cinema. In defence against Hollywood, dualistic conceptions of culture—art versus industry, self-realization versus entertainment—proved self-defeating. The dismissal of American film as advertising or assembly-line merchandise, intended to damn it irredeemably, simply confirmed the interrelatedness of commercial and creative impulses which German filmmakers had to accept to rival Hollywood. Competitive pressure from Hollywood therefore not only accelerated rationalization of the German film industry but also progressively deprived film experts of the critical categories used to suggest cultural distinctiveness.

The extended discourse on national versus international cinema was another dualistic structure used to establish distance between Hollywood and Berlin. Here too, critical dissection of American global film hegemony exposed the options as more illusory than real.[8] Broadly speaking, contemporaries concluded that the juggernautlike force of American cinema derived from its marriage of three achievements—a distinct identity, popular appeal and cultural respectability. As a trinity these permitted American movies to establish themselves not only as the dominant national cinema but also as the archetype of cinema, the yardstick for all others. Consequently, Americanization in cinema went beyond matters of cutting rhythms, fashions or advertising campaigns. It implied appropriation or replication of the particular achievements which made Hollywood preeminent.

In the early 1920s prestige and profit, at home and abroad, appeared within the grasp of German filmmakers. In short order American inroads began to frustrate realization of these ambitions and to force a particular construction on the way in which they were pursued. The essential task for Weimar cinema became to duplicate the American feat, that is, to win a position domestically and internationally comparable to that enjoyed by Hollywood. To do so meant creation of a distinct product which would generate the type of consensus which American cinema enjoyed in the United States. A decidedly un-American motion picture identity which did not possess broad appeal clearly would not shake Hollywood's hegemony. Conversely, adoption of the American model in the interests of international sales, enormously tempting though it proved, meant engaging American production at its strongest points and thereby condemning German cinema to derivative and subordinate status. Confrontation with Hollywood therefore highlighted the challenge of establishing production both German and publicly relevant.

The 1920s witnessed a somewhat erratic but ongoing quest to realize these twin objectives in the guise of a German national cinema. Despite the term it was neither nationalistic nor politically motivated. Rather it connoted that synthesis of recognizability, prestige and popularity which Hollywood had attained. Although multiple variables conditioned that synthesis, two overlapping relationships were primary—between filmmaker and audience and between Germany and the world. The first challenge was to give German cinema a profile at home comparable to Hollywood's in the United States. The second was to extend that profile abroad. Since contemporaries generally believed that successfully meeting the former would assure the latter, the problem boiled down to establishing a reliable, mutually-reinforcing link between producer and consumer.[9]

Though self-evident, this particular problem resisted simple solutions. As discussion in chapter five indicated, experts reasoned that, by contrast with the United States, Germany was a socially and culturally fragmented nation. Regional, confessional, political and intellectual differences presented substantial if not insurmountable obstacles to truly shared cinema experience. In particular, the expectations imposed on cinema by the cultivated segment of German society, represented within as well as outside the industry, complicated general conquest of the German public realm. Under these circumstances Weimar cinema exhibited admirable diversity but lacked a center, a representative type. Between Expressionism, psychological drama or literary adaptations and sentimental romances, military farces and patriotic spectacles German production appealed to a wide range of social and intellectual groups but failed to unite them. Squeezed by domestic resistance and foreign competition it required a formula to reconcile cultivation and general accessibility.[10]

At the level of critical discourse the demand for realism became the principal expression of contemporary concern to create a national cinema and more homogenous audience. But that recommendation collided with recognition that Germany offered far too divided a community to permit realistic treatment of topical issues. To the extent that its films shared aversion to realistic, contemporary settings and themes, they mirrored the lack of social and political consensus in the Weimar Republic.[11] A national cinema presupposed a degree of social and cultural homogeneity, linking filmmakers and moviegoers, which Weimar lacked. The only escape from the social instability and cultural conflict which constituted the cinema's *Sitz im Leben* would come from their amelioration. To establish a solid nexus between producer and consumer meant participation in the task of defining and creating the nation.[12]

Insofar as America exemplified the social and cultural symmetry required to sustain a national cinema, it was model and ally to Weimar cinema. Nevertheless, Americanization continued to elicit very ambivalent responses. Trade experts recommended adoption of a series of organizational, performing and filmic techniques, and more broadly recognized the symbiosis of American cinema and society, but they rarely advocated fundamental social and cultural democratization as the prerequisite of a national cinema. Similarly, more distanced observers such as Roland Schacht or Herbert Ihering, who traced Hollywood's ascendancy to the peculiarities of American culture, were still loathe to open the door to *Amerikanismus*. This instinctive aversion to the prospect of Berlin becoming New York was not, however, the whole key to ambivalence. There was rationale as well as reflex response in German discourse on the filmic ramifications of Americanization. Since wholesale borrowing appeared to permit further subjugation by Hollywood, imitation offered a treacherous way forward. On the assumption that German and American mentalities differed in fundamentals, many experts also argued that catering to the latter would not open doors to the American market. Berlin could not be New York. Finally, evidence that cultural differences could be overcome within specific styles or genres justified pursuit of a separate identity. The lesson drawn from slapstick, for example, was the need not to imitate but to cultivate a comparably unique and popular German genre.

The simultaneous transition to talking motion pictures and realization by German cinema of its long-standing aspiration to national primacy appear causally related. The number and variety of American imports declined as domestic producers proved adept in early sound pictures, so adept that Germany also experienced widening European export prospects.[13] In the language of the mid-1920s, Germany finally had spawned a national cinema. Some observers believed, however, that this attainment had more organic causes. In their opinion the sound revolution ran parallel with a national revolution in tastes as well as politics. Nationalist rhetoric strikingly confirms, however, even as it conceals, the immensity of the American film shadow. The national cinema was dressed as an endogenous creation which escaped Hollywood, but it emerged out of almost unbroken dialogue with American cinema and duplicated the American achievement as analyzed by German observers in the 1920s. In the early 1930s prestige, profit and national distinctiveness appeared reconciled at last.

The discourse of national cinemas elided crucial aspects of Hollywood's significance for Berlin. In pragmatic terms, both the attractiveness of the American market and the potency of the American model encouraged large-scale borrowing from early in the Weimar period. No plea for cultural independence could gainsay that Hollywood, not Germany, ruled the film world. No claim of optimal market potential for distinctively German pictures or warning against unauthentic Americanisms prevented at least the larger producers from attempting to gauge and satisfy the tastes of American viewers. Insofar as they collaborated directly with American partners for exchange of motion pictures these tendencies were institutionalized. The discourse of national revolution should not therefore obscure the extent to which domestic revival drew on American precedents.

Particularly revealing for the later Weimar period was policy at UFA after the takeover of Alfred Hugenberg and associates in 1927. Whatever his political agenda, Hugenberg and his right-hand man, Ludwig Klitzsch, were committed to contesting Hollywood's home turf. Rapid revision of the Parufamet agreements and repayment of the accompanying loan did not mean that UFA intended to solve the problem of German film production without reference to Hollywood. On the contrary, not only did UFA follow Hollywood's lead in rationalization of production and borrowing of sound technology, but it continued to make the American market a top priority. Most telling in the last regard was the decision to reacquire the services of Erich Pommer in 1927. Pommer made no secret of his outlook: two years in Hollywood convinced him that the American film mentality, which he characterized as naive and unproblematic, was the key to international success.[14] UFA entrusted its most expensive and representative productions, first silent and then sound, to the man best situated between Berlin and Hollywood to create pictures appealing to American viewers. It thus deliberately entrusted its international image to a self-confessed convert to the Hollywood system.[15]

Given the dramatic increase in UFA's relative weight in German production with the industrial concentration attendant upon the transition to sound, Pommer's second German career has more than passing significance. Commercially, and perhaps artistically, his pictures belie the scepticism about hybridization of Hollywood and Berlin so prevalent in the 1920s.[16] They also throw intriguing light on the question of national provenance. By terms of the import legislation Pommer's productions clearly qualified as German. Yet if a picture made by Lubitsch or Murnau in America had earlier been seen as profoundly German, there are grounds for judging Pommer's early sound pictures as the offspring of a cross-cultural marriage. In the framework of national cinemas, Hollywood had now, by invitation, returned to Berlin in the person of the former champion of German cinema art.

Since concern here is with discourses rather than influences, such a conclusion suggests the ambiguity of Berlin's encounter with Hollywood as much as the triumph of Americanization. With limited means to predict how Weimar cinema would have evolved had Hollywood not been omnipresent, it is impossible to apportion credit neatly to exogenous and endogenous factors. Independently, neither Hollywood nor Berlin represented static entities; in practice each developed through interaction with the other. The assumption that cinema had become irreversibly internationalized by the 1920s is as tenable as the case for national cinemas. Exchange was so voluminous and adoption or assimilation by one cinema of another's methods and techniques so routine that the web of influence and counterinfluence cannot be fully disentangled.

What remains indisputable is that America was the dominant partner in the encounter between Hollywood and Berlin. Decades later there is still reason to question whether, in the formulation of Edward Buscombe, a revolt against Hollywood is a revolt against the cinema. Contemporaries already perceived that internationalization and Americanization were dangerously close to synonymous. There was an extremely fine line between a national cinema which enjoyed international recognition and absorption by Hollywood. Significantly, the discourse of the more visionary commentators tacitly admitted this. They awaited the filmic *Gesamtkunstwerk* which would obliterate stylistic and market distinctions. National would become international, technology would prove humanly liberating, commerce would become *Kunst,* idea would become image, the word would be made cinematic flesh. Even though their terminology derived from dualistic assumptions, their arguments clearly intended to foster the kind of synthesis evidenced by Hollywood.

In retrospect it can hardly be doubted that without Hollywood some form of this problem would have received critical attention. The motion picture, bound by commercial and ideological dictates to seek consensus, badly strained the bounds of bourgeois *Kultur.* Some attempt had to be made to reconcile nineteenth-century cultural norms, essentially middle-class in purview, and a medium which belonged originally to a lower-class subculture. Weimar witnessed a number of strategies to ease this strain, as well as severe erosion of the the social stratification on which it was based. Insofar as the national cinema presupposed formation of an increasingly homogenous movie-going public, the growing number of urban white-collar workers and the blurring of class boundaries which the National Socialists later idealized in the *Volksgemeinschaft* were noteworthy developments in the 1920s. Despite political polarization and fragmentation, Weimar's socioeconomic experience was increasingly democratized.[17] Nevertheless, it was pressure from Hollywood which focused the cinematic challenge, for it was Hollywood which demonstrated the indivisibility of cinematic and broader cultural consensus. It was thus perfectly appropriate that the eclipse of Hollywood's presence coincided with the rise of a movement which recognized in film a device to override class distinctions and make *Kultur* both serve and command the *Volk.*

Notes

INTRODUCTION

1. A general introduction is Frank Costigliola, *Awkward Dominion* (Ithaca: Cornell University Press, 1984). The essential sources for Weimar Germany are Earl Beck, *Germany Rediscovers America* (Tallahassee: Florida State University Press, 1968); Peter Berg, *Deutschland und Amerika, 1918–1929* (Lübeck/Hamburg: Matthiesen Verlag, 1963); Manfred Buchwald, "Das Kulturbild Amerikas im Spiegel deutscher Zeitungen und Zeitschriften 1919–1932" (Ph.D. Dissertation, Kiel, 1964).

2. Cf. Kristin Thompson, *Exporting Entertainment* (London: British Film Institute, 1985), p. 168. On the particularly intriguing Soviet case see the paper by Denise J. Youngblood, "'Americanitis': The *Amerikanshchina* in Soviet Cinema," *Journal of Popular Film & Television*, 19 (1992), 148–156, and her *Movies for the Masses: Popular Cinema and Soviet Society in the 1920s* (Cambridge: Cambridge University Press, 1992).

3. For Germany, see Anton Kaes, *Kino-Debatte: Texte zum Verhältnis von Literatur und Film, 1909–1929* (Tübingen: Niemeyer, 1978); Viktor Žmegač, "Exkurs über den Film im Umkreis des Expressionismus," *Sprache im technischen Zeitalter*, 35 (1970), 243-257; Gary Stark, "Cinema, Society and the State: Policing the Film Industry in Imperial Germany," in Gary Stark and B. K. Lackner (eds.), *Essays on Culture and Society in Modern Germany* (Arlington: Texas A & M Press, 1982), pp. 122–166; Manuel Lichtwitz, "Die Auseinandersetzung um den Stummfilm in der Publizistik und Literatur 1907–1914" (Dissertation, Göttingen, 1986); Heinz-B. Heller, *Literarische Intelligenz und Film* (Tübingen: Niemeyer, 1985). Cf. on France: Richard Abel, "American Film and the French Literary Avant-Garde," *Contemporary Literature*, 17 (Winter 1976), 84–109, and his edited collection *French Film Theory and Criticism 1907–1939*, 2 vols. (Princeton, Princeton University Press, 1988); Franz-Josef Albersmeier, *Die Herausforderung des Films an die französische Literatur* (Heidelberg: Carl Winter, 1985).

4. There is no comprehensive account of Americanization in interwar Europe. Apart from Costigliola, *Awkward Dominion*, see on England, D. L. LeMahieu, *A Culture for Democracy* (Oxford: Clarendon Press, 1988); on France, David Strauss, *Menace in the West: The Rise of*

French Anti-Americanism in Modern Times (Westport, CT: Greenwood Press, 1978). Also useful is the introductory essay by C. W. E. Bigsby, "Europe, America and the Cultural Debate," in Bigsby (ed)., *Superculture: American Popular Culture and Europe* (Bowling Green: Bowling Green University Popular Press, 1975), pp. 1–26; and the general article by Erich Angermann, "Die Auseinandersetzung mit der Moderne in Deutschland und den USA in den 'Goldenen zwanziger Jahren'," in Georg Eckert and Otto-Ernst Schüddekopf (eds.), *Deutschland und die USA, 1918–1933* (Braunschweig: Albert Limbach, 1968), pp. 53–64.

5. A general introduction to the extensive literature on European images of the United States is Hugh Honor, *The New Golden Land: European Images of America* (New York: Pantheon, 1975). On German opinion cf. Theresa Mayer Hammond, *American Paradise: German Travel Literature From Duden to Kisch* (Heidelberg: Carl Winter, 1980); Erhard Schütz, *Kritik der literarischen Reportage* (Munich: Wilhelm Fink Verlag, 1977); Alexander Ritter (ed.), *Deutschlands literarisches Amerikabild* (Hildesheim: Georg Olms, 1977).

6. See Bigsby, "Europe, America and the Cultural Debate," pp. 6–8; LeMahieu, *A Culture for Democracy,* pp. 117–121.

7. Cf. Heller, *Literarische Intelligenz und Film,* pp. 28; 45–53.

8. For Hollywood's expansion, discernible already before the war, see Thompson, *Exporting Entertainment,* pp. 36ff.

9. On Britain cf. Robert Murphy, "Under the Shadow of Hollywood," in Charles Barr (ed.), *All Our Yesterdays: Ninety Years of British Cinema* (London: British Film Institute, 1986), pp. 47–58; Peter Miles and Malcolm Smith, *Cinema, Literature and Society: Elite and Mass Culture in Interwar Britain* (London: Croom Helm, 1987), pp. 163–179. For France see Strauss, *Menace in the West,* pp. 145–151; and on Italy see James Hay, *Popular Film Culture in Fascist Italy* (Bloomington: Indiana University Press, 1987), pp. 64–98.

10. Victoria de Grazia, "Mass Culture and Sovereignty: The American Challenge to European Cinemas, 1920–1960," *Journal of Modern History,* 61 (1989), 53–87. Cf. the new study by Ian Jarvie, *Hollywood's Overseas Campaign. The North Atlantic Movie Trade, 1920–1950* (Cambridge: Cambridge University Press, 1992). On the *Kulturfilm* see Barry Fulks, "Film Culture and *Kulturfilm:* Walter Ruttmann, the Avant-Garde Film, and the *Kulturfilm* in Weimar Germany and the Third Reich" (Ph.D. Dissertation, University of Wisconsin, 1982), pp. 62-63.

11. Chapter four examines the less optimistic views of Siegfried Kracauer and Lotte Eisner.

12. The well-known British film journal *Close-Up* (1927–1932) reflects the contemporary admiration for German cinema as a counterpoint to Hollywood.

13. Cf. Siegfried Kracauer, *From Caligari to Hitler* (Princeton: Princeton University Press, 1947), and the summaries in Gordon Craig, *Germany 1866–1945* (New York: Oxford University Press, 1978), pp. 495–496; Walter Laqueur, *Weimar: A Cultural History, 1918–1933* (London: Weidenfeld & Nicolson, 1974), pp. 230–249.

14. Kracauer, *From Caligari to Hitler*. For critical appraisals of this text see Barry Salt, "From Caligari to Who?" *Sight and Sound*, 48 (1979), 119–123; Thomas Elsaesser, "German Silent Cinema: Social Mobility and the Fantastic," *Wide Angle*, 5 (1982), 14–25; Patrice Petro, "From Lukács to Kracauer and Beyond: Social Film Histories and the German Cinema," *Cinema Journal*, 22 (1983), 47–70. Kracauer has recently been the focus of considerable attention. See, for instance, the special issues of *New German Critique*, no. 40 (1987), on Weimar film theory, and no. 54 (1991), on Kracauer.

15. Lotte H. Eisner, *The Haunted Screen*, trans. by Roger Greaves (London: Thames and Hudson, 1969). The first monographic treatment was by Rudolf Kurtz, *Expressionismus und Film* (Berlin: Verlag der Lichtbildbühne, 1926).

16. Essential reading are several articles by Thomas Elsaesser: "German Silent Cinema," cited above; "Film History and Visual Pleasure," in Patricia Mellencamp and Philip Rosen (eds.), *Cinema Histories/ Cinema Practices* (Frederick, MD.: University Publications of America, 1984), pp. 47–84; "Lulu and the Meter Man: Pabst's *Pandora's Box* (1929)," in Eric Rentschler (ed.), *German Film and Literature: Adaptations and Transformations* (London and New York: Methuen, 1986), pp. 40–59. Less comprehensive than their titles suggest and conceptually problematic but still stimulating are Helmut Korte (ed.), *Film und Realität in der Weimarer Republik* (Munich: Carl Hanser Verlag, 1978); Paul Monaco, *Cinema and Society* (New York: Elsevier, 1976); Bruce Armstrong et al., "Alptraumfabrik? Der deutsche Film in den Zwanziger Jahren," in Reinhold Grimm and Jost Hermand (eds.), *Faschismus und Avantgarde* (Königstein: Athenäum, 1980), pp. 115–130.

17. Cf. for instance, Ilona Brennicke and Joe Hembus, *Klassiker des deutschen Stummfilms 1910–1930* (Munich: Goldmann, 1983); David Cook, *A History of Narrative Film* (New York: W. W. Norton & Co., 1981), pp. 107–132.

18. For a sampling see the papers from the Luxemburg conference on Weimar cinema in 1989 collected in Walter Schatzberg and Uli Jung (eds.), *Filmkultur zur Zeit der Weimarer Republik* (Munich: Saur,

1991). Cf. the special issue of *New German Critique* on Weimar film theory noted above; Axel Marquardt and Heinz Rathsack (eds.), *Preußen im Film* (Reinbek bei Hamburg: Rowohlt, 1981); Thomas Plummer, et al., *Film and Politics in the Weimar Republic* (New York: Holmes and Meier, 1982); Patrice Petro, *Joyless Streets* (Princeton: Princeton University Press, 1989); Bruce Murray, *Film and the German Left in the Weimar Republic* (Austin: University of Texas Press, 1990); Jürgen Kinter, *Arbeiterbewegung und Film, 1895-1933* (Hamburg: Medienpädagogik-Zentrum, 1986).

19. Recent contributions include Eric Rentschler (ed.), *The Films of G. W. Pabst* (New Brunswick: Rutgers University Press, 1990); Wolfgang Jacobsen, *Erich Pommer: Ein Produzent macht Filmgeschichte* (Berlin: Argon, 1989); Ursula Hardt, "Erich Pommer: Film Producer for Germany" (Ph.D. Dissertation, University of Iowa, 1989); Reinhold Keiner, *Thea von Harbou und der deutsche Film bis 1933* (Hildesheim: Georg Olms Verlag, 1984); Helga Belach, *Henny Porten: Der erste deutsche Filmstar* (Berlin: Hände und Spener, 1986).

20. In addition to the material cited in note 3 see *Hätte ich das Kino! Die Schriftsteller und der Stummfilm* (Marbach: Schiller-Nationalmuseum, 1976); Fritz Güttinger, *Der Stummfilm im Zitat der Zeit* (Frankfurt a.M.: Deutsches Filmmuseum, 1984), and his *Kein Tag ohne Kino* (Frankfurt a.M.: Deutsches Filmmuseum, 1984).

21. Klaus Kreimeier's new company history—*Die Ufa-Story. Geschichte eines Filmkonzerns* (Munich: Carl Hanser Verlag, 1992)—is important in its own right and partially answers this need. Klaus Petersen of the University of British Columbia is currently completing a study of censorship in the Weimar Republic.

22. See Wolfgang Jacobsen, "Produktion: Erich Pommer," in Schatzberg and Jung (eds.), *Filmkultur zur Zeit der Weimarer Republik*, pp. 215–229; Eric Rentschler, "Mountains and Modernity: Relocating the '*Bergfilm*'," *New German Critique*, no. 5 (1990), 137–161, especially, 148–150. Cf. Thomas Brandlmeier, "Vom Expressionismus zur Neuen Sachlichkeit," in *Die UFA - auf den Spuren einer großen Filmfabrik* (Berlin: Elefanten, 1987), pp. 34-53.

23. Research on Erich Pommer has begun to bring this phenomenon into focus. On Soviet cinema in Weimar culture see Gertraude Kühn, Karl Tümmler, Walter Wimmer (eds.), *Film und revolutionäre Arbeiterbewegung in Deutschland, 1918–1932*, 2 vols. (Berlin: Henschelverlag, 1975). For a selective compilation on Hollywood in Germany see *Klassiker des amerikanischen Stummfilms im Spiegel der deutschen Kritik* (Berlin: Stiftung Deutsche Kinemathek, 1977).

24. Kristin Thompson documents American inroads abroad in *Ex-*

porting Entertainment. The best brief overview is Victoria de Grazia, "Mass Culture and Sovereignty." Jarvie, *Hollywood's Overseas Campaign,* covers Canada and the United Kingdom. Older surveys include John Harley, *World-Wide Influences of the Cinema* (Los Angeles: University of Southern California Press, 1940); Robert Sklar, *Movie-Made America* (New York: Random House, 1975), pp. 215–227; Frank Costigliola, *Awkward Dominion,* pp. 176–178. Seminal on the formation of the Hollywood narrative tradition is David Bordwell, Janet Staiger and Kristin Thompson, *The Classical Hollywood Cinema* (New York: Columbia University Press, 1985).

25. On Australia see Glen Lewis, *Australian Movies and the American Dream* (New York: Praeger, 1987); Peter Hamilton and Sue Mathews, *American Dreams: Australian Movies* (Sydney: Currency Press, 1986). On England and Italy see note 9 above.

26. On middle-class suspicion of foreign images see Heller, *Literarische Intelligenz und Film,* p. 28; Lichtwitz, "Die Auseinandersetzung um den Stummfilm," pp. 106–107.

27. For developments in Germany see Hans Barkhausen, *Filmpropaganda für Deutschland im Ersten und Zweiten Weltkrieg* (Hildesheim: Georg Olms, 1982), pp. 37–52.

28. See, for instance, what is often touted as the first theory of cinema: Béla Balázs, *Der sichtbare Mensch* (first published in 1924), in his *Schriften zum Film,* vol. I (Berlin: Henschelverlag, 1982), p. 57.

29. For characterizations from the German perspective see Emilie Altenloh, *Zur Soziologie des Kino* (Jena: E. Diederichs, 1914), pp. 10–13.

30. See Monaco, *Cinema and Society,* p. 68, which details its relevance while conceding its rhetorical convenience (p. 74) and then uses it as a label (p. 160).

31. Cf. Thompson, *Exporting Entertainment,* pp. 168–170; Petro, "From Lukács to Kracauer," pp. 57–58. The latter's criticisms of Monaco do not, however, resolve the difficult question of Hollywood's popularity in Germany. See chapter five below.

32. Expressionism foremost among them. Apart from Kracauer and Eisner see Andrew Tudor, *Image and Influence* (London: George Allen and Unwin, Ltd., 1974), chap. 7; S. E. Bronner and D. Kellner (eds.), *Passion and Rebellion* (New York: Universe Books, 1983), chaps. 18–21; Francis Courtade, *Cinéma Expressioniste* (Paris: Henri Veyrier, 1984). As Barry Salt has recently argued, the concept of national cinemas rests more on subject matter than formalist elements. See his *Film Style and Technology: History and Analysis* (London: Starword, 1983), p. 179.

33. On the general question of national film cultures cf. Keith

Reader, *Cultures on Celluloid* (New York: Quartet Books, 1981); Philip Rosen, "History, Textuality, Nation: Kracauer, Burch, and Some Problems in the Study of National Cinemas," *Iris*, 2 (1984), 69–84; Edward Buscombe, "Film History and the Idea of a National Cinema," *Australian Journal of Screen Theory*, no. 9/10 (1981), 141–153.

34. Figures vary somewhat depending on the year to which they refer. George Sadoul, *Histoire Générale du Cinéma* (Paris: Denoël, 1975), vol. V, p. 408, compares 3,731 German to 18,000 American cinemas in 1921.

35. Lary May, *Screening Out the Past* (New York: Oxford University Press, 1980); Douglas Gomery, "Film and Business History: The Development of an American Mass Entertainment Industry," *Journal of Contemporary History*, 19 (1984), 89–102.

36. Cf. LeMahieu, *A Culture for Democracy*, pp. 291–292; David Shi, "Transatlantic Visions: The Impact of the American Cinema upon the French Avant-Garde," *Journal of Popular Culture*, 14 (1981), 583–596.

37. Elsaesser, "Film History and Visual Pleasure," pp. 68–81.

38. Kaes, *Kino-Debatte*. The introduction is available in English as "The Debate about Cinema: Charting a Controversy (1909–1929)," *New German Critique*, no. 40 (1987), 7–33.

39. Peter Stead, "Hollywood's Message for the World: the British Response in the Nineteen Thirties," *Historical Journal of Film, Radio and Television*, 1 (1981), 19–32; Paul Swann, *The Hollywood Feature Film in Postwar Britain* (London: Croom Helm, 1987).

40. Hay, *Popular Film Culture in Fascist Italy*.

41. David Shi, "Transatlantic Visions"; Thomas Elsaesser, "Two Decades in Another Country: Hollywood and the Cinephiles," in C. W. E. Bigsby (ed.), *Superculture*, pp. 199–216.

42. Barry Salt, *Film Style and Technology*, pp. 213–218.

43. Cf. the comments in the preface to Bigsby (ed.), *Superculture*, pp. xi–xii.

44. In striking confirmation of Hollywood's normative status Frederick Ott, *The Great German Films* (Secaucus: Citadel Press, 1986), pp. 38–44, emphasizes the Germanization of Hollywood, rather than the reverse, and juxtaposes it to Soviet influence on German cinema. On the German "invasion" see Graham Petrie, *Hollywood Destinies* (London: Routledge & Keagan Paul, 1985).

45. Cf. Eric Rentschler, "How American Is It: The U.S. as Image and Imaginary in German Film," *German Quarterly*, 54 (1984), 603–620, especially pp. 614 and 618: "America figures as a crucial stage in a larger process, a process bound in the quest of a national cinema for a sense of cultural identity." "What is really at stake is one's image of oneself."

46. Cf. Anton Kaes, "Brecht und der Amerikanismus im Theater der 20er Jahre: Unliterarische Tradition und Publikumsbezug," *Sprache im technischen Zeitalter*, 56 (1975), 359–371; and his introduction to *Kino-Debatte*, pp. 15–17.

47. Costigliola, *Awkward Dominion*, p. 169.

48. LeMahieu, *A Culture for Democracy*, pp. 90–91. For a healthy reminder of how assumptions about Hollywood's primacy in cinema can yield erroneous conclusions see Reyner Banham, "'Mediated Environments' or: 'You can't build that here'," in Bigsby (ed.), *Superculture*, pp. 70–71. Swann, *The Hollywood Feature Film in Postwar Britain*, p. 42.

49. Hay, *Popular Film Culture in Fascist Italy*, p. 84. Cf. the admission on p. 79.

50. The limitations in the German case are discussed in chapter five. Cf. Swann, *The Hollywood Feature Film in Postwar Britain*, p. 8, who did have access to public opinion surveys.

51. On *Der letzte Mann* cf. Hkt., "Der Lebensoptimismus im amerikanischen Film," *Germania*, 15 May 1926; Karl Freund interview of 1 June 1964; University of California at Los Angeles, Special Collections, 542, box 2, pp. 6–7. On *Metropolis* see Enno Patalas, "*Metropolis*, Bild 103," in Elfriede Ledig (ed.), *Der Stummfilm. Konstruktion und Rekonstruktion* (Munich: Schaudig, Bauer und Ledig, 1988), pp. 153–162. Cf. John Willett, *The New Sobriety: Art and Politics in the Weimar Period* (London: Thames and Hudson, 1978), p. 146; Cook, *A History of Narrative Film*, p. 122.

52. Salt, "From Caligari to Who?," p. 123, and *Film Style and Technology*, pp. 213, 238; Elsaesser, "Film History and Visual Pleasure," p. 68.

53. As Salt, *Film Style and Technology*, p. 179, admits.

54. In an interview with George Huaco in 1962 in Huaco's *The Sociology of Film Art* (New York: Basic Books, 1965), p. 36, Pommer claimed "it would have been impossible to try and imitate Hollywood or the French. So we tried something new." Cf. Ursula Hardt, "Erich Pommer: Film Producer for Germany," pp. 123–124; 159–160. Cf. Elsaesser, "Film History and Visual Pleasure," pp. 68–70, who cautions against straightforward cause-effect models.

55. Peter Bächlin, *Der Film als Ware* (Frankfurt a.M.: Athenäum Fischer, 1975); Armstrong et al., "Alptraumfabrik?," p. 120. On marketing of popular novels in Weimar see Lynda King, *Best-Sellers by Design: Vicki Baum and the House of Ullstein* (Detroit: Wayne State University Press, 1988).

56. See Charles Maier, "Between Taylorism and Technocracy: Eu-

ropean Ideologies and the Vision of Industrial Productivity in the 1920s," *Journal of Contemporary History,* 5 (1970), 27–61; Helmut Lethen, *Neue Sachlichkeit, 1924–1932* (Stuttgart: J. B. Metzlersche, 1970); Thomas Hughes, *American Genesis* (New York: Viking, 1989), chaps. 6 and 7.

CHAPTER 1: THE SETTING

1. The essential source on German cinema before 1914, which focuses on film genres and theory, is Heide Schlüpmann, *Unheimlichkeit des Blicks* (Basel: Stroemfeld/Roter Stern, 1990). Cf. Paolo Cherchi Usai and Lorenzo Codelli (eds.), *Before Caligari. German Cinema, 1895–1920* (Pordenone: Le Giornate del Cinema Muto, 1990).

2. I have used the figures compiled by Alexander Jason, *Handbuch der Filmwirtschaft,* 3 vols. (Berlin: Verlag für Presse, Wirtschaft und Politik, 1930–1932), vol. I, p. 61. Cf. Hans Wollenberg, *Fifty Years of German Film* (London: Falcon Press, 1948), pp. 15–16; Hans Traub (ed.), *Die UFA: Ein Beitrag zur Entwicklungsgeschichte des deutschen Filmschaffens* (Berlin: UFA-Buchverlag, 1943), p. 155.

3. Jason, *Handbuch der Filmwirtschaft,* vol. I, p. 61.

4. Cf. Rolf-Peter Baacke, *Lichtspielhausarchitektur in Deutschland. Von der Schaubude bis zum Kinopalast* (Berlin: Verlag Frölich & Kaufmann (1982), a recent, derivative account; Uta Berg-Ganschow and Wolfgang Jacobsen, "Kino-Marginalien," in their . . . *Film . . . Stadt . . . Kino . . . Berlin . . .* (Berlin: Argon Verlag, 1987), pp. 17–56; Lothar Binger, Hans Borgelt and Susann Hellemann, *Vom Filmpalast zum Kinozentrum Zoo-Palast* (Berlin: Zentrum am Zoo Geschäftsbauten AG, 1983); Petra Schaper, *Kinos in Lübeck* (Lübeck: Verlag Graphische Werkstätten, 1987).

5. Roger Manvell and Heinrich Fraenkel, *The German Cinema* (London: J. M. Dent & Sons, 1971), pp. 3–7; Wollenberg, *Fifty Years of German Film,* pp. 10–11.

6. Annemarie Schweins, "Die Entwicklung der deutschen Filmwirtschaft" (Ph.D. Dissertation, Nürnberg, 1958), p. 6; Karl Zimmerschied, *Die deutsche Filmindustrie, ihre Entwicklung, Organisation und Stellung im Staats- und Wirtschaftsleben* (Stuttgart: Poeschel Verlag, 1922), p. 152.

7. See Heide Schlüpmann, "The First German Art Film: Rye's *The Student of Prague* (1913)," in Rentschler (ed.), *German Film and Literature,* pp. 9–24; Marcus Bier, "Max Reinhardt und die PAGU - der Weg zur deutschen Filmkunst," in *Die UFA - auf den Spuren einer großen Filmfabrik,* pp. 14–32. On the *Autorenfilm* and *Das Kinobuch* see Heller,

Literarische Intelligenz und Film, pp. 67ff; Lichtwitz, "Die Auseinandersetzung um den Stummfilm," pp. 319–343.

8. Stark, "Cinema, Society and the State," p. 157; Karl Wolffsohn (ed.), *Jahrbuch der Filmindustrie,* 5 vols. (Berlin: Verlag der Lichtbildbühne, 1922–1933), vol. III (1926–1927), p. 255.

9. See Alfred Kallmann, "Die Konzernierung in der Filmindustrie, erläutert an den Filmindustrien Deutschlands und Amerikas" (Ph.D. Dissertation, Würzburg, 1932), pp. 9–13.

10. There is a good, brief sketch of these developments in Jürgen Spiker, *Film und Kapital* (Berlin: Volker Spiess, 1975), pp. 18ff. Also see Barkhausen, *Filmpropaganda für Deutschland,* pp. 78ff.

11. On UFA the esential work is now Kreimeier, *Die Ufa-Story,* pp. 34–43. Cf. Spiker, *Film und Kapital,* pp. 24–27; J.-C. Horak, "Ernst Lubitsch and the Rise of UFA, 1917–1922" (M.Sc. Thesis, Boston University, 1975), pp. 31ff. The press statement is quoted in Schweins, "Die Entwicklung der deutschen Filmwirtschaft," pp. 34–35.

12. On the interaction of film and literature see the introduction, note 3, and Thomas Koebner, "Der Film als neue Kunst. Reaktionen der literarischen Intelligenz," in Helmut Kreuzer (ed.), *Literaturwissenschaft-Medienwissenschaft* (Heidelberg: Quelle & Meyer, 1977), pp. 1–31. Lichtwitz, "Die Auseinandersetzung um den Stummfilm in der Publizistik und Literatur," pp. 53–54, notes that until 1912 the bulk of outside concern for the cinema came not from literary interests but from pedagogues, lawyers, pastors and doctors.

13. There was, of course, overlap between the campaign to protect the traditional cultural hierarchy and that to preserve the established social system. See Stark, "Cinema, Society and the State"; Schlüpmann, *Unheimlichkeit des Blicks,* pp. 189–243; Volker Schulze, "Frühe kommunale Kinos und die Kinoreformbewegung in Deutschland bis zum Ende des ersten Weltkriegs," *Publizistik,* 22 (1977), 61–71.

14. Wollenberg, *Fifty Years of German Film,* p. 15. Monaco, *Cinema and Society,* pp. 20–21, summarizes the expansive trend.

15. Monaco, *Cinema and Society,* p. 21, accepts a figure of over two million. Jason, *Handbuch der Filmwirtschaft,* vol. I, p. 69; vol. III, p. 69, derived a total of 340 million patrons annually from the tax revenue they provided.

16. Schweins, "Die Entwicklung der deutschen Filmwirtschaft," p. 38; Heinz Kuntze-Just, "'Guten Morgen, Ufa!' Die Geschichte eines Filmkonzerns," *Film-Telegramm,* no. 47 (1954) - no. 25 (1955); here no. 49 (1954), 17.

17. Norbert Grünau, "Die finanzielle und wirtschaftliche Entwicklung der Filmindustrie in Deutschland" (Ph.D. Dissertation, Mün-

ster, 1923), pp. 69–72. On the other corporations and the role of the banks see Kallmann, "Die Konzernierung in der Filmindustrie," pp. 20–25, and Schweins, "Die Entwicklung der deutschen Filmwirtschaft," pp. 50–60. On the question of market monopoly see Monaco, *Cinema and Society*, pp. 29–30.

18. The contemporary proliferation of dissertations on motion pictures, mostly on their economic and legal ramifications, indicates the new-found appreciation. See especially the study by Grünau cited above and those by Franz Hayler, "Die deutsche Film-Industrie und ihre Bedeutung für Deutschlands Handel" (Ph.D. Dissertation, Würzburg, 1926); and Fritz Meyer, "Kunstgewerbe und ökonomisches Prinzip (Der Aufbau der Filmindustrie)" (Ph.D. Dissertation, Berlin, 1924).

19. See Stark, "Cinema, Society and the State," pp. 154–158.

20. Monaco, *Cinema and Society*, pp. 52–53.

21. *Verhandlungen der verfassungsgebenden Deutschen Nationalversammlung*, vol. 328, pp. 1590–1597. Only when the Independent Socialists charged that censorship masked political intentions did the exchange become heated.

22. The meeting of socialist and conservative minds illustrates cinema's transgression of conventional political categories. Cf. Spiker, *Film und Kapital*, pp. 28–29.

23. *Verhandlungen der Nationalversammlung*, vol. 330, pp. 3164–3202.

24. USPD opinion was split. One deputy raised hackles by charging the government with solicitude for youth at the movies when they had had no compunction about sending seventeen year-olds to their death in the war. See ibid., vol. 333, pp. 5167–5183, here 5173–5177.

25. Ibid., pp. 5175, 5179–5183.

26. The USPD sought to gain working-class representatives of the film industry on the boards; the Zentrum wanted local authorities to have supplementary censorship rights. Ibid., pp. 5169, 5180.

27. The final version of the legislation is reproduced in Gerd Albrecht, *Nationalsozialistische Filmpolitik* (Stuttgart: F. Enke, 1969), pp. 510–520. Its development from draft through committee stages can be followed in *Verhandlungen der Nationalversammlung*, vol. 341, pp. 2045–2053; 2484–2511.

28. Cf. Wolfgang Becker, *Film und Herrschaft* (Berlin: Volker Spiess, 1973), p. 72; Welch, "The Proletarian Cinema and the Weimar Republic," p. 5. Becker emphasizes the ease with which the legislation of 1920 was modified to suit the more explicit nationalist ends of 1934 (pp. 85–88). Welch stresses the function of censorship in preserving "the existing political and economic order."

29. *Verhandlungen der Nationalversammlung*, vol. 328, p. 1593; vol. 330, p. 3202; vol. 333, pp. 5174–5177.

30. Early in the decade the proportion was much higher—over two-thirds. Monaco, *Cinema and Society*, p. 54. On the broader campaign to guard youth from the entertainment industry see Klaus Petersen, "The Harmful Publications (Young Persons) Act of 1926. Literary Censorship and the Politics of Morality in the Weimar Republic," *German Studies Review*, 15 (1992), 505–523; Margaret Stieg, "The 1926 German Law to Protect Youth Against Trash and Dirt: Moral Protectionism in a Democracy," *Central European History*, 23 (1990), 22–56.

31. Ignaz Wrobel (Kurt Tucholsky), "Kino-Zensur," *Die Weltbühne*, 16 (1920), vol. II, pp. 308–310. The Appeal Board spent much of its time listening to protests against restricted rulings.

32. Spiker, *Film und Kapital*, p. 33.

33. Zimmerschied, *Die deutsche Filmindustrie*, pp. 128–130, gives several pages of figures for 1921 which yield this average. Monaco, *Cinema and Society*, p. 46, cites several extreme cases.

34. Cf. prewar attitudes noted in Stark, "Cinema, Society and the State," p. 152. That film reformers remained frustrated by the standard of cinema entertainment was reflected in municipal sponsorship of special programs aiming to provide acceptable educational films.

35. The practice predated the war. Cf. Altenloh, *Zur Soziologie des Kino*, pp. 42–43.

36. Jason, *Handbuch der Filmwirtschaft*, vol. I, p. 69. Cf. the chart of rates for 1924 and 1925 in cities of over 100,000 inhabitants in *Lichtbildbühne*, 30 May 1925, p. 12.

37. Cf. Monaco, *Cinema and Society*, pp. 59–61 on the impact of the motion picture law and taxation on German production.

38. *Verhandlungen des Deutschen Reichstages*, vol. 341, pp. 2511–2513.

39. Thomas Elsaesser, "Social Mobility and the Fantastic," pp. 14–25; "Film History and Visual Pleasure," pp. 70–71.

40. Every major city had elegant first-run theaters to attract the middle class. See Lichtwitz, "Die Auseinandersetzung um den Stummfilm," pp. 71–73, 84ff. Cf. Altenloh, *Zur Soziologie des Kino*, pp. 19–20. On variations in Berlin see Berg-Ganschow and Jacobsen, "Kino-Marginalien," p. 48.

41. The sociology of Weimar cinema is relatively unexplored. Altenloh's prewar *Zur Soziologie des Kino* remains seminal. Otherwise cf. Anton Kaes, "Mass Culture and Modernity: Notes Toward a Social History of Early American and German Cinema," in Frank Trommler and Joseph McVeigh (eds.), *America and the Germans*, (Philadelphia:

University of Pennsylvania Press, 1985), vol. II, pp. 317–331; Miriam Hansen, "Early Silent Cinema: Whose Public Sphere?" *New German Critique*, no. 29 (1983), 147–184; Dietrich Mühlberg, "Anfänge proletarischen Freizeitverhaltens und seiner öffentlichen Einrichtungen," *Weimarer Beiträge*, 27 (1981), 124–138; Siegfried Kracauer, "The Mass Ornament," *New German Critique*, no. 5 (1975), 67–76; Jörg Schweinitz, "Kino der Zerstreuung. Siegfried Kracauer und ein Kapitel Geschichte der theoretischen Annäherung an populäre Filmunterhaltung," *Weimarer Beiträge*, 33 (1987), 1129–1144.

42. The essential reference for early German film criticism, fundamental for Weimar despite its prewar focus, is Helmut Diederichs, *Anfänge deutscher Filmkritik* (Stuttgart: Verlag Robert Fischer & Uwe Wiedleroither, 1986). Also useful is Heinz-B. Heller, "Anfänge der deutschen Filmpresse," in Berg-Ganschow and Jacobsen (eds.), . . . *Film . . . Stadt . . . Kino . . . Berlin . . .* , pp. 117–126.

43. Despite recent interest in early literary encounters with the cinema, this particular interaction has scarcely been explored. See René Jeanne and Charles Ford, *Le Cinéma et la Presse, 1895–1960* (Paris: A. Colin, 1961); Ewald Sattig, "Die Deutsche Filmpresse" (Ph.D. Dissertation, Leipzig, 1937); Ena Bajons, "Film und Tagespresse" (Ph.D. Dissertation, Vienna, 1951); Günter Kaltofen, "Die publizistische Bedeutung des Filmischen" (Ph.D. Dissertation, Leipzig, 1950).

44. Helmut Diederichs, "Die Anfänge der deutschen Filmpublizistik 1895 bis 1909," *Publizistik*, 27 (1982), 55–71.

45. Kaes, *Kino-Debatte;* Heller, *Literarische Intelligenz und Film*. Kurt Pinthus's claim to have pioneered film criticism with *Quo vadis?* in 1913 is misleading: "Die erste deutsche Filmkritik," *Querschnitt*, 11 (1931), 139.

46. W. Thielemann, "Zeitgemässe Filmkritik," *Kinematograph*, 24 December 1913. On perspectives before 1914 see Diederichs, *Die Anfänge deutscher Filmkritik*, pp. 36–83.

47. Cf. "Das Kino und die Tagespresse," *Kinematograph*, 20 January 1915; "Kino, Fach- und Tagespresse," *Lichtbildbühne*, 15 January 1916, pp. 12–14; E. A. Dupont, "Kinematographie und Tagespresse," *Der Film*, 1 April 1916, pp. 9–11. Also see the careful strategy outlined by Alfred Fiedler, "Die 'Deutsche Filmkorrespondenz'," *Der Film*, 28 December 1918, pp. 36, 49. On prewar precedents cf. Heller, "Anfänge der deutschen Filmpresse," p. 122.

48. Cf. Carl Hedinger, "Ueber Filmkritik und Anderes," *Lichtbildbühne*, 17 April 1915, pp. 16, 19; Julius Urgiss, "Zum Thema: 'Fachkritik'," *Lichtbildbühne*, 5 June 1915, pp. 16–18; R. Genenncher, "Film-

kritik und Presse," *Kinematograph*, 28 April 1915. This last maintained only the trade press could provide the combination of expertise and objectivity required for meaningful criticism.

49. On the varieties of film criticism see Heller, "Anfänge der deutschen Filmpresse," pp. 123–126.

50. Ibid., pp. 125–126; Werner Sudendorf, "Täglich: *Der Film-Kurier*," in Berg-Ganschow & Jacobsen (eds.), *. . . Film . . . Stadt . . . Kino . . . Berlin . . .*, pp. 127–132; Thomas Schorr, "Die Film- und Kinoreformbewegung und die deutsche Filmwirtschaft," (Ph.D. Dissertation, Munich, 1990), focuses on *Kinematograph*. Sabine Hake has prepared a manuscript that treats film criticism in this period in greater detail.

51. On the contemporary distinction between trade criticism and that of the daily press cf. W. Warstat, "Filmkritik," *Bücherei und Bildungspflege*, 1 (1921), 41–44; "Filmkritik," *Lichtbildbühne*, 1 August 1925, p. 26.

52. For a list of newspapers with regular (usually weekly) film sections see Wolffsohn (ed.), *Jahrbuch der Filmindustrie*, vol. I (1922–1923), pp. 231–232; vol. II (1923–1925), pp. 378–379.

53. Sattig, "Die Deutsche Filmpresse," pp. 28, 32.

54. Equally or more prominent persons such as Kurt Tucholsky, Walter Hasenclever or Alfred Kerr treated movies too sporadically to merit description as film critics.

55. There are brief sketches of several front-ranking critics (among them Haas, Balázs, Pinthus, Schacht, Siemsen) in Hans-Michael Bock (ed.), *CineGraph. Lexikon zum deutschsprachigen Film* (Munich: Edition Text, and Kritik, 1984ff.). Also see, on Haas, Wolfgang Jacobsen, Karl Prümm and Benno Wenz (eds.), *Willy Haas. Der Kritiker als Mitproduzent* (Berlin: Edition Hentrich, 1991); Dietrich Kuhlbrodt, "Der Fachkritiker," in Berg-Ganschow & Jacobsen (eds.), *Film . . . Stadt . . . Kino . . . Berlin*, pp. 133–138; on Ihering, Jürgen Ebert, "Der 'sachliche' Kritiker," ibid., pp. 139–144; on Pinthus, Brigitta Lange, "Extrakt, Steigerung, Erregung, Komposition," ibid., pp. 145–148.

56. On blurring of the distinction between authorship and journalism see Erhard Schütz, *Romane der Weimarer Republik* (Munich: Wilhelm Fink Verlag , 1986), pp. 35–36. For retrospective minimizing of connection with the cinema see the memoirs of Axel Eggebrecht, *Der halbe Weg* (Reinbek bei Hamburg: Rowohlt, 1975), and Willy Haas, *Die literarische Welt: Erinnerungen* (Munich: Paul List Verlag, 1957). Cf. the more balanced reflections of Hans Sahl, *Memoiren eines Moralisten* (Zurich: Ammann Verlag, 1983), and Lotte H. Eisner, *Ich hatte einst ein schönes Vaterland* (Munich: Deutscher Taschenbuch Verlag, 1984).

57. Fritz Olimsky, "Tendenzen der Filmwirtschaft und deren Auswirkung auf die Filmpresse" (Ph.D. Dissertation, Berlin, 1931), pp. 31-32. R. (Alfred Ruhemann), "Kritik und Film," *Der Welt-Film*, 25 May 1922, pp. 409–410. A number of critics noted how rare the gift of observation and training essential to serious film criticism was in Germany. See Max Schach, "Filmkritik," *Das Tagebuch*, 3 (1922), 1358–1361; Hans Siemsen, "Kino. Kritik. Und Kino-Kritik," *Die neue Schaubühne*, 5 (1925), 36–37; Roland Schacht, "Eine Dramaturgie des Films," *Der Kunstwart*, 40 (1927), 265.

Kinematograph, for example, presentedf anonymous criticism for most of the 1920s, a practice which had been controversial even in the previous decade. See Egon Jacobsohn, "Anonyme Film-Kritik," *Licht-bildbühne*, 12 June 1915, pp. 12–14. See the survey of personalities and interests among trade critics in the later twenties in "Männer der Feder: Ein kritischer Rundgang durch die Gefilde der Fachkritik," *Filmkünstler und Filmkunst*, no. 10–11 (1929).

59. Doctoral graduates include Kracauer, Kurt Pinthus, Roland Schacht, Hans Sahl, Max Prels, Wolfgang Martini and Hans Wollenberg.

60. In general see Marc Ferro, "Film as Agent, Product and Source of History," *Journal of Contemporary History*, 18 (1984), 357–360. Hans Sahl's, *Memoiren eines Moralisten*, pp. 99–103, reflect this passion vividly. Axel Eggebrecht's apparent indifference to cinema in his memoirs, *Der halbe Weg*, must be set against his contemporary polemic, "Das Kino ist Kunst," *Film-Kurier*, 17 July 1925.

61. See Laroche, "Die Kinokritik," *Der Kritiker*, 23 August 1919, pp. 9–10.

62. Herbert Ihering, "Der Film als Industrie," *Berliner Börsen-Courier*, no. 35, 21 January 1923; "Filmkritik," *Freie Deutsche Bühne*, 1 (1919), 21–23. On the parallel with defensive attitudes originating before 1914 see Heller, *Literarische Intelligenz und Film*, p. 59; Ferro, "Film as Agent," p. 358.

63. Eisner, *Ich hatte einst ein schönes Vaterland*, p. 81, reports one publisher's way around the problem: assign her only those pictures suited to her preferences.

64. The problem was not new to Weimar. See Julius Urgiss, a screenwriter and critic for *Kinematograph*, responding to the more insidious charge that his uncomplimentary reviews were designed to force a company to *begin* advertising with the paper: "Zumutungen an die Presse," *Kinematograph*, 10 January 1917. Illustrations from the 1920s include a case in Frankfurt cited by Hans Siemsen, "Die Situation der deutschen Filmkritik," *Die Weltbühne*, 23 (1927), vol. II, pp.

144–147, and conflicts in Dresden and Augsburg reported by Walter Steinhauer, "Film und Presse," *Süddeutsche Filmzeitung*, 7 October 1927, pp. 3–4.

65. See the reports in *Der Welt-Film*, 25 May 1922, pp. 410–412; Cf. Heller, "Anfänge der deutschen Filmpresse," p. 123.

66. Cf. Bundesarchiv Koblenz, UFA (henceforth cited as BA-UFA with folio number) R109I/1026a, 3 May 1927; 20 July 1927; 21 July 1927; R109I/1026b, 5 October 1927.

67. BA-UFA R109I/1026b, 26 March 1928. It also referred the case to Spio, the umbrella organization of German producers. BA-UFA R109I/1027a, 26 October 1928.

68. "Scherl-Aros-Feige," *Lichtbildbühne*, 8 March 1927. Ihering labeled Rosenthal a *Reklameschriftsteller*. Cf. H.S. (Hans Sahl), "Warnung vor einem Filmkritiker," *Montag Morgen*, 24 February 1930.

69. It was also not uncommon for a critic to work for more than one paper at a time. For attitudes early in the decade see "Die 'Korruption' in der Filmpresse," *Der Film*, 30 August 1919, pp. 25–27. A guide to the incestuous nature of the industry is Kurt Mühsam and Egon Jacobsohn, *Lexikon des Films/Wie ich zum Film kam* (Berlin: Lichtbildbühne, 1926). Hans David, "Film-Kritiker und -Autor," *Deutsche Presse*, 2 December 1921, pp. 2–3.

70. W. Haas, "Fachkritik und literarische Kritik," *Film-Kurier*, 15 April 1922.

71. In *Berliner Börsen-Courier*, no. 233, 20 May 1923.

72. Hans Siemsen, "Kino. Kritik. Und Kino-Kritik," *Die neue Schaubühne*, 5 (1925), 34.

73. Siemsen led with "Die Situation der deutschen Filmkritik," *Die Weltbühne*, 23 (1927), vol. II, pp. 144–147. Haas replied with "Die Unabhängigkeit der Filmkritik," *Film-Kurier*, 28 July 1927, and provoked a lengthy rejoinder from Siemsen, "Standesregeln, Nebenverdienst und Film," *Die Weltbühne*, 23 (1927), vol. II, pp. 337–342. Haas shot back with "Der Sinn der Filmkritik," *Die Literarische Welt*, 16 September 1927, p. 7, and Siemsen replied with "Kleiner Roman aus der Naturgeschichte des deutschen Films," *Die Weltbühne*, 23 (1927), vol. II, pp. 489–492. For other perspectives see (Felix) Gong, "Die unsichtbare Bestechung," *Deutsche Republik*, 2 (1927), 40–42, and Hans Georg Brenner, "Die Situation der Filmkritik," *Die neue Bücherschau*, 7 (1927), 189–190.

74. Jost Hermand and Frank Trommler, *Die Kultur der Weimarer Republik* (Munich: Nymphenburger, 1978) pp. 265–266, argue that serious film criticism appeared in only a handful of publications. Heller, "Die Anfänge der deutschen Filmpresse," p. 123, mentions apart

from the political-cultural journals, *Frankfurter Zeitung* and *Berliner Börsen-Courier*. Brennicke and Hembus, *Klassiker des deutschen Stummfilms 1910–1930*, p. 7, claim that even serious critics cannot be trusted. On trade papers cf. Kreimeier, *Die Ufa-Story*, p. 144.

75. This is particularly observable in socialist and communist papers. The industry obviously judged the need to present its product, and the attraction of that product, greater than the negative impact of critical opinion. The implications of its judgment for the relationship between the working class and its political press is a subject I am presently investigating in more detail.

76. See *Preußen im Film*, vol. 5 of Axel Marquardt and Heinz Rathsack (eds.), *Preußen. Versuch einer Bilanz* (Reinbek bei Hamburg: Rowohlt, 1981).

77. On *Potemkin* see Kühn, Tümmler and Wimmer (eds.), *Film und revolutionäre Arbeiterbewegung*, vol. I, pp. 323–369. On Universal's adaptation of the Remarque novel see Modris Eksteins, "War, Memory and Politics: The Fate of the Film *All Quiet on the Western Front*," *Central European History*, 13 (1980), 60–82.

78. Rainer Berg, "Zur Geschichte der realistischen Stummfilmkunst in Deutschland—1919 bis 1929" (Ph.D. Dissertation, Freie Universität Berlin, 1982).

79. Willy Haas pointed out that Hugenberg had invested far too much to turn out nationalistic propaganda if the public balked. Hugenberg, no less than his democratic financial rivals, would have to orient production around business considerations. Haas, "Filmkrise und kein Ende," *Die Literarische Welt*, 15 April 1927, p. 7.

80. Rainer Berg, "Zur Geschichte der realistischen Stummfilmkunst," pp. 48, 155–156; See "Weg von der Politik," *Lichtbildbühne*, 25 October 1924, p. 23.

81. A contemporary statement along these lines from beyond trade circles is Mario Mohr, "Der Film als kulturelle und politische Macht," *Der Kritiker*, 8 (1926), 138–140.

82. See especially Kreimeier, *Die Ufa-Story*, pp. 85, 100–114. Cf. Laqueur, *Weimar*, p. 231; Welch, "The Proletarian Cinema," p. 3, who suggests that the "overall thematic cluster is most easily associated with the political right." Thomas Plummer tries to advance a political reading of the Weimar cinema in the introduction to his *Film and Politics in the Weimar Republic*, but admits many films defy classification in political terms. Armstrong et al., "Alptraumfabrik?," pp. 121, 129.

83. The recurring refrain on the far left was that film was an instrument of bourgeois repression. Cf., for instance, Axel Eggebrecht, "Die bürgerliche Filmgefahr," *Rote Fahne*, 14 June 1922; Hans Siemsen,

"Tendenz-Filme," *Die Weltbühne*, 24 (1928), vol. I, pp. 23–25. In general see Linda Schulte-Sasse, "Film Criticism in the Weimar Press," in Plummer et al., *Film and Politics in the Weimar Republic*, pp. 47–59.

84. Laqueur, *Weimar*, pp. 31–32, speaks of opposing camps in literature, theater, music and the cinema. He later concedes (pp. 231, 249) that the last is a dubious entry. On socialist and communist approaches to film see Richard Weber, "Der Volksfilmverband," in the reprint of *Film und Volk* (Cologne: Prometh Verlag, 1978), pp. 5–27; Heller, *Literarische Intelligenz und Film*, pp. 137–156.

CHAPTER 2: GERMAN-AMERICAN FILM RELATIONS

1. See Thompson, *Exporting Entertainment*, pp. 1–27. Apart from French firms, Denmark's Nordisk had extensive branch operations in Germany: Altenloh, *Zur Soziologie des Kino*, pp. 9–10, 15–17.

2. Eisner, *The Haunted Screen*, p. 7, dates the period of bloom from the end of the war to the midtwenties, as does Kracauer, *From Caligari to Hitler*, pp. 3–5; 134–137. Cf. Kreimeier, *Die Ufa-Story*, p. 90; Pommer's contemporary statement, "Internationale Film-Verständigung," *Das Tagebuch*, 3 (1922), 993–995.

3. See, for instance, Hermand and Trommler, *Die Kultur der Weimarer Republik*, pp. 262–263; Armstrong et al., "Alptraumfabrik?" p. 124; Kreimeier, *Die Ufa-Story*, pp. 152–153.

4. Since together American and domestic pictures controlled eighty percent or more of the market, these figures essentially trace the contours of domestic film consumption. Thompson, *Exporting Entertainment*, p. 107, reproduces a chart for all features censored from 1923–1929.

5. Wolffsohn (ed.), *Jahrbuch der Filmindustrie*, vol. III, pp. 256–257.

6. For an early sample of the mix of art and business see "Film-Amerika in Berlin," *Berliner Tageblatt*, 18 June 1922. Inflation made travel to the United States expensive until 1924; thereafter transatlantic journeys became common.

7. See de Grazia, "Mass Culture and Sovereignty." An illuminating study of Hollywood's targeting of foreign markets is Ruth Vasey, "Diplomatic Representations: Mediations Between Hollywood and its Global Audiences, 1922–1939" (Ph.D. Dissertation, University of Exeter, 1990). Cf. Jarvie, *Hollywood's Overseas Campaign*, part III.

8. See "Das Problem der Übergangswirtschaft," *Der Film*, 2 June 1917, pp. 11–16, which boasted *Der Film* had initiated trade discussion of adjustments to peace shortly before the United States declared war.

9. Cf. Alfred Rosenthal, "Kinopolitische Streifzüge," *Kinemato-*

graph, 12 December 1917; "Der Film dem Weltmarkt," *Kinematograph*, 27 March 1918.

10. "Organisation ist Not?" *Lichtbildbühne*, 9 November 1918, p. 14, defends UFA's critical position in this struggle.

11. See, for instance, renewed ties between Oskar Einstein Co. and Universal: *Lichtbildbühne*, 18 January 1919, p. 77, and *Erste Internationale Film-Zeitung*, 25 January 1919, p. 15. Cf. "Die ersten Amerikaner sind eingetroffen," *Kinematograph*, 29 January 1919, and complaints about film smuggled into Germany via Holland, Italy and the occupied Rhineland: *Der Film*, 1 February 1919, pp. 30–31. Advertisements for American pictures began to multiply in mid-1919. For covert advertising see opinion on resumption of import, "Die Internationalisierung des Films," *Erste Internationale Film-Zeitung*, 11 October 1919, pp. 34–38, in which UFA director Carl Bratz, Oskar Einstein and others had opportunity to justify their business commitments.

12. See Bundesarchiv-Filmarchiv Berlin/UFA (henceforth BA-FB/UFA) 379 (Dafco). Cf. Kuntze-Just, "Guten Morgen, Ufa!," *Film-Telegramm*, no. 49 (1954), 15; Hans Hagge, *Das gab's schon zweimal. Auf die Spuren der Ufa* (Berlin: Henschelverlag, 1959), pp. 20–22; Horak, "Ernst Lubitsch," p. 77.

13. *Film-Kurier* introduced "Die amerikanische Gefahr für die Filmindustrie," on 6 June 1919 and in a series of articles from 10–13 June 1919. Cf. "Einfuhr amerikanischer Filme durch die Nordische," *Der Film*, 7 June 1919, pp. 25–26. "Wer hat nun recht?" *Kinematograph*, 25 June 1919. For justification of UFA's conduct see C. Kersten, "'Dafco'," *Lichtbildbühne*, 12 July 1919, p. 10.

14. See reports on early conferences with trade representatives in *Der Film*, 8 February 1919, pp. 29–30, and 15 February 1919, pp. 31–32. The debate can be followed in "Organisation der Einfuhr," *Lichtbildbühne*, 30 August 1919, pp. 12–13; *Film-Kurier*, 30 August, 2, 6, 19, 21, 23, 25 September 1919. Cf. "Wie stellt sich der Theaterbesitzer zur Internationalisierung des Films," *Erste Internationale Film-Zeitung*, 18 October 1919, pp. 36–38.

15. Cf. the "Bericht über Situation der UFA" dated December 1919, and marked strictly confidential in BA-UFA R109I/1287, especially pp. 9–13; payment charts, Dafco to UFA, 14 November 1919, in BA-FB/UFA 379. To that point UFA and Nordisk had paid roughly one-quarter of the almost $3 million they owed American firms for distribution rights. When the contract was signed the dollar was worth 14 marks. By the end of 1919 the dollar equivalent was forty-two marks.

16. The path to resolution can be followed in *Film-Kurier*, 31 Au-

gust, 1 and 15 September, 24 November, 6 and 8 December 1920, 6 and 7 January 1921.

17. The excess for the years 1922–1924 was 49,000, 56,000 and 134,000 meters respectively. Hayler, "Die deutsche Film-Industrie," p. 179. On import trends generally see Jason, *Handbuch der Filmwirtschaft*, vol. I, pp. 19, 51.

18. Jason, *Handbuch der Filmwirtschaft*, vol. I, pp. 18–20.

19. In 1921 and 1922 Universal provided almost fifty percent of American imports. Most of the remainder came from several other large concerns—Famous Players (Paramount), Goldwyn and Metro. On distribution practices see Thompson, *Exporting Entertainment*, p. 107.

20. Bundesarchiv-Potsdam, Reichswirtschaftsministerium 31.01/ 5424, pp. 81–83. Cf. *Der Film*, 7 August 1921, p. 20.

21. On *Madame Dubarry* in America see the article from *Das Tagebuch* by Leopold Schwarzschild quoted in Brennicke and Hembus, *Klassiker des deutschen Stummfilms*, p. 246. On *Caligari* see Michael Budd, "The National Board of Review and the Early Art Cinema in New York: the Cabinet of Dr. Caligari as Affirmative Culture," *Cinema Journal*, 26 (1986), 3–18; "The Cabinet of Dr. Caligari: Conditions of Reception," *Cine-Tracts*, 3 (Winter 1981), 41–49.

22. Cf. "Amerikaner in Berlin," *Der Film*, 11 September 1920, pp. 26–27; "Auf dem Wege zur Überfremdung," *Der Film*, 13 November 1920, pp. 21–22; "Rückblick," *Kinematograph*, 21 November 1920. For the original contracts see "Engagement Pola Negris nach Amerika," *Film-Kurier*, 10 December 1920; "UFA und Ben-Blumenthal-Rachmann," *Film-Kurier*, 21 December 1920; "Auch May geht nach Dollarika," *Der Film*, 25 December 1920, p. 21.

23. See "Die UFA und Amerika," *Film-Kurier*, 31 January 1921; "UFA-Famous Players," ibid., 15 February 1921; "UFA und Famous Players," ibid., 3 March 1921 and "Die Verträge der Amerikaner," ibid., 4 March 1921; "Unklare Situation," *Lichtbildbühne*, 12 March 1921, pp. 33–34. Olimsky, "Tendenzen der Filmwirtschaft," p. 44, claims the Americans demanded majority shares in UFA.

24. There is a useful summary in "Die amerikanische Expansion," *Der Film*, 23 April 1921, pp. 25–26. Other notable EFA employees included Emil Jannings, Harry Liedtke, the screenwriter Hans Kraely and the cameraman Theodor Sparkuhl. For discussion of American motives see Jan-Christopher Horak, "Rin-Tin-Tin erobert Berlin oder Amerikanische Filminteressen in Weimar," in Schatzberg and Jung (eds.), *Filmkultur zur Zeit der Weimarer Republik*, 258–260.

25. Bundesarchiv-Potsdam, Reichswirtschaftsministerium 31.01/ 5424, pp. 38–47.

26. Ibid., pp. 86–87.

27. The other three were Paul Wegener's *Herzog Ferrante*, Dimitri Buchowetzki's *Peter der Grosse* and Georg Jacoby's *Napoleons kleiner Bruder*. The balance sheet is presented in "Der Untergang der EFA," *Film-Kurier*, 23 November 1922.

28. See "Auflösung der Efa," *B.Z. am Mittag*, 19 November 1922. Negri left Germany in 1922. Lubitsch made an initial trip overseas in December 1921 after completing *Das Weib des Pharao*, returned to direct *Die Flamme* and then departed again in November 1922. See Horak, "Ernst Lubitsch," pp. 113, 118–119.

29. *Der Film*, 8 January 1921, p. 25. Cf. Lubitsch's article "Deutsche Filme und die Welt," *Film-Kurier*, 5 July 1921. Davidson uttered equally loyal statements about producing German pictures in *Film-Kurier*, 25 April 1921. Bratz joined the chorus: *Der Film*, 23 October 1921, p. 48.

30. Cf. -o- (Robert Volz), "Der Sprung nach dem Dollar," *Tägliche Rundschau*, 24 April 1921; Caius, "Amerika kommt!" *Kinematographische Monatshefte*, May 1921, pp. 15–16; "Überfremdung?" *Lichtbildbühne*, 23 April 1921, pp. 11–12; Zimmerschied, *Die deutsche Filmindustrie*, pp. 82–84; Hayler, "Die deutsche Film-Industrie," pp. 111–112; W. Haas, "Reflexionen vor einem indischen Grabmal," *Film-Kurier*, 18 May 1921.

31. Olimsky, "Tendenzen der Filmwirtschaft," p. 43. For other post mortem analyses see "Der Untergang der EFA," *Film-Kurier*, 23 November 1922; W. Haas, "November-Films," *Das blaue Heft*, 4 (1922), 129–131; "EFA," *Kinematograph*, 26 November 1922, and the material cited in Brennicke and Hembus, *Klassiker des deutschen Stummfilms*, pp. 246–247.

32. Olimsky, "Tendenzen der Filmwirtschaft," pp. 26–27, claims ten percent for 1923. Spiker, *Film und Kapital*, pp. 36–37, cites a figure of thirty to forty percent over the period 1921–1923.

33. Sklar, *Movie-Made America*, p. 215. The phenomenon was not peculiar to Germany or the interwar period. Cf. Swann, *The Hollywood Feature Film*, p. 94. How bizarre circumstances were even in 1920 can be seen in the boast of Paul Davidson that in one week in New York *Madame Dubarry* more than recovered its entire production costs. See "Der deutsche Film im Ausland," *Berliner Tageblatt*, 5 April 1921.

34. Cf. "Amerikana," *Film-Kurier*, 31 January 1921; "Amerikanische Spielfilme nach deutschem Muster," ibid., 30 March 1921; and three articles in *Berliner Tageblatt*: "Der deutsche Film im Ausland," 5 April 1921, "Eine Krisis in der amerikanische Filmindustrie," 6 June 1921; "Der deutsche Film als Exportmittel," 13 July 1921.

35. "Ein deutscher Weltrekord: Ein deutscher Film schlägt Griffith und Chaplin," *Lichtbildbühne*, 5 November 1921, p. 41; "Neues vom Auslande," *Kinematograph*, 1 January 1922. Cf. Joseph Delmont's remarks in "Der deutsche Film in 1921," *Der Film*, 1 January 1921, pp. 34–35, and the very deprecatory opinions of Hollywood expressed in "Amerikas Film-Produktion und -Export," *Film-Kurier*, 3 May 1921.

36. Rudolf Berg, "Amerika und der deutsche Film," *B.Z. am Mittag*, 11 June 1922.

37. "Amerika und die Amerikaner," (interview with Rosenfeld), *Kinematograph*, 29 July 1923, p. 9. E. H. Correll, "Das amerikanische Problem," ibid., 19 August 1923, p. 13. All three experts took at face value American complaints about the ponderous, morbid and unedifying quality of German films. Cf. "Mary Pickford in Berlin," *Lichtbildbühne*, 22 April 1924.

38. "Die Krisis in den Glashäusern," *Berliner Tageblatt*, 21 January 1923.

39. Cf. warnings about gearing films to foreign audiences in order to dump them abroad from Balthasar (Roland Schacht), "Vor der Drohung des Auslands," *Freie Deutsche Bühne*, 2 (1921), 719, and "Rückblick," p. 1030; Paul Ickes, "Produktions-Politik," *Film-Kurier*, 28 February 1922; C. K. Brand, "Die Filmkrise," *Berliner Tageblatt*, 25 October 1921; Homunculus, "Im Zeichen des Dollars," *Reichsfilmblatt*, 1 September 1923, pp. 12–16. In January 1921 a dollar cost sixty-five marks.

40. Wolffsohn (ed.), *Jahrbuch der Filmindustrie*, vol. I, pp. 346–347. On the chaos resulting from collapse of the mark see Max Schach, "Panik?" *Berliner Börsen-Courier*, no. 411, 2 September 1923, p. 7. UFA's retreat to distribution and theater operations was earlier noted by J-s. (Paul Ickes), "Die UFA-Dividende," *Film-Kurier*, 27 November 1922; Egon Jacobsohn, "Das Film-Jahr 1922," *B.Z. am Mittag*, 31 December 1922.

41. Aros, (Alfred Rosenthal), "Die Eroberung Deutschlands," *Kinematograph*, 10 June 1923, pp. 5–6. Willy Haas, "Film-Resümee 1922–23," *Das blaue Heft*, 4 (1923), 447–449. Wolfgang Martini, "Münchener Filmbrief," *Kinematograph*, 1 October 1923, pp. 2–3.

42. See BA-UFA R109I/1026a, 23 September 1927, pt. 16. Cf. BA-UFA R109I/1027a, 6 July 1928, pt. 2, where threatened loss of three to four million marks in American earnings if export versions were not ready on time sparked the decision to work around the clock to meet a deadline.

43. Long-term, official loans alone totaled over $1.4 billion between 1924 and 1930. Werner Link, "Der amerikanische Einfluss auf

die Weimarer Republik in der Dawesplanphase (Elemente eines 'pene-trierten Systems')," in H. Mommsen, D. Petzina, B. Weissbrod (eds.) *Industrielles System and politische Entwicklung in der Weimarer Republik* (Düsseldorf: Droste, 1974), p. 489. More generally see William C. McNeil, *American Money and the Weimar Republic* (New York: Columbia University Press, 1986).

44. Kallmann, "Die Konzernierung in der Filmindustrie," p. 27; "Eine amerikanisch-deutsche Alliance," *Lichtbildbühne,* 19 July 1924, p. 20; "Phoebus - Metro - Goldwyn," ibid., 11 October 1924, p. 20.

45. Cf. in *Lichtbildbühne:* "United Artist - Ifa," 22 August 1925, p. 11; "United Artists in Deutschland," 5 September 1925, pp. 14–15; "First National verleiht," 1 May 1926, p. 20; Thompson, *Exporting Entertainment,* p. 111.

46. Horak, "Rin-Tin-Tin erobert Berlin," emphasizes the resis-tance to reciprocity on the part of the American companies.

47. For the race to Berlin see ibid., pp. 262–263; Kreimeier, *Die Ufa-Story,* p. 152.

48. See BA-UFA R109I/510, indexed as UFA Films Inc. N.Y., with the letter from von Stauss to F. W. Jones in New York (1 August 1924) outlining the aims of the new company. UFA simultaneously sought to raise its American profile through personal diplomacy in Holly-wood. See "Empfang in Los Angeles," *Lichtbildbühne,* 15 November 1924, p. 17.

49. See BA-UFA R109I/1046, Geschäftsbericht 1924–1925, in which expenditures in all branches of the firm were portrayed as ex-cessive given the general economic situation, but absolutely necessary in the face of American inroads. Cf. Kuntze-Just, "Guten Morgen, Ufa!" *Film-Telegramm,* no. 1 (1955), 10.

50. The press statement is reproduced in "An der Jahreswende," *Süddeutsche Filmzeitung,* 8 January 1926, p. 1.

51. Paul Elsberg, "Was steht in den UFA Verträgen?" *Vossische Zei-tung,* 8 January 1926. The pact with Universal was also for ten years and brought UFA a further loan of $275,000.

52. Roland Schacht commented that there had obviously been some major blunders in UFA management to allow Hollywood an entrance. "Blick auf die Walstatt," *Das blaue Heft,* 8 (1926), 25–26.

53. -g. (G. Herzberg), "Ein König im Exil," *Film-Kurier,* 5 May 1926, claimed that tumultuous howling and whistling had become the norm for almost every American premiere in Berlin. Cf. the reception of Erich Stroheim's *Greed* discussed in chapter four.

54. "und der deutsche Film?" *Vossische Zeitung,* 1 January 1926. The trade press withheld judgment on the condition that UFA re-

mained a *German* company making *German* motion pictures. See Dr. R. V. [Robert Volz], "An der Jahreswende," *Süddeutsche Filmzeitung,* 8 January 1926, p. 1; "Der neue Kurs," *Lichtbildbühne,* 2 January 1926, pp. 9–11.

55. BA-UFA R109I/121: Agreement between Universum-Film Aktiengesellschaft and Famous-Players-Lasky Corporation regarding distribution of "UFA" Pictures in America, pt. 1c. This folio includes both English and German copies of the pact.

56. Ibid., pt. 1d.

57. BA-UFA R109I/121: Agreement between Metro-Goldwyn Pictures Corporation and UFA Filmvertrieb Gesellschaft regarding distribution of Metro-Goldwyn Pictures in Germany, pt. 2l.

58. Heinrich Stürmer (Kurt Pinthus), "Deutscher oder amerikanischer Film?" *Das Tagebuch,* 6 (1925), 1699–1703.

59. Herbert Ihering, *Von Reinhardt bis Brecht: vier Jahrzehnte Theater und Film,* 3 vols. (Berlin: Aufbau Verlag, 1958–1961), vol. II, pp. 508–509.

60. See Schacht's remarks in "Blick auf die Walstatt," *Das blaue Heft,* 8 (1926), 23–26; "Der Anmarsch der Sieger," ibid, 57.

61. Cf. the affirmative assessment of Erich Pommer's role in Kurt Mühsam, "Friedliche Eroberung," *Lichtbildbühne,* 24 May 1924, pp. 10–11; "Das Programm der UFA," ibid., 5 September 1925, pp. 13–14. Later assessments are much more mixed. Cf. Roland Schacht's indictment in "Filme," *Das blaue Heft,* 8 (1926), 114–119; Fried. (Otto Friedrich), "Erich Pommer," *Deutsche Allgemeine Zeitung,* no. 49, 30 January 1926; Wolffgang Fischer, "Hie Deutschland—hie Amerika!" *Deutsche Filmwoche,* 26 March 1926; Hermann Treuner, "Der Amerikavertrag der Ufa und der deutsche Film," *Der Reichsbote,* 13 March 1926.

62. UFA was to release twenty pictures from Paramount and twenty-one from Metro-Goldwyn. The actual feature releases numbered eleven and fifteen respectively, plus fifteen from First National and twelve from Warner Bros. See BA-UFA R109I/2440, Verleih-Abteilung der UFA, pp. 23–25, 33a. The First National contracts are in BA-FB/UFA 257.

63. -z. (Robert Volz), "Die UFA beherrscht das Feld," *Süddeutsche Filmzeitung,* 14 August 1925; "Die UFA und Amerika," *Film-Kurier,* 7 August 1925.

64. See "Filmpolitik der Stunde," *Lichtbildbühne,* 12 September 1925, pp. 9–10; "Die amerikanischen Verträge und wir," *Reichsfilmblatt,* 15 August 1925, pp. 11–12; "UFA-Politik," *Lichtbildbühne,* 8 August 1925, pp. 9–10.

65. Otto Kriegk, *Der deutsche Film im Spiegel der UFA: 25 Jahre Kampf und Vollendung* (Berlin: UFA-Buchverlag, 1943), pp. 118, 124–127, styled Hugenberg a national hero for rescuing UFA from American-Jewish hands. Traub, *Die UFA*, pp. 63–66, 95, expressed similar opinions. UFA published a record of its fortunes in about 1943—*Die UFA* (n.p., n.d.)—which opened with the year 1927, thus excising the pre-Hugenberg period from its history.

66. For champions of cinema art like Willy Haas the decline of German film coincided with but was not caused by Hugenberg's purchase of UFA. See his remarks in "Filmkrise und kein Ende," *Die Literarische Welt*, 15 April 1927, p. 7; Cf. Michael Kurd, "Das Schicksal der UFA," *Welt am Abend*, 17 December 1926; Horak, "Ernst Lubitsch," p. 121.

67. G.H. (Georg Herzberg), "Madame Dubarry und wir," *Film-Kurier*, 6 August 1925.

68. Cf. Arthur Heichen, "Der Amerikavertrag der UFA," *Berliner Tageblatt*, no. 13, 8 January 1926; "Der neue Kurs," *Lichtbildbühne*, 2 January 1926, p. 10; the government report in Bundesarchiv-Reichskanzlei R43I/2498, p. 267; Funk, "Voran UFA," *Welt am Montag*, 22 March 1926, claimed these clauses offered Germany the chance to claim its rightful place in the cinematic sun.

69. Cf. the denial "Falsche Gerüchte," *Lichtbildbühne*, 17 April 1926, p. 7, and the later sharp attack on UFA "Wenn Verträge verschwiegen werden," ibid., 5 May 1927; Axel Eggebrecht, "Deutscher Filmfrühling 1927," *Die Weltbühne*, 23 (1927), vol. I, p. 755.

70. No time was wasted in pressing for revision of the Parufamet contract. See BA-UFA R109I/1026a, 2 May 1927, pt. 2, and 13 August 1927, pt. 2. Cf. BA-UFA R109I/1046, Geschäftsbericht 1927–1928, and details in Kuntze-Just, "Guten Morgen, Ufa!" *Film-Telegramm*, no. 4 (1955), 13. Once sound pictures complicated an already unhappy relationship the pact was annulled. See BA-UFA R109I/1027b 15 August 1930, pt. 6; 16 September 1930, pt. 9.

71. Details are in chapter four.

72. See Beissel's articles: "Die amerikanische Gefahr," *Reichsfilmblatt*, 23 February 1924, pp. 9–10; "Nochmals die amerikanische Gefahr," ibid., 8 March 1924, p. 5. Cf. the rebuttal "Immer für deutsche Interessen!" *Lichtbildbühne*, 15 March 1924, pp. 16–17.

73. "Ist das deutsche Kinopublikum amerikamüde?" *Reichsfilmblatt*, 6 December 1924, p. 13.

74. See *Reichsfilmblatt*, 20 September 1924, pp. 35–36; 18 October 1924, pp. 32–33; 24 January 1925, pp. 42–43; 28 February 1925, pp. 52–53; 11 July 1925, pp. 11–12; 19 September 1925, p. 16.

75. *Reichsfilmblatt:* 23 January 1926, pp. 9–10; 30 January 1926, pp. 14–15; 13 March 1926, p. 4.

76. See "Der König im Exil," *Der Film,* 9 May 1926, p. 18, and on "Mädchenscheu" and "Ein Dieb im Paradies," ibid., 7 March 1926, pp. 19 and 21.

77. Careful editing became a trade panacea. "Das ist das alte Lied . . . ," *Film-Kurier,* 7 April 1926; "Deutsche 'Verarbeitung'," *Film-Kurier,* 10 May 1926; "Die UFA gegen den amerikanischen Film," *Lichtbildbühne,* 10 May 1926; "Negativ-Dramaturgie," *Lichtbildbühne,* 18 May 1926; Aros, "Der Film der Zukunft," *Kinematograph,* 23 May 1926, pp. 2–3.

78. "Der Reichsverband in Abwehrstellung," *Süddeutsche Filmzeitung,* 21 May 1926, p. 2; "Boykott oder Bündnis?" *Film-Kurier,* 20 March 1926. Pr., "Reichsverband und amerikanischer Film," *Lichtbildbühne,* 22 May 1926, pp. 14–16.

79. Large, vertically integrated concerns like UFA, had conflicting interests in this matter.

80. See Aros, "Blick in die Zukunft," *Kinematograph,* 7 March 1926, pp. 5–6; "Die amerikanische Gefahr," ibid., 9 May 1926, pp. 5–6.

81. Rosenthal also identified vested interests at work. He distinguished between German firms working with Hollywood and profiting thereby, and those facing competition without American partners and trying to avenge themselves by clamorous warnings about the "American danger." "Blick in die Zukunft," *Kinematograph,* 7 March 1926, p. 5.

82. See Rosenthal, "Antiamerikanische Offensive," ibid., 16 March 1926, pp. 5–6; "Merkwürdige Film-Politiker," ibid., 20 May 1926, pp. 5–6. Cf. Willy Haas, "Meine Meinung," *Die Literarische Welt,* 11 June 1926, p. 2, who claimed that the "respectable trade press" was calling for international cooperation in recognition of the fact that American setbacks in Germany meant setbacks for the native cinema.

83. "Platz für den amerikanischen Film," *Lichtbildbühne,* 5 June 1926, pp. 7–10.

84. Fritz Olimsky, "Filmbilanz," *Berliner Börsen-Zeitung,* 1 January 1926, p. 4.

85. That UFA had accepted American funding even though its board had representatives from a score of large and small German banks disturbed some commentators. Cf. -ns, "War der Ufavertrag notwendig?" *Der Deutsche,* 3 January 1926; Hermann Treuner, "Der Amerikavertrag der Ufa und der deutsche Film," *Der Reichsbote,* 13 March 1926; Avk., "U.F.A. = U.S.A.," *Neue Preussische Kreuzzeitung,* 16 December 1926.

86. Herbert Ihering, "Die Zukunft der UFA," *Berliner Börsen-Courier*, 11 January 1926, p. 2.

87. See the editorial afterword which corrected Arthur Heichen, "Der Amerikavertrag der UFA," *Berliner Tageblatt*, 8 January 1926. Heichen compared Parufamet very unfavorably with the Dawes Plan because he believed it would check rather than stimulate German production.

88. Analogies to Versailles and Locarno were suggested in "Vor der Entscheidung," *Lichtbildbühne*, 12 December 1925, p. 9; "Das Ufa-Problem," ibid., 15 March 1926. The broader parallel with the Dawes Plan is mentioned by Kuntze-Just, "Guten Morgen, Ufa!" *Film-Telegramm*, no. 1 (1955), 10.

89. Hermann Rosenfeld, "National und Paramount," *Film-Kurier*, 11 January 1925.

90. "Universal-Bruckmann," *Lichtbildbühne*, 3 October 1925, p. 14; "In Sachen: Bruckmann-Universal," *Bruckmann-Nachrichten*, November 1925; "Bruckmann-Warner Bros.," *Lichtbildbühne*, 9 April 1926.

91. See "Die große Fox-Schau in der Alhambra," *Lichtbildbühne*, 10 October 1925, p. 14; "Deutsche-Fox Produktion," ibid., 6 February 1926, p. 23; "F.E.F. Fox Europa Film-Produktions G.m.b.H.," ibid., 12 June 1926, p. 14.

92. "United Artists - Phoebus," ibid., 3 May 1926; Kurt Mühsam, "Amerika filmt in Deutschland," *B.Z. am Mittag*, 1 April 1927.

93. Curt Kramarski, "Die Amerikanisierung des deutschen Films," *Welt am Montag*, 23 April 1928; Kurt Mühsam, "Deutsch-amerikanische Filmgemeinschaften," *B.Z. am Mittag*, 10 June 1927.

94. For the pattern of responses see Kurt Mühsam, "Europäische Kultur-amerikanische Technik," *B.Z. am Mittag*, 19 October 1928; "Amerika kommt zu uns!" *Film-Journal*, 20 May 1927; "Amerika als deutscher Produzent," *Film-Kurier*, 7 May 1926; "Deutsch-amerikanische Filmunion," *Film-Kurier*, 9 June 1927.

95. "Dr. Bausback über die deutsch-amerikanischen Filmbeziehungen," *Lichtbildbühne*, 14 and 15 June 1926.

96. On Pommer see chapter eight.

97. See "Die Einkreisung," *Lichtbildbühne*, 25 July 1925, pp. 5–6; "Amerikanisierung und deutsche Filmindustrie," ibid., 29 August 1925, pp. 9–10.

CHAPTER 3: THE INITIATION 1921–1923

1. Pabst's remark is cited in K.M. (Kenneth MacPherson), "Die Liebe der Jeanne Ney," *Close-Up*, 1 (December 1927), 17–27, here pp.

18–19. Cf. Willy Haas, "Die Amerikaner beleidigen uns . . !?" *Film-Kurier*, 5 November 1924.

2. Cf. Rainer Pommerin, *Der Kaiser und Amerika* (Cologne/Vienna: Böhlau Verlag, 1986), pp. 208–209; Frank Trommler, "The Rise and Fall of Americanism in Germany," in Trommler and McVeigh (eds.), *America and the Germans*, vol. II, pp. 332–342.

3. The characterization of American as cultureless refused to die. Cf. Beck, *Germany Rediscovers America*, pp. 2–3; Laqueur, *Weimar*, p. 32.

4. Some American pictures appeared among approximately 250 smuggled into the country during 1919 and 1920. Traub, *Die UFA*, p. 40.

5. See, for example, "Die Krisis des französischen Films," *Der Film*, 3 August 1918, p. 55. Cf. in *Kinematograph:* "Französische Filmsorgen," 22 August 1917; "Neues vom Ausland—Der südamerikanische Markt," 5 September 1917; "Neues vom Ausland-Russland," 7 November 1917.

6. Cf. the review of "Gehetzte Menschen," *Lichtbildbühne*, 20 March 1919, p. 29, and Egon Jacobsohn's reviews in *Kinematograph*, 2 April 1919. Cf. reviews of "Schmutziges Geld," *Der Film*, 10 May 1919, p. 34; *Lichtbildbühne*, 24 May 1919, p. 29; *Der Film*, 28 February 1920, p. 47, and 17 April 1920, p. 48.

7. "Neues vom Ausland," *Kinematograph*, 27 February 1918; "Das Ende des amerikanischen Filmtrusts," *Der Film*, 14 September 1918, pp. 53–54.

8. Egon Jacobsohn reviewed Ernst Lubitsch's *Carmen* from this perspective: *Kinematograph*, 15 January 1919, as did a critic in *Lichtbildbühne*, 21 December 1918, p. 71. The international cinema was likewise the yardstick in Alfred Rosenthal's comments on *Veritas vincit:* "Der Triumph des deutschen Films," *Erste Internationale Film-Zeitung*, 15 April 1919. Ludwig Brauner adopted the same approach in reviews of Paul Leni's *Prinz Kuckuck* and Fritz Lang's *Die Spinnen: Kinematograph*, 1 October 1919, and 8 October 1919. Most explicit in this regard was a panegyric for Lubitsch's *Madame Dubarry* by Arthur Liebert, which claimed that more works of this caliber would end America's international dominance: *Der Film*, 20 September 1919, p. 46.

9. Karl Figdor in *Erste Internationale Film-Zeitung*, 25 October 1919, p. 36.

10. See "Der Filmautor—Der deutsche Film in Frieden," *Kinematograph*, 30 April 1919.

11. *Erste Internationale Film-Zeitung*, 18 October 1919, pp. 42–43.

12. Urban Gad, "Der amerikanische Grossfilm," *Lichtbildbühne*, 15

March 1919, pp. 14–16, and 22 March 1919, pp. 28–30. Cf. Robert Bogyansky, "Der deutsche Film," *Film-Kurier*, 4 March 1920; *Lichtbildbühne*, 26 July 1919, p. 21.

13. See Thomas Saunders, "History in the Making: Weimar Cinema and National Identity," in Bruce Murray and Christopher Wickham (eds.), *Framing the Past* (Carbondale: Southern Illinois University Press, 1992), pp. 42–67.

14. "Die Amerikaner," *Kinematograph*, 13 August 1919.

15. Karl Figdor in *Erste Internationale Film-Zeitung*, 3 January 1920, p. 24.

16. "Stockholmer Kino-Bericht," *Kinematograph*, 10 July 1918. "Der amerikanische Film," *Erste Internationale Film-Zeitung*, 22 November 1919, pp. 30–32. Historians would disagree with the value judgments and choice of language, but the essential contrast sketched by Genenncher is that taken up by Kracauer, Eisner et al.

17. See the summary in A. Hellwig, "National Kinoreform," *Soziale Kultur*, 38 (1918), 218–223.

18. Saunders, "History in the Making."

19. In review of *Liebe* in *Der Film*, 21 December 1919, p. 39; *Lichtbildbühne*, 1 February 1919, p. 26. Hans Richter (ed.), *Das Kinojahrbuch, 1921* (Berlin: H. Richter Verlag, 1921), vol. III, pp. 9–10. Cf. Ihering, *Von Reinhardt bis Brecht*, vol. I, p. 448. Cf. the later reflections of Heinz Michaelis, "Wahrer und falscher Internationalismus im deutschen Film," *Film-Kurier*, 5 January 1923.

20. See Buscombe, "Film History and the Idea of a National Cinema."

21. "Die Schicksalstunde der deutschen Filmindustrie," *Erste Internationale Film-Zeitung*, 19 June 1920, pp. 10–11. Cf. P. Schmitt, "Von der Weltgeltung des deutschen Films," *Der Türmer*, 20 (1918), 256–258 for a nationalist lament about prewar compulsion to view the world through French glasses.

22. See Heller, *Literarische Intelligenz und Film*, pp. 39–44, 67–98. Cf. Bier, "Max Reinhardt und die PAGU," p. 29.

23. See Hugo Zehder, *Der Film vom Morgen* (Berlin/Dresden: Rudolf Kaemmerer, 1923). Elsaesser, "German Silent Cinema," notes the self-conscious character of these ambitions.

24. Siemsen was a member of the left-wing splinter Socialist Workers' Party. See Wolfgang Jacobsen's biographical sketch in H.-M. Bock (ed.), *CineGraph*. Siemsen's own writings, now collected as *Schriften*, 3 vols. (Essen: Torso Verlag, 1985–1989) are indispensable, especially those from the collection of travel anecdotes and reflections, *Wo hast du dich denn herumgetrieben: Erlebnisse* (Munich: Kurt Wolff Verlag,

1920) which includes commentary on the war and capitalism and a biting attack on militarism ("Potsdam oder Döberitz," pp. 58–69). Through the mid-1920s Siemsen wrote film reviews for *Die Weltbühne* and edited the film section of the liberal *8 Uhr-Abendblatt*.

25. Siemsen, "Film-Reform?" *Die Weltbühne*, 15 (1919), vol. I, pp. 292–294. Cf. Rudolf Kurtz, "Der Reform-Film," ibid., pp. 117–119; Laroche, "Kinokritik," *Der Kritiker*, 1, 25 (1919), 9–10.

26. Siemsen, "Die Filmerei," *Die Weltbühne*, 17 (1921), vol. I, pp. 101–105.

27. Cf. Paul Beyer, "Film! Kunst?" *Der Kritiker*, 3 (March 1921), 88–90; Hugo Zehder, *Der Film von Morgen*, especially Siemsen's "Das Filmmanuskript," pp. 52–60; eu. (Erich Hamburger?), "Das Tier im Film," *Berliner Tageblatt*, 4 March 1923. Béla Balázs, *Der Sichtbare Mensch*, in his *Schriften zum Film*, vol. I, pp. 108–112. Cf. Joseph Zsuffa, *Béla Balázs, The Man and the Artist* (Berkeley: University of California Press, 1987), pp. 109–122.

28. In a chapter from *Wo hast du dich denn herumgetrieben* entitled "Amerika" (pp. 108–111), Siemsen wrote in 1920 that he had wanted to visit America until he read about grain growers there destroying their harvest while malnutrition was prevalent in Europe. He blamed this lunacy, like the war, on the logic of capitalism and lost all desire to see America. His respect for American film was nonetheless genuine.

29. See Albersmeier, *Die Herausforderung des Films an die französische Literatur*, pp. 32–34.

30. See Yvan Goll, "Das Kinodram," *Die neue Schaubühne*, 2 (1920), 141–143, and Claire Goll, "Amerikanisches Kino," ibid., pp. 164–165. Both are reproduced in Kaes, *Kino-Debatte*, pp. 136–139; 146–148.

31. Rudolf Kurtz, "Kampf ums Kino: Wider Hans Siemsen," *Die Weltbühne*, 17 (1921), vol. I, pp. 166–168; with reply from Peter Panter (Kurt Tucholsky), "Für Hans Siemsen," pp. 168–170. For the reprint and Haas's rejoinder see *Film-Kurier*, 10 and 11 February 1921.

32. Siemsen, "Deutsche Filme," *Die Weltbühne*, 17 (1921), vol. II, pp. 253–257.

33. Ludwig Wolff, "Brief an Hans Siemsen," ibid., 315–316. Cf. "Friede," *Kinematograph*, 9 July 1919; K. Figdor, "Ensemble- oder Star-System im Exportfilm?" *Erste Internationale Film-Zeitung*, 25 October 1919, pp. 36–37.

34. Siemsen, "Erwiderung an Ludwig Wolff," *Die Weltbühne*, 17 (1921), vol. II, pp. 358–360.

35. Hans Glenk, "Auslandsfilme," ibid., pp. 415–417.

36. Glenk spoke of Pickford in a way which suggested he too had seen the film; he was in all likelihood also familiar with Haas's review.

37. Haas, "Ein Mary-Pickford-Film in Berlin," *Film-Kurier*, 28 February 1921.

38. Haas, "Die Degeneration der Filmkunst," ibid., 6 April 1921. Not long after, Béla Balázs, then resident in Vienna, saw an ideal future in the synthesis of European art and American technology: "Achtung! Amerika kommt!" in his *Schriften zum Film*, vol. I, pp. 154–155.

39. One expert, disgruntled by the fact that with five years of foreign production to choose from German distributors were importing miles of these serials, accurately estimated that a single American company, Universal, was swallowing up one-half of the import quota: Quintus Fixlein, "Filmwirtschaft: Auslese des Schlechtesten," *Das Tagebuch*, 2 (1921), 1026–1027. Cf. Wolffsohn (ed.), *Jahrbuch der Filmindustrie*, vol. I, p. 165.

40. *Der Film*, 3 July 1921, pp. 46, 49. Cf. the preview based on foreign experience by H.K., "Der amerikanische Sensationsfilm," *Vorwärts*, 15 April 1921.

41. Brauner's review of "Goliath Armstrong" in *Kinematograph*, 1 May 1921. Cf. ina (Paul Medina), "Tarzan," *Film-Kurier*, 7 May 1921; 1f., "Tarzans Roman," *Film-Kurier*, 27 August 1921, and "Mit Büchse und Spaten," in *Film-Kurier*, 3 September 1921, and *Berliner Börsen-Courier*, no. 317, 10 July 1921, p. 13. C. F. W. Behl, editor of *Der Kritiker*, argued that two features almost always distinguished American movies—"sugary femininity and brutal manliness": *Freie Deutsche Bühne*, 2 (1921), 1194.

42. Laupp, "Film," *Der Kritiker*, August 1921, p. 16. A convenient point of entry to the range of opinion on the early American sensationalist films is the short-lived journal *Film und Presse*, nos. 17/18–33/34, 1921, which presented a digest of contemporary reviews. Cf. the poll among producers before the first wave of American films which linked the popularity of sensationalism to public restlessness and the industry's desire to capture markets abroad: "Die Produktion der neuen Saison," *Der Film*, 26 March 1921, pp. 28–29. Laqueur, *Weimar*, pp. 234–235, explains the postwar preference for what he calls horror films as a demand for stimulation as intense as the war.

43. For reactions to "Goliath Armstrong" see *Der Film*: 30 April 1921, p. 39; 10 July 1921, p. 26; 17 July 1921, p. 47; 24 July 1921, p. 38.

44. Cf. *Kinematograph*, 1 May 1921, and 7 August 1921, on "Goliath Armstrong;" 3 July 1921, 10 July 1921, 17 July 1921 on *The Red Ace*.

45. See folio at Deutsches Institut für Filmkunde, Frankfurt, Filmprüfstelle Berlin, 15 September 1921, and Film-Oberprüfstelle Berlin, 22 September 1921; henceforth DIFF-FP and DIFF-FO respectively.

46. Cf. DIFF-FP, 15 October 1921; DIFF-FO, 20 October 1921.

47. DIFF-FP, 23 June 1922.

48. DIFF-FO, 5 July 1922.

49. Cf., for example, DIFF-FO, 22 July and 25 August 1922; 11 November 1921; DIFF-FP, 23 June 1922.

50. Cf. DIFF-FP, 9 October 1923; DIFF-FO, 16 October 1923.

51. DIFF-FP, 8–9 October 1923. The absence of mitigating circumstances was clearly stated: "The film piles one sensation on another. There is no thought, no psychological motivation in it . . . . Its style is beyond that of the worst trashy novel."

52. DIFF-FO, 1 November 1923.

53. DIFF-FO, 22 June 1923.

54. Cf. DIFF-FP, 13 December 1923; DIFF-FO, 21 December 1923.

55. "Der deutsche Film im Ausland," *Berliner Tageblatt,* 5 April 1921; Fritz Engel, "Amerika-Film," ibid., 17 July 1921.

56. Urban Gad, "Warum siegt der amerikanische Film?" *Lichtbildbühne,* 20 August 1921, p. 15. It may be more than coincidental that Gad came under fire just weeks later for sacrificing stylistic consistency in order to incorporate American sensationalism: Krft. (Arthur Krefft), "Insel der Verschollenen," *Der Kritiker,* 3 (December 1921), 219–222.

57. For a dissenting view see L. A. Hermann, "Schiefe Urteile über die amerikanische Produktion," *Kinematograph,* 6 November 1921.

58. Paul Meissner, "Amerikaner," *Film-Kurier,* 17 October 1921. Without mentioning Siemsen by name Meissner commented acidly that after the warnings issued about Hollywood's superiority American film had proven imposing only in its length.

59. *Der Film,* 5 March 1922, p. 44.

60. Siemsen, "Deutsch-amerikanischer Filmkrieg," *Die Weltbühne,* 17 (1921), vol. I, pp. 219–222.

61. gl. (Oscar Geller?), "Aus der Praxis," Kinematograph, 18 September 1921. Cf. the more modest recommendation of Herbert Ihering responding to "Goliath Armstrong:" "This American film is a crude, vulgar affair, and one should be careful not to imitate it in Germany . . . . Nevertheless, one should still take note of it, one should still take a lesson from its resolution in foregoing assumptions, in shortening, in omission of motivation. That seems to me to be the task: to exploit for the expression of acting in Germany the tempo which the Americans have for daredevil acrobatic stunts." *Berliner Börsen-Courier,* no. 341, 24 July 1921, p. 9.

62. Siemsen, "Deutsch-amerikanischer Filmkrieg," *Die Weltbühne,*

17 (1921), vol. II, p. 221, observed that Berlin's film critics had "no taste for the boundless naiveté of a film like "Goliath Armstrong." Cf. Franz Schulz, "Definitionen zum Film," in Zehder, *Der Film von Morgen*, p. 46: "The disdain toward the cinema, especially among cultivated, respected Germans, can be traced to the native dogma that boredom is a necessary attribute of art."

63. Paul Ickes, "Vorstellungen und Irrtümer," *Film-Kurier*, 27 June 1921. No critic praised the sentimental, moralizing qualities of the film. Cf. reviews of "Die fremde Frau" by -d- (F. Podehl), *Der Film*, 28 August 1921, p. 50; L. Brauner, *Kinematograph*, 4 September 1921; and -a. (P. Medina), *Film-Kurier*, 25 August 1921. Brauner used the term *Kammerspiel* to describe the focus on emotional/psychological conflict.

64. Max Prels, "Verbotene Frucht," *Kinematograph*, 25 June 1922. Cf. Paul Medina, "Amerika und wir," *Film-Echo*, 19 June 1922, who noted the financial freedom Hollywood enjoyed to work for a national audience, one it understood, rather than chasing an unpredictable international market, as Germans were doing with emphasis on historical pageants.

65. Balthasar, "Inland und Ausland," *Das blaue Heft*, 3 (1922), 957. M.Z., "Kinoides," *Der Kritiker*, 4 (June 1922), 15: "The how may be quite nice, but the what is too foolish. . . . So the villain gets his just punishment, so passionate love overcomes class prejudices triumphantly: it is too banal, too inconsequential in its banality."

66. *Vossische Zeitung*, no. 609, 27 December 1921.

67. Paul Ickes, "Viola Dana," *Film-Kurier*, 29 August 1922, Cf. J.S. (Julius Sternheim?), "Im Reiche des weissen Elefanten," *Film-Kurier*, 22 May 1922; *Berliner Tageblatt*, 18 March 1923.

68. Frank Furter, "Viola Dana," *Das Tagebuch*, 3 (1922), 1107–1108.

69. For the broad distinctions of type and quality see "Sechs Fox-Filme," *Lichtbildbühne*, 22 July 1922, p. 42; Bz., "Der Fox-Film," *Vossische Zeitung*," no. 343, 22 July 1922. For specific, slashing criticism of the historical pictures see J-s (Paul Ickes), "Die Königin von Saba," *Film-Kurier*, 19 July 1922; F.K., "Nero," *Film-Kurier*, 22 July 1922.

70. Aros (Rosenthal), "Fox-Parade," *Film-Echo*, 24 July 1922. Cf. Willy Haas' response to *Daddy-Long-Legs* discussed above; Kreimeier, *Die Ufa-Story*, p. 151.

71. *Kinematograph*, 6 August 1922, p. 123.

72. Wolfgang Martini, "Vom Wesen des amerikanischen Films. Vom Wesen des Films überhaupt," *Süddeutsche Filmzeitung*, 14 September 1923, pp. 1–2. Cf. Erich Hamburger, "Harald Lloyd [sic]," *Berliner Tageblatt*, 4 May 1924.

73. See R-th. (Joseph Roth?), "Foxfilme in der Alhambra," *Berliner Börsen-Courier*, no. 341, 23 July 1922, p. 8: "Among us doctrinaires the controversy over the question: is film art or not? has never been terminated. The Fox films demonstrate the superfluity of this controversy. . . . Sometimes the event on which the film is based is banal—but then details and nuances are enriched by the acting. Sometimes the subject is an improbable exaggeration—but then the details are of gripping truthfulness. By laying, therefore, a real foundation for castles of fantasy, as it were, one commands the interest of the most demanding viewer. This basically constitutes the success of American films."

74. A. K. Rosen-Lohr, "Der amerikanische Film in Deutschland," *Film-Kurier*, 14 January 1922: "One cannot take America too seriously as the homeland of film. It has the advantage that the leap there from a mechanical invention like cinematography to an art form like film-art is not as great as in old Europe. Pioneering in America, in which the forests still resound with the ax clearing the land, in which steel is bent into technical wonders, has the right mind for the immediate art of film. For it is an art form for industrial pioneers who have a feeling for the thirst of film for ever new impressions of a changed locality." Cf. Hans Tintner, "Umwege zum Weltgeschmack," *Süddeutsche Filmzeitung*, 15 December 1922, pp. 6–7.

75. See the review of *My Boy* in *Der Film*, 16 September 1923, p. 24; Hi (Fred Hildenbrandt), "Jackie," *Berliner Tageblatt*, 5 September 1923; E.H. (Erich Hamburger), "König Jackie," *Berliner Tageblatt*, 30 March 1924; and Egon Jameson (Jacobsohn), *Mein Lachendes Spree-Athen* (Berlin: Haude & Spenersche, 1968), pp. 24–34.

76. By contrast, *The Sheik*, starring Rudolph Valentino, and D. W. Griffith's *Orphans of the Storm* provoked very mixed reactions. For general perspectives see Walter Thielemann, "Der amerikanische Film," *Reichsfilmblatt*, 22 December 1923, pp. 7–8; Kurt Pinthus, "Die Insel der verlorenen Schiffe," *Das Tagebuch*, 4 (1923), 1790–1791. For later reflections by Fritz Lang on the appeal of Hollywood's action, romance and comedy see "Was ich in Amerika sah," *Film-Kurier*, 13 and 17 December 1924.

77. Cf. Fulks, "Film Culture and *Kulturfilm*," p. 8.

CHAPTER 4: THE HOLLYWOOD INVASION

1. A summary is in Willett, *The New Sobriety*, pp. 95–104. The bibliography in Beck, *Germany Rediscovers America*, pp. 289–306, gives some indication of escalating interest in the United States. The statistics

compiled by Wilhelm Pocher, "Die Rezeption der englischen und amerikanischen Literatur in Deutschland in den Jahren 1918–1933" (Ph.D. Dissertation, Jena, 1972), pp. 18–19, show that over the period 1923–1928 German articles published on contemporary American literature increased 400 percent

2. On its reception see Lethen, *Neue Sachlichkeit*, pp. 20–24, and Peter Berg, *Deutschland und Amerika*, pp. 99–107. Cf. reactions to Walt Whitman cited in Sahl, *Memoiren eines Moralisten*, p. 58.

3. On *Amerikanismus* see Anton Kaes (ed.), *Weimarer Republik. Manifeste und Dokumente zur deutschen Literatur 1918–1933* (Stuttgart: J. B. Metzlersche, 1983), pp. 265–286; Peukert, *Die Weimarer Republik*, pp. 178–190; Hermand and Trommler, *Die Kultur der Weimarer Republik*, pp. 49–57, 314.

4. Cf. Lethen, *Neue Sachlichkeit*, pp. 25–26; Beck, *Germany Rediscovers America* pp. 244–245, whose concern to show that the German perception of America was seriously flawed mars his analysis of German perceptions. Contemporaries recognized that America was largely an abstraction. Cf. the essays reprinted in Kaes (ed.), *Weimarer Republik;* Alfred Ehrentreich, "Americana," *Die Tat*, 19 (1928), 789–792: "In the final analysis it is ideologically not at all a matter of America itself, but of what type of intellectual culture we endorse."

5. On social realism and politicization see Korte (ed.), *Film und Realität;* Murray, *Film and the German Left;* Rainer Berg, "Zur Geschichte der realistischen Stummfilmkunst."

6. For a pithy summary of sentiments see "Volkes Stimme," *Lichtbildbühne*, 24 January 1925, p. 14.

7. Adolf Halfeld, *Amerika und der Amerikanismus* (Jena: E. Diederichs, 1927), pp. x and 237. This work is a compendium of the contrasting stereotypes applied by nationalists to Germany and the United States.

8. Hans Buchner, *Im Banne des Films: Die Weltherrschaft des Kinos* (Munich: Deutscher Volksverlag, 1927), pp. 24–25, 78, 80. A brief analysis of Buchner is in Rainer Berg, "Zur Geschichte der realistischen Stummfilmkunst," pp. 195–196. For parallels with France see Strauss, *Menace in the West*, p. 141.

9. In this regard see the shrewd guesses of Buchwald, "Das Kulturbild Amerikas," p. 112, which still, however, fail to penetrate stereotypes applied to American film.

10. G.H. (Georg Herzberg), "Madame Dubarry und wir," *Film-Kurier*, 6 August 1925 (italics in original).

11. Willy Haas, "Nostra culpa?" *Film-Kurier*, 16 November 1925; David Melamerson, "Unsere Stellung zum Auslandsfilm in der neuen Saison," *Kinematograph*, 30 August 1925.

12. Pinthus wrote under the pen name Heinrich Stürmer, "Deutscher oder amerikanischer Film?" *Das Tagebuch*, 6 (1925), 1702.

13. Hanns Brodnitz, "Zur Psychologie der Filmkrise," *Film-Kurier*, 8 June 1926; H. Sp. (Hans Spielhofer) reviewing "Durch Feuer und Flammen," *Süddeutsche Filmzeitung*, 17 September 1926, p. 3.

14. On Schacht see my contribution to *CineGraph*. For his migration from literature to the cinema and conception of film criticism see his "Filmproduktion und Filmkritik," *B.Z. am Mittag*, 25 November 1923, and "Deutsche und Amerikaner," *Das blaue Heft*, 5 (1 December 1923), 26. His emphasis on mass sensibilities is explained in *Freie Deutsche Bühne*, 1 (1920), 919. The cinema's fate at the hands of German intellectuals is lamented in "Filmhandlung und Stoffgebiet," *Das blaue Heft*, 5 (1 March 1924), 17–21, and 124–126. All Schacht's film essays in *Das blaue Heft* appeared under the pseudonym Balthasar.

15. Balthasar, "Rundschau-Filmpolitik," *Das blaue Heft*, 3 (1922), 532–533 and 1022–1023; also "Deutsche und Amerikaner," ibid., 5 (1 December 1923), 26–27.

16. "Der Carlos-Film," ibid., 5 (1 April 1924), 16–19.

17. "Amerikanische Invasion," ibid., 5 (1924), 199–200.

18. This review was reprinted under the caption "Entlarvung," in *Der Bildwart*, 2 (1924), 643–644.

19. "Beginn der Filmsaison," *Das blaue Heft*, 6 (1 October 1924), 23–24. "The intellectual paltriness of the whole thing, the balletlike style of the first part [and] the primitiveness of the second would have been overlooked because for the price there was still something to watch. Only when an attempt was made to dupe the Berliner did he start to rebel."

20. Ibid., p. 24.

21. "Bilanz," ibid., 6 (1925), 556–557; "Ausgangssituation," ibid, 7 (1 October 1925), 32.

22. "Ausgangssituation," ibid., p. 34.

23. Cf. Paul Beyer, "Abgesang," *Film-Kurier*, 12 January 1924.

24. See, for example, the lead article "Ein Welterfolg . . .?" *Lichtbildbühne*, 23 August 1924, p. 9. Cf. reviews in *Kinematograph*, 24 August 1924, p. 11; *Der Bildwart*, 2 (15 September 1924), 94–96; *Der Kunstwart*, 38 (January 1925), 191–192. More general, caustic reflections are found in Franz Blei, "Die zehn Gebote," *Berliner Tageblatt*, 14 August 1924; Fritz Engel, "Die zehn Gebote aus Amerika," ibid., 22 August 1924.

25. Georg Mendel, "Wie lange noch," *Lichtbildbühne*, 11 May 1926.

26. See Joe May, "Wir und ihr Film," *Das Tagebuch*, 3 (1922), 1217; Aros (Rosenthal), "Deutschland und Amerika," *Kinematograph*, 18 November 1923, p. 5.

27. Cf. Walter Flitner, "Amerikanisierung?" *Reichsfilmblatt*, 12 January 1924, pp. 16–19; Fritz Berger, "Der amerikanische Filmgeschmack," *Der Film*, 18 May 1924, pp. 20–24.

28. Cf. "Das Kentucky Derby," *Süddeutsche Filmzeitung*, 27 June 1924, p. 3; e.b. (Erna Büsing), *Vorwärts*, no. 302, 29 June 1924.

29. On *King of Kings* see the reviews by Willy Haas in *Film-Kurier*, 29 October 1927; Kurt Pinthus in *Das Tagebuch*, 8 (1927), 1814–1815; Hans Wollenberg in *Lichtbildbühne*, 28 October 1927; Harry Kahn in *Die Weltbühne*, 23 (1927), vol. II, pp. 755–757.

30. "Amerika, hörst Du die Pfiffe?" *Film-Kurier*, 10 September 1926. Also on *Ben Hur* see *Film-Kurier*, 8 September 1926; *Süddeutsche Filmzeitung*, 22 October 1926, p. 8; the exhaustive critique in *Der Bildwart*, 4 (1926), 788–791; Kracauer's review of 23 October 1926 from the *Frankfurter Zeitung* in the folio at the Schiller Museum in Marbach, henceforth cited as Kracauer Folio, Marbach; *Reichsfilmblatt*, 11 September 1926, pp. 18–19.

31. Willy Haas, "Charleys Tante," *Film-Kurier*, 26 September 1925; "Premiere im UFA-Palast," *Reichsfilmblatt*, 3 October 1925, p. 14. Interestingly, *Lichtbildbühne*, 26 September 1925, pp. 25–26, expressed admiration for the new style. Rainer Berg, "Zur Geschichte der realistischen Stummfilmkunst," pp. 98–99, implies that this development was the start and finish of anti-American protest, which it clearly was not. UFA put the program on the road with Rappé: *Frankfurter Volksstimme*, 7 October 1925 and 25 November 1925.

32. On the former see May, *Screening out the Past*.

33. "Verlorene Töchter," *Kinematograph*, 17 August 1924, p. 13. This was one of the pictures Schacht lumped with the new wave of American imports which were beneath discussion.

34. *Vossische Zeitung*, no. 390, 17 August 1924. For Mendel's comments see "Verlorene Töchter," *Lichtbildbühne*, 16 August 1924, p. 34. Almost identical sentiments came from *Berliner Tageblatt*, 17 August 1924.

35. *Vorwärts*, no. 386, 17 August 1924.

36. "Du sollst nicht begehren deines Nächsten Weib," *Vorwärts*, no. 446, 21 September 1924. The tone here was sharper than in the trade press; the message was similar. Cf. *Lichtbildbühne*, 20 September 1924, p. 29; *Kinematograph*, 28 September 1924, p. 18.

37. *Der Film*, 21 September 1924, p. 41. Cf. Pinthus's blistering attack on American moral obtuseness in *Das Tagebuch*, 5 (1924), 1158–1159.

38. *Reichsfilmblatt*, 20 September 1924, pp. 35–36.

39. See the remarks by Ludwig Scheer, president of the National

Association of German Exhibitors in *Reichsfilmblatt,* 31 July 1926, p. 4.

40. Although the historical section came under fire in some quarters for externalizing and trivializing sacred history the modern part did most to offend. Cf. Fritz Goetz in *Vossische Zeitung,* no. 399, 22 August 1924; Ternova in *Der Kritiker,* 6 (October 1924), 16.

41. Kurt Pinthus, "Die zehn Gebote," *Das Tagebuch,* 5 (1924), 1235–1236.

42. Ibid., p. 1236. Cf. the review in *Vorwärts,* no. 398, 24 August 1924: "To the major questions which concern mankind the American cinema answers with a miserable little tract which may be good over there to dupe the masses but has no place any more in Europe."

43. Martin Beheim-Schwarzbach, "Goldrausch oder Rauschgold," *Film-Journal,* 11 June 1926. Cf. Walter Steinhauer: "The customary female type in American film . . . is slowly becoming unbearable. One can no longer quite swallow this blond, overly sentimental virtue." *Reichsfilmblatt,* 16 January 1926, p. 36.

44. See the review of "Das goldene Land," *Vorwärts,* no. 102, 1 March 1925; Ludwig Scheer in *Reichsfilmblatt,* 31 July 1926, p. 4; and especially Axel Eggebrecht in *Die Weltbühne,* 22 (1926), vol. I, pp. 229. Sentiments in this area are no more aptly captured than in the surprise and admiration for films perceived as an assault on the cult. See Kracauer, "Girldämmerung," Kracauer Folio, Marbach, 22 June 1928; (Felix) Gong, "Zwei Amerikas," *Deutsche Republik,* 2 (1928), 1161; Wolfgang Petzet, "Amerikadämmerung," *Der Kunstwart,* 41 (1928), 269–270; especially Hans Kafka, "Neben dem Theater," *Das blaue Heft,* 10 (1928), 427–428. On the phenomenon in general see Fritz Giese, *Girlkultur: Vergleiche zwischen amerikanischem und europäischem Rhythmus und Lebensgefühl* (Munich: Delphin-Verlag, 1925); Günter Berghaus, "*Girlkultur*—Feminism, Americanism, and Popular Entertainment in Weimar Germany," *Journal of Design History,* I (1988), 193–219.

45. Haas, "Was uns an der amerikanischen Filmmoral befremdet," *Film-Kurier,* 5 November 1925. Hans Tintner, "Die zehn Gebote des amerikanischen Films," *Film-Kurier,* 11 April 1925, deals only marginally with ethical questions.

46. Rainer Berg, "Zur Geschichte der realistischen Stummfilmkunst," pp. 93–99, acknowledges a crisis at middecade under the impact of the American invasion but then all but ignores the repercussions of this crisis in his discussion of developments from 1926 to 1929.

47. A critical biography is Richard Koszarski, *The Man You Love to Hate* (New York: Oxford University Press, 1983).

48. This plot summary is cursory even for the two and a half hour version of the film which saw public release. As Stroheim created it, the picture would have run for seven and a half hours. The script has been published: Joel Finler (ed.), *Greed. A Film by Erich von Stroheim* (London: Lorimer, 1972). For a selection of stills from the film see Herman Weinberg, *The Complete Greed of Erich von Stroheim* (New York: Avon Press, 1972).

49. For a brief description of the premiere and its aftermath see "Skandal im UFA-Palast," *Lichtbildbühne*, 17 May 1926. Heinrich Fraenkel, *Unsterblicher Film* (Munich, 1956), vol. I, p. 126, claims perfect recall of the premiere, but does not even mention that the showing was canceled and the film withdrawn. He presumably was present at the first show, for which he records considerable enthusiastic applause drowned out by whistles and laughter. He remarks as well that the "literary" press was ecstatic—an overstatement—while the box-office results were disappointing—an understatement. For a report which linked the uproar to chauvinistic protest against Stroheim himself see Joseph Delmont, "Der Skandal im UFA-Palast," *Süddeutsche Filmzeitung*, 21 May 1926, p. 10.

50. There were similar scenes over enlightenment films in the post-war period and over *Fridericus Rex* in 1922.

51. Cf. Balthasar, "Leckerbissen," *Das blaue Heft*, 8 (1926), 304–305; F. Olimsky, "Gier nach Geld," *Berliner Börsen-Zeitung*, no. 223, 16 May 1926, p. 6, who both conceded that the film had artistic merit, especially in the acting. *Vorwärts*, no. 227, 16 May 1926, also noted a nationalist protest directed against Stroheim. *Film-Echo*, 17 May 1926.

52. See "Die UFA gegen den amerikanischen Film," *Lichtbildbühne*, 10 May 1926.

53. *8 Uhr-Abendblatt*, no. 109, 12 May 1926 (my emphasis).

54. One critic advised shifting its venue from the UFA-Palast am Zoo to the smaller UFA theater on the Kurfürstendamm which specialized in *Kulturfilme*. UFA's show theater, geared to pomp and glitter, was the least appropriate place in which to release serious motion pictures: *Germania*, 15 May 1926.

55. *Berliner Tageblatt*, 16 May 1926. In substance Fritz Olimsky (see note 51 above) and Max Freyhan in *Deutsche Allgemeine Zeitung*, 15 May 1926, agreed without relating this criticism to German practice.

56. *Lichtbildbühne*, 15 May 1926, p. 20.

57. *Germania*, 15 May 1926. Cf. reviews by Felix Henseleit in *Reichsfilmblatt*, 15 May 1926, p. 10, and those by Ernst Blass and Max Freyhan already cited. Henseleit saw a preliminary press performance and

predicted that the German public would be "aghast in the face of this film." Albert Schneider, *Der Film*, 16 May 1926, p. 11, attended the premiere and remarked that the audience failed to comprehend this rare masterpiece.

58. Haas, "Gier nach Geld," *Film-Kurier*, 15 May 1926. While conceding certain pluses this review is decidedly negative.

59. See "Publikum als Scharfrichter," *Montag Morgen*, 17 May 1926, p. 4.

60. Ernst Blass, "Normalfilme," *Berliner Tageblatt*, no. 287, 20 June 1926.

61. Erwin Gepard, scriptwriter and critic, decided that not Stroheim but the Kurfürstendamm public was mentally deficient; no German director could presently rival Stroheim's accomplishment: *Der Deutsche*, 16 May 1926.

62. See BA-UFA R109I/2440, Revisions-Abteilung, 13 December 1926, Anlage 3, which shows gross distribution receipts of RM 280.85 for May 1926, clearly the box office from the first showing on opening night. Between June and September the film earned another RM 2507, evidence that it did show elsewhere, if not widely or with great success.

63. The Soviet breakthrough came just two weeks before *Greed* with the premiere of Sergei Eisenstein's *Battleship Potemkin*. Haas, "Meine Meinung," *Die Literarische Welt*, 11 June 1926, p. 2, opened the door for revisionist appraisals.

64. "Streik," *Film-Kurier*, 26 February 1927. Roland Schacht, "Russische Filme, amerikanische und deutsche," *Der Kunstwart*, 40 (April, 1927), 55–57, also linked reflections on *Greed* to a discussion of the unique impact of Soviet pictures, chief among them *Strike*.

65. Helmut Brandis, "Gier und Geld," *Film-Kurier*, 24 December 1927.

66. Georg Kruse, "Neue Wege des Films," *Der Kunstwart*, 42 (October, 1928), 62–66.

67. Cf. Harry Kahn, "Alte Filme," *Die Weltbühne*, 24 (1928), vol. II, pp. 103–104; Arnheim, "Erich von Stroheim in der Kamera," in his *Kritiken und Aufsätze zum Film* (Frankfurt a.M.: Fischer, 1977), pp. 204–208.

68. UFA's sabotage is alleged in Kurt Kersten, "Gier nach Geld," *Film und Volk*, August, 1928, pp. 10–11. Haas, "Meine Meinung," *Die Literarische Welt*, 13 August 1926, p. 2, credited the scandal to a combination of National Socialist agitators and a sincerely outraged audience. Cf. the suspended judgment of Willi Wolfradt in *Das Kunstblatt*, 10 (1926), 390. *Kinematograph*, 16 May 1926, p. 13, called the premiere

of a Metro-Goldwyn picture amidst protests against this firm for re-release of the hate film, *The Four Horsemen of the Apocalypse,* scarcely tactful, but did not relate this to the critique of the film. A number of critics (Schacht, Schneider and Delmont) accused UFA of misman-agement of the premiere

69. "Amerikanische Filme und das deutsche Publikum," *Lichtbild-bühne,* 30 June 1926.

CHAPTER 5: EXCURSUS

1. Cf. Bordwell, Staiger and Thompson, *The Classical Hollywood Cinema;* Janet Staiger and Douglas Gomery, "The History of World Cinema: Models for Economic Analysis," *Film Reader,* 4 (1979), 35–44; and the pioneering study by Lary May, *Screening out the Past.*

2. Cf. the formulations by Buscombe, "Film History and the Idea of National Cinema," pp. 141–143; Thompson, *Exporting Entertain-ment,* pp. x, 1, 100; de Grazia, "Mass Culture and Sovereignty," pp. 57-61; Salt, "From Caligari to Who?" p. 123; Miles and Smith, *Cinema, Literature and Society,* pp. 166–177; Staiger and Gomery, "The History of World Cinema," pp. 36–38.

3. See the summary by Roland Schacht in *Das blaue Heft,* 5 (1 Febru-ary 1924), 14. Cf. UFA's annual report for 1924–1925 and 1925–1926 in BA-UFA R109I/1046. Variations on the theme are S-r. (Albert Schneider), "Immer die Anderen!" *Film-Journal,* 11 March 1927; Kurt Mühsam, "Der Film für junge Mädchen," *B.Z. am Mittag,* 16 Septem-ber 1927; "Der Weltmarkt des Films," *Film-Kurier,* 28 April 1928.

4. The American danger thus became a weapon in the struggle against the entertainment tax and censorship. See the pamphlet by Walther Plugge, *Film und Gesetzgebung,* commissioned by Spio (Spitz-enorganisation der deutschen Filmindustrie) and his article, "Welt-wirkung des Films," in BA-Reichskanzlei R43I/2498, pp. 222–236; 237–243. Cf. the report from the ministry of finance of 8 June 1926 on regulation of the entertainment tax, ibid., pp. 263–268. A useful summary of the German predicament is Alfred Ruhemann, "Der Film / Sache der Nation," *Süddeutsche Filmzeitung,* 12 March 1926, pp. 1–2.

5. "Und dennoch 1:1," *Film-Kurier,* 26 November 1926: "Film is not merchandise! . . . Indeed, precisely because film is not merchan-dise we can compete with America. . . . In the cinema *Geist* can balance the monetary supremacy of the competition." Cf. Walther Rilla, "Ge-danken über eine Produktion," *Film-Kurier,* 7 April 1928.

6. Hans Pander, "Die 'amerikanische Filmgefahr'," *Der Bildwart*, 4 (1926), 227.

7. "Die Fehler der Amerikaner," *Film-Kurier*, 28 May 1926.

8. K.W., (Karl Wolffsohn), "Ist die deutsche Filmindustrie amerikanisiert?" *Lichtbildbühne*, 24 April 1926, pp. 7–8.

9. Salt, "From Caligari to Who?" p. 123, duplicates this pattern when he takes for granted German preference for American films in the 1920s.

10. Irmalotte Guttmann, *Über die Nachfrage auf dem Filmmarkt in Deutschland* (Berlin: Gebr. Wolffsohn, 1928), p. 12. Jason, *Handbuch der Filmwirtschaft*, vol. I, pp. 9–10. Cf. the plea for "Mehr System," *Lichtbildbühne*, 14 February 1925, p. 15.

11. Averaged over the years 1925–1930, the results showed 67.6 percent of the votes for native pictures, 19.3 percent for America and 13.1 percent for European imports; Jason, *Handbuch der Filmwirtschaft*, vol. I, p. 60.

12. There was, to be sure, a steady increase in participation, from 350 theaters (8 percent of the total) in 1925–1926 to 1138 cinemas (21.9 percent of the total) in 1929–1930. Ibid., p. 60. UFA did not permit its cinemas to participate.

13. Guttmann, *Über die Nachfrage*, p. 11; Georg Mendel, "Was sind Umfragen wert?" *Lichtbildbühne*, 9 February 1926.

14. "Die Düsseldorfer Tagung," *Reichsfilmblatt*, 31 July 1926, pp. 3–4.

15. See Aros, "Tagung mit Zwischenfällen," *Kinematograph*, 1 August 1926, p. 10. Cf. "Zahlen allein beweisen nichts," ibid., 8 August 1926, pp. 11–12. Double features, frequently one German and the other American, bedeviled attempts to compare audience preferences.

16. BA-UFA R109I/2440, pp. 26–27. This report, which runs to sixty pages, with tables giving precise distribution returns, is one of the most revealing documents of UFA's troubles and troublesome relations with Hollywood in this period.

17. Guttmann, *Über die Nachfrage*, pp. 17–18, 25, 36.

18. Ibid., pp. 51–52, 59.

19. Ibid., pp. 65–67.

20. "Betrifft Lage der Parufamet Ende April 1927" (29 April 1927) in BA-FB/UFA 258, pp. 3–6.

21. Ibid. pp. 1–2. For a detailed breakdown of receipts at season's end see "Parufamet Erträge, 7. April 1927," in BA-FB/UFA 258.

22. See the correspondence of November and December 1926, especially Gabriel to Bausback, 20 November 1926, and Bausback to Parufamet, 8 December 1926, in BA-FB/UFA 435.

23. Guttmann, *Über die Nachfrage*, p. 8, fn. 2, justified the emphasis on successful films with the argument that they circulated more thoroughly than the failures and thus reflected market trends more accurately.

24. See Anlage 2 of Parufamet to UFA, 23 February 1928, in BA-FB/UFA 258.

25. Kracauer's conclusion for Berlin in his "Cult of Distraction: On Berlin's Picture Palaces," *New German Critique*, No. 40 (Winter 1987), 91–96, should not be taken as representative of the country. Cf. Sandra Coyner, "Class Consciousness and Consumption: The New Middle Class During the Weimar Republic," *Journal of Social History*, 10 (1977), 310–331.

26. Experts tagged UFA with colossal lack of discrimination in its selection of American motion pictures, particularly those from Paramount and Metro-Goldwyn. Cf. Roland Schacht's remarks in *Das blaue Heft*, 8 (1926), 305–306; "Zahlen allein beweisen nichts," *Kinematograph*, 8 August 1926, p. 12. For the high initial costs incurred by UFA in cornering the import trade see BA-UFA R109I/2440, pp. 31–32.

27. For exceptions see Alfred Rosenthal, "Europäische Flimmerwahrheit," *Kinematograph*, 11 April 1926, pp. 3–6: "For once it must be openly stated: we have devoted too much money, too much energy and too much intelligence to useless artistic experiments." Cf. "Reine Bahn," *Film-Kurier*, 24 April 1926, which insisted that the German film dilemma was not a financial problem but one of "idealism, intellect, spirit and ideas."

28. Pander, "Die 'amerikanische Filmgefahr'," pp. 228–231. Cf. Ejott, "Taylorisierung der Filmindustrie?" *Film-Kurier*, 19 January 1924.

29. Cf. his comments in "Deutsche und Amerikaner," *Das blaue Heft*, 5 (1 December 1923), 26; "Prestige und Produktion," ibid., 6 (1925), 245.

30. Cf. his "Drei Frauenfilme," ibid., 9 (1927), 135; "Stagnation," ibid., 8 (1926), 197.

31. "Deutsche und amerikanische Filme," *Der Kunstwart*, 39 (1926), 267–269, here p. 268.

32. Schacht, "Das Problem der deutschen Filmproduktion," ibid., 40 (1927), 416–419, here p. 417. This article draws together the major threads in Schacht's critical writing.

33. Cf. for instance, P.V., "Mut zur Kolportage," *Film-Kurier*, 9 May 1924; W. H. (Haas), "Der Kitsch ist kein Geschäft mehr!" ibid., 22 December 1924.

34. See Schacht, "Abstieg zum Kitsch!" *Das blaue Heft*, 6 (1924),

133–138, for an early formulation of this point in conjunction with discussion of popular movies. Cf. his "Filme," *Der Kunstwart,* 40 (1927), 263–265. Better known comparisons are Carlo Mierendorff, "Hätte ich das Kino," *Die Weissen Blätter,* 7 (1920), 86–92 (reprinted in Kaes, *Kino-Debatte,* pp. 139–146.); Franz Schulz, "Definitionen zum Film," in Zehder, *Der Film von Morgen,* pp. 44–51; Adolf Behne, "Die Stellung des Publikums zur modernen deutschen Literatur," *Die Weltbühne,* 22 (1926), vol. I, pp. 774–777.

35. Peukert, *Die Weimarer Republik,* pp. 181–188, argues that some intellectuals who decried Americanization favored progress but sought to salvage human freedom and dignity in the process. On these progressive defenders of cultural values cf. Heller, *Literarische Intelligenz und Film,* p. 124.

36. Ihering, *Von Reinhardt bis Brecht,* vol. I, p. 492; vol. II, p. 513.

37. Cf. "Filmschau," *Berliner Börsen-Courier,* no. 341, 24 July 1921, p. 9; "Jannings- und Jackie-Coogan-Filme," in *Von Reinhardt bis Brecht,* vol. I, pp. 462–464; "Filmrückschritt," *Berliner Börsen-Courier,* no. 92, 24 February 1925. "Das alte Nest," *Berliner Börsen-Courier,* no. 143, 25 March 1923, p. 7; *Von Reinhardt bis Brecht,* vol. II, pp. 479–481, which explores this theme in response to *The Ten Commandments.*

38. Ihering, *Von Reinhardt bis Brecht,* vol. II, pp. 506–507.

39. On the context for this ambivalence see Fulks, "The *Kulturfilm,*" pp. 138–141.

40. Pinthus, "Die Film-Krisis," *Das Tagebuch,* 9 (1928), 574–580. Pinthus encouraged the study by Guttmann and made reference to her findings before they were published. His generalization from her conclusions brought a lengthy rejoinder, complete with the statistics produced two years previously, by Ludwig Scheer: "Film-Krisis?" *Lichtbildbühne,* 14 April 1928.

41. *Das Tagebuch,* 9 (1928), 716.

42. Ibid., p. 760. For analyses of the film crisis which follow Balázs closely see Hermand and Trommler, *Die Kultur der Weimarer Republik,* pp. 278–281; Zsuffa, *Béla Balázs,* pp. 172–175. Cf. the general criticism of Balázs's thesis in Peukert, *Die Weimarer Republik,* p. 187.

43. Political polarization in the cinema became problematic precisely because the competition in America and Russia could afford to be "unpolitical." Their "realism" catered to a specific market, whereas Berlin's encountered division. See Rainer Berg, "Zur Geschichte der realistischen Stummfilmkunst," pp. 12–13, 268.

44. (Hans-Walther) Betz, "Filmkrise? Krise des Geschmacks," *Der Film,* 23 May 1928, pp. 1–2. Cf. Kurt Pinthus's reference to American and Russian work as proof of popular interest in contemporary

themes in *Das Tagebuch*, 9 (1928), 578–579; Willy Haas, "Die Krise der deutschen Filmindustrie," *Die Literarische Welt*, 12 February 1926, pp. 3–4.

45. Rainer Berg's "Zur Geschichte der realistischen Stummfilm-kunst," focuses on trade opinion, but fails to emphasize the extent to which the industry adopted the slogan to counter American intrusions.

46. *Das Tagebuch*, 9 (1928), 761.

CHAPTER 6: COMIC REDEMPTION

1. An earlier version of this chapter appeared as "Comedy as Redemption: American Slapstick in Weimar Culture," *Journal of European Studies*, xvii (1987), 253–277.

2. Dr. Brann, "Vier Fox-Grotesken," *Der Film* (Kritiken der Woche), 5 May 1928, p. 1.

3. On France see Shi, "Transatlantic Visions," pp. 587–590; Richard Abel, "The Contribution of the French Literary Avant-Garde to Film Theory and Criticism (1907–1924)," *Cinema Journal*, 15 (1975), pp. 23–24. On Spain cf. C. Brian Morris, "Charles Chaplin's Tryst with Spain," *Journal of Contemporary History*, 18 (1983), 517–531. On England see LeMahieu, *A Culture for Democracy*, pp. 43–53. More generally on Chaplin as public phenomenon cf. David Robinson, *Chaplin: The Mirror of Opinion* (Bloomington: Indiana University Press, 1984); David Marland, *Chaplin and American Culture* (Princeton, Princeton University Press, 1989); Timothy Lyon, *Charlie Chaplin: A Guide to References and Resources* (Boston: G. K. Hall, 1979).

4. Charles Chaplin, *My Autobiography* (London: The Bodley Head, 1964), pp. 285–293. There is a summary in Robinson, *Chaplin: The Mirror of Opinion*, pp. 52–59. Erich Burger, *Charlie Chaplin. Bericht seines Lebens* (Berlin: Rudolf Mosse, 1929), p. 93, mistakenly claims that Berliners had no opportunity to acquaint themselves with Chaplin's work before his visit.

5. On the very different reception when Chaplin returned to Berlin a decade later see Arnold Hollriegel, *Lichter der Großstadt* (Leipzig: E. P. Tal Co., 1931); Wolfgang Gersch, *Chaplin in Berlin* (Berlin: Henschelverlag, 1988).

6. Hans Siemsen, "Chaplin," *Die Weltbühne*, 18 (1922), vol. II, pp. 367–368. Cf. the views of the French poet Cendrars cited in Willett, *The New Sobriety*, p. 33.

7. Karl Lütge, "Das deutsche Lustspiel in Vergangenheit und Zukunft," *Kinematograph*, 19 February 1922; *Illustrierte Film-Woche*, no.

30, 1922. Cf. *Der Film*, 16 October 1921, p. 45; "Chaplin im Warenhaus," *Kinematograp*, 18 December 1921; "Filmschau," *Berliner Börsen-Courier*, no. 1, 1 January 1922.

8. See *Der Film*, 16 October 1921, p. 45; *Kinematograph*, 18 December 1921; *Berliner Börsen-Courier*, no. 1, 1 January 1922, and no. 389, 20 August 1922, p. 7; *Süddeutsche Filmzeitung*, 12 January 1923, p. 6. On Harry Sweet cf. *Berliner Tageblatt*, 5 August 1923.

9. M.Z., "Kinoides," *Der Kritiker*, 4 (June 1922), 14.

10. Haas, "Einwände gegen Chaplin," *Das Tagebuch*, 3 (1922), 1073–1074. Cf. *Berliner Börsen-Courier*, no. 329, 16 July 1922, p. 8. Similar opinions are cited in Morris, "Charles Chaplin's Tryst with Spain," p. 519.

11. Contrary to Monaco, *Cinema and Society*, p. 74. Cf. reports from Düsseldorf and Leipzig in "Aus der Praxis," *Kinematograph*, 30 October 1921; "Chaplin als Sträfling," *Film-Kurier*, 12 November 1921; H.W. (Hans Wollenberg), "Die Chaplin-Quelle," *Lichtbildbühne*, 15 October 1921, p. 44.

12. For a polemical formulation of this point see K. Lütge, "Das deutsche Lustspiel in Vergangenheit und Zukunft," *Kinematograph*, 19 February 1922.

13. Cf. the introduction to Klaus Kreimeier (ed.), *Zeitgenosse Chaplin* (Berlin: Oberbaum Verlag, 1978) for a more politicized reading.

14. Cf. "Buster Keaton als Cowboy," *Kinematograph*, 26 December 1926, p. 26; Hans Wollenberg, "Der Sportstudent," *Lichtbildbühne*, 9 November 1926, p. 2; Dr. Neulander, "Filmchronik," *Der Kritiker*, 8 (February 1926), 32; "Ben Akiba hat gelogen," *Vorwärts*, no. 433, 13 September 1925; Heinz Pol on Harold Lloyd in *Vossische Zeitung*, no. 57, 7 March 1926.

15. Paul Sorgenfrei, "Der Faktor 'Publikum' im Rechenexempel des Kinos," *Süddeutsche Filmzeitung*, 23 April 1926, p. 1; S-r. (Albert Schneider), "Mädchenscheu," *Der Film*, 7 March 1926, p. 19; Hermann Bräutigam, "Woran wir kranken!" *Reichsfilmblatt*, 28 March 1925, pp. 14–15, who claimed Lloyd was the only American comedian still popular in Germany; B.S., "Humor im Film," *Süddeutsche Filmzeitung*, 6 August 1926, pp. 2–3.

16. maxim (Maxim Ziese), "Buster Keaton, der Matrose," *Deutsche Allgemeine Zeitung*, no. 13, 9 January 1926.

17. Cf. Severin Rüttgers, "Kultur, Kunst und Film," *Deutsches Volkstum*, 7 (1925), 359–365; Hans Steckner,"Kunst und Kino," *Die Tat*, 16 (1924), pp. 470–473.

18. In this case upon first encounter with a Chaplin short: Pinthus, "Sehenswerte Filme," *Das Tagebuch*, 2 (1921), 1288–1289.

19. Heinz Pol, "Filmschau," *Vossische Zeitung*, no. 335, 18 July 1922, embraced Chaplin as therapeutic, as the "only right fare in these times when one would like to crawl away and hide in one's gloom." Cf. Pinthus, "Sehenswerte Filme," p. 1289.

20. "Fatty-Lustspiele," *Kinematograph*, 22 July 1923, p. 9. Cf. *Film-Kurier*, 11 October 1921 and 25 November 1921 for suggestions that German film humor seemed moribund by contrast.

21. Joseph Aubinger, "Die geteilte Wohnung," *Süddeutsche Filmzeitung*, 9 November 1923, p. 3. Paul Ickes, "Grotesken," *Film-Kurier*, 5 December 1922.

22. Hans Siemsen, *Charlie Chaplin* (Leipzig: Feuer-Verlag, 1924). Contrary to Lyons, *Charles Chaplin*, p. 99, this is not a "standard biography." Later books in Chaplin's honor are L. A. Hermann, *Chaplin's wunderbarer Aufstieg* (Berlin: Otto Dreyer, n.d.); Erich Burger, *Charlie Chaplin. Bericht seines Lebens*.

23. Siemsen, "Chaplin—Der Politiker," *Die Weltbühne*, 18 (1922), vol. II, pp. 415–416. Several months after Chaplin visited Berlin Siemsen reported that the comedian had toured the working-class districts rather than the fashionable Kurfürstendamm: "Chaplin," *Der Querschnitt*, 1 (1921), 213–214.

24. See the other articles in the series in *Die Weltbühne*, 18 (1922), vol. II, pp. 367–368; 385–387; 447–448; 473–474.

25. A partial exception by Claire Goll, then resident in Paris, is "Amerikanisches Kino," *Die neue Schaubühne*, 2 (1920), 164–165. Cf. the recent analysis by Sabine Hake, "Chaplin Reception in Weimar Germany," *New German Critique*, no. 51 (1990), 87–111; here pp. 88–89.

26. Strictly speaking, the first feature release of this type was *The Kid* (1921), which premiered in Berlin in late November 1923. The import of shorts grew rather than diminished; features remained a small minority of the total.

27. See the summary by Wolfgang Petzet, "Der Stand des Weltfilms," *Der Kunstwart*, 42 (1928), 116–121, here p. 117.

28. The perception of otherness took root with the Fox releases of 1922. It occasionally included regret that Germany failed to imitate. Cf. Walter Thielemann, "Neue Fox-Filme," *Reichsfilmblatt*, 15 December 1923, p. 16; hfr. (Heinrich Fraenkel), "Ein Wolkenkratzer der Filmkomik," *Lichtbildbühne*, 3 May 1924, p. 28; Aros (Rosenthal), "Harold Lloyd im UFA-Palast," *Film-Echo*, 2 November 1925; R.O. (R. Otto), "Reprisen amerikanischer Grotesken," *Film-Kurier*, 28 June 1927.

29. See Schacht's remarks on *Safety Last* in *Das blaue Heft*, 5 (1 June

1924), 91–92, and *Girl Shy* in ibid., 8 (1926), 197–198. The contrast between Buster Keaton and Reinhold Schünzel is in ibid., 9 (1927), 566–567; 647. Cf. H.A. (Hans Alsen), "Fox-Grotesken," *8 Uhr-Abendblatt*, 11 July 1925.

30. *Das Tagebuch*, 6 (1925), 106. Also see F.S. (Fritz Scharf), "Um Himmelswillen," *Vorwärts*, no. 561, 27 November 1927; Hans Pander in *Der Bildwart*, 5 (1927), 548; 6 (1928), 316; 7 (1929), 284.

31. hfr. (Heinrich Fraenkel), "Ein Wolkenkratzer der Filmkomik," *Lichtbildbühne*, 3 May 1924, p. 28. Cf. "Der neue Harold Lloyd," *Kinematograph*, 8 November 1925, p. 20; Hans Frey, "Film," *Der Kritiker*, 9 (March 1927), 38; Hassreiter, "Harolds liebe Schwiegermutter," *Der Film*, 3 November 1928, p. 177; "Eine Spitzenleistung in der Filmgroteske," *Reichsfilmblatt*, 3 May 1924, pp. 12–13; s-r. (Albert Schneider), "Der General," *Film-Journal*, 1 April 1927.

32. For a concise interpretation of contemporary artistic expectations see Elsaesser, "German Silent Cinema: Social Mobility and the Fantastic."

33. Rudolph Arnheim, "Film," *Das Stachelschwein*, 3 (August 1927), 50. Cf. the earlier argument of Willi Wolfradt, "Kino," *Das Kunstblatt*, no. 11/12, 1923, pp. 358–360.

34. *Die Weltbühne*, 17 (1921), vol. II, 219.

35. Kurt Pinthus, "Film," *Das Tagebuch*, 5 (1924), 645, commenting here on Harold Lloyd's *Safety Last*.

36. Hans Siemsen, "Goldrausch," *Die Weltbühne*, 22 (1926), vol. I, p. 391.

37. Alfred Polgar, "Chaplin," *Die Weltbühne*, 20 (1924), vol. II, pp. 28–29. Cf. his "Amerikanischer Groteskfilm," *Berliner Tageblatt*, 16 July 1924; Pinthus, "Vom deutschen, amerikanischen und schwedischen Film," *Kulturwille*, 1 November 1925, in Pinthus Folio, Marbach. For recent strictures on intellectual rhapsodies cf. John McCabe, *Charlie Chaplin* (New York: Doubleday, 1978), pp. ix–x; Robinson, *Chaplin: The Mirror of Opinion*, pp. vi–viii.

38. Cf. Wilfried Wiegand (ed.), *Über Chaplin* (Zurich: Diogenes, 1978), pp. 15–18.

39. Use of animals for "dramatic" films was in any case an American specialty. One need only contemplate *Madame Dubarry* handled in this fashion in Germany to indicate the measure of irreverence which such a picture displayed. See *Der Film*, 1 July 1927, p. 12.

40. See Arnheim's remarks in *Das Stachelschwein*, 2, 20, (1925), 46–47. Cf. Felix Henseleit in *Reichsfilmblatt*, 30 May 1925, p. 39: "With his refreshing humor he uproots movie kitsch, a movie kitsch which has been tolerated for decades and almost gained recognition."

Schacht in *Das blaue Heft,* 6 (1925), 189. Ihering, *Von Reinhardt bis Brecht,* vol. II, pp. 497–498; Kurt Pinthus on Keaton's *The Navigator* in *Das Tagebuch,* 7 (1926), 73–74.

41. "Buster Keaton der Student," *Film-Journal,* 23 October 1927: "Insofar as slapstick is perceived as deliberate parody of real life, this film is Buster Keaton's best." Cf. rth. (Joseph Roth), "Filme," *Frankfurter Zeitung,* no. 103, 8 February 1925; *Das blaue Heft,* 6 (1925), 189–190; "Um Himmelswillen," *Vorwärts,* no. 561, 27 November 1927; *Lichtbildbühne,* 3 July 1926, p. 19.

42. Keaton's *The General* was both lauded for exposing the absurdity of war and heroics and criticized for failure to denounce war consistently. Cf. Kurt Pinthus, "Nochmals: Buster Keaton," *Das Tagebuch,* 8 (1927), 597; Ihering, *Von Reinhardt bis Brecht,* vol. II, pp. 532–534; Wolf Zucker, "Der General," *Die Weltbühne,* 23 (1927), vol. I, pp. 602–603. Harold Lloyd's *Why Worry?* became a powerful, if perhaps unintentional antimilitarist picture: see "1000:1—Harold Lloyd," *Vorwärts,* no. 517, 1 November 1925.

43. -l. (Walter Kaul?), "Fox-Grotesken," *Berliner Börsen-Courier,* no. 229, 17 May 1925, p. 6. Remy Hardt, "Ausgerechnet Wolkenkratzer," *Der Kritiker,* 6 (May/June 1924), 15–16, praised the early sections of this film for their "clever, almost ingenious observation of the things of life."

44. See *Das blaue Heft,* 6 (1924), 100–103; here pp. 101–102. Cf. remarks of Hans Spielhofer in *Süddeutsche Filmzeitung,* 12 March 1926, p. 4.

45. *Das blaue Heft,* 6 (1925), 519. Cf. Schacht's "Buster Keaton als Matrose," *B.Z. am Mittag,* 5 January 1926; *Der Kunstwart,* 40 (1927), 274.

46. Eggebrecht's comments are in *Die Weltbühne,* 22 (1926), vol. I, p. 350. Cf. Felix Henseleit, "Buster Keatons erste Flitterwoche," *Reichsfilmblatt,* 21 February 1925, p. 40; Dr. M-l. (Georg Mendel), "Buster Keaton, der Cowboy," *Lichtbildbühne,* 22 December 1926, pp. 3–4.; E.K., "Ben Akiba hat gelogen," *Deutsche Allgemeine Zeitung,* no. 430, 12 September 1925; m., "Fox-Grotesken," *Film-Kurier,* 11 July 1925 and 14 August 1925; Hanns Brodnitz, "Der Film am Scheideweg," *Berliner Börsen-Courier,* no. 357, 2 August 1925, p. 6.

47. See Pinthus's "Lustspiel-Grotesken," *Das Tagebuch,* 5 (1924), 1007–1008; and his review of Keaton's *The Navigator,* ibid., 7 (1926), 73–74. Cf. Kracauer Folio, Marbach, for articles from *Frankfurter Zeitung:* no. 35, 24 February 1924; no. 44, 9 March 1924; no. 14, 29 January 1926; no. 90, 24 July 1926; no. 142, 22 December 1926. Also see W.H. (Willy Haas), "Von Tanzgirls, Lausbuben und dem Kater

Felix," *Film-Kurier,* 31 July 1926, and "Fox-Grotesken," *Film-Kurier,* 25 June 1927.

48. Cf. "Der Student," *Vorwärts,* no. 502, 23 October 1927; H. W-g. (Hans Wollenberg), "Grotesken im Capitol," *Lichtbildbühne,* 28 June 1927.

49. For general perspectives see Kinter, *Arbeiterbewegung und Film;* Bert Hogenkamp, "The Proletarian Cinema and the Weimar Republic: A comment," *Historical Journal of Film, Radio and Television,* i (1982), 177–179; Murray, *Film and the German Left in the Weimar Republic.*

50. "He manages to make other people [look] ridiculous with his appearance alone. He only has to make an appearance . . . and all surroundings are suddenly wrong and he is right and the whole world has become ridiculous. . . . And he shows how ludicrous it is to be a grown-up man who takes himself seriously." Kurt Tucholsky, "Der berühmteste Mann der Welt," in his *Gesammelte Werke* (Reinbek bei Hamburg: Rowohlt, 1960), vol. I, pp. 1004–1007, here p. 1006. This article first appeared in *Prager Tageblatt* in July 1922. Cf. his review of *The Kid* in *Die Weltbühne,* 19 (1923), vol. II, pp. 564–566.

51. Siemsen, "Chaplin-Der Politiker," *Die Weltbühne,* 18 (1922), vol. II, pp. 415–416.

52. See Kreimeier (ed.), *Zeitgenosse Chaplins,* pp. 10–13, and *"Erobert den Film": Proletariat und Film in der Weimarer Republik* (Berlin: Neue Gesellschaft für bildende Kunst, 1977), pp. 25–26.

53. Cf. T. K. Fodor, "Soziologie der Groteske," *Arbeiterbühne und Film,* no. 7 (1930), 26–28; Mersus, "St. Charlie oder Ein Chaplin-Film, der nie gedreht wird," ibid., no. 4 (1931), 30–32; "Die Rote Fahne bei Chaplin," *Die Rote Fahne,* 3 March 1931; O. Biha, "Zeitschau der Kulturbarbarei," *Die Linkskurve,* no. 4 (1931), 1–5. All are reproduced in Kreimeier (ed.), *Zeitgenosse Chaplins,* pp. 87–102.

54. Gerhart Pohl, "Grotesk-Filme," *Film und Volk,* no. 7 (1929), 12–15. On the politics of Chaplin's visit in 1931 see Gersch, *Chaplin in Berlin,* especially pp. 120ff.

55. Pander's review of "Zirkus," *Der Bildwart,* 6 (1928), 246–247. Pander defined this "human content" through Chaplin's film persona—an outsider in a hostile world who survived in spite of himself. Pinthus's "Amerikanische Filmkomiker" in Pinthus Folio, Marbach (1926). For adulation of Chaplin distinguished by revulsion toward almost everything else associated with the cinema see Gerhard Ausleger, *Charlie Chaplin* (Hamburg: Pfadweiser Verlag, 1924). Cf. Hake, "Chaplin Reception in Weimar Germany," pp. 92–93.

56. Ihering, *Von Reinhardt bis Brecht,* vol. II, pp. 514–515.

57. Dr. R.P. (R. Pabst), "Goldrausch," *Süddeutsche Filmzeitung,* 20

August 1926, p. 3. Cf. Schacht's views in *Das blaue Heft*, 8 (1926), 144–145; *Der Kunstwart*, 39 (1926), 392; Kracauer's review in Kracauer Folio, Marbach, no. 127, 6 November 1926. Cf. Ausleger, *Charlie Chaplin*, p. 25, who labeled *The Kid* a "social work of art—not a socialist one. That would mean imputing to it a fixed purposefulness. For that Charlie Chaplin is too human."

58. Siemsen, "Goldrausch," *Die Weltbühne*, 22 (1926), vol. I, 390–392.

59. See note 10 above.

60. Haas, "Goldrausch," *Film-Kurier*, 17 February 1926.

61. Cf. Gerhart Pohl, "Charlie Chaplin: Ein Symptom für die amerikanische Kulturdämmerung," *Die Glocke*, 11 (1925), 406–408. Pohl did not see Chaplin as "the epitome of what was wrong with the movies" (Beck, *Germany Rediscovers America*, p. 164), but as a genius who had invented the formula which would make America a cultural force via cinema. Cf. his "Grotesk-Filme," *Film und Volk*, no. 7 (August/September, 1929), pp. 12–15. For an opinion resembling the one Beck credits to Pohl see Wilhelm Michel, "Chaplin, der Held des Untermenschlichen," *Der Kunstwart*, 41 (1928), 126–128.

62. Peter Panter (Kurt Tucholsky), "The Kid," *Die Weltbühne*, 19 (1923), vol. II, pp. 564–566. Siemsen, "So kommt man an den Suff," *Die Weltbühne*, 21 (1925), vol. II, pp. 62–63.

63. This is nicely illustrated by the censorship decision to lift the restriction on *The Kid* as suitable for adults only because of the overriding element of human affection it displayed: DIFF-FP, 7 November 1923; DIFF-OP, 8 November 1923. See R.K. (Rudolf Kurtz), "Zirkus," *Lichtbildbühne*, 8 February 1928. Cf. Shi, "Transatlantic Visions," pp. 587–590; Hake, "Chaplin Reception in Weimar Germany," p. 91.

64. Hans Feld, "Lache mit," *Film-Kurier*, 15 December 1927.

65. Henseleit, "Sherlock Holmes jr.," *Reichsfilmblatt*, 30 May 1925, p. 39.

66. F. H-t. (Henseleit), "Der General," ibid., 9 April 1927, p. 37.

67. Max Feige, "Der Mann mit den 1000 Bräuten," *Der Film*, July 1926, p. 18. Hans-Walther Betz, "Buster Keaton, der Student," *Der Film* (Kritiken der Woche), 22 October 1927, p. 4.

68. Cf. English intellectual opinion cited in LeMahieu, *A Culture for Democracy*, p. 115.

69. Haas, "Unser Kronzeuge," *Film-Kurier*, 15 March 1926.

70. Siemsen, "Chaplin," *Die Weltbühne*, 18 (1922), vol. II, pp. 473–474.

71. For a detailed examination of Chaplin's visit, focused on the German public sphere, see Gersch, *Chaplin in Berlin*. Hake, "Chaplin

Reception in Weimar Germany," pp. 97–99, emphasizes the cultural ambiguity of Chaplin's image.

72. Siemsen, "Deutsch-amerikanischer Filmkrieg," *Die Weltbühne*, 17 (1921), vol. II, pp. 219–222; Rauol Sobel and David Francis, *Chaplin: Genesis of a Clown* (London: Quartet Books, 1977), p. 139.

73. Cf. Kaes, *Kino-Debatte*, pp. 12–15; Heller, *Literarische Intelligenz und Film*, pp. 199–200; Fritz Usinger, "Charlie Chaplin und die Bedeutung des Grotesken in unserer Zeit," *Der Literat*, 20, 1 (1978), 1–2.

74. Ernst Blass, "Harold Lloyds 'Mädchenscheu'," *Berliner Tageblatt*, no. 112, 7 March 1926.

75. -ma. (Maxim Ziese), "Um Himmelswillen: Harold Lloyd!" *Deutsche Allgemeine Zeitung*, no. 553, 26 November 1927. Cf. the earlier argument of eu. (Erich Hamburger?) in *Berliner Tageblatt*, 17 December 1922.

CHAPTER 7: GERMAN-AMERICAN PRODUCTION IN HOLLYWOOD

1. -ma. (Maxim Ziese), "Murnau: 'Sonnenaufgang'," *Deutsche Allgemeine Zeitung*, no. 541, 19 November 1927.

2. On the film emigration see John Russell, *Strangers in Paradise. The Hollywood Émigrés 1933–1950* (London: Faber & Faber, 1983). The German experience is covered by Maria Hilchenbach, *Kino im Exil: Die Emigration deutscher Filmkünstler 1933–1945* (Munich: K. G. Saur, 1982); Jan-Christopher Horak, *Fluchtpunkt Hollywood* (Münster: MAKS-Publ., 1986); *German Film Directors in Hollywood* (San Francisco: Goethe Institute, 1978).

3. Graham Petri, *Hollywood Destinies*, examines several leading émigré artists of this period, including Lubitsch and Murnau. Horak, *Fluchtpunkt Hollywood*, pp. 2–6 offers a brief overview with emphasis on Hollywood's economic motivation in hiring German personnel.

4. Lya de Putti earned her ticket cast opposite Emil Jannings in *Varieté;* Camilla Horn was introduced as Gretchen in Murnau's *Faust*. Wilhelm Dieterle later recalled the standing joke in Berlin film circles that if the phone rang in a restaurant it had to be Hollywood calling to make someone an offer. See the interview by Tom Flinn, "William Dieterle: The Plutarch of Hollywood," *The Velvet Light Trap*, no. 15 (Fall 1975), 23–28, here p. 24.

5. Pola Negri starred in twenty-one American pictures between 1923 and 1928—the romance and fame are chronicled in her *Memoirs of a Star* (New York, Doubleday, 1970). Greta Garbo, though much more tenuously linked to Germany, could also be mentioned here

since she starred in G. W. Pabst's *Die freudlose Gasse* en route to Hollywood. Vilma Banky was Hungarian.

6. Carl Mayer, the screenwriter for (among other classics) *The Cabinet of Dr. Caligari* and *Der letzte Mann*, scripted two of Murnau's American works, *Sunrise* and *Four Devils*, but never pursued an independent career in America as did Kraely.

7. Kreimeier, *Die Ufa-Story*, p. 146. For contemporary reactions cf. "Auszug und Nachwuchs," *Kinematograph*, 11 April 1926, pp. 9–10; "Europa wird geplündert," *Film-Journal*, 8 October 1926; Gregor Rabinovitsch, "Europas Gefährdung," *Film-Kurier*, 5 October 1926; Georg Mendel, "Deutscher Ausverkauf?" *Lichtbildbühne*, 8 March 1926, and "Deutsche Filmfürsten im Exil," ibid., 6 May 1926.

8. This is not intended, of course, as an explanation for émigré behavior. Germans went to Hollywood because the Americans wanted them and could afford to employ them on substantial projects. See the opinions of Emil Jannings, "Deutschland-Amerika," *B.Z. am Mittag*, 5 January 1926, and Murnau in "Murnau ist heute abgereist," *Film-Kurier*, 22 June 1926.

9. F. Henseleit, "Stellt Amerika sich um?" *Reichsfilmblatt*, 13 March 1926. Cf. Roland Schacht's opinions in *Das blaue Heft*, 9 (1927), 259; Dr. R. Otto, "Verbeugt euch vor Europa! Europäischer Geist im amerikanischen Film," *Film-Kurier*, 26 March 1926. In response to EFA, Willy Haas had compared America's plundering of European culture to ancient Rome's plundering of Greece. He hoped it would result in the maturation of American culture: "Reflexionen vor einem indischen Grabmal," *Film-Kurier*, 18 May 1921.

10. See, for instance, "Jannings bei Paramount," *Film-Kurier*, 7 October 1926; s-r. (A. Schneider), "Begeht der deutsche Film Harakiri?" *Film-Journal*, 22 October 1926; J. (Ernst Jäger), Ostergruss," *Film-Kurier*, 3 April 1926.

11. Robert Ramin, "Kolonie oder Konkurrenz," *Kinematograph*, 30 January 1927, pp. 9–10. Ramin commented acidly on the oaths of loyalty from German émigrés who claimed they intended only brief careers in Hollywood and then remained indefinitely, a barb obviously directed at Lubitsch.

12. On the continuity in Lubitsch's style see Horak, "Ernst Lubitsch and the Rise of UFA." Cf. Salt, "From Caligari to Who?" p. 123, who calls Lubitsch the only German director with an instinctive sense for American cutting rhythms and camera angles. Jacqueline Nacache, *Lubitsch* (Paris: Edilig, 1987), pp. 39–50. Sabine Hake, *Passions and Deceptions. The Early Films of Ernst Lubitsch* (Princeton: Princeton University Press, 1992), is now essential reading.

13. A sketch of this phase of his career is provided by Helmut Prinzler in *Ernst Lubitsch* (Paris: Cahiers du cinéma, 1985), pp. 29–43; Robert Carringer and Barry Sabath, *Ernst Lubitsch: A Guide to References and Resources* (Boston: G. K. Hall, 1978). Eight of Lubitsch's American pictures were scripted by Kraely before they parted company in 1930. For the terms of Lubitsch's employment see the contracts of 12 July and 7 August 1923 in Warner Bros. Archives—University of Southern California (henceforth WBA-USC), 2729, packet no. 3.

14. Ernst Ulitzsch, "Der deutsche und der amerikanische Lubitsch," *Kinematograph*, 31 August 1924, pp. 15–16.

15. Th. (W. Theile), "Rosita," *Der Film*, 31 August 1924, p. 39.

16. Theile, "Die Ehe im Kreise," ibid., 7 September 1924, p. 31.

17. Hans Siemsen, "Kino. Kritik. Und Kino-Kritik," *Die neue Schaubühne*, 5 (1925), 39–40, blamed the nonsense spouted about these two pictures on critical myopia, by which he meant preformed mental categories which impaired vision.

18. Dr. M-l (Georg Mendel), "Rosita," *Lichtbildbühne*, 30 August 1924, p. 30. Cf. W.H. (Willy Haas) in *Film-Kurier*, 29 August 1924; *Süddeutsche Filmzeitung*, 19 September 1924, p. 9; *Reichsfilmblatt*, 6 September 1924, p. 59.

19. hfr., "Die Ehe im Kreise," *Lichtbildbühne*, 6 September 1924, pp. 41–42.

20. *Film-Kurier*, 2 September 1924. Cf. *Reichsfilmblatt*, 6 September 1924, p. 60. Josef Aubinger, *Süddeutsche Filmzeitung*, 10 October 1924, p. 2, argued that although success followed from the marriage of "German *Geist* and American efficiency" the former enjoyed precedence.

21. Warschauer's review is in *Die Weltbühne*, 20 (1924), vol. II, pp. 552–553. Cf. "Die Ehe im Kreise," *Vossische Zeitung*, no. 418, 3 September 1924.

22. See note 17 above.

23. *Das Tagebuch*, 5 (1924), 1277–1278.

24. Cf. Lo., "Drei Frauen," *Der Film*, 6 September 1925, p. 18; Cf. the preview from New York "Lubitsch, der 'Amerikaner'," *Lichtbildbühne*, 7 October 1924; reviews by W.K. (Walter Kaul) in *Berliner Börsen-Courier*, 5 September 1925, p. 5; and D. (K. H. Döscher?) in *Vorwärts*, no. 421, 6 September 1925.

25. Otto Friedrich, "Drei Frauen," *Deutsche Allgemeine Zeitung*, no. 430, 12 September 1925. Cf. the review in *Welt am Montag*, 7 September 1925.

26. Haas's review is in *Film-Kurier*, 4 September 1925. For the gen-

eral discussion see "Warum das deutsche Manuskript keine Weltgeltung hat," ibid., 29 July 1926.

27. On *Forbidden Paradise* cf. Robert Ramin in *Film-Echo*, 7 December 1925 (Lubitsch, "with all concessions to a world audience, still proves that he matured in Berlin"); Haas in *Film-Kurier*, 5 December 1925; *Welt am Montag*, 7 December 1925. Georg Mendel in *Lichtbildbühne*, 5 December 1925, p. 16, charged Lubitsch with lack of tact and artistic degeneration. Roland Schacht argued by contrast that precisely the absence of German influence had raised this film to extraordinary heights: "Here is shown who really has culture and why the American, not the German cinema conquers the world." *Das blaue Heft*, 7 (1925), 187–188.

28. Cf. Felix Henseleit, "Das neue Kammerspiel," *Reichsfilmblatt*, 13 February 1926, pp. 14–15; reviews of "Küss mich noch einmal," *Kinematograph*, 14 February 1926, p. 23; Dr. R.P(abst) in *Süddeutsche Filmzeitung*, 31 July 1926, p. 4.

29. Willy Haas, "Küss mich noch einmal," *Film-Kurier*, 8 February 1926. Cf. his reflections on Chaplin's *A Woman of Paris* in *Film-Kurier*, 16 September 1924.

30. See the exchange of cables between Jack and Harry Warner in WBA-USC, 2729, packet no. 2 (January/February 1926). Cf. James Harvey, *Romantic Comedy in Hollywood from Lubitsch to Sturges* (New York: Alfred A. Knopf, 1987), pp. 5–7. On the limitations of Lubitsch's appeal beyond the Kurfürstendamm see "So ist Paris," *Kinematograph*, 16 January 1927, p. 22. BA-UFA R1091/2440, Revisions-Abteilung, 13 December 1926, Anlage 3, shows *Three Women* and *Kiss Me Again* were high cost imports which did poorly at the box office.

31. Georg Mendel, "Deutscher Ausverkauf?" *Lichtbildbühne*, 8 March 1926, and "Deutsche Filmfürsten im Exil," ibid., 6 May 1926.

32. "Auszug und Nachwuchs," *Kinematograph*, 11 April 1926, pp. 9–10; Cf. "So ist Paris," ibid., 16 January 1927, p. 22, on the predictability of Lubitsch's American productions. "Gefährdete Zusammenarbeit," *Film-Kurier*, 12 October 1926. Cf. Gong, "Meisterfilme," *Deutsche Republik*, 1 (1927), 801, who named Lubitsch as the sole German director to profit artistically from the transplant to Hollywood. Fritz Olimsky, "Saisonbeginn," *Berliner Börsen-Zeitung*, no. 389, 22 August 1926, p. 7.

33. Ihering, *Von Reinhardt bis Brecht*, vol. II, pp. 508–509.

34. ibid., vol. I, pp. 435–36: Ihering remarked in late 1922 when reviewing a Mary Pickford picture that poor German films usually were weak because they were not moving pictures; Hollywood productions were by contrast always moving pictures, though not without

other flaws. Also see his discussion, "Der Film als Industrie," *Berliner Börsen-Courier*, no. 35, 21 January 1923.

35. For reflections on Negri's fate in Hollywood see Georg Mendel, "Bella Donna," *Lichtbildbühne*, 20 September 1924, p. 30; "Belladonna," *Vorwärts*, no. 446, 21 September 1924; -ma., "Maripose, die Tänzerin," *Deutsche Allgemeine Zeitung*, no. 166, 10 April 1926; Albert Schneider in *Der Film*, 11 April 1926, p. 18; Willy Haas in *Film-Kurier*, 7 April 1926; Hans Pander, "Qualen der Ehe," *Der Bildwart*, 6 (1928), 726.

36. Cf. reviews of "Lieb mich und die Welt ist mein," *Der Kritiker*, 9 (25 April 1927), 54; *Das blaue Heft*, 9 (1927), 259–260; *Film-Kurier*, 16 April 1927; *Film-Journal*, 22 April 1927; *Deutsche Allgemeine Zeitung*, no. 182, 20 April 1927.

37. On Veidt see, for instance, reviews of "Der Mann der lacht" by Eric Kluge in *Welt am Montag*, 4 March 1929, and Fritz Walter in *Berliner Börsen-Courier*, 3 March 1929, p. 10. Paul Leni, a graphic artist and set designer prior to becoming a director and known for visual imagination more than thematic concentration, received somewhat less than average sympathy: Cf. Schacht, "Spuk im Schloss," *B.Z. am Mittag*, 26 August 1927, and *Das blaue Heft*, 9 (1927), 569; Haas's review in *Film-Kurier*, 25 August 1927; Georg Herzberg, "Der Chinesenpapagei," *Film-Kurier*, 13 December 1927; *Deutsche Allgemeine Zeitung*, 17 December 1927.

38. On Pommer see Wolfgang Jacobsen, *Erich Pommer*; Ursula Hardt, "Erich Pommer."

39. Elsewhere I have treated his Hollywood pictures as part of the initial wave of war movies: "Politics, the Cinema, and Early Revisitations of War in Weimar Germany," *Canadian Journal of History*, XXIII (1988), 39–40.

40. See reviews of "Hotel Stadt Lemberg" by Albert Schneider in *Film-Journal*, 7 January 1927; E.S.P. in *Lichtbildbühne*, 6 January 1927; Schacht in *Das blaue Heft*, 9 (1927), 50–51.

41. *Kinematograph*, 9 January 1926, p. 19; Felix Henseleit in *Reichsfilmblatt*, 8 January 1927, p. 34.

42. Cf. the comments by Kurt Pinthus on *The Marriage Circle* and Willy Haas on *Three Women* cited above.

43. The standard monograph on Murnau is Lotte H. Eisner, *Murnau* (London: Secker and Warburg, 1973). A succinct and elegant reading is Thomas Elsaesser, "Secret Affinities," *Sight & Sound*, 58 (Winter 1988/89), 33–39. For an overview of Murnau's career stressing the sharp discontinuity between its German and American phases see *Friedrich Wilhelm Murnau. Ein großer Filmregisseur der 20er Jahre*

(Stuttgart: Deutscher Sparkasse, 1981). Robert Allen, "William Fox Presents 'Sunrise'," *Quarterly Review of Film Studies*, 2 (1977), 327–338. On American opinion see Steven Lipkin, "'Sunrise': A Film Meets its Public," ibid., pp. 339–355; cf. Dudley Andrew, "The Gravity of 'Sunrise'," ibid., pp. 356–379, especially pp. 363–368.

44. "Sonnenaufgang," *Film-Journal*, 20 November 1927.

45. Pander's review of "Sonnenaufgang" in *Der Bildwart*, 6 (1928), 727–728. Cf. *Kinematograph*, 20 November 1927, p. 17; the programmatic remarks of Hans Wollenberg in *Lichtbildbühne*, 18 November 1927; Eugen Gürster, "Filme und solche, die es werden wollten," *Der Kunstwart*, 41 (1928), 404–406, who called *Sunrise* the first real fruit of German-American movie cooperation. For quibbles about plot and characterization see Haas's review in *Film-Kurier*, 18 November 1927; Ziese in *Deutsche Allgemeine Zeitung*, no. 541, 19 November 1927; Hans Erdmann in *Reichsfilmblatt*, 26 November 1927, p. 28, and Roland Schacht in *Das blaue Heft*, 9 (1927), 707–708.

46. (Felix) Gong, "Nach 'Sonnenaufgang'," *Deutsche Republik*, 2 (1927), 247–249. Cf. American judgments cited in Lipkin, "'Sunrise'," pp. 350–352.

47. On Jannings see his *Theater/Film—Das Leben und ich* (Berchtesgaden: Zimmer & Herzog, 1951); Herbert Holba, *Emil Jannings* (Ulm: Günter Knorr, 1979).

48. Cf. Hans Pander, "Der Weg allen Fleisches," *Der Bildwart*, 6 (1928), 128–129; (Felix) Gong, "Jannings via Hollywood," *Deutsche Republik*, 2 (1927), 312–313; *Kinematograph*, 27 November 1927, p. 21.

49. Pander's review is a notable exception. The split image is forcefully projected by Eugen Gürster, "Der Weg allen Fleisches," *Der Kunstwart*, 41 (1928), 335–337. Cf. Munkepunke, *1000% Jannings* (Hamburg-Berlin: Prismen Verlag, 1930), pp. 108–109.

50. Haas's review in *Film-Kurier*, 22 November 1927.

51. Cf. *Film-Journal*, 27 November 1927, and the review by Felix Henseleit in *Reichsfilmblatt*, 26 November 1927, p. 38.

52. Hans Wollenberg, "Der Weg allen Fleisches," *Lichtbildbühne*, 22 November 1927. Cf. the earlier unsigned lead article, "Die Lehren des amerikanischen Janningsfilms," ibid., 15 October 1927, pp. 9–10. For similar sentiments on *The Last Command* (directed by Joseph von Sternberg) and *The Patriot* (which teamed Jannings with Lubitsch and Kraely) see *Deutsche Republik*, 3 (1928), 22–24, and 3 (1929), 726–727; *Der Film* (Kritiken der Woche), 2 March 1929, pp. 261–262; *Film-Kurier*, 20 September 1928. Even Ihering, *Von Reinhardt bis Brecht*, vol. II, pp. 562–564, acknowledged the artistry with which Lubitsch and Jannings crafted *The Patriot* as a popular film.

53. Rudolf Arnheim, "Film," *Das Stachelschwein,* no. 1 (January 1928), 52; Ihering, *Von Reinhardt bis Brecht,* vol. II, p. 542. Ihering's review betrayed considerable bitterness at Jannings's surrender to Hollywood and at the reluctance of others to criticize his conduct honestly. Cf. "Jannings: 'Der Weg allen Fleisches'," *Deutsche Allgemeine Zeitung,* no. 546, 22 November 1927.

54. Pinthus reviewed these films simultaneously in *Das Tagebuch,* 8 (1927), 1036–1037. Cf. John Baxter, *The Hollywood Exiles* (London: MacDonald and Jane's, 1976), p. 40.

55. *Die Weltbühne,* 23 (1927), vol II, p. 867. This, of course, was an artistic judgment, not a commercial one. As already noted, the trade press spoke highly of Jannings's American work as box-office value.

56. In his autobiography Jannings treats the three pictures which received a generally favorable German press—*The Way of All Flesh, The Last Command, The Patriot*—and then elides the other three to discuss his return to Germany: *Theater/Film—Das Leben und ich,* pp. 179–188. Cf. the parallel approach of Ludwig Berger in his memoirs, *Wir sind vom gleichen Stoff, aus dem die Träume sind* (Tübingen: Rainer Wunderlich Verlag, 1953), pp. 240–270.

57. Even though the latter was directed by Ludwig Berger. See Herbert Holba, *Emil Jannings,* pp. 27–29. On *The Street of Sin* cf. reviews of "Der König von Soho" in Ihering, *Von Reinhardt bis Brecht,* vol. II, pp. 569–571; *Deutsche Allgemeine Zeitung,* no. 248–249, 2 June 1929; *Der Film* (Kritiken der Woche), 2 June 1929, p. 337. On *Sins of the Fathers* see, for instance, "Sünden der Väter," *Film-Echo,* 20 January 1930; *Reichsfilmblatt,* 18 January 1930.

CHAPTER 8: THE COMING OF SOUND

1. Cf. Schweins, "Die Entwicklung der deutschen Filmwirtschaft," pp. 88–106; Ludwig Klitzsch, "Neujahrswünsche an den *Film-Kurier,* 1 January 1930," and "Rede zur UFA-Konvention, 1930," in his *Bekenntnis zum deutschen Film,* which explain UFA's position.

2. Jason, *Handbuch der Filmwirtschaft,* vol. III, p. 37.

3. Wolffsohn (ed.), *Jahrbuch der Filmindustrie,* vol. V, pp. 338–339.

4. Dubbing eventually became standard practice, but first attempts met considerable critical resistance. *Lummox,* screened in January 1930, was judged a disaster as film and as sound. See the reviews of "Der Tolpatsch" in *Berliner Börsen-Zeitung,* no. 22, 14 January 1930, p. 3; *Der Film,* 18 January 1930, p. 11; *Lichtbildbühne,* 14 January 1930.

5. Douglas Gomery, "Tri-Ergon, Tobis-Klangfilm, and the Coming of Sound," *Cinema Journal,* 16 (Fall 1976), 51–61; "Economic struggle

and Hollywood Imperialism: Europe Converts to Sound," *Yale French Studies,* no. 60 (1980), 80–93.

6. Titles were present in the original film, which was shot as a silent in 1927.

7. Whether or not UFA deliberately sabotaged the premiere of *Greed,* it definitely sabotaged the showing of *The Wedding March,* which it considered anti-German. See the board decision in BA-UFA R1091/ 1027b, 8 July 1929, pt. 5.

8. "Der Tonfilm-Krieg geht weiter," *Vossische Zeitung,* no. 129, 31 May 1929, sketches the difficulties prior to the premiere. On the difficulties gaining admission even for critics see *Der Bildwart,* 7 (1929), 620; M. Georg Folio, Marbach, 5 June 1929.

9. See reviews of "Der singende Narr" by Felix Gong in *Deutsche Republik,* 3 (1929), 1151–1153; Hans Spielhagen in *Film und Volk,* no. 6 (July 1929), 7–8; R.K. (Rudolf Kurtz) in *Lichtbildbühne,* 4 June 1929; Manfred Georg Folio, Marbach, 5 June 1929; Maxim Ziese, *Deutsche Allgemeine Zeitung,* no. 252–253, 5 June 1929.

10. Wolfgang Petzet in *Der Kunstwart,* 43 (1930), 274–275; Hans Pander in *Der Bildwart,* 7 (1929), 621–622; Ihering, *Von Reinhardt bis Brecht,* vol. II, pp. 571–573. Cf. reviews by Gong and Ziese cited in the previous note.

11. For an ironic survey of critical scepticism toward sound see "E.A. Dupont an seine Kritiker," *Film-Kurier,* 2 November 1929. Among the targets of Dupont's witticisms were Herbert Ihering, Ernst Blass and Heinz Pol.

12. Z. (Maxim Ziese), "Tonfilm auch bei der UFA," *Deutsche Allgemeine Zeitung,* no. 165–166, 11 April 1929. Cf. Oscar Geller, "Wie lange noch . . . ," *Deutsche Filmzeitung,* 22 March 1929, p. 1.

13. Walter Tritsch, "Gesicht des Films von 1929," *Deutsche Allgemeine Zeitung,* no. 598–599, 28 December 1929; "Johnny braucht Geld," *Film-Rundschau,* 18 February 1930; "Das Glück des Anderen," *Film-Rundschau,* 15 April 1930.

14. Rudolf Arnheim, "Die traurige Zukunft des Films," *Die Weltbühne,* 26 (1930), vol. II, pp. 402–404. Cf. Hans-W. Betz, "Submarine," *Der Film* (Kritiken der Woche), 15 June 1929, p. 346; Alfred Polgar, "Von Geräuschen und rauher Freundschaft," *Das Tagebuch,* 10 (1929), 1035–1036; Georg Folio, Marbach, 13 June 1929; *Der Bildwart,* 7 (1929), 619–620; Hans Sahl, *Memoiren eines Moralisten,* pp. 106–107.

15. Gong, "Die Arche Noah," *Deutsche Republik,* 3 (1929), 1450–1453, here p. 1452. These remarks came, ironically, in response to the silent version of the film.

16. See especially reviews of *The Singing Fool* and *Submarine* in *Film-künstler und Filmkunst*, no. 9 (1929). For a denial that picture and sound could be combined artistically see Egon Larsen, "Tonfilm-Dämmer-ung," *Der Zwiebelfisch*, 22 (1928/29), 281–287.

17. Oscar Geller, "Des stummen Filmes Selbstverteidigung," *Deutsche Filmzeitung*, 9 May 1930, pp. 2–3: "Silent film, let that be heavily emphasized again and again, raised itself to the level of art—*sound film is exclusively business, industry, 'trade'.*" Cf. Manfred Georg, "Cilly im Farbtopf," Georg Folio, Marbach, 21 March 1930, who likened American film production to the manufacture of Ford cars and saw sound as a major setback to its isolated artistic achieve-ments.

18. See Hugo G. Schmitt, "Ruf nach Filmvertiefung!" *Deutsche Filmzeitung*, 8 March 1929, pp. 1–4. On disenchantment with film because of sound cf. Elsaesser, "Two Decades in Another Country," p. 201.

19. W. Ertel-Breithaupt, "Produktionskatastrophe und Gesin-nungskrise," *Filmkünstler und Filmkunst*, no. 6 (1929).

20. "Deutschland amerikanische Filmkolonie?" *Der Film*, 15 April 1929, pp. 1–2. Manfred Georg called the successful premiere of *The Singing Fool* a dangerous triumph for America in that German produc-tion was two years behind Hollywood. Georg Folio, Marbach, 5 June 1929.

21. See the warnings in "Wir achten zu wenig auf Holywood [sic]," *Kinematograph*, 4 December 1930; "Nach Titta Ruffo Michael Boh-nen," *Lichtbildbühne*, 10 April 1929, a lament about Hollywood's hiring of European opera talent for sound pictures; "Amerikanische 'An-leihen'," *Deutsche Filmzeitung*, 9 May 1930, pp. 3–4.

22. For an extended treatment of Hollywood's hegemonic intent from the postwar period through the conversion to sound see Ebbe Neergaard, "Amerikas Film-Herrschaft," *Die Weltbühne*, 27 (1931), vol. II, pp. 219–224. Fear of American takeover was especially acute in the early sound period when the Munich-based Emelka faced bank-ruptcy and possible sale to American interests. Trade reaction in Mu-nich was sharp. See the articles in *Deutsche Filmzeitung*, "Wird der deutsche Film an Amerika verkauft?" 14 February 1930, pp. 1–2; "Soll Film-Europa amerikanische Provinz werden?" 21 February 1930, pp. 1–2; Oscar Geller, "Unter amerikanischer Kontrolle," 16 May 1930, pp. 1–3; and "Hände weg von deutschem Kulturgut!" 30 May 1930, pp. 1–2. Also see Richard Muckermann, "Politischer Hugen-berg oder deutscher Film?" *Film-Rundschau*, 25 March 1930.

23. Franz Schulz, "Tonfilm in London," *Das Tagebuch*, 10 (1929), 946–949.

24. Willy Haas, "Rückblick, Gruss und Appell," *Film-Kurier*, Sondernummer, 1 June 1929.

25. See the reflections of Z. (Maxim Ziese), in *Deutsche Allgemeine Zeitung*, no. 165–166, 11 April 1929.

26. Six months previously Haas had put it bluntly: "Today nearly all persons who want art and need art to live view film just as they viewed film in 1914: namely, with absolute uninterest." Haas, "Prognose," *Die Literarische Welt*, 4 January 1929, p. 1. Cf. Kurt J. Bachrach, "Die 'Geistigen' und der Film," *Deutsche Filmzeitung*, 18 October 1929, p. 1.

27. Hans Spielhofer, "Hoffnung auf Film als Gesamtkunstwerk," *Deutsche Filmzeitung*, 17 May 1929, pp. 1–3. For a commercialized program which neither Haas nor Spielhofer would have endorsed see "Wenn ich Herr Küchenmeister wäre," *Lichtbildbühne*, 7 October 1929, which recommended imitation of Hollywood's musical comedies to exploit Germany's stage talent and musical tradition.

28. "Umwertung aller Werte," *Lichtbildbühne*, 22 February 1930.

29. "Die amerikanisch-deutsche Situation," ibid., 4 March 1930.

30. "Die Abstimmung des 'Film-Kurier'," *Film-Kurier*, 2 June 1930. Detailed results for 1929–1930 are in the Sondernummer, 31 May 1930.

31. "Marktrevolution durch Tonfilm," ibid., 11 July 1931. Cf. the tabulations at the beginning of the year, "Der deutsche Film in Front" and "Tonfilm drängt Auslandsfilme zurück" in the Sondernummer, 1 January 1931.

32. The reversion to older behavior patterns is again revealing. Immediately after the war theater owners had desired the novelty of foreign pictures and the check these would provide to price dictation by native producers. Later, when Hollywood dominated the market, they complained of American price control. Now they once again opposed cultural independence because it would eliminate competition. See Wolfgang Petzet, "Das künftige Filmkontingent," *Der Kunstwart*, 45 (1932), 738–739.

33. Fritz Olimsky, "Die nationale Wendung," *Berliner Börsen-Zeitung*, no. 537, 16 November 1930, p. 4.

34. "Bleibe im Lande," *Kinematograph*, 14 November 1930. Cf. Ludwig Klitzsch, "Rede auf der UFA-Konvention, 1931."

35. Kuno Renatus, "Vom falschen und vom echten deutschen Film," *Deutsche Allgemeine Zeitung*, no. 461, 1 October 1932; Georg Foerster, "Stirbt der Film am Wort?" *Deutsche Allgemeine Zeitung*, no. 317, 9 July 1932; Karl Sabel, "Filmwende? Von Hollywood zum deutschen Qualitätsfilm," *Film-Rundschau*, 1 March 1932. Even a sharp

opponent of motion picture autarky conceded that different languages projected different "intellectual worlds:" Wolfgang Petzet, "Die Wirtschaftskrise des Tonfilms," *Der Kunstwart*, 45 (1932), pp. 670–673.

36. The article by Karl Sabel cited in the previous note is particularly rich in stereotypes which were popular a decade earlier.

37. "Der deutsche Film," *Deutsche Filmzeitung*, 3 June 1932, pp. 1–2.

38. For the import regulations of 1930 and their official justification in the name of Germany's economic and cultural integrity see Bundesarchiv-Reichskanzlei R431/2500, pp. 67–72. The amended regulations are also reproduced as "Die Einfuhr-Bestimmungen," *Lichtbildbühne*, 16 July 1930. For the subsequent revisions see Henning v. Boehmer and Helmut Reitz, *Der Film in Wirtschaft und Recht* (Berlin: Carl Heymanns Verlag, 1933), pp. 64–66.

39. See the arguments by hs. (Hermann Sinsheimer), "Schutz dem deutschen Film," *Berliner Tageblatt*, no. 312, 3 July 1932; Wolfgang Petzet, "Das künftige Filmkontingent," *Der Kunstwart*, 45 (1932), 739; P.M., "Kontingent oder künstlerischer Film?" *Berliner Tageblatt*, no. 563, 27 November 1932.

40. R.A., "Die Einengung des deutschen Marktes," *Deutsche Filmzeitung*, 25 November 1932, p. 4.

41. Stephan Ehrenzweig, "Die Film-Saison beginnt," *Das Tagebuch*, 13 (1932), 1355–1357; here p. 1357.

42. Dietrich's German releases included *Morocco, Blond Venus, Dishonored* and *Shanghai Express*, all directed by von Sternberg. Eight Greta Garbo vehicles, four films by Lubitsch and four starring Harold Lloyd were released in Germany in these three years.

43. See, for instance, Felix Henseleit, "Liebesparade," *Reichsfilmblatt*, 29 November 1930; E. Jäger, "Love-Parade," *Film-Kurier*, 25 November 1930; Ihering, *Von Reinhardt bis Brecht*, vol. III, pp. 321–322. Cf. on *Monte Carlo*, H.-W. Betz in *Der Film*, 7 July 1931, p. 51; Pinthus in *8 Uhr-Abendblatt*, 3 July 1931; Georg Herzberg in *Film-Kurier*, 3 July 1931.

44. See especially Rudolf Arnheim, "Garbo und Gassenhauer," *Die Weltbühne*, 27 (1931), vol. I, 509–510; W.G.H. (W. G. Hartmann), "Greta Garbo: 'Helgas Fall und Aufstieg'," *Deutsche Allgemeine Zeitung*, no. 572, 6 December 1932; Kurt London, "Mata Hari," *Der Film*, 17 September 1932, p. 4.

45. Cf. H.T., "Schanghai Express," *Lichtbildbühne*, 12 April 1932; Felix Henseleit, "X 27," *Reichsfilmblatt*, 9 January 1932; Manfred Georg, "Schanghai-Express," Georg Folio, Marbach, 12 April 1932.

46. Both Garbo and Dietrich suffered on this count. See especially the reviews of *Dishonored*, a film whose closing scenes elicited mocking laughter from the premiere audience: F. H. Lehr, "Marlene wird ausgelacht!" *Deutsche Allgemeine Zeitung*, no. 13, 9 January 1932; Pinthus, "Spektakel um Marlene," *8 Uhr-Abendblatt*, 7 January 1932.

47. Cf. Hermann Sinsheimer: "'X 27' im Capitol," *Berliner Tageblatt*, no. 11, 7 January 1932; "Marlene Dietrich: 'Schanghai Express'," no. 173, 12 April 1932; and "Die blonde Venus," no. 550, 19 November 1932. Cf. W. Freisburger, "Die blonde Venus," *Film-Rundschau*, 22 November 1932.

48. Kurt Pinthus, "Eine Stunde mit Dir," *8 Uhr-Abendblatt*, 5 August 1932. Cf. K. L. (Kurt London) on the same in *Der Film*, 6 August 1932, p. 4.

49. Rudolf Arnheim, in *Die Weltbühne*, 28 (1932), vol. I, pp. 62–63. Cf. E.E. Schwabach, "Die Filmsaison 1931/32," *Die Literarische Welt*, 27 May 1932, p. 7; Fritz Olimsky, "Marlene Dietrich in 'X 27'," *Berliner Börsen-Zeitung*, no. 10, 7 January 1932, p. 4; K.W., "Die blonde Venus," *Berliner Börsen-Courier*, no. 542, 19 November 1932, pp. 2–3; Petzet, "Chronik des Films," *Der Kunstwart*, 45 (1932), 611–612; "Richtungen der neuen Produktion," ibid., 46 (1933), 389–391.

50. See, for example, Heinz Pol, "Halleluja," *Vossische Zeitung*, no. 237, 4 October 1930; and Fritz Olimsky in *Berliner Börsen-Zeitung*, no. 462, 3 October 1930, p. 3; Hermann Sinsheimer, "King Vidors Neger-Film," *Berliner Tageblatt*, no. 467, 3 October 1930; Georg Folio, Marbach, 8 October 1930; Kurt Pinthus in *8 Uhr-Abendblatt*, 3 October 1930. On the limited appeal of these pictures see the comments on the former in *Kinematograph*, 3 October 1930; *Reichsfilmblatt*, 4 October 1930; and on the latter in *Lichtbildbühne*, 29 April 1932.

51. Manfred Georg, "Amerikanische Tragödie," Georg Folio, Marbach, 29 April 1932. Cf. reviews by Kurt Pinthus in *8 Uhr-Abendblatt*, 29 April 1932; Charlotte Demmig in *Film-Rundschau*, 3 May 1932; Wolfgang Martini in *Deutsche Filmzeitung*, 1 July 1932, p. 5; Wolfgang Petzet in *Der Kunstwart*, 45 (1932), 739; Ihering, *Von Reinhardt bis Brecht*, vol. III, pp. 364–365.

52. See "Tagebuch der Zeit," *Das Tagebuch*, 13 (1932), 2046–2047, which compared American courage in film to the hypersensitivity shown by German censors, and Franz Schulz, "Film-Moral in Hollywood und Berlin," *Das Tagebuch*, 14 (1933), 189–193.

53. The conspicuous exception to this rule was *Menschen hinter Gittern*, made in Hollywood with a German cast headed by Heinrich George. See, for example, Ihering, *Von Reinhardt bis Brecht*, vol. III, pp. 348–350; Petzet in *Der Kunstwart*, 45 (1931), 208; Rudolf Arnheim, *Die Weltbühne*, 27 (1931), vol. I, pp. 930–931.

54. See, for example, Hans Feld, "Olympia," *Film-Kurier*, 8 November 1930; Georg Herzberg, "Die heilige Flamme," ibid., 5 May 1931; "Liebe auf Befehl," *Lichtbildbühne*, 18 February 1931.

55. See the arguments of Fritz Olimsky in "Mordprozess Mary Dugan," *Berliner Börsen-Zeitung*, no. 60, 5 February 1931, p. 3, and "Geist und Ungeist beim Film," ibid., no. 192, 25 April 1931, p. 14. The Paramount production base near Paris came under especially heavy criticism. Cf. "Jede Frau hat etwas," *Deutsche Filmzeitung*, 19 June 1931, p. 6; "Paramount auf Irrwegen," *Lichtbildbühne*, 7 January 1932, which called its output the laughingstock of Europe; Fränze Schnitzer, "Der amerikanische Film in Deutschland," *Berliner Tageblatt*, no. 16, 10 January 1932.

56. Otto Wilhelm, "Die abhängige UFA," *Deutsche Allgemeine Zeitung*, no. 85, 20 February 1926.

57. Cf. Manfred Georg, "Frankenstein," Georg Folio, Marbach, 19 May 1932; Pinthus, "Sie werden lachen . . . !" *8 Uhr-Abendblatt*, 19 May 1932; hs. (Hermann Sinsheimer), "Frankenstein," *Berliner Tageblatt*, no. 235, 19 May 1932.

CONCLUSION

1. Cf. Salt, "From Caligari to Who?" p. 123; Monaco, *Cinema and Society*, pp. 72–74, generally accepts the claims of the *Film-Kurier* poll.

2. Cf. Hake, "Chaplin Reception," p. 108; Kaes, "Literary Intellectuals and the Cinema," pp. 21–23.

3. See Miles and Smith, *Cinema, Literature and Society*, p. 177, for the claim that America created the sole model of narrative cinema which has proven marketable in the western world.

4. Cf. Berg, *Deutschland und Amerika*, p. 132; Hermand and Trommler, *Die Kultur der Weimarer Republik*, pp. 55–58; Hughes, *American Genesis*, p. 293.

5. Berg, *Deutschland und Amerika*, p. 131.

6. Cf. Kaes, *Kino-Debatte*, p. 17; Beck, *Germany Rediscovers America*, pp. 244–245; Stark, "Cinema, Society and the State," p. 165; Strauss, *Menace in the West*, pp. 90, 176.

7. See the general yet penetrating remarks in Schütz, *Romane der Weimarer Republik*, pp. 18–19.

8. Cf. on this point LeMahieu, *A Culture for Democracy*, pp. 98–99, who opposes aesthetic and commercial impulses; Hay, *Popular Film Culture in Fascist Italy*, pp. 9–10, 72–73; Elsaesser, "Cinema—The Irresponsible Signifier or 'The Gamble with History': Film Theory or Cinema Theory," *New German Critique*, no. 40 (1987), 70; 84.

9. Cf. the options discussed by Buscombe, "Film History and the Idea of a National Cinema," pp. 143–148.

10. Kreimeier, *Die Ufa-Story*, pp. 100, 109, refers to UFA, in its early years, as a media department store, offering whatever promised commercial or critical success.

11. See, for instance, Fritz Lang, "Was ich in Amerika sah," *Film-Kurier*, 17 December 1924; and the recommendations of Ihering, "Wohin geht der deutsche Film?" *Von Reinhardt bis Brecht*, vol. II, pp. 530–532. On temporal displacement see Elsaesser, "German Silent Cinema." Eric Rentschler's recent argument that consensus was attained through the *Bergfilm* throws an interesting light on the remoteness of Weimar's film "center" from everyday life: see his "Mountains and Modernity," pp. 145–146.

12. This argument is developed more fully in my "History in the Making." Cf. Buscombe, "Film History and the Idea of a National Cinema," pp. 150–151, who treats this as a production problem.

13. Ludwig Klitzsch, "Rede zur UFA Konvention, 1930," noted that Germany was in a favorable position to move into European film markets where native producers were unable to meet the demand for high quality sound pictures. In 1931 he reported surprisingly favorable results with foreign versions. The following year foreign earnings were up forty-five percent over 1930–1931. See the speeches in Klitzsch, *Bekenntnis zum deutschen Film*.

14. Erich Pommer, "Der internationale Film," *Film-Rundschau*, 6 November 1928.

15. BA-UFA R109I/1473. This folio, indexed as Erich Pommer, includes a copy of the PSC-UFA contract of 16 August 1930. Article 2 stipulated that in choice of subject matter and nature of production these films were to be suitable for "the whole world, especially for distribution in America." Cf. the programmatic debate on cultivating the American market in BA-UFA R109I/1028b, 26 January 1932, pt. 1 and Anlage.

16. The list includes *Melodie des Herzens, Der blaue Engel, Drei von der Tankstelle, Der Kongress tanzt, Bomben auf Monte Carlo*. One can debate the artistic merits of these productions relative to works like *Faust* or *Tartüff* made under Pommer's supervision in the mid-1920s. Their commercial value is certain.

17. Hermand and Trommler, *Die Kultur der Weimarer Republik*, pp. 70–71, cite remarks by Siegfried Kracauer from 1926 to this effect, but date the critical divide to 1923. Cf. Kracauer, "Kult der Zerstreuung," in his *Das Ornament der Masse* (Frankfurt a.M.: Suhrkamp, 1977), pp. 311–317, here p. 313, who identified mass society in Berlin as the model of the new, homogenous *Weltstadt-Publikum*.

Select Bibliography

Included here are the main archival, periodical and secondary sources. Chapter notes provide more complete references.

ARCHIVAL SOURCES AND GOVERNMENT PUBLICATIONS

Bundesarchiv Koblenz
  R109I/UFA
  R43I/2497–2500 Reichskanzlei, Film und Presseangelegenheiten
Bundesarchiv Potsdam
  13.01 Reichswirtschaftsministerium
Bundesarchiv-Filmarchiv Berlin
  UFA
Deutsches Institut für Filmkunde, Frankfurt a.M.
  Filmprüfstelle; Film-Oberprüfstelle, Berlin
Deutsches Literaturarchiv, Marbach
  Siegfried Kracauer
  Kurt Pinthus
  Manfred Georg
Verhandlungen des Deutschen Reichstages
Verhandlungen des verfassungsgebenden Deutschen
  Nationalversammlung
Warner Bros. Archive, University of Southern California

PERIODICALS

Arbeiterbühne und Film (Film und Volk)
Berliner Börsen-Courier
Berliner Börsen-Zeitung
Berliner Tageblatt
Der Bildwart
B.Z. am Mittag
Deutsche Allgemeine Zeitung
Deutsche Filmwoche
Deutsche Republik
8-Uhr-Abendblatt
Erste Internationale Film-Zeitung (Die Film-Welt)

Der Film
Film-Echo
Film-Journal
Filmkünstler und Filmkunst
Film-Kurier
Film-Rundschau
Film und Presse
Frankfurter Zeitung
Freie Deutsche Bühne (Das blaue Heft)
Kinematograph
Kinematographische Monatshefte
Der Kritiker
Der Kunstwart (Deutsche Zeitschrift)
Lichtbildbühne
Die Literarische Welt
Montag Morgen
Die neue Bücherschau
Die neue Schaubühne
Der Reichsbote
Reichsfilmblatt
Rote Fahne
Das Stachelschwein
Süddeutsche Filmzeitung (Deutsche Filmzeitung)
Das Tagebuch
Tägliche Rundschau
Vorwärts
Vossische Zeitung
Welt am Abend
Welt am Montag
Die Weltbühne

MEMOIRS AND ANTHOLOGIES

Arnheim, Rudolf. *Kritiken und Aufsätze zum Film.* Frankfurt a.M.: Fischer, 1977.

Balázs, Béla. *Schriftum zum Film.* 2 vols. Berlin: Henschelverlag, 1982–1984.

Berger, Ludwig. *Wir sind vom gleichen Stoff, aus dem die Träume sind.* Tübingen: Rainer Wunderlich, 1953.

Chaplin, Charles. *My Autobiography.* London: The Bodley Head, 1964.

Eggebrecht, Axel. *Der halbe Weg.* Reinbek bei Hamburg: Rowohlt, 1975.

Eisner, Lotte H. *Ich hatte einst ein schönes Vaterland.* Munich: Deutscher Taschenbuch Verlag, 1984.
Haas, Willy. *Die literarische Welt: Erinnerungen.* Munich: Paul List Verlag, 1957.
Hätte ich das Kino! Die Schriftsteller und der Stummfilm. Marbach: Schiller-Nationalmuseum, 1976.
Ihering, Hebert. *Von Reinhardt bis Brecht: vier Jahrzehnte Theater und Film.* 3 vols. Berlin: Aufbau Verlag, 1958–1961.
Jannings, Emil. *Theater/Film—Das Leben und Ich.* Berchtesgaden: Zimmer and Herzog, 1951.
Kaes, Anton, ed. *Kino-Debatte: Texte zum Verhältnis von Literatur und Film, 1909–1929.* Tübingen: Niemeyer, 1978.
Klassiker des amerikanischen Stummfilms im Spiegel der deutschen Kritik. Berlin: Stiftung Deutsche Kinemathek, 1977.
Klitzsch, Ludwig. *Bekenntnis zum deutschen Film.* N.p., n.d.
Kreimeier, Klaus, ed. *Zeitgenosse Chaplin.* Berlin: Oberbaum Verlag, 1978.
Kühn, Gertraude, Karl Tümmler, and Walter Wimmer, eds. *Film und revolutionäre Arbeiterbewegung in Deutschland, 1918–1932.* 2 vols. Berlin: Henschelverlag, 1975.
Negri, Pola. *Memoirs of a Star.* New York: Doubleday, 1970.
Sahl, Hans. *Memoiren eines Moralisten.* Zurich: Ammann Verlag, 1983.
Siemsen, Hans. *Schriften.* 3 vols. (Essen: Torso Verlag, 1985–1989).
Weber, Richard. *Film und Volk.* Köln: Prometh Verlag, 1978.
Wiegand, Wilfried, ed. *Über Chaplin.* Zurich: Diogenes, 1978.
Zehder, Hugo, ed. *Der Film von Morgen.* Berlin/Dresden: Rudolf Kaemmerer, 1923.

OTHER SOURCES

Abel, Richard. "American Film and the French Literary Avant-Garde." *Contemporary Literature* 17 (Winter 1976), 84–109.
———. "The Contribution of the French Literary Avant-Garde to Film Theory and Criticism (1907–1924)." *Cinema Journal* 15 (Spring 1975), 18–40.
Altenloh, Emilie. *Zur Soziologie des Kino.* Jena: E. Diederichs, 1914.
Angermann, Erich. "Die USA in den 'Goldenen Zwanziger Jahren.' " In *Deutschland und die USA, 1918–1933,* ed. George Eckert and Otto-Ernst Schüddekopf, pp. 53–64. Braunschweig: Albert Limbach, 1968.
Armstrong, Bruce, et al. "Alptraumfabrik? Der deutsche Film in den Zwanziger Jahren," In *Faschismus und Avantgarde,* ed. Reinhold

Grimm and Jost Hermand, pp. 115–30. Königstein: Athenäum, 1980.

Ausleger, Gerhard. *Charlie Chaplin.* Hamburg: Pfadweiser Verlag, 1924.

Baacke, Rolf-Peter. *Lichtspielhausarchitektur in Deutschland. Von der Schaubude bis zum Kinopalast.* Berlin: Verlag Frölich and Kaufmann, 1982.

Bächlin, Peter. *Der Film als Ware.* Frankfurt a.M.: Fischer, 1975.

Beck, Earl. *Germany Rediscovers America.* Tallahassee: Florida State University Press, 1968.

Becker, Wolfgang. *Film und Herrschaft.* Berlin: Volker Spiess, 1973.

Berg, Peter. *Deutschland und Amerika, 1918–1929.* Lübeck/Hamburg: Matthiesen Verlag, 1963.

Berg, Rainer. "Zur Geschichte der realistichen Stummfilmkunst in Deutschland—1919 bis 1929." Ph.D. dissertation, Freie Universität Berlin, 1982.

Berg-Ganschow, Uta and Wolfgang Jacobsen, eds. *... Film ... Stadt ... Kino ... Berlin. ...* Berlin: Argon Verlag, 1987.

Bigsby, C. W. E., ed. *Superculture: American Popular Culture and Europe.* Bowling Green: Bowling Green University Popular Press, 1975.

Bock, Hans-Michael, ed. *CineGraph: Lexikon zum deutschsprachigen Film.* Munich: Edition Text + Kritik, 1984–.

Boehmer, Henning von, and Helmut Reitz. *Der Film in Wirtschaft und Recht.* Berlin: Carl Heymanns Verlag, 1933.

Brennicke, Ilona and Joe Hembus. *Klassiker des deutschen Stummfilms 1910–1930.* Munich: Goldmann, 1983.

Buchner, Hans. *Im Banne des Films: Die Weltherrschaft des Kinos.* Munich: Deutscher Volksverlag, 1927.

Buchwald, Manfred. "Das Kulturbild Amerikas im Spiegel deutscher Zeitungen und Zeitschriften 1919–1932." Ph.D. dissertation, Kiel, 1964.

Burger, Erich. *Charlie Chaplin: Bericht seines Lebens.* Berlin: Rudolf Mosse, 1929.

Buscombe, Edward. "Film History and the Idea of a National Cinema," *Australian Journal of Screen Theory,* no. 9/10 (1981), 141–153.

Carringer, Robert, and Barry Sabath. *Ernst Lubitsch: A Guide to References and Resources.* Boston: G. K. Hall, 1978.

Cook, David. *A History of Narrative Film.* New York: W. W. Norton and Co., 1981.

Costigliola, Frank. *Awkward Dominion.* Ithaca: Cornell University Press, 1984.

de Grazia, Victoria. "Mass Culture and Sovereignty: The American

Challenge to European Cinemas, 1920–1960." *Journal of Modern History* 61 (1989), 53–87.

Diederichs, Helmut. "Die Anfänge der deutschen Filmpublizistik 1895 bis 1909." *Publizistik* 27 (1982), 55–71.

———. *Anfänge deutscher Filmkritik.* Stuttgart: Verlag Robert Fischer and Wiedleroither, 1986.

Eisner, Lotte H. *The Haunted Screen.* Trans. Roger Greaves. London: Thames and Hudson, 1969.

———. *Murnau.* London: Secker and Warburg, 1973.

Eksteins, Modris. "War, Memory, and Politics: The Fate of the Film *All Quiet on the Western Front.*" *Central European History* 13 (1980), 60–82.

Elsaesser, Thomas. "Cinema—The Irresponsible Signifier or, 'The Gamble With History': Film Theory or Cinema Theory." *New German Critique* no. 40 (1987), 65–89.

———. "Film History and Visual Pleasure." In *Cinema Histories/Cinema Practices,* ed. Patricia Mellencamp and Philip Rosen, pp. 47–84. Frederick, MD: University Publications of America, 1984.

———. "German Silent Cinema: Social Mobility and the Fantastic." *Wide Angle* 5 (1982), 14–25.

———. "Secret Affinities." *Sight and Sound* 58 (Winter 1988/89) 33–39.

"Erobert den Film": Proletariat und Film in der Weimarer Republik. Berlin: Neue Gesellschaft für bildende Kunst, 1977.

Friederich Wilhelm Murnau. Ein großer Filmregisseur der 20er Jahre. Stuttgart: Deutscher Sparkasse, 1981.

Fulks, Barry. "Film Culture and *Kulturfilm:* Walter Ruttmann, the Avant-Garde Film, and the *Kulturfilm* in Weimar Germany and the Third Reich." Ph.D. Dissertation, University of Wisconsin, 1982.

Gersch, Wolfgang. *Chaplin in Berlin.* Berlin: Henschelverlag, 1988.

Giese, Fritz. *Girlkultur: Vergleiche zwischen amerikanischem und europäischem Rhythmus und Lebensgefühl.* Munich: Delphin-Verlag, 1925.

Gomery, Douglas. "Economic Struggle and Hollywood Imperialism: Europe Converts to Sound." *Yale French Studies* no. 60 (1980), 80–93.

———. "Film and Business History: The Development of an American Mass Entertainment Industry." *Journal of Contemporary History* 19 (1984), 89–102.

———. "Tri-Ergon, Tobis-Klangfilm, and the Coming of Sound." *Cinema Journal* 16 (Fall 1976), 51–61.

Grünau, Norbert. "Die finanzielle und wirtschaftliche Entwicklung der Filmindustrie in Deutschland." Ph.D. dissertation, Münster, 1923.

Guttmann, Irmalotte. *Über die Nachfrage auf dem Filmmarkt in Deutschland.* Berlin: Gebr. Wolffsohn, 1928.

Hagge, Hans. *Das gab's schon zweimal. Auf die Spuren der Ufa.* Berlin: Henschelverlag, 1959.

Hake, Sabine. "Chaplin Reception in Weimar Germany." *New German Critique* no. 51 (1990), 87–111.

————. "Girls and Crisis—The Other Side of Diversion." *New German Critique* no. 40 (1987), 147–164.

————. *Passions and Deceptions. The Early Films of Ernst Lubitsch.* Princeton: Princeton University Press, 1992.

Halfeld, Adolf. *Amerika und der Amerikanismus.* Jena: E. Diederichs, 1927.

Hansen, Miriam. "Early Silent Cinema: Whose Public Sphere?" *New German Critique* no. 29 (1983), 147–184.

Hardt, Ursula. "Erich Pommer: Film Producer for Germany." Ph.D. dissertation, University of Iowa, 1989.

Harley, John. *World-Wide Influences of the Cinema.* Los Angeles: University of Southern California Press, 1940.

Hay, James. *Popular Film Culture in Fascist Italy.* Bloomington: Indiana University Press, 1987.

Hayler, Franz. "Die deutsche Film-Industrie und ihre Bedeutung für Deutschlands Handel." Ph.D. dissertation, Würzburg, 1926.

Heller, Heinz-B. *Literarische Intelligenz und Film.* Tübingen: Niemeyer, 1985.

Hermand, Jost, and Frank Trommler. *Die Kultur der Weimarar Republik.* Munich: Nymphenburger, 1978.

Hermann, L. A. *Chaplin's Wunderbarer Aufstieg.* Berlin: Otto Dreyer, n.d.

Holba, Herbert. *Emil Jannings.* Ulm: Günter Knorr, 1979.

Hollriegel, Arnold. *Lichter der Großstadt.* Leipzig: E. P. Tal Co., 1931.

Horak, Jan-Christopher. "Ernst Lubitsch and the Rise of UFA, 1917–1922." M.Sc. Thesis, Boston University, 1975.

————. "Rin-Tin-Tin erobert Berlin oder Amerikanische Filminteressen in Weimar." In Walter Schatzberg and Uli Jung, eds. *Filmkultur zur Zeit der Weimarer Republik.* pp. 255–270. Munich: Saur, 1992.

Huaco, George. *The Sociology of Film Art.* New York: Basic Books, 1965.

Jacobsen, Wolfgang. *Erich Pommer: Ein Produzent macht Filmgeschichte.* Berlin: Argon, 1989.

Jarvie, Ian. *Hollywood's Overseas Campaign. The North Atlantic Movie Trade, 1920–1950.* Cambridge: Cambridge University Press, 1992.

Jason, Alexander. *Handbuch der Filmwirtschaft.* 3 vols. Berlin: Verlag für Presse, Wirtschaft und Politik, 1930–1932.

Kaes, Anton. "Brecht und der Amerikanismus im Theater der 20er Jahre: Unliterarische Tradition und Publikumsbezug." *Sprache im technischen Zeitalter* 56 (1975), 359–371.

———. "Mass Culture and Modernity: Notes Toward a Social History of Early American and German Cinema." In *America and the Germans*, ed. Frank Trommler and Joseph McVeigh, pp. 317–331. Philadelphia: University of Pennsylvania Press, 1985.

Kallmann, Alfred. "Die Konzernierung in der Filmindustrie, erläutert an den Filmindustrien Deutschlands und Amerikas." Ph.D. dissertation, Würzburg, 1932.

Keiner, Reinhold. *Thea von Harbou und der deutsche Film bis 1933*. Hildesheim: Georg Olms Verlag, 1984.

Kinter, Jürgen. *Arbeiterbewegung und Film, 1895–1933*. Hamburg: Medienpädagogik-Zentrum, 1986.

Koebner, Thomas. "Der Film als neue Kunst. Reaktionen der literarischen Intelligenz." In *Literaturwissenschaft-Medienwissenschaft*. ed. Helmut Kreuzer, pp. 1–31. Heidelberg: Quelle and Meyer, 1977.

Korte, Helmut, ed. *Film und Realität in der Weimarer Republik*. Munich: Carl Hanser Verlag, 1978.

Kracauer, Siegfried, *From Caligari to Hitler*. Princeton: Princeton University Press, 1947.

———. "Kult der Zerstreuung." In *Das Ornament der Masse*, pp. 311–317. Frankfurt a.M.: Suhrkamp, 1977.

———. "The Mass Ornament." *New German Critique* no. 5 (1975), 67–76.

Kreimeier, Klaus. *Die Ufa-Story. Geschichte eines Filmkonzerns*. Munich: Carl Hanser Verlag, 1992.

Kriegk, Otto. *Der deutsche Film im Spiegel der UFA: 25 Jahre Kampf und Vollendung*. Berlin: UFA-Buchverlag, 1943.

Kuntze-Just, Heinz. " 'Guten Morgen, Ufa!' Die Geschichte eines Filmkonzerns." *Film-Telegramm* no. 47–49 (1954), 25 (1955).

Kurtz, Rudolf. *Expressionismus und Film*. Berlin: Verlag der Lichtbildbühne, 1926.

Laqueur, Walter. *Weimar: A Cultural History, 1918–1933*. London: Weidenfeld and Nicolson, 1974.

LeMahieu, D. L. *A Culture for Democracy*. Oxford, Clarendon Press, 1988.

Lethen, Helmut. *Neue Sachlichkeit, 1924–1932*. Stuttgart: J. B. Metzlersche, 1970.

Lyons, Timothy. *Charlie Chaplin: A Guide to References and Resources*. Boston: G. K. Hall, 1979.

Manvell, Roger, and Heinrich Fraenkel. *The German Cinema.* London: J. M. Dent and Sons, 1971.

Marland, David. *Chaplin and American Culture.* Princeton: Princeton University Press, 1989.

Marquardt, Axel, and Heinz Rathsack, eds. *Preußen im Film.* Reinbek bei Hamburg: Rowohlt, 1981.

"Mass Culture in Imperial Germany." Special Issue, *New German Critique* no. 29 (Spring/Summer 1983).

May, Lary. *Screening Out the Past.* New York: Oxford University Press, 1980.

McCabe, John. *Charlie Chaplin.* New York: Doubleday, 1978.

Meier, Charles. "Between Taylorism and Technocracy: European Ideologies and the Vision of Industrial Productivity in the 1920s." *Journal of Contemporary History* 5 (1970), 27–61.

Meyer, Fritz. "Kunstgewerbe und ökonomisches Prinzip (Der Aufbau der Filmindustrie." Ph.D. dissertation, Berlin, 1924.

Miles, Peter, and Malcolm Smith. *Cinema, Literature, and Society: Elite and Mass Culture in Interwar Britain.* London: Croom Helm, 1987.

Monaco, Paul. *Cinema and Society.* New York: Elsevier, 1976.

Morris, C. Brian. "Charles Chaplin's Tryst with Spain." *Journal of Contemporary History* 18 (1983), 517–531.

Mühlberg, Dietrich. "Anfänge proletarischen Freizeitverhaltens und seiner öffentlichen Einrichtungen." *Weimarer Beiträge* 27 (1981), 124–138.

Murphy, Robert. "Under the Shadow of Hollywood." In *All Our Yesterdays: Ninety Years of British Cinema,* pp. 47–58. ed. Charles Barr. London: British Film Institute, 1986.

Murray, Bruce. *Film and the German Left in the Weimar Republic.* Austin: University of Texas Press, 1990.

Murray, Bruce, and Christopher Wickham, eds. *Framing the Past: The Historiography of German Cinema and Television.* Carbondale: Southern Illinois University Press, 1992.

Nacache, Jacqueline. *Lubitsch.* Paris: Edilig, 1987.

Olimsky, Fritz. "Tendenzen der Filmwirtschaft und deren Auswirkung auf die Filmpresse." Ph.D. dissertation, Berlin, 1931.

Patalas, Enno. "*Metropolis,* Bild 103." In *Der Stummfilm: Konstruktion und Rekonstruktion,* ed. Elfriede Ledig, pp. 153–162. Munich: Schaudig, Bauer und Ledig, 1988.

Petrie, Graham. *Hollywood Destinies.* London: Routledge and Keagan Paul, 1985.

Petro, Patrice. "From Lukács to Kracauer and Beyond: Social Film Histories and the German Cinema." *Cinema Journal* 22 (1983), 47–70.

————. *Joyless Streets*. Princeton: Princeton University Press, 1989.

Plummer, Thomas, et al. *Film and Politics in the Weimar Republic*. New York: Holmes and Meier, 1982.

Prinzler, Helmut. *Ernst Lubitsch*. Paris: Cahiers du Cinéma, 1985.

Reader, Keith. *Cultures on Celluloid*. New York: Quartet Books, 1981.

Rentschler, Eric, ed. *German Film and Literature: Adaptations and Transformations*. London and New York: Methuen, 1986.

————. "How American is It? The U.S. as Image and Imaginary in German Film." *German Quarterly*, 54 (1984), 603–620.

————. "Mountains and Modernity: Relocating the '*Bergfilm*.' " *New German Critique* no. 51 (1990), 137–161.

Richter, Hans, ed. *Das Kinojahrbuch*. Berlin: H. Richter Verlag, 1921.

Robinson, David. *Chaplin: The Mirror of Opinion*. Bloomington: Indiana University Press, 1984.

Rosen, Philip. "History, Textuality, Nation: Kracauer, Burch, and Some Problems in the Study of National Cinemas." *Iris* 2 (1984), 69–84.

Salt, Barry. *Film Style and Technology: History and Analysis*. London: Starword, 1983.

Saunders, Thomas. "Comedy as Redemption: American Slapstick in Weimar Culture." *Journal of European Studies* 17 (1987), 253–277.

————. "History in the Making: Weimar Cinema and National Identity." In *Framing the Past. The Historiography of German Cinema and Television*, ed. Bruce Murray and Christopher Wickham, pp. 42–67. Carbondale: Southern Illinois University Press, 1992.

————. "Politics, the Cinema, and Early Revisitations of War in Weimar Germany." *Canadian Journal of History* 23 (1988), 21–40.

Schatzberg, Walter, and Uli Jung, eds. *Filmkultur zur Zeit der Weimarer Republik*. Munich: Saur, 1992.

Schlüpmann, Heide. *Unheimlichkeit des Blicks*. Basel: Stroemfeld/Roter Stern, 1990.

Schütz, Erhard. *Romane der Weimarer Republik*. Munich: Wilhelm Fink Verlag, 1986.

Schweinitz, Jörg. "Kino der Zerstreuung: Siegfried Kracauer und ein Kapitel Geschichte der theoretischen Annäherung an populäre Filmunterhaltung" *Weimarer Beiträge* 33 (1987), 1129–1144.

Schweins, Annemarie. "Die Entwicklung der deutschen Filmwirtschaft." Ph.D. dissertation, Nürnberg, 1958.

Shi, David. "Transatlantic Visions: The Impact of the American Cinema upon the French Avant-Garde." *Journal of Popular Culture* 14 (1981), 583–596.

Siemsen, Hans. *Charlie Chaplin*. Leipzig: Feuer-Verlag, 1924.

Sklar, Robert. *Movie-Made America.* New York: Random House, 1975.

Spiker, Jürgen. *Film und Kapital.* Berlin: Volker Spiess, 1975.

Staiger, Janet, and Douglas Gomery. "The History of World Cinema: Models for Economic Analysis." *Film Reader* 4 (1979), 35–44.

Stark, Gary. "Cinema, Society and the State: Policing the Film Industry in Imperial Germany." In *Essays on Culture and Society in Modern Germany,* ed. Gary Stark and B. K. Lackner, pp. 122–166. Arlington: Texas A & M Press, 1982.

Stead, Peter. "Hollywood's Message for the World: the British Response in the Nineteen Thirties." *Historical Journal of Film, Radio and Television* 1 (1981), 19–32.

Strauss, David. *Menace in the West: The Rise of French Anti-Americanism in Modern Times.* Westport, Conn.: Greenwood Press, 1978.

Swann, Paul. *The Hollywood Feature Film in Postwar Britain.* London: Croom Helm, 1987.

Thompson, Kristin. *Exporting Entertainment.* London: British Film Institute, 1985.

Traub, Hans, ed. *Die UFA: Ein Beitrag zur Entwicklungsgeschichte des deutschen Filmschaffens.* Berlin: UFA-Buchverlag, 1943.

Trommler, Frank. "The Rise and Fall of Americanism in Germany." In *America and the Germans,* ed. Frank Trommler and Joseph McVeigh, pp. 332–342. Philadelphia: University of Pennsylvania Press, 1985.

Tudor, Andrew. *Image and Influence.* London: George Allen and Unwin, Ltd., 1974.

Die UFA—auf den Spuren einer großen Filmfabrik. Berlin: Elefanten Press, 1987.

Usai, Paolo Cherchi, and Lorenzo Codelli, eds. *Before Caligari: German Cinema, 1895–1920.* Pordenone: Le Giornate del Cinema Muto, 1990.

"Weimar Film Theory." Special Issue *New German Critique* no. 40 (Winter 1987).

Welch, David. "The Proletarian Cinema and the Weimar Republic." *Historical Journal of Film, Radio and Television* 1 (1981), 3–18.

Willet, Ralph. *The Americanization of Germany, 1945–1949.* London: Routledge, 1989.

Willett, John. *The New Sobriety: Art and Politics in the Weimar Period.* London: Thames and Hudson, 1978.

Wolffsohn, Karl, ed. *Jahrbuch der Filmindustrie.* 5 vols. Berlin: Verlag der Lichtbildbühne, 1922–1933.

Wollenberg, Hans. *Fifty Years of German Film.* London: Falcon Press, 1948.

Youngblood, Denise. " 'Amerikanitis': the *Amerikanshchina* in Soviet Cinema." *Journal of Popular Film & Television* 19 (1992), 148–156.
————. *Movies for the Masses: Popular Cinema and Soviet Society in the 1920s.* Cambridge: Cambridge University Press, 1992.
Zimmerschied, Karl. *Die deutsche Filmindustrie, ihre Entwicklung, Organisation und Stellung im Staats- und Wirtschaftsleben.* Stuttgart: Poeschel Verlag, 1922.
Žmegač, Viktor. "Exkurs über den Film im Umkreis des Expressionismus," *Sprache im technischen Zeitalter* 35 (1970), 243–257.

Index

Designer: U.C. Press Staff
Compositor: Maryland Composition Company, Inc.
Text: 10/13 Baskerville
Display: Baskerville
Printer: Malloy Lithographing, Inc.
Binder: John H. Dekker & Sons